# Broken English/
# Breaking English

# Broken English/ Breaking English

## A Study of Contemporary Poetries in English

## Rob Jackaman

Madison • Teaneck
Fairleigh Dickinson University Press
London: Associated University Presses

Associated University Presses
2010 Eastpark Boulevard
Cranbury, NJ 08512

Associated University Presses
Unit 304
The Chandlery
50 Westminster Bridge Road
London SE1 7QY, England

Associated University Presses
P.O. Box 338, Port Credit
Mississauga, Ontario
Canada L5G 4L8

The paper used in this publication meets the requirements of the American National Standard for Permanence of Paper for Printed Library Materials Z39.48–1984.

Library of Congress Cataloging-in-Publication Data

Jackaman, Rob, 1945-
  Broken English/breaking English : a study of contemporary poetries in English / Rob Jackaman.
    p. cm.
  Includes bibliographical references and index.
  ISBN 0-8386-3991-7 (alk. paper)
  1. English poetry—20th century—History and criticism. 2. Commonwealth poetry (English)—History and criticism. 3. American poetry—History and criticism. 4. English language—Versification. 5. English language—Variation. I. Title.
  PR601.J325 2003
  821'.9109—dc21

                                                        2003004817

PRINTED IN THE UNITED STATES OF AMERICA

# Contents

# Acknowledgments

I WOULD LIKE TO ACKNOWLEDGE THE ASSISTANCE OF A NUMBER OF people and institutions without whose support this book would not have been possible. They are:

The University of Canterbury, Christchurch, New Zealand for library, word-processing, printing, and other facilities; and for granting me a year's study leave during which I was able to complete my research for the project, and do most of the composition of the final manuscript.

The English Department at the University of Canterbury for a research grant, and for postal and secretarial assistance.

The University of Sydney in Australia for research facilities during my period in the English Department there as a Visiting Scholar; and colleagues in that department, particularly Dr. David G. Brooks, for hospitality and constructive discussion of my project.

International House in the University of Sydney for accommodation and hospitality.

Queen's University at Kingston, Ontario, Canada for research facilities during my period in the English Department there as a Visiting Scholar; and colleagues in that department, particularly Professor Les Monkman, for hospitality and constructive discussion of my project.

King's College, Cambridge, United Kingdom for hospitality; and the University of Cambridge for research facilities.

Christine Retz and the editorial team at Associated University Presses for their assistance, and care in handling my manuscript.

ॐ ॐ ॐ ॐ ॐ

As well, grateful acknowledgment is made for the following permissions to quote:

From *The Fact of a Doorframe: Poems Selected and New, 1950–1984* by Adrienne Rich. Copyright © 1984 by Adrienne Rich. Copyright © 1975, 1978 by W.W. Norton & Company, Inc. Copyright © 1981 by Adrienne Rich. Used by permission of the author and W.W. Norton & Company, Inc.

From *On Lies, Secrets, and Silence: Selected Prose 1966–1978* by Adrienne Rich. Copyright © 1979 by W.W. Norton & Company, Inc. Used by permission of the author and W.W. Norton & Company, Inc.

The lines from "Sources," from *Your Native Land, Your Life: Poems by Adrienne Rich.* Copyright © 1986 by Adrienne Rich. Used by permission of the author and W.W. Norton & Company, Inc.

Excerpts from *Preoccupations: Selected Prose 1968–1978* by Seamus Heaney. Copyright © 1980 by Seamus Heaney. Used by permission of the author, Faber and Faber Ltd., and Farrar, Straus and Giroux, LLC.

# Broken English/
# Breaking English

# 1

## Introductory Discussion:
## Poetry and Purity (and Other Fictions)

IF MY INITIAL THEME OF PURITY SEEMS OLD-FASHIONED, PERHAPS IT'S
to some degree the responsibility of Donald Davie—not to mention
my late mother! Growing up in immediately post-Second-World-War
England, I remember that my mother favored a particular type of
sausage which was marketed under the name of "Purity Brand." I
mention this eminently nonliterary fact not merely as an early excursion into irrelevant autobiography, but because at about the same
moment (the early 1950s), a literary study appeared whose primary
marketing strategy was remarkably similar to that of the aforemen-
tioned forcemeat artifact—the appeal in a dingy postwar world of
the notion of purity. The study in question is, of course, Donald
Davie's *Purity of Diction in English Verse* (1952).[1]

It's not my current intention (though it may later turn out to be
so) to draw disparaging analogies between the poetry of that time
(which came to be identified with a pressure group known as "The
Movement") and sausages (the homogeneous filling, just enough to
fill out the product, though almost without flavour of any kind; the
barely adequate skin, colorless and virtually transparent; the ease of
handling and consumption, yet concomitant lack of nourishment
and sustenance). Rather, I wish to draw attention to Davie's use of
the word (and concept) "Purity" as a promotional device.

As any recent literary critic will tell us, the idea of purity is significantly predicated on its opposite, its "other" or its absence: impurity.
An awareness of this situation (though many years before the new
wave of literary commentators theorized it) presumably accounts to
some degree for Davie's concern in the early 1950s to persuade his

readers of purity's desirability—perhaps even inevitability—in English verse (the term "English" here being, for him, exclusive to poetry written in Britain as opposed to written in the English language worldwide). One of the key literary historical data here is the rise of what is consigned by implication to the category of the "impure"— *American* influence on the *eastern* side of the Atlantic, not only in politics and economics, but as well culturally and—specific to the present case—through poetry written in American English. Irrespective of quality, the sheer volume of material, and its ever-more ready accessibility to a British readership might be seen as a daunting challenge to the "purely" British cultural context.

And this is only the threat from *outside*, which can to some extent be neutralized by xenophobic rhetoric, manipulation of the marketplace, carefully orchestrated bias in reviewing and the wielding of editorial power, and so forth. The *laager* mentality generated by "Movement" writers to meet the trans-Atlantic challenge is harder to maintain, however, when there is also a threat from *inside*, when English writers writing in English in England don't conform to a preordained hard core of Englishness, however strongly this latter may be propagandized. My main argument in this book, indeed, is that such a reductive hard core notion of "Englishness" in poetry is no longer possible, was never desirable, and has been progressively subverted over the last thirty or forty years by "impure" writers both inside and outside the British Isles whose efforts have been directed precisely towards the breaking of English as a monopoly concern: hence (inevitably) my title, *Broken English/Breaking English*.

Breaking English implies, on the one hand, an act of cultural vandalism (which is roughly how Movement writers thought of challenges to their literary and linguistic hegemony and autonomy); and, on the other, an act of liberating iconoclasm, breaking new ground, ushering in the break of a new poetic day, and so on. Further, the label of "Broken English" might be made to refer disparagingly to "inauthentic" forms of the language spoken by the disadvantaged and colonized, whose native tongue is other than standard English; or it might connote vital new pidgins and kriols asserting equal rights (writes) from the cultural margin, partly dismantling received monopolistic English in favor of a multiplicity of different but equally valid voices.[2]

Perhaps, though, we should begin by returning to the articulation and establishment of the idea of English as a literary discourse unsullied and indivisible, and consider the influential volume, *Purity of Diction in English Verse* .

ॐ   ॐ   ॐ   ॐ   ॐ

Donald Davie's starting point in the book is an attempted refutation of the (then) conventional critical opinion that the eighteenth century represented something of a trough in the great onward surge of English poetic discourse. He begins by pondering the question

> whether it is true that in the eighteenth century literary English was metaphorically impoverished. In the last hundred years most literary historians have found this metaphorical poverty falling, like a shadow, over most English poetry written between the death of Pope and the publication of *Lyrical Ballads.* (1)

In the face of this consensus, Davie asserts:

> I have come to believe that what seems poverty is sometimes economy; and that this economy in metaphor produces effects which I call "poetical," to which, it seems to me, most readers of our day are blind. The effect seems to me to be morally valuable . . . (1)

Quite what the "moral value" may be isn't entirely clear, though Davie reiterates the phrase on the following page (2), linking it to the statement that "the diction is pure" (again, whatever that may mean). An act of clarification appears to be in the air when he goes on to say, "I want to understand what I mean when I make these judgments"; but at this stage one gets the distinct impression that these are simply assertions of personal value judgement, serving some as yet unstated agenda—which actually emerges half a page later, when Davie makes a virtue out of the old-fashioned tenor of his argument by stating, "I do not argue for a new criterion, only for an old one which has fallen out of use." The point here, though, turns out to bear not only (perhaps not even principally?) on the eighteenth century, but on the 1950s as well; for, as he admits, "I am interested in . . . [purity of diction] because I think it relevant, indeed indispensable, to the poetry of Goldsmith's contemporaries, *and to that of my own"* [my emphasis].

The introduction to *Purity of Diction in English Verse,* then, sets up what is perceived as a desirable (even salutary) moral value in a par-

ticular kind of poetic diction deemed to have existed in the poetry of
the mid- to late- eighteenth century, an era conveniently removed
from the (debased) present, yet somehow still relevant to and perhaps even continuous with it. Purity is sited in a stable historical spot
in the past, long before any threats from American cultural imperialism (or Lend-Lease, for that matter), long before the embarrassing
excesses of Dylan Thomas and the New Apocalypse movement of the
1940s, and long before the Suez crisis that was perhaps the final kiss
of death to British notions of empire. Further, this "purity" locates itself—or is located by Davie—not in the clamoring foreign symbolist
urge so popular with expatriate modernist writers early in the twentieth century (not to mention the francophiliac fringe in the 1930s and
1940s), but in the unpretentious minor English tradition, as exem-
plified (in Davie's choice of relatively small-scale literary heroes) by
"Johnson, Goldsmith, Collins and Cowper" (32). *English Verse* indeed.

This ideal of English verse diction is to be supported, we see as we
read on through the book, by good English common sense, involving "a selection from the language on *reasonable* principles and for a
*reasonable* purpose" (6; my emphasis). Further, "poise and good
breeding" will come into the picture too—as Davie asserts is the case
with Shelley, who enjoyed "the birth and breeding of a gentleman,
and that cannot be irrelevant" (158). The Shelley on display here, incidentally, is not the author of a "poetry which overflows the soul,
but [of a poetry which is] the considered expression of an intelligent
man" (159). Such poets have a high calling which imposes what
Davie describes as "a web of responsibilities," involving "conserving
the genres and the decorum" evolved by "past masters," maintaining
"a consistent tone and point of view," and in general preserving
"chastity and propriety in language" (16–17).

As if purity weren't enough, chastity now becomes a writerly linguistic issue too, as is signaled by the fact that chapter 2 of *Purity of
Diction* is actually entitled "The Chastity of Poetic Diction." Here,
"chastity" is made up of a number of virtues such as "propriety," "re-
straint and economy"; and it sets itself up against any "deviation
from propriety," against "extravagance" and (particularly) against
"hyperbolical and highly metaphorical language" (18), not to mention (though Davie *has* mentioned it, a few pages earlier, in the context of the non-English poet, J. M. Synge) "poems which were experiments" and "poetic diction of an unusually elaborate and eccentric
kind" (9).

The chaste and responsible writer of English must use his or (very occasionally) her pure diction "not to extend meaning, but to work over areas already explored" (33). This significant limitation of range will serve to focus poetic energies, generating what Davie (appropriating Matthew Arnold) describes as "'the tone of the center'" both in literary-political and in geographical terms; he asserts, "A chaste diction is 'central,' in Arnold's sense; it expresses the feeling of the capital, not the provinces." He goes on: "The effect is a valuable urbanity, a civilized moderation and elegance" (26–27). The centralized power of the dominant discourse must be maintained by strict observance of poetic purity and chastity. Failure to do so carries dire consequences: as Davie says, this time borrowing from the unlikely source of Ezra Pound in his *ABC of Reading* (though the two men might well not have agreed over precise definitions of the terms used), "A people that grows accustomed to sloppy writing is a people in process of losing grip on its empire and on itself" (93). What could be worse, with the independence of India in the recent past and the Suez débacle just around the corner? No wonder, perhaps, that a hint of hysteria (or at least despair) creeps into Davie's voice at times. So, as he reviews radical experiment with poetic diction he's driven into the following gigantic exaggerations:

> To abandon syntax in poetry [and he's presumably targeting free verse here] is not to start or indulge a literary fashion; it is to throw away a tradition central to human thought and conduct, as to human speech. (98)

> One could almost say, on this showing, that to dislocate syntax in poetry is to threaten the rule of law in the civilized community. (99)

One "rule of law" which Davie doesn't cover in his book, but which will prove significant to our discussion later, and is therefore appropriate to introduce here, is the law of the dictionary-makers. Dictionaries fit well with much of what Davie has to say in *Purity of Diction in English Verse:* they, too, seek (or at least have done so in the past) to centralize, regulate, legislate, and purify the language, however absurd that enterprise may be for a linguistic hybrid and mishmash such as English. The first authority to attempt to systematize the English language was, of course, Dr. Johnson, who figures prominently throughout Davie's book, quoted uniformly therein with approval as a normative influence. The principal family of English dictionaries is undoubtedly the Oxford series, centered on the "civilized community" of the University of Oxford which Davie shared with most of his Movement colleagues. Even a retrenchment to "purity" is shared, in the face of threats to literary, linguistic, and literal empire: as John Willinsky points out in his fascinating study, *Empire of Words: the Reign of the* OED (1994):

> With the first signs of the crumbling of the empire and the shifting of power in the English-speaking world to the United States, the Society of Pure English was formed in 1915 with a mission to protect the language from the "obnoxious condition" of British colonials engaged in "habitual intercourse" with "other-speaking races"—"It would seem that no other language can ever have had its central force so dissipated" (cited by [Philip] Dodd, 1986, p. 15). For such xenophobia, as with the spirit of imperialism that ran before it, the *OED* was no less a unifying monument to what was pure, to what had to be preserved. (203)

I'm not necessarily suggesting that Davie shares the xenophobic agenda of the Society of Pure English (uncomfortable as the echo with his title may be, and intransigently xenophobic though some of his Movement colleagues undoubtedly were or are). Neither am I suggesting that the current personnel of the *OED* are involved in any way in an imperial rearguard action.[3] But the canonical status and authority of both the Oxford University Press (notably through its literary anthologies), and the Oxford English Dictionary series are significant data that remain to be considered later in this study.

꒰꜔ ꒰꜔ ꒰꜔ ꒰꜔ ꒰꜔

From the other side of the empire and of the dictionary, the other side of "purity" and of the Atlantic, things appear in a somewhat different light from that shed by Donald Davie. His eyes are clearly not the eyes of (for the sake of argument) Walt Whitman. The latter is actually dealt with in passing in *Purity of Diction in English Verse*— though not, predictably, as a culture hero or exponent of either purity or chastity. In his chapter on Gerard Manley Hopkins, Davie quotes Hopkins's modest comparison of his own work with that of Whitman—the English Victorian innovator crediting the American late-nineteenth century innovator with an extreme energy which dramatizes "savagery" and a "rhythm in its last ruggedness and decomposition into common prose" (173). This, however, doesn't suit

Davie's purposes, and he asserts:

> The upshot of this is that Hopkins does not use his special rhythms in order to catch the movement of living speech. That is Whitman's policy but it is only Hopkins' starting-point. His rhythms differ from Whitman's (and by implication they are superior to Whitman's) sheerly because they are reduced to or elaborated into a system. Hopkins is systematic where Whitman is casual. (174)

Whether the value-judgments are dressed up in terms of an opposition between being systematic and being casual, or for that matter being "pure" or "impure," it's obvious that Davie's paradigm consistently privileges the English over the non-English. Seen more sympathetically from the American side of things, the alternative to the notion of purity doesn't seem to be *im*purity, but (rather as Hopkins had apprehended) something like energy or dynamism, however savage.

Probably the most famous initial datum here is the "barbaric yawp" of Walt Whitman in his *Leaves of Grass* of 1855. While I'm not going back into history quite as far as Davie does in my efforts to contextualize these introductory remarks about rival dictions, it might be as well to note in defense of my method that Whitman is in many respects (like Gerard Manley Hopkins) an achronological figure in the making of poetry in English. That is, to outwear a cliché, he was a writer born before his true time; and it's more fitting to see his significance in terms of the trajectory of the poetry of the first half of the twentieth century rather than the latter half of the nineteenth. His infuence as regards theories of diction has been on William Carlos Williams, Ezra Pound, e. e. cummings, and (notably, as we shall see later) Allen Ginsberg rather than on Ralph Waldo Emerson or James Greenleaf Whittier: Whitman's yawp continues to resonate through the modernist and postmodern moments. In 1855 he had written:

> The spotted hawk swoops by and accuses me. . . . he complains of my
>      gab and my loitering.

> I too am not a bit tamed. . . . I too am untranslatable,
> I sound my barbaric yawp over the roofs of the world.[4]

This is the voice of the new America in the face of the old world —not pretty, perhaps, even discordant and rough; but urgent, natural, and above all untamed and embued with a sense of its own power which is unmediable through the colonizing English discourse ("untranslatable"). It is a free voice echoing widely (as well as wildly) across a huge landscape so different from the inherited narrow (culturally as well as geographically) perspective of the England that had once ruled America, an old England which is part of the European civilization Whitman describes as "the small theater of the antique" (6).

Width becomes a keynote, in fact, in many of Whitman's pronouncements: in his preface to *Leaves of Grass*, for instance, he emphasizes the "crampless and flowing breadth" of America with its "crowds" and "prolific and splendid extravagance" (5)—phenomena mimed in the amplitude of his own work, of course. And where Davie's approach is *ex*clusive, Whitman aims to be *in*clusive, as is evidenced by the number of unutterably tedious catalogs that feature as part of the texture of *Leaves of Grass*. The democracy of objects and ideas created in the text even incorporates the old order that attempts to retain its narrowing authoritarian power: "America does not repel the past or what it has produced under its forms or amid other politics or the idea of castes or the old religions. . . . accepts the lesson with calmness . . ." (5). These opening words of the preface reflect the confidence of the cultural Darwinism that pervades the work at this point, the conviction that America is the fittest, and it will indeed survive (an opinion vindicated, ineluctably, by the course of twentieth-century history). America *is* the new world, and a new world demands a new language, even if that language turns out to be (an evolutionary variant of) English. And, in contrast to the insular old grammars, laws, poetic forms and political power élites on the eastern side of the Atlantic, "American bards . . . shall be kosmos . . . without monopoly or secrecy . . . hungry for equals night and day" (15).

Inevitably, though, the dominant colonial discourse will be the starting point; and indeed it yields some advantage, as Whitman is quick to point out. He argues:

> The English language befriends the grand American expression . . .
> it is brawny enough and limber and full enough. . . . It is the powerful
> language of resistance . . . it is the dialect of common sense. . . . It is the
> chosen tongue to express growth faith self-esteem freedom justice
> equality friendliness amplitude prudence decision and courage. (25)

So far so good; and yet there are dangers implicit in appropriating English for American purposes, a theme he explores in two self-reviews of his poetry published in 1855 (and guaranteeing a sympathetic critical baptism for his work!). In the review entitled "An English and an American Poet"[5] Whitman examines the conundrum of a new nation still joined to the old world through its language, and therefore everything implicit in that language (power structures, political codes, precedents, and prejudices both cultural and other). He notes: "The poetry of England, by the many rich geniuses of that wonderful little island, has grown out of the facts of the English race, the monarchy and aristocracy prominent over the rest, and conforms to the spirit of them." However, as a result of England's "little island"-ness (what he describes a few lines later as "small geography") and its nonegalitarian structure, Whitman points out that "what very properly fits a subject of the British crown may fit very ill an American freeman" (his democratic point being in interesting contrast to Donald Davie's admiration of Shelley's "birth and breeding of a gentleman"!). Consequently, the great canon of Eng. Lit. doesn't properly pertain here, and

> In the verse of all those undoubtedly great writers, Shakespeare as much as the rest, there is the air which to America is the air of death. The mass of the people, the laborers and all who serve, are slag, refuse. . . . What play of Shakespeare, represented in America, is not an insult to America, to the marrow in its bones?

In any event, irrespective of the democratizing or nondemocratizing linguistic gesture, the contemporary models offered by the English literary canon don't pass muster: they are rather colorfully described by Whitman as the work of "jinglers and snivellers and fops"; or "danglers" whom American writers follow at their peril. The largest figure on the (then) literary horizon was "Alfred Tennyson" (with the "Lord" scrupulously omitted); but Whitman sees him as "the bard of ennui and of the aristocracy," and goes on to tag the elements of Tennyson's work as "unnatural," "emasculated," "impotent," and "sickly."

In the face of all this, thank God for Walt Whitman. The other anonymous self-review, entitled "Walt Whitman and his Poems" (Murphy, 29–37), opens with an energetic assertion of cultural independence and power: "An American bard at last! One of the roughs, large, proud, affectionate, eating, drinking, and breeding, his costume manly and free, his face sunburnt and bearded, his postures strong and erect. . . ." It hardly needs to be emphasized that the way Whitman describes himself is in almost caricatural opposition to the here unspoken norms of Victorian society in England. He is "rough" rather than smooth (sophisticated); "large" rather than small; "affectionate" rather than restrained to the point of affectlessness; prepared to acknowledge his natural human needs and appetites rather than disavowing them; practising flamboyance rather than decorum; having an out-doorsy hirsuteness rather than a parlor pallor (later making a point of emphasizing that he is "No . . . tea-drinking poet"); and—perhaps most telling of all—being "erect" (in several senses, no doubt) rather than a "dangler," "emasculated" and "impotent." Whitman's silliness in his self-advertising and self-indulgence at this point (and at many others) shouldn't deflect us from seeing that what we have here is perhaps the first early-modern example of what we might now call a countercultural paradigm generated out of disaffection with the dominant discourse in English.

Whitman himself describes it as a sort of cultural Declaration of Independence to match the political Declaration of 1776 which doesn't yet (in 1855 that is) seem to have filtered down to a literary level. He writes: "We shall start an athletic and defiant literature. We realize now how it is, and what was most lacking. The interior American republic shall also be declared free and independent." Until the arrival of his own work, this spiritual, psychological, and cultural republic hasn't eventuated because, in spite of winning a military war of independence, America continues to "dress by London and Paris modes" (Whitman going on a few lines later to criticize the imported stuffiness of the head-to-toe bathing suit), to "receive what is received there" and to "obey the authorities" and "settle disputes by the old tests." In the midst of all of this, "Where in American literature" Whitman asks rhetorically (how else?), "is the first show of America?" The answer, of course, is—only in *Leaves of Grass*.

In this work, in fact, so independent is the poet's assertion of cultural identity that

> Not a whisper comes out of him of the old stock talk and rhyme of poetry—not the first recognition of gods or goddesses, or Greece or Rome. No breath of Europe, or her monarchies or priestly conventions, or her notions of gentlemen and ladies, founded on the idea of

caste, seems ever to have fanned his face or been inhaled into his lungs.

And when the peerless Walt Whitman steps into the literary arena he talks

> ... like a man unaware that there was ever hitherto such a production as a book, or such a being as a writer. Every move of him has the free play of the muscle of one who never knew what it was to feel that he stood in the presence of a superior.[6] Every word that falls from his mouth shows silent disdain and defiance of the old theories and forms. Every phrase announces new laws. . . .

The "new laws" in question involve Whitman's famous formal innovations as regards poetry in English. Firstly there is the restatement, in changed (or further evolved) cultural circumstances, of the Romantic notion of organic principles in poetic growth and form. Conventionally (and, of course, in Donald Davie's and The Movement's view of things), rhyme and uniformity circumscribe and demarcate poetic energies; but for Whitman—as he argues in his preface to *Leaves of Grass*—"The rhyme and uniformity of perfect poems show the *free growth* of metrical laws and bud from them as unerringly and loosely as lilacs or roses on a bush, and take shapes as compact as the shapes of chestnuts and oranges and melons and pears. . . ." (11). Compared to these chthonic poetic energies (manifesting the virtues of ancient fertility rituals [the lilacs], elemental notions of love and mysticism [the rose], and various forms of natural fruitfulness), "the gaggery and gilt of a million years will not prevail."

Armed with the concept of organic (as opposed to learned and acculturated) energies, and the ideal of "free growth," the poet goes on to develop what we now call "free verse," manifested most obviously in the long lines of "Song of Myself" that subscribe to no preconceived models of regularized and rigid form, but expand and flex as required by the ideas and images which they embody. Like the hawk that inspired the original "barbaric yawp," this kind of form allows the poem to fly free across the page, and ignore or deny the symmetries imposed by convention and tradition. Pioneering in this area in poetry written in the English language, Whitman arguably became not only the father of American verse, but as well the father of modern verse in English more widely, his experiments with form significantly influencing many modernist writers more than half a century after *Leaves of Grass* was first published.

A further datum supporting Whitman's efforts to "make it new"[7] is the fact that language itself (at least as he sees it) is organic, liberating, and in step with the new world constantly evolving. His remarks in this area are contained in two interesting prose pieces, the essay "Slang in America" (1165–70) and the compilation of notes entitled "An American Primer."[8] The very first words of "Slang in America" indicate his desire to democratize the language—as opposed to narrowing it down by an authoritative (and authoritarian) prescription. He writes: "View'd freely, the English language is the accretion and growth of every dialect, race, and range of time, and is both the free and compacted composition of all. From this point of view, it stands for Language in the largest sense, and is really the greatest of studies." As usual, Whitman parades his vocabulary of freedom and size, two of his favorite metaphors (both in the prose and the poetry). The concept of English propagandized here is clearly quite different from that circumscribed and straitened version promoted by Donald Davie with his notion of "*Purity of Diction*," or by the dictionaries of the time with their tendency to render language static and stable through canonical legislation. For Whitman, language is neither pure nor stable—and nowhere is this more linguistically evident than in the main topic of his essay, *slang*. He writes: "Slang, profoundly consider'd, is the lawless germinal element, below all words and sentences, and behind all poetry, and proves a certain perennial rankness and protestantism in speech." And he goes on later in the same paragraph to add, "Slang, too, is the wholesome fermentation or eructation of those processes eternally active in language": under these circumstances, the "barbaric yawp" almost becomes the (linguistic) barbaric *burp*! The lawless germinal ferment that is language according to Whitman, untrammelled by conventional proprieties or social niceties, is mediated not by a governing political élite or its equivalent in the academies or University Presses, but by the *people*: "Language, be it remember'd, is not an abstract construction of the learn'd, or of dictionary-makers, but is something arising out of . . . long generations of humanity, and has its bases broad and low, close to the ground." And, as far as Whitman is concerned, it is the *American* primer where this will be most evident, since, just as America represents the cutting edge of new democracy and (increasingly) technology, so too its language must represent the cutting edge of

English. In "An American Primer" he catalogs this phenomenon, writing that "These States are rapidly supplying themselves with new words, called for by new occasions, new facts, new politics, new combinations." Predictably, he goes on to list copious examples from a range of fields, showing (among other things) that technological and linguistic expansion inevitably go hand in hand: "*Factories, mills, and all the processes of hundreds of different manufacturers grow thousands of words.*" His conclusion, once again, is that while people on the western side of the Atlantic owe a huge debt of gratitude to the parent language (America's "greatest inheritance" being "the English language"), nevertheless

> American writers are to show far more freedom in the use of words.— Ten thousand native idiomatic words are growing, or are to-day already grown, out of which vast numbers could be used by American writers, with meaning and effect . . . —words that would give that taste of identity and locality which is so dear in literature.

❧ ❧ ❧ ❧ ❧

Whitman's pioneering work in scrutinizing the parent language, and asserting the rights of the offspring to a new identity, albeit still sheltering under the generic umbrella of "English," was to be carried on in a slightly different context by another eminent American poet of a later generation—William Carlos Williams. Where Whitman had examined the cultural relationship with *old* England, Williams was to perform this task with reference to *New* England. The importance of New England, and of the Puritan heritage, to the American cultural matrix is well documented, and scarcely needs to be rehearsed here. Suffice it to say that from the publication of Nathaniel Hawthorne's *The Scarlet Letter* in 1850 and Herman Melville's *Moby Dick* in 1851, New England has had a dominant role in the literature in English of the United States, and seems to hang on in the cultural consciousness long after its overt foundational significance has faded into history.

The text in which Williams primarily addresses the phenomenon is a collection of prose essays entitled *In the American Grain* of 1925. Though Puritanism as it developed in New England is arguably a primarily American impulse, Williams treats it as a colonizing strategy, and traces it back to the original European voyages of discovery: from his perspective, Columbus and Raleigh become culture villains rather than heroes, and are responsible for the disease that is at the root of all things American, and which needs to be acknowledged and then remedied. This enterprise will involve, initially, a reviewing or rewriting of the settler myths, a recasting not skewed by blind patriotism or false national pride of a kind often found "in the American grain." So Williams begins:

> History, history! We fools, what do we know or care? History begins for us with murder and enslavement, not with discovery. No, we are not Indians but we are men of their world. . . . It is we who ran to the shore naked, we who cried, "Heavenly Man!" These are the inhabitants of our souls, our murdered souls. . . . [9]

This is hardly the sentiment of the traditional Thanksgiving dinner party, which is precisely the point: that kind of celebration, of sentimental construction, needs to be subverted or undermined. Williams in 1925 acknowledges the reciprocal nature of the experience of first contact, and in particular the reciprocal *harm* caused, both to colonizer and colonized—a notion that other literary and cultural theorists have only arrived at much more recently. The local peoples may lose their lands and lives; but the invaders don't really end up on the profit side of the ledger either, because they lose their souls.

From this point, Williams marshals his argument through a series of related metaphors. The native inhabitants are part of a teeming, hot, luminous, natural world full of life and movement; the colonizers, by contrast, are cold, dark, sterile, empty, and static. So, on the one hand the Rousseauesque noble savage inhabits a world of "Thickets with striped leaves, ferns emerging from the dark, palms, the heat, the moon, the stars, the sun in a pool of swampwater. Fish fly. In the water seals. . ." (335). On the other hand, we meet Sir Walter Raleigh, setting up the abortive colony of Virginia: "It is Raleigh, anti-tropical. It is the cold north, flaring up in ice again" (338). Similarly, in the essay entitled "Voyage of the Mayflower" (340–45), it is the Pilgrims who become metaphors of cold and sterility: their ship may be "May" (new possibilities, spring, fertility) and "flower" (natural fecundity and beauty), but they themselves turn into "little pips" beset "by winter's cold." So the voyage is not a triumph but a disaster: the settler American "grain" may have begun with the "seed of Tudor England's lusty blossoming" but quickly it became "spent" and turned "hard and little," a "nadir" rather than a splendid zenith. As

Williams acknowledges, they were "The first to come as a group" and thus became "the first American democracy"; but Whitman's hugely positive trigger-word of "democracy" is used ironically by Willams now, because the only thing they manage to do is to "succeed in making everything like themselves"—imposing a homogeneous cultural vision in the classic colonizing manner. Unable to face or accommodate difference, the native *other*, they simply retrench to "their tight-locked hearts"; and the divine logos which might have created a genuine new world (as it did in the beginning, according to the Book of Genesis) becomes for them merely a defense mechanism: "The jargon of God, which they used, was their dialect by which they kept themselves surrounded as with a palisade." The result is (once more) the loss of the soul: as Williams puts it, "And the soul? a memory (or a promise), a flower sheared away—nothing." The word "nothing" and its equivalents ("emptiness," "zero") resonate through the essay like a grim litany, ironically counterpointed by the repetition of "flower," "petals," "seed," "germination"—the absences that highlight the Puritan void. He even says at one point in the essay: "Puritans, as they were called, if they were pure it was more since they had nothing in them of fulfillment than because of positive virtues" (an argument it's tempting to use, as well, with what the Movement made of Donald Davie's notion of "Purity of Diction" years later in England). Like Hawthorne and Melville before him, Williams sees Puritanism as *death*-oriented rather than life-oriented. His (predictable) referent here is "Salem"; and he moves on from a brief discussion of historical witch-burning to remind his readers of the *continuity* of this destructive and negative impulse:

> And it is still to-day the Puritan who keeps his frightened grip upon the throat of the world lest it should prove him—empty. . . .
>    The result of that brave setting out of the Pilgrims has been an atavism that thwarts and destroys. The agonized spirit, that has followed like an idiot with undeveloped brain, governs with its great muscles, babbling in a text of the dead years.

The grim vision of America, perhaps echoed with slightly less intensity in Williams's poem "To Elsie" (poem 18 of *Spring and All* [17–20]), and re-articulated (as we shall see later), in Ginsberg's angry *Howl*, is carried on to the end of the essay, where the (brave) new world is described as having "become 'the most lawless country in the civilized world,' a panorama of murders, perversions. . . ."

So far, all of this horror may not seem particularly relevant to our main area of concern, poetic dictions in English (other than through the chance—or perhaps significant—echo between Davie's enshrined "Purity" and Whitman's and Williams's target, Puritanism). In fact, however, the analysis of extracts of *In the American Grain* which I've undertaken above *does* have real significance here, because part of the Puritan cultural consciousness inherited from America's early European colonial origins inevitably involves literature and, in particular, literary forms that may need to be cast aside. To put it in another manner, *ways of saying* not tainted by earlier histories may need to be evolved in the face of the destructive weight of the past: a diction *other* than that generated by the dominant colonizing discourse may be required. This brings us back to the same sort of argument generated earlier by Walt Whitman: for him the English language of England may be contaminated by an antidemocratic authoritarianism, still powerful, however effete it may appear. For Williams, the English language inherited from England and transplanted into early European America is also contaminated, but by a Puritanism which has imposed itself first on the native population and then on the consciousness of the colonizers, with disastrous consequences. What can be done with the "jargon of God" that the Puritans (according to Williams) used as "their dialect"; what can be made of their "text of the dead years"?

Obviously, one answer is to rewrite the dialect, to reject the dead elements. In the specific world of poetic diction this may come down to a rebellion against old forms of saying. As Williams noted, "Ready-made forms are sinister cookie-cutters impressed on the daily flux" (a culinary metaphor he gleaned from a childhood helping his mother in the kitchen).[10] He continued (using a metaphor from childhood holidays watching seafood being packed):

> "I was early in life sick to my very pit with order that cuts off the crab's feelers to make it fit into the box." Before creation may evolve, there must be a destruction of the box—the rhyme scheme mesmerized by the pendulum swing, perhaps, or the "fascist" sonnet form. The type of the modern artist is Whitman, who "broke through the deadness of copied forms which keep shouting above everything that wants to get said to-day, drowning out one man with the accumulated weight of a thousand voices in the past. . . ."

In order to achieve growth and health, then, it may be necessary to resist the conformist pressures of an authoritarian past, to write (as Whitman had suggested) using organic rather than closed and artificially symmetrical forms, and to shout above the dead. In the essay, "A Point for American Criticism" of 1929 (373–83) Williams emphasizes that a large part of what must be rejected is "the English viewpoint," which is "an old basis, without further capacity for extension and nearly ready to be discarded forever." The old must give way (again) to the new: "Forward is the new. It will not be blamed. It will not force itself into what amounts to paralyzing restrictions." He goes on, following another Whitmanesque theme, to cite America's sheer size (presumably geographical *and* cultural) as a key datum in the argument:

> And this is the opportunity of America! to see large, larger than England can.
> An appearance of synchrony between American and English literature has made it seem, especially at certain times, as if English criticism could overlay the American strain as it does the English. This cannot be so. The differences are epochal. Every time American strength goes into a mold modeled after the English, it is wholly wasted.

The cookie cutters and rigid boxes (even, possibly, the sausage machines with which I began!) must be set aside, then; the fascism of the totalitarian sonnet form must be subverted; all molds must be thrown out. Instead, the poet must rely on his or her own energies, and the strength of the materials to hand. To avoid cultural contamination from outside or from the past it may be necessary simply to make statements without slavish observance of old systems of saying—a task Williams undertakes in his poem "This is Just to Say" (33).

This very brief objectivist work tells of Grand Theft/Plums, recounting a situation in which the speaker in the text has purloined fruit from a shared refrigerator and has clearly enjoyed the experience. Presumably, in spite of the poem's extreme brevity, there's a double irony in the title here: that is, in spite of the apparent simplicity of the exercise, the writer implicitly ponders the *difficulty* of just saying anything (given the cultural baggage we bring into the frame) without lapsing into flat banality; and at the same time our attention is drawn to what is *not* just said in the verbal formulation—that is, we note the *absence* of fascistic sonnets, dictionary definitions, the English literary canon, and so on.

A more famous attempt at just saying, at purifying poetic diction in English in a way Davie would surely never have countenanced, occurs in Williams's "The Red Wheelbarrow" of 1923 (21). For anyone used to traditional English poetry, with its rich textures and rhythms, metaphorical usages, and complex rhyme schemes, this poem is a veritable nightmare of economy. A particular embarrassment for academics trying to explicate it to first year undergraduates (as I know only too well from personal experience), "The Red Wheelbarrow" resists conventional interpretation, in spite of Williams's assurance in the first line that a great deal may depend on it. The poem creates a viewing space for the objects within it (the wheelbarrow, the chickens) and, like Ezra Pound's similar excursion into Imagism,[11] seeks to go back to basics, constructing poetic diction and reality from the ground up, subverting our preconceptions and the textual tactics we might wish to apply.

"The Red Wheelbarrow" is poem 21 in the title sequence of Williams's volume, *Spring and All*. The first poem in the sequence, though not normally read in quite this way, strikes me as exploring a surprisingly similar textual area to that of the notorious wheelbarrow. Many commentators see poem 1 (15–16) in the context of Williams's career as a doctor, the spring in question simply being (reasonably enough) the birth of a new human life in sympathy with the new natural season (though Williams is careful to de-sentimentalize this notion, highlighting the grimness and pain in the process). To this obvious reading might be added, however, the suggestion that the birth in question is a *cultural* one, the awakening of a new American poetic (basic, unsentimental, down to earth, and as utilitarian as a gardening utensil) that is struggling to emerge from its historical antecedents, long after that original Declaration of Independence in 1776, or even the call by Whitman for literary independence in 1855. Seen in this light, the bushes that "grip down" with their roots in Williams's poem become metaphoric of American poets discovering a new consciousness, gaining sustenance from their own land and becoming fresh growths of an evolving language or idiom of the local.

かか かか かか かか かか

This may well be an overreading, on my part, of the text of the first poem in *Spring and All;* but, irrespective of individual readings of individual poems, it's evident that an act of rewriting poetic English is taking place, a re-casting of the dictions and forms inherited from the colonial past. My argument here is that the efforts of Whitman and of Williams constitute early attempts at what one might describe as "Breaking English," subverting or undermining the discourse of the parent nation—just as Davie's efforts (and those of dictionary makers) constitute attempts at enshrining or purifying that discourse. Whitman's example was to be influential in the formulation of cultural new-worldism not only in America but also (for instance) in Australia, where his break with English models struck a sympathetic chord in writers such as Bernard O'Dowd, a speaker for the emergent Australian nation seeking alternative cultural paradigms to the colonial ones at Federation (in 1901). Davie's thesis, on the other hand, was to prove foundational to the invention of the Movement, the dominant literary phenomenon in England early in the contemporary era. These are the drawn battlelines of a conflict that we can now pursue into that period.

# 2

## Gentility and its Alternatives

IN 1962 ALFRED ALVAREZ PRODUCED AN ANTHOLOGY ENTITLED *The New Poetry*. The title itself is, of course, something of a liability, since it ceases to be strictly accurate in the moment that it announces itself. This doesn't seem to have deterred subsequent anthologists, however, from adopting the same title (see, for instance, Michael Hulse, David Kennedy, and David Morley's *The New Poetry* [1993]), a tactic specifically explained and defended in the introduction to that volume (which we may need to review later) as an act of avant-garde solidarity emphasizing the continuity of the urge to be "fresh," "risk-taking" and "plural in . . . forms and voices" (16). For the moment, though, I want to turn to the introductory essay of the earlier anthology, drawing attention not only to its assertion of newness, but particularly to information contained in the second half of the title of that essay: "The New Poetry or *Beyond the Gentility Principle*" (21–32, my emphasis).

The word "New" in the title of both the essay and the book(s) seems to serve the same kind of marketing imperative that I suggested in the previous chapter motivated the use of the label "Purity" in Donald Davie's pantheon—though where Davie looked *back* for his sanctions, Alvarez (and Hulse et al.) obviously look *forward*. The product being purveyed by Alvarez, it rapidly becomes apparent, rather than being "pure English" is evidently *American*, an evolutionary step "Beyond" the status quo argued by Davie in the mid-1950s. In a prefatory note (17) Alvarez mentions the inclusion in his selection of the poetry of two writers from America who established themselves *before* the 1950s (the decade with which he otherwise begins his chronological sweep). He justifies the inclusion on the grounds that these writers (Robert Lowell and John Berryman) have already concerned themselves "with problems that some of the new generation of poets over here are beginning to face": this remark clearly puts the Americans in the position of being the "New" and the "Beyond" asserted in Alvarez's title. This position is further emphasized, as he notes in the "Preface to the Revised Edition" (dated 1965), when the anthology is expanded to include poetry by Sylvia Plath and Anne Sexton, who had been "Inexplicably" omitted (Alvarez's own word) from a Penguin anthology of contemporary American poetry (18). He decides that his own anthology is the place to remedy such an omission, particularly since it is precisely the work of these two poets which—as he puts it—"makes sense" of his introductory remarks. Again, then, Alvarez is giving strategic pride of place in an otherwise dominantly British anthology to American poets, of both the older and younger generations.

His introductory essay begins, though, with reference to an *earlier* generation of revolutionary Americans who impinged on the English literary scene: the Modernists. Alvarez returns to an opinion he first formulated in his book, *The Shaping Spirit* (1958), "that the experimental techniques of Eliot and the rest never really took on in England because they were essentially an American concern: attempts to forge a distinctively American language for poetry" (Alvarez, *The New Poetry*, 21). He cites Thomas Hardy's remark to Robert Graves that "*vers libre* could come to nothing in England," and adds his own comment that "Since about 1930 the machinery of modern English poetry seems to have been controlled by a series of negative feed-backs designed to produce precisely the effect Hardy wanted." English poetry resisted the first American attempt at literary colonization, then. The net outcome of the governing "feed-backs," however, is scarcely auspicious, at least as Alvarez sees the situation. The most recent formative negative reaction has produced a distaste for "wild, loose emotion" of the kind vented in some poetry (notably that of the Dylan Thomas–inspired New Apocalypse group) during the 1940s. The result, typified by "the Movement" and Robert Conquest's anthology *New Lines*, is "academic-administrative verse, polite, knowledgeable, efficient, polished," the work of writers who have in common (by Conquest's own admission) "little more than a negative determination to avoid bad principles." (Alvarez, *The New Poetry*, 23). The flattening, homogenizing effect of this is illustrated famously by Alvarez at this point when he quotes a twelve-line Movement poem which turns out to be his own fabrication, made up of lines from eight of the nine poets included in that anthology. His assertion is that this exercise demonstrates the "unity of flatness" evident in Movement poetry as a whole, articulating the voice of "the post-war Welfare State Englishman," the "man next door" (24–25).

In itself there may be nothing wrong with this: after all, why shoudn't the man next door have a voice in poetry? After a decade of linguistic inflation at the hands of war propagandists and of New Apocalyptic posturers, a down-to-earth common sense might prove salutary. The problem, though, as Alvarez puts it, revolves around "the delicate question of how common common sense should be" (25). He suggests that overreliance on a no-nonsense attitude has the effect of artificially stabilizing appearances, creating the impression that "life in England goes on much as it always has, give or take a few minor changes in the class system." Moreover—and this seems to be the nub of the argument—"the concept of gentility still reigns supreme. And gentility is a belief that life is always more or less orderly, people always more or less polite, their emotions and habits more or less decent and more or less controllable; that God, in short, is more or less good" (25). The problem with this normalized and normalizing view of Englishness is that it wilfully ignores (or smooths out) the history of the twentieth century, which is a catalog of "forces of disintegration which destroy the old standards of civilization. Their public faces are those of two world wars, of the concentration camps, of genocide, and the threat of nuclear war" (26). Under these circumstances, the sort of retreat offered by Donald Davie into "Purity," into low-key minor eighteenth-century poetry, is understandable perhaps, but unhelpful. What Alvarez sets up as an alternative to this literary gentility is a new poetry willing to engage with "the full range of . . . experience," which will eschew "either the conventional response or choking incoherence" (28), but that will nevertheless contrive to articulate "experience on the edge of disintegration and breakdown" (29). And if English poetry doesn't offer any models for this, American poetry in English certainly does, Alvarez asserts—in the persons of the "new generation of poets" in the United States in the 1940s "when English poetry was at its nadir" (28), Lowell and Berryman.

That such models are being heeded on the eastern side of the Atlantic in the 1950s is suggested by the work of (say) Ted Hughes, in whom Alvarez finds new energies and power. The introductory essay of *The New Poetry* concludes with an interesting comparison of two "horsey" poems: Philip Larkin's "At Grass" and Hughes's "A Dream of Horses." One might note, in passing, how, predictably enough, the Larkin poem deals with retirement and pasture while Hughes concerns himself with the typically Surrealist realm of dream (which, I've argued at length elsewhere, forms a key component of Hughes's poetic vision[1]). This difference aside, Alvarez notes how Larkin's horses —fine as the poem is in itself—"emotionally . . . belong to the world of the R.S.P.C.A." (30); whereas Hughes's horses, inhabiting a poem that presents "a powerful complex of emotions and sensations" have "a violent, impending presence" (31). Obviously, from Alvarez's perspective, this "presence" is promising; but in spite of the promise he concludes somewhat cautiously that while "a good deal of poetic talent exists in England at the moment," its growing to fruition depends on avoiding a typically English pitfall: "whether or not it will come to anything largely depends . . . on the degree to which the poets can remain immune to the disease so often found in English culture: gentility" (32).

✌  ✌  ✌  ✌  ✌

So much for the dismissal of gentility: but what of those poets who, far from immunizing themselves against the disease, succumbed to it willingly? Before we proceed to look at the work of the Americans singled out in Alvarez's essay, it's perhaps appropriate to glance, however briefly, at the efforts of the Movement, and in particular those of its brightest exponent, Philip Larkin. I don't wish to go beyond what's necessary in order to establish a significant context here for my later remarks: certainly I don't intend to indulge in a detailed survey, something which has been done already by far too many critical commentators (including myself).[2] Nevertheless, gentility (if nothing else) requires that we at least call in to visit the Movement before moving beyond.

In the main Movement anthologies, edited by Robert Conquest, *New Lines* (1956) and *New Lines—II* (1963), it becomes immediately evident that Donald Davie's *pre*scription ("Purity") and Alfred Alvarez's *pro*scription ("Gentility") are both to be embraced cheerfully (or at least as cheerfully as a Movement poet can manage): far from being labeled a "disease," the gentility principle is clearly seen as part of a new drive towards "health." In the first *New Lines* volume, Conquest in fact claims that "this collection has been made" as a result of "the belief that a genuine and healthy poetry of the new period has established itself" (xi). And Davie himself amplifies this somewhat in the first part of his essay "The Poet in the Imaginary Museum" when he notes that English poets in the 1950s "are putting the house of English poetry in order," an exercise that (he adds) involves building "an altogether humbler structure on a far narrower basis" and creating work that "is severely limited in its aims, painfully modest in its pretensions."[3] All of this seems to be in keeping with the agenda Davie had set out in *Purity of Diction in English Verse*, and he admits—in his 1967 postscript to that document—that "Under a thin disguise the book was, as it still is, a manifesto" that Movement writers such as Kingsley Amis "read with enthusiasm" (197).

As will be evident from what I've already said above, and earlier, "Purity" and "Gentility" involve not only poetic diction, but also the way that that diction is mediated, and the materials that the diction is called upon to articulate. To put it at its crudest, the concepts we're dealing with inevitably imply an attitude to *content* as well as to form and language: that is, if "Purity" is the primary governing notion for the diction of 1950s English poetry, then "Gentility" governs approach and subject-matter. Like all other discourses, the "English" that is to be either broken or conserved carries in itself information over and above the merely linguistic (as Whitman had noted a century before the Movement came to prominence). Davie's notion of poetic diction seems to pivot (as we saw in the previous chapter, and in total contrast to what Whitman desired) on values associated with "the birth and breeding of a gentleman" (*Purity of Diction*, 158). In practice this involves "poise and good breeding" (which seems to be very close to the "Gentility" that Alvarez disparages), propriety, decorum, consistent tone and point of view, stability, civilized moderation and urbanity, common sense, lack of extravagance or pretension, and a willingness to obey the traditional laws governing the regulation of syntax.[4]

This setup comes, as we've already discovered, from Davie's fossicking in the minor poetry of the late-eighteenth century—an area of literary history also favored by another early Movement sympathizer, G. S. Fraser, when he spoke of "the notion of a new Augustanism" (*Poetry Now* [1956], 17). The immediate *twentieth*-century model, though, is Edward Marsh's series of *Georgian Anthologies* commencing in 1912 (the era, in a very different context, of Pound's and Eliot's early poetry). In fact, at some points the introduction to the Movement's *New Lines* actually seems to echo Marsh's prefatory note to the first collection of *Georgian Poetry* (1912): when the editor, Robert Conquest, talks, for instance, of "the belief that . . . a genuine and healthy poetry of the new period" is in the process of formation (xi) he is more or less reiterating, more than four decades later, the Georgian editorial statement of "the belief that English poetry is now once again putting on a new strength and beauty" (n. p.).

The principal theorists of the Movement were very keen to emphasize the Georgian connection for a couple of reasons. To begin with, it allowed them to assert a continuity with a minor native English tradition of poetry whose "Purity" had been restated and re-enacted (wittingly or otherwise) at the start of the modern period. Secondly, as a corollary to this, a Georgian lineage allowed the Movement to bypass the powerful Modernist impulse which, according to most written literary histories, dominated at least the first half of the twentieth century. Such sidetracking is necessary because Modernism has come from *outside* the native tradition to offend against many of the principles enshrined in a "proper" English poetic diction—notably those to do with the regularizing of syntax and form (which free verse clearly undermines). That is, in spite of sometimes masquerading as English, Modernism is in fact American, and therefore, in a word, "impure."

In the face of this expatriate, almost colonizing, phenomenon, it becomes critical for the Movement to reassert the truly English English poetic dispensation, something which Philip Larkin does in a *Listener* interview with Anthony Thwaite on 12 April 1973. Therein he puts forward the notion

> . . . that there might have been what I'll call, for want of a better phrase, an English tradition coming from the nineteenth century with people like Hardy, which was interrupted partly by the Great War, when many English poets were killed off, and partly by the really tremendous impact of Yeats, whom I think of as Celtic, and Eliot, whom I think of as American. (473)

Such a tradition, debilitated but not entirely obliterated by the twin disasters of armed conflict and Modernism, can be reactivated by following the example of the various "survivors"—not only Hardy, but Graves, and (a little later) Auden (until he renounced his British nationality), and Empson. And the continued good health of Georgianism is even vouchsafed in a kind of latter-generation Georgian, and favorite of the Movement (particularly Larkin)—John Betjeman. John Wain, another of the *New Lines* contributors, in his *Essays on Literature and Ideas* (1963) obviously sees Betjeman as virtually the incarnation of gentility, a champion of "The English middle class, and particularly its upper layer [which] has lived for fifty years in a world less and less organized for its comfort, appreciative of its virtues, indulgent of its failings." (168) In the unlikely event of being called on to consider anything as un-English as passion as a literary theme, Betjeman can be relied on (unlike Lowell, or Berryman, or Ginsberg, or Plath) to keep a stiff upper lip, and keep the party clean: Wain writes,

> He is at his best when describing passion before puberty; after holding Wendy's hand in a game of hide-and-seek at a party, the little boy gets home and sinks into a delicious dream of love, "safe inside my Slumberwear." Adult sex relations, which insist that at some point the lover gets out of his Slumberwear, are seen mainly as a disruptive and ugly calamity. (169)

As far as I can tell, this essay is not written tongue-in-cheek, though it's otherwise rather hard to believe. Irrespective of Sir John's slumberwear, however, he clearly occupies a significant spot in the Movement pantheon. Larkin, commenting on Betjeman's *Collected Poems* in 1971, found therein the work of

> . . . a robust and responsive writer, registering "Dear old, bloody old England" with vivacious precision and affectionate alliteration. . . . I have sometimes thought that this collection of Betjeman's poems would be something I should want to take with me if I were a soldier leaving England: I can't think of any other poet who has preserved so much of what I should want to remember. . . . ("It Could Only Happen in England," reprinted in *Required Writing* [1983], 214)

Over and above this, Larkin awards a strategic role to Betjeman in his own somewhat idiosyncratic view of twentieth-century literary history. He writes:

> For it is as obvious as it is strenuously denied that in this century English poetry went off on a loop-line that took it away from the general reader. Several factors caused this. One was the aberration of modernism, that blighted all the arts. . . . One, I am afraid, was the culture-mongering activities of the Americans Eliot and Pound. In any case, the strong connection between poetry and the reading public that had

been forged by Kipling, Housman, [and] Brooke . . . was destroyed as
a result. It is arguable that Betjeman was the writer who . . . restored direct intelligible communication to poetry. . . . (ibid., 216–17)

He even concludes with the somewhat staggering speculation that
perhaps "as Eliot dominated the first half of the twentieth century,
the second half will derive from Betjeman" (218).

The degree to which such a suggestion owes its existence to a desperate rearguard attempt to reclaim English poetry for the English,
and snatch it from the (literary) nouveau riche Americans must remain a matter of speculation. Curiously, though, Larkin found himself in a position to enforce what would otherwise appear a highly
implausible structuring of literary history. This occurred as a result
of his being appointed (among other things) the editor of the *Oxford Book of Twentieth-Century English Verse* in 1966 (though the anthology itself didn't come out until 1973).

ﾟﾟﾟﾟﾟﾟﾟ  ﾟﾟﾟ  ﾟﾟﾟ  ﾟﾟﾟ  ﾟﾟﾟ

In an earlier book on this subject, I've already examined at significant length the phenomenon of the Movement's principal exponents (and particularly Larkin) maneuvering themselves into positions of great literary power, mainly editorial and executive. While I
don't wish to duplicate that endlessly tedious list here, it's important
to my argument to mention at least some details which will support
my contention (hinted at above) that the Movement essentially
adopted a *laager* mentality in its self-created custodianship of the purity and gentility of English poetry in the mid-twentieth century—a
tactic designed primarily to combat and exclude the threat from
American poetries in English at the same period, beginning with the
loathed Modernists, and moving on to those writers whom (we've already noted) Alfred Alvarez was to champion in his anthology, *The
New Poetry*. This sketch of the efforts made to resist the breaking of
English will also allow me to expand somewhat on my remarks in the
previous chapter concerning the canonicity of dictionaries, particularly those generated by the Oxford University Press presiding over
its empire of words; and as well it will enable me to air some views of
its parent academic body, Oxford University itself.[5]

In a sense, at this time, Oxford University seems to have been virtually a *laager* within the larger *laager* of a post-Suez England, relying
on earlier traditions to bolster a view of empire (in this case *academic*

empire) scarcely in touch with the contemporary world. Alfred Alvarez—unlikely, of course, to be a neutral observer in this context—
points out in his essay "The Limits of Analysis" that the process of
textual analysis used widely in American scholarship (not to mention, as well, at Cambridge University), and developed significantly
by various Modernist critics had, by the time of his writing (1959),
"still hardly penetrated" academe in Oxford, "one-third of the syllabus for a Bachelor of Arts degree in English [continuing to be] . . .
made up of Anglo-Saxon, Middle English and Modern Philology, a
less daring method . . . of ensuring some element of 'mind train-
ing.'" (in *Beyond All This Fiddle* [1968], 232). American approaches to
poetry, therefore, become irrelevant, particularly since (as Alvarez
notes elsewhere) "American writing begins where the Oxford syllabus used to end, around 1830" ("American Critics" in ibid., 272).
Oxford becomes—or remains—, then, a bastion of (probably) purity
and (certainly) gentility: Alvarez rather cruelly describes the scene as
follows:

> Granted the monks are no longer quite so monkish. Most, sometimes
> to their own surprise are married and live in considerable elegance. . . .
> The port is still excellent and the prejudice remains. Not that it often
> manifests itself in distasteful ways. In public manners the mild, gentle-
> manly ideal still prevails. . . .[6] Issues come and issues go while those
> Oxford spires dream on forever, unperturbed by the smoke fuming
> from the practical spires of Cowley. ("Oxford," ibid., 291)

He goes on to speak of a "vast, complacent courtesy" (292), a
"trance of self-admiration" which is "also self-perpetuating" (294),
and a retrogressive attitude whereby any undergraduate who "wants
to read what is being written now . . . must do so as best he may in his
spare time. It won't help him to his degree" (300). Alvarez's conclusion to all of this is that, while American literature continues elsewhere on its own independent trajectory and "is still happening,"
English literature has all already happened, so that "all we can do, as
readily and as sensitively as possible, is remould our idea of the tradition in order to include whatever tiny fragment of contemporary writing seems important ("The Poet in the University," ibid., 300). Such a
comment on contemporary writing in England in the mid-1950s
might seem to be somewhat sour and jaundiced; but on the other
hand, it might just as easily be seen as a fairly accurate reflection of
what Larkin and other Movement apologists were doing at the time.

This situation might not matter much at all, were it not for the strategic position that Oxford (and its Press) has come to occupy. The complaint of an ivory-towerish intellectualism and an entrenched conservatism is, after all, one that could be leveled at very many—if not all—tertiary education institutions. One of the reasons that this criticism is particularly significant when directed at *Oxford*, though, is that Oxford University has become identified as a key site, not only of learning, but of the mediation of the English language and, both indirectly and directly, of literary canon-formation. It may not be metropolitan in a strict geographical sense, but internationally it has long been recognized as a significant center (perhaps *the* significant center) in the production of English written culture, especially through its family of English dictionaries, and through its comprehensive collection of apparently "definitive" literary anthologies. Its prestige, authority, and influence is enormous worldwide, in a different dimension from any other English academic publishing house. John Willinsky in *Empire of Words* tells us that the dictionaries, led of course by the *OED*, enjoy "worldwide sales of five million books a year," and that in the late-1980s in Britain the top three nonfiction hardcover bestsellers were the *POD* (*Pocket Oxford Dictionary*), the *LOD* (*Little Oxford Dictionary*), and the *COD* (*Concise Oxford Dictionary*)! This, he suggests, "could reasonably be considered as the last powerful outreach of an imperial age" (13).[7]

So Oxford now becomes a center of the empire after the empire, as it were—an empire, moreover, whose significance goes far beyond mere word-lists: as Willinksy (again) points out:

> The *OED*, after all, does more than provide a catalog of some 300, 000 English words. It defines the scope of the English language, attesting to both its historical reach and global currency; it establishes the possibility of fixed points of meaning, definite senses, located in the publishing activity of a number of writers. Through its use of supporting quotations for each entry, this dictionary defines who has given this language shape and meaning, then and now. (7)

To me, the key words in this statement are "defines" and "establishes," for these precisely indicate the role that the *OED* has assumed, irrespective of editorial intention, either in 1884 or 1984: that is, it becomes a *definitive* account of English, published from an *Establishmentarian* orientation by an Establishmentarian organ. Its function is normative and standardizing—which is not necessarily a bad thing, so long as nonstandard usages are not totally suppressed, and standards are not used to exclude and silence alternatives. However, given the status of the Oxford imprint, the temptation is to assume that such standards *are* effectively absolute, though in fact they may be arbitrary, and indeed fictitious (as Professor Roy Harris claims in *The Language Machine* [1987], when he talks about "the *myth* of standard English").[8] Perhaps the appropriate question to ask is *not* "What is the standard?" but "*Is there* a standard?"—just as, at risk of appearing tedious, one might ask Donald Davie not "What is 'Purity of Diction'?" but rather "Is there such a thing as 'Purity of Diction'?"

This talk of dictionaries may all seem to be some distance from the poetry which is supposed to be the main concern of this book; but in fact the format of the *OED* brings us into more immediate contact with literature than one might at first suspect. A few pages ago, I pointed in passing to Oxford University's role in literary canon-formation both indirectly and directly. The direct route comes through the OUP network of anthologies widely used in schools and tertiary institutions, which we will need to look at in a particular context in a moment; but the indirect route comes through the *OED* itself, as has been noted by Tony Crowley in his book, *The Politics of Discourse* (1989). John Honey, summarizing Crowley in his own book, *Language Is Power,* (prior to disagreeing violently with him) writes that, according to Crowley, the original "*OED* compilers' reliance on literary language as the basis for their conception of standard English" had the de facto effect of actually creating a literary canon where previously there had been none. Consequently the canon (according to Crowley) is a fiction, promoted by the *OED*, and arising out of "'the need for it that had been produced by the work of the linguistic historians'" (94).[9] Whether one goes quite this far or not, though, there can be no doubt that the *OED* procedure of citing literary sources as examples of linguistic usage has the effect of creating a kind of literary English Establishment backed by the authority of the Oxford imprint.[10]

That authority is more obvious, of course, in the Oxford anthologies themselves. It's not my present intention to review these *in extenso*, but one particular volume commends itself to us as being of special significance—the *Oxford Book of Twentieth-Century English Verse* of 1973, edited by Philip Larkin. Here was a case where Movement orthodoxy and Oxford orthodoxy joined forces—though not for the first time. It might be worth pointing out here that in fact the majority of the Movement personnel were undergraduates at Oxford University at about the same time, and therefore it's not entirely surprising that they shared similar conservative attitudes to English poetry. In particular, both Larkin and Kingsley Amis had had the same tutor at Oxford, Gavin Bone. Bone was responsible for writing a book, *Anglo-Saxon Poetry* (1945), which the commentator John McDermott in his extraordinarily-titled study, *Kingsley Amis: an English Moralist* (1989) described as having "both a vigorous emphasis on Englishness ('the importance of the native stock') and a dismissive attitude to modernism, brushing aside T. S. Eliot as 'an American critic'" (13). And Blake Morrison notes that John Wain, another of the Movement's long-term Oxford connections, was tutored as an undergraduate there by C. S. Lewis who "shared Gavin Bone's prejudice against Modernist poetry, fearing Eliot as anti-Christian and Pound as a 'harmful charlatan'" (*The Movement*, 14). Clearly, then, a formative anti-Modernism was brewing in the classrooms of Oxford in the years leading up to the 1950s. It was to come to full fruition on the printing presses of Oxford twenty years later.

When Larkin undertook the editorial task, he was in no doubt as to what he was doing: he said, in a letter to Judy Egerton (quoted in Andrew Motion's *Philip Larkin: a Writer's Life* [1993], 405), "I am drawing English poetry in my own image." What this involved, essentially, was articulating the Movement paradigm—which we've seen before—of admirable Georgians and despicable Modernists. He wrote, in a letter to the OUP of 20 January 1966, "I am interested in the Georgians, and how far they represented an 'English tradition' that was submerged by the double impact of the Great War and the Irish-American-continental properties of Yeats and Eliot. . . ." (quoted in Motion, *Philip Larkin*, 361). If the Delegates at the Press were uncomfortable at this, they were evidently soothed by Larkin's assurance elsewhere in the letter that he did not wish "an Oxford book of this character to be eccentric"—though in fact the end product was in some ways very eccentric indeed. As John Gross was to put it in his essay "The Anthologist" (in the compilation, edited by Anthony Thwaite, *Larkin at Sixty* [1982]): "Not only do a great many of the choices in the anthology bear the stamp of Larkin's outlook and personality; they also cohere and interreact, so that we are left with a distinctive picture of the world. The result is a book . . . which deserves a permanent place in the Larkin canon" (86). The use of the term "Larkin canon" here is somewhat ambiguous: presumably Gross intends us to read it as "the canon of Larkin's work"—but it might just as appropriately mean "the canon evolved by Larkin," since that's basically what's produced in the anthology. As Motion suggests, "Larkin used the *Oxford* book to define and promote the taste by which he wished to be relished. A year after publication he told a colleague at Hull, 'Rumour has it that Kingsley is to revise—or re-do—the *Oxford Book of Light Verse*. We shall have stamped our taste on the age between us in the end'" (434). Nor were Amis and Larkin the only Movement personnel to "stamp their taste on the age" as reflected in Oxford anthologies. As well, over the next thirty or so years, there was (almost inevitably) Donald Davie, who edited the *New Oxford Book of Christian Verse*; D. J. Enright, who edited the *Oxford Book of Contemporary Verse*, the *Oxford Book of Death*, and (in less macabre mood) the *Oxford Book of Friendship*; and John Wain, who edited the *Oxford Anthology of English Poetry*.

Outside the specific purview of the OUP, Larkin himself, of course, was to flex his literary muscles in any number of posts. This is in spite of his disavowal to the contrary in an interview for *Paris Review*, where he said,

> I'm somewhat withdrawn from what you call "the contemporary liter-
> ary community," for two reasons: in the first place, I don't write for a
> living, and so don't have to keep in touch with literary editors and
> publishers and television people in order to earn money; and in the
> second, I don't live in London. (in *Required Writing*, 65)

This evasion notwithstanding, Larkin amassed an impressive list of friends and acquaintances in the publishing world, even as he continued to live in Hull: this list includes contacts with the BBC, the *Daily Telegraph*, *Encounter*, the *Guardian*, the *Listener*, the *New Statesman*, the *Spectator*, and *The Times*. As regards the positions and awards he gained, among many others there were the Chair of the Poetry Book Society; the Editorship of the *PEN New Poems* series; membership of the committee for the National Manuscripts Collection of Contemporary Poets; membership of the committee for the Eric Gregory awards scheme for young poets, and of the Compton Fund Committee; membership of the Advisory Committee of the Queen's Gold Medal for Poetry; nomination for the Professorship of Poetry at Oxford (a post, incidentally, held by his friend and fellow Movement contributor, John Wain, from 1973–78); Chair of the Booker Prize Committee; the official decoration of CBE, and subsequently Companion of Honour; and nomination for Poet Laureate.[11]

My point here, somewhat ponderously managed, perhaps, is that Larkin and many of his associates were literary entrepreneurs as well as writers, and formed a formidable lobby and power élite for imposing their tastes on English poetry (at least that written in England) for a number of years. And those tastes, as we've already seen, tend very much in favor of the Georgian, the native status quo, and against the Modernist, the expatriate experimental. So it's no surprise, when we turn to Larkin's version of twentieth-century poetry as collected and reflected in the *Oxford Book*, to find that its constitution is significantly different from that of the previous version, which had been edited by a man described by Larkin himself as "Celtic"[12] (which was almost certainly *not* intended as a compliment)—W. B. Yeats. Yeats had been editor in 1935, over thirty years before Larkin was appointed; so naturally one wouldn't expect the contents of the two anthologies to be anywhere near identical. Even given this circumstance, though, some striking data emerge in a comparison.

The big scandal of Yeats's reign as *Oxford* editor had been his total exclusion of the work of Wilfred Owen (much to the discomfort of the Delegates at the Press). Not surprisingly, since Owen represents one of the components of Larkin's view of English poety damaged by the Great War, he is now reinstated with seven poems. The same is the case with Robert Graves, from whose work eleven poems are selected (again, none in Yeats's version of the anthology). Similarly with other First World War poets, Larkin pubishes seven from Sassoon (four in Yeats); six from Brooke (one in Yeats); nine from Edward Thomas (one in Yeats); two from Rosenberg (none in Yeats); and four from Muir (again, none in Yeats). Larkin's choices clearly bolster the impression a reader would get of the significant *bulk* (if nothing else) of this more or less Georgian material. As much might be said, too, of the particular Movement favorites from the minor native line: Larkin opts for eight poems by Housman (five in Yeats); thirteen by Kipling (two in Yeats); twelve by Betjeman (none in Yeats); and a staggering *twenty-seven* by Hardy (four in Yeats).

On the other side of the coin, much of the space liberated to make way for this strong local showing comes, predictably enough, from the Modernist share of things. Larkin does, admittedly, offer fairly substantial selections from the "Celtic" Yeats and the "American" Eliot, presumably on the grounds that, even from a Movement perspective, these writers are scarcely negligible. But Pound is nowhere to be seen; and Herbert Read (who perhaps strayed too close to Modernism, Surrealism, and the New Apocalypse for Larkin's liking) is represented by only one poem (as opposed to a full seventeen pages in Yeats's selection). And—most notorious of all—David Jones is conspicuous by his total absence from the Larkin text, in spite of significant pressure from the Delegates at the Press to include him.

Of course, selections in any anthology are apt to be somewhat idiosyncratic, and every editor in one way or another rewrites literary history; but Larkin's version of twentieth-century English poety is so loaded as to have provoked adverse criticism even from friends and sympathizers. Donald Davie, for instance, in retrospect rather surprisingly complained:

> And thus conclusively—so some angrily thought and said—was the clock put back to the languid and all too English amateurishness which two Americans and an Irishman had bullied us out of sixty years before. To such observers it seemed that the volume was a monument to our insular complacency, and a device for perpetuating it. (in *Under Briggflatts: a History of Poetry in Great Britain 1960–1988* [1989], 114)

Larkin, meanwhile, was unrepentant; and—as Andrew Motion points out—was prepared to indulge in more of the same:

> More vigorously and entertainingly than the *Oxford* anthology, *Required Writing* defends what is local, well-made, modest and accessible. Early Auden, Hardy, William Barnes, Edward Thomas, Housman, Owen, Betjeman and Pym are praised, Eliot and Pound derided. . . . At every turn the English line is proclaimed as more resilient and various than its detractors admit: more entertaining and likely to produce work which is beautiful or true or both. (*Life*, 502–3)

What this amounts to, given Larkin's (and Oxford's) prestige, his wide circle of influential acquaintance, and his popularity—even dominance—as a literary figure over twenty or so years, is a concerted attempt to preserve the Englishness of English poetry (its "Purity," its "Gentility"), to resist attempts at breakage of its stranglehold on the British poetry marketplace. This might have as much to do with the history of publicity campaigns as of literature; and Larkin's entrepreneurial efforts may be seen somewhat cynically in the context of packaging deals; but the fact remains that the front established (*E*stablished) here is a truly formidable one.

જી      જી      જી      જી      જી

Before moving on to the other dispensation, Alvarez's *New Poetry* Americans, there only remains the necessity of putting some brief text into the context examined above. The answer to the question, "What was Movement poetry actually like?" is of course a highly significant one for us here, albeit already conveniently available in any number of locations.[13] The obvious answer, too, is an easy one, since Movement poetry (and to some degree Larkin's own *corpus* in the late-1950s) is eminently *generalisable*, uniform, homogeneous. Without wishing to over-crudify, one might say that at the heart of the Movement is Bleaney: I refer, of course, to Larkin's eponymous character in the poem, "Mr. Bleaney" (*Collected Poems*, 102–3).[14]

At the start of the poem we're ushered into a bed-sitter by a land-lady who (in Larkin's own recorded rendition of the text) has something of a whine in her voice, guaranteed to make us feel at our *un*ease. Being uncomfortable is something of a prerequisite for admission to many of Larkin's poems of this period—not so uncomfortable as to validate complaint, or real anxiety, or provoke the search for any positive remedy, but discomfort nonetheless. The room is one of several rented premises we encounter in the course of the *Collected Poems*—the "upstairs" of "Negative Indicative" (79) with its "plain room smelling of soap" and "the grate choked with a frill" that precludes warmth of any description; the unpleasantly thin "emaciate attic" of "Unfinished Poem" (60); the "desolate attic" in "Deceptions" (32), which turns out to be not a literal attic, but metaphoric of grim "fulfilment"; and the "High Windows" of Larkin's own upstairs apartment (in the collection of that name) from which he used to look down (literally and figuratively) on his (poetic) subjects. These elevated vantages enable withdrawal and spectation (if not quite voyeurism), much as do the moving trains from whose windows Larkin so often seems to be peering without risk of engagement or involvement. In the room that used to house Mr. Bleaney (who has now moved on and is therefore—echoing the emptinesses so common in this poetry—only an absence in the text) what the replacement tenant sees from the window is a garden; or, to be more accurate in the postlapsarian world of Bleaneydom, a shabby and untidy building site. Downstairs, as the foretaste of a low-key suburban, domestic hell, perhaps, the TV blathers away, communicating something that it's probably best not to hear. Inside, all the furnishings continue the theme of dinginess and discomfort, and as readers invited into this space we begin to feel that this may all be no more (nor less) than we deserve, *our* place, along with the poet—a small-scale punishment of tedium and malaise for our undisclosed (but presumably small) sins. Or, rather, it's *not* our place, since that would be to fit in somehow: the many flats in Larkin's work (and by that I mean "rentable accommodations" rather than depressed moments—of which there are also many) emphasize that our stay is temporary, not based on ownership (which would be too definite, too permanent, not to mention too affluent).

And speaking of affluence (or the lack of it), there's Mr. Bleaney's place of work—"the Bodies." This reference may at first be puzzling if we can't identify it—and certainly it seems disconcerting, even ominous: *whose* bodies are we called on to deal with here? We know that our own bodies are in a sense rented accommodation just like Bleaney's room; further, when we see the vacant lot outside, we may wonder if this is something out of a low-budget horror movie and there are corpses (bodies) buried at the bottom of the garden. Then we realize that the primary reference is to the car bodies plant in Coventry (Larkin's home territory), the vast automated factory in the English Midlands (affectionately but dubiously known as the "black country"), a place heavily devastated by bombing during the Second World War (so that perhaps the littered view beyond Bleaney's window is in fact a bomb-site?).[15] Mortality, horror, war, heavy industry, automation—all add to our sense of discomfort, so that by the time we learn in line nine that in "Mr. Bleaney's room" there is in fact "no room" (though the impression somehow remains of *emptiness*, literal as well as metaphorical), we begin to wonder quite where we are, what's going on, and to what terminus the negatives are leading. And the poet is unable to help us, as he builds up for his climax, an eight-line crescendo culminating in the monumentally *un*ringing statement, "I don't know": if he doesn't know, then how can we (and does it really matter)?

"Mr. Bleaney" showcases many Movement themes and mannerisms—the life of the "Less Deceived"[16] (sub)urban Englishman in the drab and slightly damaged 1950s, expecting little and getting less, uncomfortable yet uncomplaining; the poetic statement based on anticlimax, and negativity, and a refusal to answer (or usually even address) the big questions; the form and technique undemonstrative yet highly controlled and competent. So far, so good, particularly in the hands of a poet of Larkin's caliber; and yet, as these "Less Deceived" gestures become reiterated in poem after Movement poem, they become remarkably unsatisfying, because no alternative seems to present itself: where do we go for a change? The Movement answer seems to be, "nowhere." In an earlier book I suggested that the 1950s saw the emergence of what I called the "SBP"—the Standard British Poet, like a measure of weight (fairly light) or volume (not too much). Such a writer always provides a guaranteed product that is uniformly the same on every occasion (like the merchandise in any number of international fast food chains or even—to go back to where I began my discussion—a Purity Brand pork sausage); but if you want something different, you have to look somewhere else, which may be tricky if the Movement has taken over all available commercial space. In order to see what we may be missing if we only buy Movement brand, perhaps some market research in the form of a *comparison* might be appropriate at this point.

In fact, a number of convenient comparisons offer themselves, and for an interesting reason. Following a tactic employed by their admired Augustan forebears, various Movement writers decided that it would be desirable to "improve" the work of that 1940s tear-away and unruly genius, Dylan Thomas, in much the same way that Dryden had decided to "improve" Shakespeare, and Pope to "smooth out" Donne. This act of rewriting, or appropriation (something one can do with impunity, of course, when one governs the empire), furnishes opportunities to compare "before" with "after," the original with the "normalized" or regulated versions. The usual texts cited in this regard are D. J. Enright's "On the Death of a Child," which appeared in *New Lines*, and performs a Movement salvage operation on Thomas's "A Refusal to Mourn the Death, by Fire, of a Child in London" (originally published in his 1946 volume, *Deaths and Entrances*, and conveniently available in the 1988 *Collected Poems*).[17] Or there's Donald Davie's "A Baptist Childhood" or Larkin's "I Remember, I Remember" (in *New Lines—II* and *New Lines* respectively), both of which attempt to "redeem" Thomas's "Fern Hill" (also from *Deaths and Entrances*).[18] In the space available here, I want to concentrate on these latter.

Thomas's poem (134–35) is relatively long and expansive (just under 470 words, in comparison to the stingy 80 or so words of Davie and the approximately 280 words of Larkin in the "purified" texts). "Fern Hill" thus gives an impression, in its physical presence on the page, of amplitude, even plenitude. This fullness is amplified by the poet's use of present participles—"singing," "running"—that create a feeling of continuing growth, energy, extension. His theme, bound to be a red rag to the bullish Movement writers who were (literally) to a man "Against Romanticism" (as Kingsley Amis had put it),[19] is a romanticized vision of childhood. From the outset, as if to offend against notions of a pure and chaste diction which were to be formulated in the next decade, Thomas creates a kind of verbal ecstasy, rich and dense—the "lilting house," the "rivers of . . . light." Reiteration of "green" and "golden" produces a gorgeous technicolor view of the farm at Fern Hill, which (many miles away, literally and figuratively, from Movement suburbanism) might almost be a prelapsarian paradise where the protagonist (quite unlike Mr. Bleaney) feels himself to be with "Adam and maiden" and is "honored," "prince," and "lordly." The fleeting suspicion that this is all an illusion, or at least only a temporary phenomenon—that in fact we're "once *below* a time" (my italics) and must suffer the ambiguous "windfall" of the light, eventually moving "out of grace"—only seems to intensify the joy and nostalgia, the desire to sing it out like a charismatic preacher.

In fact, *singing* is a key referent in the poem (appearing in a variety of grammatical guises—"singing," "songs," "sang") because it underlines the *lyric* nature of the work, the lyric mode being very much part of Thomas's stock-in-trade, though the Movement was to come out against it (Davie dismissing it in a genteel manner in *Purity of Diction in English Verse* by suggesting that lyric poetry sits rather ill with the notion of "a chaste diction" [70]). "Fern Hill"'s lyricism is bolstered by various audial effects—notably alliterations such as the rather breathless "happy as the heart" and "house high hay"; but also the complex melodic repetitions and continuities achieved in the intricate modulation of the nine-line stanzas. These are basically unrhymed (though with occasional rhymes, half-rhymes, and assonances), but with a patterned syllabic interweaving of long (lines 1, 2, 6, 7), medium (lines 3, 5, 9), and short (lines 4, 8).

Davie's "A Baptist Childhood" (*Collected Poems 1950–1970* [1972], 46) is by comparison short, plain and direct—or perhaps one should say, to use the poet-critic's own terms—"pure" and "chaste." It begins with a quote from line 2 of "Fern Hill"—"happy as the grass was green"—but that's the last we see of color and natural growth. Thomas's (and, earlier, Whitman's) joy at the grass is replaced by something joyless, darker, and colder. The pantheism of Thomas's open and "easy" nature is replaced by an interiorscape dominated by strict Scriptural law and awareness of a Fallen dispensation. Here the soul, in spite of belonging to a Baptist, must "Parch unbaptized." The poem's tight negative control of subject-matter (absolutely *no* nostalgia, *no* celebration, *no* innocence) is mimed by a strict form—three basic four-line stanzas rhyming abab, with no suggestion of flamboyance in the language, and a meticulous scrutiny (in particular) of adjectives, which are emphatically functional (albeit ingenious at times). Undoubtedly the poem is adroitly handled, clever, and controlled; but in the end (to borrow a word from Larkin's attic) it seems by comparison to Thomas's work to be rather "emaciate."[20]

Larkin's "I Remember, I Remember" (*Collected Poems*, 81–82), continuing the common theme of memories of childhood, is *more* substantial, but not more positive in tone. This time the memories— awakened by the poet's arrival (by train, as usual) in Coventry—are of what *didn't* transpire (Larkin frequently boasting at parties, incidentally, that nobody could write his biography because nothing had ever happened to him). Coventry is the same place we visited in "Mr. Bleaney," with the same implications of pollution, dereliction, industrial production lines. Unlike Thomas's green and golden Eden of Wales, the Midlands are (as I pointed out earlier) *black* country. The spontaneous natural life of "Fern Hill" (not only grass, but foxes, owls, nightjars, cocks, pheasants, horses) is replaced by the seemingly automated flow of "men with number-plates": these phenomena are actually employees returning after delivering new cars (hence the [temporary] car registration plates they carry), but the way Larkin phrases the poem makes them seem like faceless and nameless ciphers, identified only by a number (and so even lower down the scale—if such a thing were possible—than Mr. Bleaney).

Thomas's almost garrulous enthusiasm is replaced by the laconic voice of a poet who, essentially, has "sent us to Coventry," unwilling to communicate with us—except, that is, in negatives. In successive stanzas (4, 5, 6) we're told of epiphanies—spiritual, sexual, and literary—that never happened: so the air of "Fern Hill," pregnant with possibility, is replaced by that of middle 1950s middle England where, like the poet, we can expect *not* to get saved, laid, or published! The whole deal is accepted more or less passively: as "Things move" the poet sits back to look out of the window again, his view framed and estranged (to describe it as *alienated* would be to overstate the case). He looks "for a sign" (of redemption or grace, per-

haps, like the penitent in T. S. Eliot's "Gerontion"?),[21] but can't even
see the station name-board that would tell him his life has come
round in a circle, to where his "childhood was unspent." His response to this potential drama of return to origins is nothing more
than a verbal shrug—"'Oh well'"—brilliantly made to rhyme by
Larkin with "'Hell,'" so that the worst fate a Christian can suffer is
linked prosodically to a tiny gesture of resigned dismissal. Nothing is
allowed great significance here; nothing is permitted to exist on the
large scale. At most there's yet again a sense of vague discomfort, like
a poorly-fitting shoe rather than the onset of angst, or sudden defen-
estration. And the conclusion, suitably enough, is a tour de force of
unstatement, an aphorism of negativity which cements Larkin's reputation as the guru of the anticlimax: "Nothing, like something, happens anywhere."

"I Remember, I Remember" does a brilliant job of deflating what
was overinflated in "Fern Hill"; but the problem is that, once something's been deflated, it comes out *flat.* This may be effective once or
twice, but as a poetic gesture it's surely subject to the law of diminishing returns? On the other hand, the original Thomas text, like so
much of his work, involves a poetry of high risk, running the gaunt-
let of all our cynicisms and prejudices (and not always triumphing, it
must be said). But the risk at least buys the poet space, giving him
the option to be positive, to believe: when he begins his fourth
stanza, "And then to awake," for instance, there's indeed a sense of
*awakening,* of freshness—not of an Amis-style hangover, or a Bleaneyesque boredom at the thought of another day of humdrum routine.
The poem, in fact, reminds us of what we're missing in the Movement camp, the baby that seems to get thrown away with the bath-
water.

A complicating factor is the Movement's exclusivity (or do I mean
exclusionism?). They brook no competition, and offer no alternatives—an interesting contrast, incidentally, to the procedure adopted
by Alfred Alvarez in *The New Poetry,* who, while championing the
Americans he showcases therein, is able to find space for a number
of Movement poets to appear beside their contemporaries. In his introductory note to *New Lines—II* Robert Conquest admitted that the
original *New Lines* was perhaps rather narrow in its scope, and
promised on this second occasion to avoid "exclusionist theories,"
noting that his sole criterion for inclusion would be that the material
"should be (a) English and (b) poetry," and adding "This may be in-

terpreted very liberally" (xxviii). Unfortunately, in practice, the interpretation was once again very *il*liberal, and Conquest proceeded to attack the usual targets—disrupters of regular grammar, writers who rely on vivid metaphor, Modernists, and Americans. The result is a hardening of attitude rather than a liberalization, something that Blake Morrison comments on in his study, *The Movement.* He writes, "The group posture has always been one of 'consolidation'; now it has become more overtly one of defense: defense of the English language against new idioms; . . . defense of metrical laws and regular forms against free verse and 'pop poetry'" (260). This defensiveness ultimately caused disaffection even among erstwhile Movement supporters. D. J. Enright, for instance, in his interesting essay "The Brain-washed Muse: Some Second Thoughts on Tradition," wrote: "with stiff upper lips we manipulate the concepts of our masters, sliding them into increasingly ingenious and decreasingly meaningful patterns. Think of all the parrot-talk about 'tradition,' 'roots,' 'native strength,' 'impersonality,' 'irony.'. . . The din has grown in intensity as the Empire has dwindled in size." (in *The Apothecary's Shop: Essays on Literature* [1957], 227).

૭ૐ   ૭ૐ   ૭ૐ   ૭ૐ   ૭ૐ

The Movement, then, seemed to be moving itself into a dead end, although it retained significant executive power in the world of literary England. But what of the forces which were marshaling themselves to stand against the cherished notions of "Purity" and "Gentility"? In the face of the "old poetry," what of *The New Poetry*?

Alvarez's anthology, after its introductory essay positing the possibility of getting "Beyond the Gentility Principle," begins with the Americans: the ones he chooses are (from the senior generation) John Berryman and Robert Lowell, and (from the younger generation) Anne Sexton and Sylvia Plath. The ones I intend to deal with are Lowell and Plath (though the latter not until the next chapter), with a side-trip to look at Allen Ginsberg, who isn't included in Alvarez's selection but is relevant to the way Lowell's writing career proceeded, and who provides a continuity with Walt Whitman whom we visited in the previous chapter.

The selection of Lowell's work in *The New Poetry* begins with "The Quaker Graveyard in Nantucket" (43–47)[22]—straight down to the serious Modernist elements that dominated the first part of his career. The poem is dense, allusive, intertextual, complex, mythic, grand in scale, profoundly *difficult:* its family kinship with Eliot's *The Waste Land* and perhaps even Pound's *Cantos* is quite clear. This is precisely what Movement theorists were trying to suppress: Lowell represents the continuity of Modernism into a later generation, thus subverting the notion put forward by (especially) Larkin that Modernism had been an isolated phenomenon, an apparently powerful yet ultimately negligible aberration in twentieth-century English poetry. Admittedly Lowell's poetry wasn't "English" in the pure sense (in spite of being written in English), but its power and persistence was an awkward circumstance from the Movement perspective, particularly as Alvarez was importing it into England: true, Lowell's poetry may have been available on the eastern side of the Atlantic slightly before this (with the publication by Faber and Faber of *Life Studies* in 1959), but now here it was cheek by jowl with Movement work, as if there might after all be some choice.

Perhaps I should point out at this juncture that, in spite of the way I've drawn up the sides in this literary-historical battle over the language, Lowell and Larkin by no means necessarily saw their relationship in terms of a bitter *rivalry*. In fact they were acquaintances, even friends for some time, and Lowell, at least, certainly saw much to admire in Larkin's work. When, for instance *The Less Deceived* was published in an edition of one thousand copies by the St. Martin's Press in New York in 1960 (a circumstance seemingly belying Larkin's judgement that "all American publishers are Neanderthal blockheads" [quoted in Motion, *Philip Larkin*, 436]), Lowell declared, "No post-war poetry has so caught the moment, and caught it without straining after its ephemera." He went on to say that while the voice involved was "a hesitant, groping mumble" (so different, one notes, from Whitman's "barbaric yawp"!), nevertheless the work was "resolutely experienced, resolutely perfect in its artistic methods" (quoted in Motion, 328). And in a letter to Randall Jarrell, he spoke of preferring Larkin's work to that of Dylan Thomas, enthusing remarkably about "the all out enjoying amazement" he experienced from it (in Motion, 429).

The admiration, regrettably, wasn't fully reciprocated; so that Larkin, for his part, was frequently only as polite as gentility required, and sometimes not even that. He reviewed the Faber version of *Life Studies* in the *Manchester Guardian Weekly* of 21 May 1959, finding it full of "curious, hurried, off-hand vignettes" which were nevertheless often light and original (10). In private he was less charitable, describing Lowell as "a Yank version of John Heath-Stubbs" (quoted in Motion, *Philip Larkin,* 344)—a comment *definitely* not intended by Larkin as a compliment (though some writers—including Thom Gunn and Ted Hughes fared even worse at his hands). And, more trenchant still, on another occasion he labeled Lowell as "simply barmy" and as looking like "A creature that has talked too much, drunk too much and stayed up too late" (in Motion, *Philip Larkin,* 430). After Lowell's death, when invited by the widow to speak at the memorial service in September 1977 Larkin declined, saying of Lowell's poems with distasteful subtextual hypocrisy: "no one could fail to recognize and envy their vivid fertility, and comprehensive many-mindedness, but not being a lecturer on poetry and having by now fallen into a different and more meagre tradition, I am sure I could not produce the full celebration that the occasion will demand (quoted in Motion, *Philip Larkin,* 466). More meager traditions aside, perhaps it would be diplomatic to return to "The Quaker Graveyard." We find that the context for the poem is an interesting one, since Lowell is (in the volume before the history-making *Life Studies*), among other things contemplating (and implicitly rejecting) the Puritan heritage that had dominated the early colonial history of America, and against which William Carlos Williams too had complained in *In the American Grain.* The difference between Williams and Lowell is that the latter was rebelling from *inside* this heritage since he was intimately related to it by long family ties: in most versions of "The Quaker Graveyard," though not the one in *The New Poetry*, the poem is dedicated "For Warren Winslow, dead at sea," Winslow being Lowell's cousin and a member of one of the families who had arrived in the *Mayflower* in 1620.[23] As a symptom of his rejection of these blighted family connections—apart altogether from becoming a Roman Catholic, and a conscientious objector, that is— Lowell preferred to be known as "Cal" (after that highly antisocial and antipuritan Roman emperor, Caligula) rather than Robert Traill Spence Lowell IV, his official nomenclature (which cemented him firmly into the New England "aristocracy"). Rebellion and protest, then (for which he was prepared to go to jail if necessary) were part of Lowell's makeup, and part of the background to "The Quaker Graveyard."

The poem doesn't look much like a protest poem at first glance, though; rather it has the appearance of a lyric elegy, echoing (for instance) Milton's *Lycidas* (a poem from the best-known *English* Puritan poet that was probably the first lyric elegy in the language, and also dealt with the death by water of a close young friend).[24] This is an indication that Lowell was quite prepared to see himself as continuous with an English tradition when necessary or convenient, though perhaps part of the tradition of which the Movement might not have approved. Certainly, governed by their customary xenophobia, they wouldn't have assented to his notion of continuity between Milton ("*inside*" English) and himself ("*outside*" English): at one point, Larkin, parading not only his xenophobia but also his chauvinism (women in this case presumably filling the category of "*gender* foreigners"), wrote famously (or infamously) in an essay held in the Brynmor Jones Library: "I have a prejudice against foreigners which extends into literature. . . . We must construct a closed, single-sexed world" (quoted in Motion, *Philip Larkin,* 100–01). At the same time as deriving from (or trespassing on) an English tradition, though, Lowell's poem clearly performs a crossover, laden as it is with references as well to a great *American* Puritan novel, Herman Melville's *Moby Dick,* not to mention (as C. David Heymann points out in his study of the Lowell dynasty, *American Aristocracy* [1980], 353) "The Shipwreck," the introductory chapter of Thoreau's *Cape Cod.* That is, like the wartime convoys that are the poem's starting point, the work's significance isn't confined to *one* side of the Atlantic. Nor is it reduced to a humdrum catalog of routine: "Nothing," as Larkin perceived, might happen "anywhere"; but *here* something's definitely happening, in the grim action of the sea, as a life-and-death struggle (which turns out to be a death-and-death struggle) plays itself out under the blank gaze of that icon of Puritan obsession, Captain Ahab.

The lurid details are told in a vivid and loaded language totally unlike Movement English—the sea "breaking violently"; the "Light" flashing from the "matted head" of the drowned sailor; the corpse itself, depicted as "a botch of reds and whites." Such details key into a complex nexus of referents: the nineteenth-century New England whale fishery; deaths in the North Atlantic during World War II; Warren Winslow as innocent and helpless victim (of Puritan inheritance as well as wartime duty?); God's ultimate purpose (if any) in all this violence; the meaning of death and Biblical (Patriarchal) authority. This web of extended linked metaphors, and the concentration on eschatologies rather than mundane specifics, emphasize the poem's *metaphysical* nature (again, something that Conquest disapproved of on behalf of the Movement).[25] And the text's guest list of special appearances by Ahab, Moby Dick, Orpheus, Poseidon, Jonah, Christ, and God (among others) underlines how different is the territory being explored from (say) Amis's tamed landscape devoid of gods and mythic beasts in "Against Romanticism." If, ultimately, Lowell "doesn't know" (and the poem's ending strikes me as being far more ambiguous than most critics suggest), then it's an *active* not-knowing quite at odds with Larkin's passive not-knowing (and ostensibly not caring) in "Mr. Bleaney."

A language selection, diction, and tone radically different from the Established norms of "purity" and "gentility" is obviously being offered us here, then. This is even more the case when we turn to the poems Alvarez selects for *The New Poetry* from Lowell's *Life Studies*. As Jonathan Raban points out, by this stage of his career Lowell

> had relinquished the driving rhetoric and rhythm of the English Metaphysicals for a language that was closer in tone to the irregular, "talky" meter of William Carlos Williams. But quite unlike Williams's affectionate portraits of the patients in his doctor's practice, Lowell's family album is mounted in anguish, phrased in desperation. (Lowell, *Selection*, 23)

These texts might almost be custom-designed to illustrate what Conquest complained of in the introduction to *New Lines—II*, the urge "to direct poetry into the service of psychological needs of a type only peripherally relevant to art" (xxiv)—though of course it needs to be said that the definition of the word "peripherally" depends exclusively on where the boundaries are drawn! In Lowell's case, they clearly include the mental institution, as is evident in "Waking in the Blue" (Alvarez, *The New Poetry*, 49–50; Lowell, *Selection*, 67–69), the first of a long line of "hospital" poems (in his *corpus* and elsewhere). From the opening vignette of the drowsy night attendant to the (certainly more ominous) "locked razor" of the final line, the mood is generally deceptively relaxed, even "joky." Having converted to Roman Catholicism, Lowell seems to have escaped the damaged inheritance of Puritanism: as he puts it, "There are no Mayflower / screwballs in the Catholic Church." But the authority figures of the New England patriarchy are not to be so easily shaken off; and in the quiet empty moments of routine, Captain Ahab's instruments of torture and death are waiting to come out of the blue:

> Absence! My heart grows tense
> as though a harpoon were sparring for the kill.
> (This is the house for the "mentally ill.")

Certainly, by most definitions Ahab would fit into the category of "mentally ill," as would many of the witch-burners and "Scarlet Lettrists" before him in the Puritan line. I agree, in fact, with Jonathan Raban's remarks on "Waking in the Blue" when he notes that the mental patients in the text "are all rich New Englanders" who "have a long sentence of history and tradition behind them" so that perhaps the poem is ultimately precisely about "the exhausted tradition of New England" (27).

What seems to be going on here (and elsewhere in *Life Studies*, in the subtext of overt examinations of family members and ties), several thousand miles away from "gentility," is a scrutiny of the aftermath of that historical moment—as explored for instance by William Carlos Williams in *In the American Grain*—when the *pioneering* urge (motivated by notions of liberation and freedom) somehow turned disastrously into a *colonizing* urge (motivated by notions of exploitation and oppression). In this light, Lowell's work, as well as being "confessional" may be seen as expressing the need to renegotiate the subject's (and the nation's) cultural position, possibly in the process seeking a new dispensation out from under the long outmoded colonial hangover of New England. This is clearly a radically alternative tactic to that of desperately clinging to a superannuated model (as the Movement arguably did in [Old] England).

Further criticism of the existing order and society in America is voiced in another text from *Life Studies* (which isn't in Alvarez's selection, but needs to be mentioned briefly here, if only for a single-line comment on the decade in which it was written), "Memories of West Street and Lepke" (Lowell, *Selection*, 70–72). The poem is generated out of the irony of the fact that, when incarcerated in the West Street Jail in Manhattan in 1943 for being a conscientious objector and not being willing to conspire in the death and violence of war, Lowell had found himself in the same institution with (though less privileged than) Lepke Buchalter, boss of the infamous *Murder Incorporated* organization of contract killers. Writing now from the vantage of the following decade, Lowell notes that "These are the tranquillized *Fifties*"—a circumstance of which his retrospective view of the late forties reminds him because Buchalter too had been in a way "tranquillized." That is, "Czar Lepke," awaiting execution, had had his personality surgically altered so that

> Flabby, bald, lobotomized,
> he drifted in a sheepish calm,
>
> . . . . . . . . . . . . . . . . . . . . . . .
>
> hanging like an oasis in his air
> of lost connections. . . .

   The most uncomfortable aspect of this description is the haunting suspicion that the poet isn't *just* talking about Buchalter here, but about the entire culture in 1950s America (and even Western civilization as a whole). Whether it be via lobotomy or lithium, electric chair or electric shock therapy, somehow we may all be left dangling among our lost connections. How can we react except with a "sheepish calm," spiritually (if not physically) "Flabby"? Perhaps for the Movement this *would* be the appropriate response—the deadened, the distanced, (literally) cut off reaction (of the kind we commonly encounter in Larkin's work; or—even more striking—in Kingsley Amis's facetious option when faced with the various possibilities of modern living: "Right then, mine's a lobotomy" [in "Out-Patient," *Collected Poems*, 75]). For Lowell, however, some protest is in order, some criticism (overt or implied) of a world in which citizens need to be drugged, encarcerated, butchered in order to preserve a shaky status quo on "'hardly passionate Marlborough Street.'" This latter phrase refers to the Lowell connection (not yet quite lost) in respectable Boston, Marlborough Street being the desirable Lowell location location location, and the quotation within the quotation coming from that most respected and genteel of Bostonians, Henry James. The irony here is that such gentility, such remnants of the old Bostonian Puritan "aristocracy," are part of what is on the brink of disappearing in the new world now; they represent an old world doomed and not worth saving. As C. David Heymann says, *Life Studies* concerns itself precisely with "decline and fall, 'the dissipation of the old aristocracy based upon birth, wealth, family, institutional affiliation, and social bearing'" (411); and with "the death of the Lowell-Winslow dynasty" (407). He goes on, "*Life Studies* is not a study of life at all but of death, of ruination, of past glories spent. Each of the Lowells and Winslows that the poet portrays exists in a false Garden of Eden, a world of pipe dreams and broken promises" (407).

That world, reflecting the dereliction of the old order, and the "sickness" of its now less well-connected and disenchanted protagonist, is further enunciated in one of Lowell's most famous poems, "Skunk Hour" (Alvarez, *The New Poetry*, 52–54; Lowell, *Selection*, 74–75). The privileged New England élite is represented by the rather sad and lonely old lady at the start of the poem, rich and superior, yet bound to die soon. Her setting, and the setting of the poem, is a run-down New England holiday resort. In the midst of the seedy landscape, unwell, stained, skull-like and fallen, we discover that the text's speaker is actually a voyeur, a peeping tom looking "for love-cars"; and the poem is his confession. Most disconcerting of all, watching with him we see that in this modern mechanized world it's really the *cars* which have been making love as "they lay together, hull to hull." Under the circumstances it's not really news when the poet says "My mind's not right"; nor are we surprised when he goes on to echo Satan from Milton's *Paradise Lost* and Mephistopheles from Christopher Marlowe's *Doctor Faustus* (in which the protagonist sells his soul to the Devil) by saying "I myself am hell." Given Lowell's life—the jail term, the regular incarceration in mental institutions, the mania, the drugs and drunkenness (so different, one imagines, from Larkin's library career!)—this may not be much of an overstatement.

After the narrator's moment of (self) damnation, though, we come back down to earth somewhat, and end with the famous skunks who give the poem its title. Whatever these creatures signify, it's certainly neither "purity" nor "gentility"! Perhaps the coming day is the day of the scavenger, and in order to survive we need to be on the side of the skunks (who've had an unnecessarily negative press down through human history): certainly, a decade or so after Lowell's poem, Ted Hughes was to feel that we need to be on the side of the Crow. The fact that, in a world where it's right for us all to be scared, the skunks "will not scare" is somehow admirable: it's almost as if *they* become the dominant species, and humanity's sole purpose becomes to generate garbage to feed them. By the end of the poem they've become somehow *dignified*—by their *connectedness*, their sense of family, their directness, confidence, and purpose.

The skunks live on, then; but the New Englanders fade away, as we see in what was the last poem in *Life Studies* and subsequently became, in slightly rewritten form, the title poem of Lowell's next collection, "For the Union Dead" (Lowell, Selection, 95–97). Here the

landmarks of the past—"The old South Boston Aquarium," the com-
memorative monument for the Union dead (or is it the dead
Union?)—are derelict, threatened by predatory machines (the "yel-
low . . . steamshovels . . . grunting"). The site of Lowell's vivid childhood memories is being violated by the construction of a new
parking building; and now instead of real fish, "giant finned cars
nose forward like fish." This is reminiscent perhaps of the occasional
hints in Larkin's work of automated factory production lines, but developed in "For the Union Dead" on a larger scale to include certain
"protest" issues. For instance, there's the moral bankruptcy of commercialism (as represented by the advertisement for a "Mosler Safe"
that survived nuclear holocaust, which involves the crass exploitation
of a photograph of "Hiroshima boiling"). And there's the theme of
racial discrimination, highlighted in the poem by the Civil War monument itself, and by "the drained faces of Negro school-children."
There seems no place in such a picture for gentility, which has de-
generated in the mechanized environment into "a savage servility
[which]/ slides by on grease." All that humanity appears to be left
with is "Space"—which might be a reference to the NASA programme of exploration, but might also indicate the moral and spiritual void we inhabit when our connections are all lost.

The Lowell presented to an English audience by Alfred Alvarez in
these poems, then, offers us a rather different perspective on poetry
in English. He catalogs a world (almost a Puritan "empire") in decline; but in spite of himself being part (however unwillingly) of that
empire, he refuses to cling to it desperately as the Movement writers
did with theirs—unlike them, he sees the damaging restrictiveness of
the old order (culturally and otherwise) and is unwilling to condone
or promote it, either in word or deed. The same might be said of another American poet who was also highly significant in bringing
American confessionalism into English poetry in the 1960s, and who
was even more outspoken in his protests and iconoclastic attitude—
Allen Ginsberg.

ॐ   ॐ   ॐ   ॐ   ॐ

Ginsberg's poetic relationship with Lowell, and with poetry in
England, is an interesting one. Though almost ten years younger
than Lowell, he was to have a significant influence on the older
poet. In the spring of 1957, Lowell temporarily escaped the Puritan
ambience of the east coast for a reading tour of the (literally) far-

from-puritan West Coast. As C. David Heymann tells us, this also "helped him break away from the ossified, closefisted language and dandified ironies of his earlier work"; it put him in contact in San Francisco—in Lowell's own words—with "the era and setting of Allen Ginsberg" although (as he goes on somewhat unnecessarily to stress) that didn't automatically make him a "convert to the 'beats.'" (in Heymann, *American Aristocracy*, 402–3) Certainly, though, the Ginsberg connection had some effect on the east coast visitor: as Heymann says, "The Beat Poets and literary Hipsters of North Beach, with their free, Freudian, colloquial sounds, a compelling admixture of the poems of Charles Olson, Dylan Thomas [whose reading tour of the United States in the early 1950s had made him and his work notorious], Williams, Pound, Crane, and Whitman, inspired Lowell to reexamine his own literary style" (403). Years later (in 1976), during a joint reading with Ginsberg, and in the context of a comment in the *New York Times* that described him and Ginsberg as "opposite ends of the spectrum," Lowell quipped (as Heymann reports) "that they were not really so different as the *Times* would have it; if anything, they were simply opposite ends of William Carlos Williams" (494)!

As regards Ginsberg's literary relationship with England, it predictably had *nothing* to do with the Movement (his drug taking, communist upbringing, and homosexuality—not to mention his American colloquialism and messianic gestures—clearly debarring him from Davie's normalizing category of "Purity"). In this case it didn't even involve Alvarez's *The New Poetry*, which—in spite of the fact that Ginsberg would definitely have placed himself "Beyond the Gentility Principle"—didn't include his work. Rather, Ginsberg's version of poetry in English came to the local audience via a large public poetry "happening"—the first International Poetry Incarnation at the Albert Hall in London in June 1965—and its subsequent celebration in Michael Horovitz's *Children of Albion* (1969). *Children of Albion* was the next Penguin in line after *The New Poetry* and, as its subtitle *Poetry of the "Underground" in Britain* suggests, in a way it marks the next step forward.

Surprisingly, Horovitz was originally part of the Oxford connection: he'd been involved in doing a B. Litt thesis on William Blake until he saw the light in 1959, and went on (as his long, self-congratulatory "Afterwords" to *Children of Albion* [316–77] indicates at every turn) to transform the course of Eng. Lit. He became one of the founders of the avant-garde review, *New Departures*; and subsequently had a hand in its performance branch—or as he calls it, "Its travelling circus incarnation—'*Live* New Departures,'" a combination of music (mainly jazz), film, sculpture, mime and other artistic manifestations, as well as live poetry events (321). Irrespective of how one feels about Horovitz's entrepreneurial pretensions, the function performed by *Live* New Departures was a significant one—that of stretching the category "poetry" to encompass new things (even if some of them were very badly written things!).

His starting point for these new things in *Children of Albion* is 1957, not only the year after the publication of *New Lines* but as well the two hundredth anniversary of William Blake's birth. Inspired (like Ginsberg) by Blake's prophetic works, Horovitz receives a hellish (if somewhat genteel) vision of the University of Oxford which is actually a lower-key echo of the start of Ginsberg's New York "Howl!":

> At Oxford I saw budding talents buried alive, most elegantly—taught —to lie. . . . Legions of professional hollow men—brandishing standards of "The New Criticism" and "New Lines"—relaid their trenches, held the muddied field and apportioned the spoils. (316)[26]

But Horovitz is not to be lured into this cultural morass, the

> piddling wit, a trivial ingenuity that cries out for the applause of learned colleagues—
>
>> That was "The Movement"
>> —that *was*! (317)

Instead, he has apparently seen higher things, and "beheld the unfetter'd insurrection of Ginsberg and Corso through unblinkered eyes" (317), witnessing "the flexing of other (transatlantic) muscles 'at home'" (318).

Much of this muscle is provided by Ginsberg himself who, while not actually present as a contributor to the anthology, is constantly quoted and referred to in his capacity of "Beat" guru.[27] The opening poem is actually entitled "For Allen Ginsberg" (14); and his work is extensively used by Horovitz in the "Afterwords"—"Death to Van Gogh's Ear!" (346); "Howl" (347); the "Footnote to Howl" (349); and *Kaddish* (350). In addition he makes many textual guest appearances—as, for instance, on p. 326:

Came '65, and Ginsberg saw in Liverpool—
  Albion, Albion, your children dance again
  Jerusalem's rock established in the basements of Satanic Mills. . . .

The English connection is emphasized when Horovitz credits Ginsberg with the "transmission" back to the British Underground of "the heritance of Blake" (337), a heritance which somehow also implicates (astonishingly enough) John Milton—at least technically, if not morally. Horovitz explains: "Ginsberg is as instrumental with density of image & syntax, elliptical suspension of main-verb sense relief, and overlapping & run-on phrases in piling up a cumulative resonance as Milton was in his massive organ structure" (353). Resonance is clearly important to the Children of Albion, since it indicates the *audial* element in the poetic diction—creating a poetry which is related in some way to music, and particularly *jazz*, which becomes a kind of international language: "Jazz: sacred river, deeply embedded in the american idiom, was a seminal influence for many of us: underground movement, living mythology and international language of our upbringing: which addressed its primal messages to the whole world—& through which all could speak" (328–29). Jazz, then, while originating "in the american idiom," acts as a kind of cultural *lingua franca* and performs (according to Horovitz, taking his cue from the Beats) the task of "opening frontiers" and bringing diverse writers "into instantaneous connection—however widely dispersed in ethnic, musical and literary traditions" (329). One imagines that Philip Larkin, from his stance of ingrained xenophobe, would scarcely have approved. Larkin, as is well known, was a lifelong fan of jazz too (and in fact jazz reviewer for the *Daily Telegraph*), but he presumably didn't share this "Underground" attitude to it. For the writers in Horovitz's anthology, however, jazz functions on a number of levels, and primarily as a model for and adjunct to poetry performance. As well as including jazz slots in their readings, they frequently utilize a jazz-style verbal improvisation or "ad-libbing," thus opening out the text from its rigid confinement in print on the page (the example that the editor holds up for our scrutiny here being Adrian Mitchell, whose comments on improvization come from an interview conducted by George MacBeth [see 357–59]).

As well as offering new verbal freedoms, jazz and related musics also serve (other) political purposes, acting as subversive elements in the cultural process. Horovitz points out that "There's a strong line of dissent from the poetry of the work-shouts, gospel-hymns and blues singers, through that of Louis Armstrong . . ." (330). Again, this wouldn't be guaranteed to endear the phenomenon to the conservative British Establishment of the time, and Horovitz singles out from the opposition for particular (and scornful) mention "the stiff upper'd Schoolmen of 'Scrutiny'" and "the Movement" (356). Against these latter authorities he pits none other than William Carlos Williams: he quotes as follows from Williams's essay, "A Point for American Criticism":

> British criticism, like any other, is built upon the exigencies of the local literary structure and relates primarily thereto. Afterward it may turn to the appraisal of heterodox and foreign works. But if these are in nature disruptive to the first, the criticism will be found to be defensive, to preserve its origins—

Horovitz pursues the point with his own aside, followed by another telling quotation:

> & so the universities, & so the religions, & so the politics, & so the english death. But what Williams went on to say is less familiar:
>
> > Forward is the new. It will not be blamed. It will not force itself into what amounts to paralysing restrictions. It cannot be correct. It hasn't time. It has that which is beyond measurement, which renders measurement a falsification, since the energy is showing itself as recrudescent. . . . (355)[28]

And as far as Horovitz is concerned, that recrudescent energy is manifest, incarnate, in the person of Allen Ginsberg. He writes that, given current circumstances, "a high-priest like Ginsberg" is required in order "to revive Albion today" (344).

As will already be obvious, such a messianic cultural calling involves something totally different from purity and gentility: on the contrary, it subverts these notions, both in its language, the direction of its argument, and the mood of its subject-matter. The critic John Hollander in a review of *Howl* on its first appearance in 1956 writes disparagingly in *Partisan Review* that, "It is only fair to Allen Ginsberg . . . to remark on the utter lack of decorum of any kind in his dreadful little volume."[29] When we turn to the book itself (*Collected Poems*, 126–34), we realize that we're dealing with an updated version of another poet for whom the conventional decora of his day meant little, except as something to be energetically swept aside—Walt Whitman, whose "barbaric yawp" had rung out over American poetic English almost exactly a century earlier. One anonymous commentator even describes Ginsberg as "the discount-house Whitman of the Beat Generation" (in Hyde, *Poetry of Ginsberg*, 54); and in one of the best known shorter poems in *Howl*, Ginsberg actually reintroduces us to the earlier bard, though with an anachronistic setting—if not quite a "discount house" then at least "A Supermarket in California" (*Collected Poems*, 136).

What could be more appropriate as a metaphor of mid-twentieth century America's being mesmerized by material opulence (albeit in a "tranquillized" daze) than the consumable splendors available on the heavily-stacked shelves? Even the poet(s) are tempted to partake, and as Ginsberg wanders down the aisles "shopping for images" who should he bump into but Walt Whitman. The question that this imaginary (hallucinatory?) meeting implicitly poses is an interesting one: what happens to a writer when society commoditizes his or her work, swallowing it with the middle-class's phenomenal capacity to assimilate and thus defuse potential threats? The poet may continue to adopt a subversive stance, tempted to shoplift by the sheer availability of a wide range of comestibles, illicitly sampling the goods, followed by the suspicious Establishmentarian figure of "the store detective," but never having to pay since he avoids "passing the cashier." But at the end of this pleasant excursion, the rebel narrator's motivations and destinations have become unclear, so that Ginsberg has to ask his mentor, "Where are we going, Walt Whitman?" The answer is not immediately forthcoming, geographically, morally, or spiritually, and the father of American poetic English and the protest tradition is left at the end of the poem on the wrong side of "the black waters of Lethe," the river of forgetfulness in the Underworld.

Ginsberg's response to this situation seems to be an attempt *not* to forget the lead given by Whitman, but *to stay angry*, to stay on the attack with his confession turned protest. So when we turn to the title-poem of the collection, we may initially be comforted (though most critics at the time *weren't*) to find that the lines and stanzas (or paragraphs) have the same fullness and flow as Whitman's, liberated from the narrow conventions of traditional English meters; but we rapidly discover that Whitman's exuberance and optimistic energy from "Song of Myself" have been replaced by a Lowell-like confession and cultural analysis, motivated not by that earlier enthusiasm but by a more recent despair and fury: the "barbaric yawp" has become an agonized animal howl. The slow decline of "Skunk Hour" has picked up pace, resulting in a vision in which, to quote Ginsberg's uncompromising and unrelenting first line, "I saw the best minds of my generation destroyed by madness, starving hysterical naked. . . ." We're no longer in a polite (if seedy) Bleaneyesque suburb, nor in the crumbling ex-dignity of a superannuated holiday settlement, but plunged straight into the underworld heart of the modern city (in this case, New York): as William Carlos Williams warns the readership in an introductory note to *Howl*, "Hold back the edges of your gowns, ladies, we are going through hell" (*Collected Poems*, 812). The poem is dedicated to Carl Solomon, whom Ginsberg had met in the Columbia Psychiatric Institute in 1949 while both were patients there, and whose anecdotes provided much of the material for "Howl." The dedication sets the mood of mental breakdown and psychological disorder (precisely what Conquest felt, we remember, should be regarded as only *peripherally relevant* to the poetic text)[30] and the poem pursues this mood (among others) ruthlessly, becoming a litany of the names of such institutions— Bellevue, Pilgrim State, Rockland, Greystone (and, in the end, Woodlawn, the cemetery in the Bronx). Set ironically against these are the sites sanctioned enthusiastically by the State, though in their own way equally "mad," equally death-bringing—Los Alamos (where the atomic bomb was developed); Wall (which is simultaneously Wall Street, location of the New York Stock Exchange, and the Wailing Wall in Jerusalem where Jews lament Christ's Passion); and Madison Avenue, center of New York's advertising agencies, always waiting to snare stray poets:

> who were burned alive in their innocent flannel suits on Madison Avenue
> amid blasts of leaden verse & the tanked-up clatter of the iron regi-
> ments of fashion & the nitroglycerine shrieks of the fairies of advertis-
> ing & the mustard gas of sinister intelligent editors, or were run down
> by the drunken taxicabs of Absolute Reality . . . .

Nuclear destruction, the "crucifixion" of the human race, rampant and exploitative investment capitalism, the destructive lie-telling industry of modern advertising, all of these are ranged against the poet and his fellows, who are forced out onto the edges of their world. The evil genius of the negative forces is, as we discover in part two of the poem, "Moloch." In keeping with the Old Testament Hebraic tone of "Howl," Moloch was a Canaanite deity to whom human sacrifices (particularly children) were made as a propitiation: this makes him a highly suitable metaphor for Ginsberg of the modern industrial city and culture. He is presented in the context of "Solitude! Filth! Ugliness! Ashcans and unobtainable dollars! Children screaming under the stairways! Boys sobbing in armies!" His "mind is pure machinery" and his "soul is electricity and banks"; his promise (which was at one time also Whitman's vision of expansion and prosperity for the new nation) has "gone down the American river!"

And yet in spite of that, Ginsberg can still end the poem with his chant of "Holy! Holy! Holy!" In the face of huge opposition, he clings onto his vision and spiritual conviction. The text becomes a collage of landmarks (stations) of the soul and anecdotes of rebellion set against Moloch's powerful dispensation. On the one hand oblivion (Lowell's "tranquillized" world of "lost connections") beckons in "Howl"'s references to "catatonia," "lobotomy" and "the concrete void of insulin Metrazol electricity hydrotherapy psychotherapy occupational therapy pingpong & amnesia." On the other hand are the anarchic rebels against the system who refuse to fall into oblivion (submerge in Lethe), and assert their individual identities energetically (if unusually):

> who ate fire in paint hotels or drank turpentine in Paradise Alley,[31]
>     death , or purgatoried their torsos night after night
> with dreams, with drugs, with waking nightmares, alcohol and cock
>     and endless balls . . . .

And the poet's goal in all of this is "confessing out the soul to conform to the rhythm of thought," and "to recreate . . . [a] syntax and measure" which will leave him standing "naked" and "intelligent" before us—creating a speech act which is direct and unembellished.[43] This may not conform to the (then) current governing fashions as mediated by the best Academies, but perhaps that's exactly the point. After all, the university system, too, for Ginsberg is virtually part of Moloch's kingdom. In "Howl" he mentions obliquely his own rustication fom Columbia ("expelled from the academies for crazy & publishing obscene odes"); his Dada exploits at the City College of New York campus ("threw potato salad at CCNY lecturers on Dadaism"); and his presciption for surviving campus life ("passed through universities with radiant cool eyes hallucinating"). More trenchantly, in his notes when he made an audio recording of

"Howl" he said: "A word on the Academies: poetry has been attacked by an ignorant and frightened bunch of bores who don't understand how it's made, and the trouble with these creeps is they wouldn't know poetry if it came up and buggered them in broad daylight" (in Hyde, *Poetry of Ginsberg*, 83). More trenchantly yet (though still utilizing the sexual metaphors he seems to favor) he complains, "All the universities been fucking dead horse for decades and this is *Culture!*?" (in Hyde, *Poetry of Ginsberg*, 78). Equine perversions aside, prime among his targets is Norman Podhoretz of whom he writes, "I keep coming back to him it seems he has collected all the garbage in one mind, archetype" (in Hyde, *Poetry of Ginsberg*, 79)—garbage ("Filth!" "Ashcans," pollution, detritus) again being associated with Moloch. And one imagines that Professor Moloch is not only tenured in the United States at this time, but is also alive and well and living in Oxford!

ॐ  ॐ  ॐ  ॐ  ॐ

Inevitably, given the nature of Ginsberg's poetry and vision, he was bound to attract opposition and adverse criticism—not only in the United States, but as well in England when his work became readily available there (in the 1960s). He brought to poetry in English, on both sides of the Atlantic, a poetic voice and language which is active, aggressive, frequently hostile, and usually grand-scale (Biblical in mood and intensity), full of energy and power. Like Lowell, and Williams, and even Whitman before him, though in a more extreme manner than any of his forebears, he aimed to construct a poetry on different principles from what had become accepted as the conservative norm. He was, like them, in a way "breaking English" as a poetic language, or at least as a literary Establishment monopoly. It might be worth mentioning at this point (as Michael Horovitz does in *Children of Albion*, 318) that the American alternative was being promoted and made available not only by himself, and by Alfred Alvarez in *The New Poetry*, but by a new anthology of the crucial post-World War II period, Donald Allen's *The New American Poetry 1945–1960* (1960), which was followed in England by a somewhat different version (co-edited by Robert Creeley) published by Penguin in 1967, *The New Writing in the USA*.

These anthologies show that Ginsberg's writing doesn't come entirely as an aberration out of the void. On the contrary, there's a clear line of progression, if one cares to trace it. John Tytell, for instance (admittedly going back a considerable distance before the end of the Second World War) writes of Ginsberg's various antecedents that "Blake permitted entry into the prophetic tradition; Whitman offered the infusion of democratic optimism [not to mention a formal model for the longer line and breath length]; Williams inspired a new diction" (in Hyde, *Poetry of Ginsberg*, 171). One might add, carrying on this progression, that Lowell and Ginsberg and his fellow Beats between them evolved a confessional voice that is of significance to the poet we encounter at the beginning of the next chapter, Sylvia Plath.

In terms of technical innovation, as Kenneth Rexroth argued, Ginsberg "is almost alone in his generation in his ability to make powerful poetry of the inherent rhythms of our speech, to push forward the conquests of a few of the earliest poems of Sandburg and of William Carlos Williams." (in Hyde, *Poetry of Ginsberg*, 33) Ginsberg, though, tends to see himself primarily as developing technically what Whitman had pioneered. He describes the poems in *Howl* as "a series of experiments with the formal organization of the long line," going on to say that "I realized at the time that Whitman's form had rarely been further explored (improved on even)" (in Hyde, *Poetry of Ginsberg*, 81). He presumably gets from Whitman, as well, the urge to incorporate contemporary *slang* into his text—the "bop" language which was "hip" in the streets of the mid-1950s: "teahead," "yacketayakking," "lays" (in the sense of "a good lay"), "hotrod," "bum," "Cocksucker," "bullshit," "dig" (in the sense of "appreciate"), "nowhere" (as an adjective), "loned" (as a verb). Not only does this provide him with a new vocabulary, but as well at times a new syntax, as parts of speech change their function (a verb becoming a noun ["lay"]; an adverb becoming an adjective ["nowhere"]; an adjective becoming a verb ["loned"]). Under pressure, conventional sentence structure starts to bend—as, for instance, "who poverty and tatters and hollow-eyed and high sat up smoking": eminently *im*pure structurally and linguistically (not even to mention morally). Traditional rules of grammar seem to get swamped in the onward roll of Ginsberg's poetic voice, evolving what he describes as "spontaneous bop prosody" (in Hyde, *Poetry of Ginsberg*, 79) which will amplify the "early XX Century organization of new speech-rhythm prosody to build up large organic structures" (in Hyde, *Poetry of Ginsberg*, 81). Again, this seems to be essentially an act of reinventing poetic English, modernizing Whitman's original lead, an updating or re-saying of the "barbaric yawp" in a different century, a reaffirmation of literary-linguistic independence in changed (but not totally changed) cultural circumstances.

It may seem, in the course of this chapter, that I've been negotiating an either/or position with regard to poetry in English in the mid-twentieth century; but in fact that isn't the case (or my intention, at least). For, as Alfred Alvarez shows in his deployment of space in *The New Poetry*, we don't really have to make a binary choice (though we may have our personal predilections): we can have both Movement and "confessional," both English and American. As the 1950s in Britain roll inexorably onward, alternatives *do* start to emerge. Lowell first, and then Ginsberg, start to offer different directions that may be explored. Ginsberg's work, certainly, represents a step onward from Lowell (I don't intend a value judgement here) —a step which, for instance, the Movement certainly wasn't interested in taking. In the next chapter we begin with the work of Sylvia Plath, which offers a step in yet another direction (though related in some way to Lowell's and Ginsberg's work), another attempt at breaking the monopoly of "purity" and "gentility" at the heart of Establishment views of poetry in English as we move into the 1960s.

# 3

# Gendered Spaces
# and the New Poetry

## SYLVIA PLATH (AND TED HUGHES):
## A QUESTION OF SIZE

ALLEN GINSBERG'S INTRODUCTION INTO LITERARY ENGLAND, A
phenomenon we saw at the end of the previous chapter, arguably
raised the specter of the Dylan Thomas-inspired old New Apocalypse
movement, which the *New Liners* had consigned (they thought) to
oblivion years earlier. Certainly Michael Horovitz's anthology, *Children of Albion*, could be described as "Apocalyptic" (though there are
also less charitable terms which might reasonably be applied to it)—
as could much of Ginsberg's work with its messianic tone and its mil-
lennialist stances. But the *other* American of note in England at the
end of the 1950s—Sylvia Plath—isn't quite as easily pigeonholed.
True, she seems to be part of the "confessionalist" line of Lowell and
Ginsberg, but her poetry provides a somewhat different language
from theirs—the voice of a *woman* struggling to survive the "tranquillized fifties," and at a time when feminism hadn't really developed its agenda and sexual/textual politics very fully.

From a *New Lines* perspective, Plath would have appeared as doubly "impure," since she was both an American (a cultural outsider,
that is) *and* a woman (a gender outsider): quite *how far* outside a
woman's gender made her (as far as the Movement was concerned)
is revealed in lurid detail in the letters and anecdotes of Amis and
Larkin.[1] But for Alfred Alvarez, Plath represents *The New Poetry*, a
phenomenon not so much *outside* as *beyond* the conventions of poetry-writing in England at the time, and therefore (in spite of her untimely death in 1963) a hope for the future of poetry in English.

Her work is difficult to approach these days because it comes to us through the vexed perspectives of various contentious biographical and autobiographical texts, and because until relatively recently it was controlled and mediated by her husband and literary executor, Ted Hughes. Under these circumstances, one valid way to get a perspective on Plath as a poet, particularly as regards the language she evolves to articulate herself in the poetry, is to sift through what remains of her *Journals* (New York: The Dial Press, 1982) for some of the statements she made about the act of writing in English as a woman in the second half of the 1950s.

It quickly becomes apparent that Plath is aware she is trying to break into a world dominated by men: in a letter to her penpal Eddie Cohen she laments that "writing poems and letters doesn't seem to do much good" because "The big men are all deaf; they don't want to hear the little squeaking as they walk across the street in cleated boots" (14). The world of patriarchal power (symbolized throughout her writing by very large men—from the great statue-figure in "Daddy" through to the descriptions of her husband), and the arena of phallogocentric discourse become the locations in which she must compete for a voice, whether it amounts merely to a "little squeaking" or not. If size is an issue (as it seems to be for her), then she must expand her own linguistic littleness, achieving a large style and attitude—very much as Whitman had decided to do when faced with the narrowness of inherited "colonial" English a century earlier, though of course the results in Plath look nothing like Whitman's texts: in a *Journal* entry of 27 April 1953 she notes that her tactic will be "To keep cracking open my mind and my vocabulary, breaking myself into larger more magnanimous orbits of understanding" (77).

This process is evidently ongoing and not always successful. So, in a *Journal* entry of 19 February 1956 she complains about her (literary) littleness again, speaking disparagingly of her "glib poems, so neat, so small" (99). And it seems that size becomes de facto an indicator of authenticity: in the same entry she accuses herself of "Fraud, fraud" as her thesaurus, one of her favorite tools in the effort to expand her vocabulary, lies open "at 545: Deception; 546: Untruth; 547: Dupe; 548: Deceiver" (97). However, she persists with her expansion program, at one point speaking of her desire for "a bigger, freer, tougher voice: work on rhythms mostly, for freedom, yet sung, delectability of speaking as in succulent chicken." And she adds the prohibition that this must involve "No coyness, archaic cutie tricks" (*Journals*, 186).

Unlike the *New Liners* on the other side of the Atlantic, then, Plath will risk the lyric, eschew the antique (however pure or genteel); and opt for poultry rather than sausages! Anyone familiar with her early poetry, up to and even including most of *The Colossus* (1960), though, will be aware of how long and how hard she had to struggle against traditional forms and "cutie tricks"—to such a degree, in fact, that her poems in *Ariel* come as a surprise, or rather shock, even revelation. As Ted Hughes says in a foreword to the *Journals*, "When a real self finds language, and manages to speak, it is surely a dazzling event—as *Ariel* was" (xii); and again, "We respond to the speech, that fascinating substance, which is everywhere fully itself, nowhere diluted and ordinary" (xiii). Hughes wasn't, of course, by any means alone in his praise of *Ariel*, or the quality of its speech: these were equally admired by (among many others) Alfred Alvarez, who chose to exemplify this late phase of Plath's writing in his selection for *The New Poetry*, since this was where her poetry became truly "new."

One key agent in Plath's linguistic transformation of herself, the breaking of her own inherited English, was Robert Lowell. She first met him in mid-1958, after reading his poems and experiencing "excitement, joy, admiration, curiosity," saying that she could almost "taste the phrases: tough, knotty, blazing with color and fury, most eminently sayable" (*Journals*, 222). Subsequently she attended Lowell's poetry class at Boston University, and found him "like good strong shocking brandy" in comparison to other poets of the time (whom she compared to "sweet dinner wine") (*Journals*, 293–94). In somewhat less alcoholic mood, she said in a later interview:

> I've been very excited by what I feel is the new breakthrough that came with, say, Robert Lowell's *Life Studies*. This intense breakthrough into very serious, very personal emotional experience, which I feel has been partly taboo. Robert Lowell's poems about his experiences in a mental hospital, for example, interest me very much. These peculiar private and taboo subjects I feel have been explored in recent American poetry. . . .[2]

If Plath credits Lowell with a breakthrough, then the compliment is repaid later, as C. David Heymann tells us: he notes that Lowell, highly impressed with *Ariel*, argued that in this work Plath "becomes herself, becomes something imaginary, newly, wildly and subtly created—hardly a person at all, . . . but one of those super-real, hypnotic, great classical heroines" (in *American Aristocracy*, 397). Judging by the final phrase here, it seems that in the end (and at the end) Plath manages (at least in the eyes of her fellow-poet) to transform herself into something large, at whatever huge cost.

๛    ๛    ๛    ๛    ๛

The poems of Plath's which Alvarez chooses in *The New Poetry* for his subversion of "Gentility" (and how spectacularly un-genteel they are!) in fact almost choose themselves: "Lady Lazarus," "Daddy," and a strong supporting cast. I don't wish to offer full comments on any of these, since as texts they've been at the mercy of innumerable commentators for many decades now. Rather, I wish to deal primarily with those aspects germane to my present argument; and I also wish to import one further supporting poem which Alvarez doesn't select, "Tulips."[3]

"Lady Lazarus" (*The New Poetry*, 61–64; *CP*, 244–47), on an autobiographical level at least, narrates Plath's brushes with death, her suicide attempts. The governing metaphor used as a vehicle for this narration is of the Nazi concentration camps during the Second World War. One notes that both these elements go well "Beyond the Gentility Principle," achieving what Plath had seen in Lowell, the breakthrough to the hitherto taboo. Lady Lazarus herself, a specially-invented female version of a character to be found in that most canonical of texts, The Bible (see John, 11), plies what must be the *second*-oldest trade in the world, that of strip-tease artiste—something (along with suicide, and death camps) about which recent poetry in English seems in general to have been remarkably reticent.[4] This reference allows the poet to enter the world of sexual/textual politics, simultanously appearing to pandar to—while in fact satirically subverting—the convention of men's voyeuristic nature. Lady Lazarus, an object to be looked at, may seem to be constructed in the male gaze (and what better symbol of that process than a stripper?), but by the end of the poem the tables (on which she dances) have been turned, and she becomes the aggressive, assertive, strong-willed component in the equation rather than the passive puppet. The patriarchal figures, so big through most of the poem (and Plath's life) —"Herr Doktor," "Herr Enemy," and so on—have been reduced in scale, now themselves commoditized so that they become simply fodder (if not canon-fodder) for the Lady of the piece. And not only mortal men are warned off: God and Lucifer, too, receive identical treatment, presumably because of their status (in this particular poetic arena) as traditionally male authoritarian figures, in fact virtually as Nazis living on *after* what at the time would have appeared to be the historical moment of Nazism. So it's the males who become the potential victims, as the female poet, mediating *her own* text and taking charge of *her own* language, metamorphoses into a kind of phoenix turned avenging angel.

The rhymes and puns, which Plath is so disarmingly expert at manipulating, tell the story. "Herr" is a linguistic intrusion from her own patriarchal heritage, her father's German-speaking past (which is to be a central motif in the poem "Daddy"). Implicitly, in a suppressed pun, "Herr" becomes, therefore, "heir"—in a double sense (again as we shall see in "Daddy"), since she is "heir" to the strong image of her father's "fascism"; and at the same time other men (notably her husband) are waiting to carry on as heirs to the male line of dominion over women. Then "Herr" becomes "hair" (such a key element in the strip-teaser's art of seducing male power); and male resonance in the word becomes female.[5] And finally, and most significantly in the chain of transmutations, "Herr" (as we're warned in the intervening rhyme-word, "Beware") becomes "air" which the larger-than-life heroine/predator ingests and spits out, so that it's the *male* principle that's discarded, becomes abject. The hegemony of phallogocentrism, strongly underlined by the caricatural germanic insistence on and repetition of the male honorific ("Herr") is merely reduced to so much "hot air," without "real" substance: an image which (anachronistically, though not inappropriately) conjures up Ian McMillan's inflated/deflated view of macho male posturing as shrivelling balloon in the poem, "Ted Hughes is Elvis Presley."[6] More of that much later; but for now to return to the conclusion of "Lady Lazarus," the poem ends with an oblique but unsettlingly aggressive sexual threat (more subtle than—but in the end much like—that of the phallic telephone violently disconnected in "Daddy").

The "English" that Plath evolves to carry all this suggestion is an interesting one. The jingling rhymes, half-rhymes and assonances create a singsong nursery rhyme atmosphere which deliberately works against the grain of the subject-matter. It's as if, given space by convention only for a "little squeaking" voice while the big men walk all over her in their "cleated boots," Plath satirically takes advantage of the setup to which the accident of gender has consigned her, deliberately assuming a "little-girlish" tone to catalog some of the fascistic atrocities perpetrated on humanity in the name of patriarchal order. The chosen diction, while actually intensifying the horror, appears to trivialize it, from the internal rhyme of "grave cave," through the near-Hudibrastic "strip tease"/ "knees," even to the rather breathless climax just analyzed ("Herr"/"hair"/"air"). In the middle of the poem (ll. 45–49) is another concatenation of naive rhymes and assonances almost resulting in a doggerel-like quality which again, on inspection, conceals something grim and dark: "well," "hell," "real," "call," "cell." The word groupings compel us to consider how "well" it is to be in "hell" (not very, presumably, even if that's the gendered space reserved for you in the dominant dispensation); and is the "cell" mentioned here actually in "hell," or merely part of the trap evolved by the patriarchy in the everyday world to imprison women (whether that "cell" be a room in a jail, or in a nunnery, or—at more of a stretch—a biological phenomenon)?

No doubt, Plath seems to want to convince us, it all feels "real" (like "The boot in the face" in "Daddy"), and maybe women have a "call[ing]" for this kind of suffering—but in the midst of all this we have to remind ourselves that the poet is talking not merely about theater (and curtain "calls"), or dance, or even sexual performance, but about the special art of "Dying," which somewhat alters the mood. Somehow, though, we assent to all of this if only because the technical transitions are so seductive and stylish—all under control, all formally shaped for us to see and cling to like life-lines (though they may, of course, actually be *death*-lines). As readers we move jauntily from "well" to "hell"; sliding smoothly down the gradient of the half rhymes "real" and "call"; and ending, thump, in our "cell" like a highly satisfactory full-stop—though, again, it may not be very satisfactory at all. An alternative way of interpreting the form of this part of the poem is to see the rhymes as links in a chain, with the half-rhymes seeming to offer a temporary freedom or variation, only for the chain to close again with that final link ("cell"), so that we're trapped in a kind of language loop (like the "grave cave") just as Lady Lazarus is trapped in her own reiterated death-drama, at least until the end of the poem, which arguably offers some sense of liberation (or of at last fighting back).

However one interprets the text, though, one thing seems clear: to adapt what I earlier quoted Ted Hughes as saying, there's the sense here of a "real self" not so much "find[ing] language" as *inventing* a language appropriate to her situation patronized and tranquillized in the middle of a desperate decade. It may ostensibly be "English," even the casual colloquial English (or American) of the time; but if so, it's an English stretched and adapted to accommodate and reflect new (though not always positive) cultural realities, and is "nowhere diluted and ordinary" in the way that Movement English actually seemed to pride itself on being. Plath contrives to turn the language at her disposal into a highly sensitized registering instrument, however banal or childlike the surface of her writing may appear.

The poem "Tulips" (*CP*, 160–62) offers us a different "take" and a different set of tactics from that of "Lady Lazarus." One of Plath's well-known "hospital" texts, it follows in the line of such work established a few years earlier by Robert Lowell, and consists of an interior (almost subterranean) monologue exploring the existence of the tranquillized woman in the tranquillized *Fifties*. Slower in pace and fuller in line than either "Lady Lazarus" or "Daddy," "Tulips" deceptively articulates what might be described as the suburban Gothic, a mode in which Plath is almost peerless, involving uncovering the horror implicit in the apparently innocent everyday world. This act of uncovering is a gradual one, in which the female protagonist of the poem becomes progressively more and more still and white (like a corpse) until she's virtually not there: so in a way, although someone's *literally* present in the text talking to herself, it's really about absence and silence—qualities made the more striking by the increasingly higher profile of the flowers that give the poem its title. To carry on the *size* motif I introduced at the beginning of my discussion of Plath, as we go from stanza to stanza the woman becomes effectively smaller and smaller (or less and less significant) while the tulips, a present from the husband and therefore in a sense a surrogate male presence in the text, become bigger and bigger.

Apparently more conventional than "Lady Lazarus" or "Daddy"— no slang, no nursery rhymes, no compressed series of puns, no "girl-speak" (the deliberate use of a childlike diction and vocabulary such as "Achoo" and "Daddy"), no foreign languages, no syntactical truncations to upset the Movement—neverthless the language-use in the poem is interesting. As I see it, Plath constructs the text around three puns which are so straightforward as to be almost transparent—"nobody"; "eye"; and "efface": together, these add up to a powerful diagnosis of the voiceless woman's situation in the hospital world of the post-war West.

The environment of the poem is controlled by men—the "anesthetist" and the "surgeons" (who might now be women, but at this time and place *aren't*). The maleness of the environment perhaps accounts for its sterility, its regimentation (mimed by the regular seven-line stanza stucture of the poem itself), its lack of color. Everything, like a blank page, tends to white—not only, one imagines, because hospitals used to be that color, or because the season is winter and it's been snowing outside, but because white suggests *absence*: already, at the start of the poem, the passive victim (the woman) is white on white, therefore virtually invisible, and certainly estranged from her own body, which she's consigned to the doctors. So she's literally "nobody," a woman not worth taking into account, a virtually disembodied being since all but her face has been swallowed in the white sheets (which may be shrouds, or poems waiting to be written, or any other kind of blankness).

But if she has no body, she still has a *head* which, sandwiched in the bedding, is "Like an eye between two white lids that will not shut." Here we have a torture more subtle than being condemned to be a resurrection artiste like Lady Lazarus, and more painful than the barbed-wire gag we're to meet in "Daddy": her consciousness, her identity (eye = I) isn't totally obliterated, but sees all and is helpless to act in the male hospital milieu. One way of reading this is as a symbolic rendition of the plight of the female poet of the 1950s. Under the circumstances, the world understandably gets interpreted and written as inimical, the vision paranoid. The bedside family photo turns into a subterfuge in which she's "hooked" (as perhaps she's also hooked on the drugs the hospital staff are feeding her) by her duties to the husband and child. To compound the entrapment, the tulips brought in by the husband (which seem to compel our attention much more than she does) become "lead sinkers" round the patient's neck, and eventually turn into spies for the patriarchy ("I am watched"): all in all, she knows she's sunk!

And that's not even taking into account the *predatory* quality of the flowers, which "hurt" her; "turn to" (or on) her; and "eat . . . [her] oxygen." And, as well, that's not to mention their *color* (in the face of her colorlessness)—their "redness": and red is a crucial referent for Plath. As we've already seen, it's the hair color of the resurgent Lady Lazarus; it's also the color of blood (one of her favorite motifs), and of danger, excitement, passion—an emblem, in fact, of all that the Movement wished to suppress![7] But here the color seems to taunt the inert, anemic, neurotic figure in the bed. The tulips, too, become a subtle instrument of torture: their "redness talks to . . . [her] wound"; they're like a "rust-red engine" sunk irritatingly in what's left of her consciousness; and finally, as the patriarchal image becomes introjected, the tulips turn into the "bowl of red blooms" that is her heart. In the end, then, she becomes totally subjected to the image imported into the poem by the male world. Somewhere in the process she realizes "I have no face, I have wanted to efface myself"— so that first her body, and then even her eye/I (which looked likely to survive, however painfully), is obliterated. It's as if the poet at this point is trying to delete herself from her own text, as if she were some kind of Kurt Schwitters self-destruct sculpture.

In spite of that, in my reading of the work, "Tulips" is a diagnosis of the struggle *not* to be silenced. Though its tactics are quite different from many of Plath's other poems, it nevertheless constitutes an attempt to rewrite the status quo. That is, it provides another (as well as an *other*) voice, ostensibly more tranquil than that of "Lady Lazarus." The mood of the poem is almost—were it not for the muted but mounting hysteria—contemplative or meditative. As regards this hysteria (culminating in the otherwise amusing assertion that "The tulips should be behind bars like dangerous animals"), we need to be clear that this isn't Plath's own (which would allow us to dismiss her as a "Mad Girl"),[8] but something she's dramatizing for the purposes of the text. She herself was quite strict about this when she said, in a famous interview statement shortly before her death:

> I must say I cannot sympathize with these cries from the heart that are informed by nothing except a needle or a knife or whatever it is. I believe that one should be able to control and manipulate experiences, even the most terrifying . . . with an informed and intelligent mind. I think that personal experience shouldn't be . . . a mirror-looking narcissistic experience. I believe it should be generally relevant, to such things as Hiroshima and Dachau, and so on.[9]

The experience in the poem, then, must be universalized in some way, however narrowly (neurotically) personal its confines might appear. In a way, this seems to be almost exactly the *reverse* of what the *New Liners* were doing at about the same time: under the guise of voicing the thoughts (and prejudices) of the "common man" in post-war England (and thus being representative of a sizeable majority), their poetic world was actually a very narrowly circumscribed one.

When we get to what is perhaps Plath's most famous poem, "Daddy" (*The New Poetry*, 64–66; *CP*, 222–24), we're certainly immediately in a personal world that quickly expands to take in global significance. The initial individual instance provides an apprehensible point of contact and focus for a much more widespread condition, offering a manageable scale for an unimaginable situation. In this poem, starting with the presumably innocent realm of a young girl's storybook, we rapidly find ourselves transported to a much grimmer reality—that of the Nazi death camps. Linguistically, the poem introduces itself (using the same tactics we noted in "Lady Lazarus") with the disarming and apparently naive rhyme of "do" "shoe" and "Achoo" (though later in the poem the latter is to become, rather disconcertingly, "a Jew"). Already we're liberated into a language world of multiple meanings, albeit (we quickly discover) dominantly dark ones: "do" may colloquially mean "be adequate," but as well it means—in standard Anglo-American slang—"to beat up," even "to kill"; and "to fuck." This theme, where words ominously simultaneously suggest violence *and* sexuality, is carried on later in the poem with references to "screw" and "root": in every sense we're clearly a long way from notions of "Purity" here as baby talk (or "girl-speak") and slang mix with more formal dictions, and signifiers start to slide.

In the second line, we come across the "black shoe," which also has multiple resonances, though all point to the notion of constriction and domination of the female. The shoe in which the poet has lived for thirty years makes her a younger version of the nursery-rhyme character, the "old woman who lived in a shoe" and had so many children "she didn't know what to do"—presumably here a reference to the way women may be trapped by (and in) their biology. As well, there may be an oblique reference to the ancient oriental custom of foot-binding (theoretically aesthetic, but also serving the practical purpose of curtailing mobility and keeping women in the house). And certainly, too, the black shoe is related to the black man's "boot in the face" later in the poem; to the "toe" of her father's "Ghastly statue" at whose feet she lay, worshipping him; and perhaps even (outside the poem) the "cleated boots" of the "big men" from her *Journal* reminiscences (14).

This may not seem to have much to do with language, but in my reading of the poem all the forces present here ultimately come to bear precisely on the topic of *language*—or rather of the silence to which females are consigned in the phallogocentric discourse. The black shoe, for instance, obviously represents the subordinate space assigned to women by the patriarchy; but as well it may connote the language system inside which women are expected to live. Daddy's little nursery-rhyme girl seems to be in an awkward situation: she probably has a cold ("Achoo")—or is *out in the cold*, for that matter— but worse than that she may also be "a Jew," a deeply unfortunate circumstance given that she's in a concentration camp text (set in Auschwitz, or Dachau, or Belsen) and surrounded by Nazis. She wishes to communicate with Daddy, but he speaks (or spoke, until he died) German, which is foreign to her: his speech is not her speech, and so she is excluded from it, effectively silenced. In a ghastly image she complains that she has been gagged by "a barb wire snare," an instrument of torture from a (language and gender) war zone, an even more vicious version of a scold's bridle, and in keeping with "the rack and the [thumb]screw" elsewhere in the poem. As the language noose tightens the woman can only make inarticulate noises as of vomiting or attempting to clear her throat ("Ich")—though, of course, had she spoken Daddy's language she would have been able to say "I" in German ("Ich"). The inability to articulate her own identity in the language of the father is symptomatic of the plight of all daughters in the patriarchy. The solution in the poem, the ripping out of the "black telephone . . . at the root," and the killing of the large black twin vampires—father and son-in-law—seems somehow rather hollow except as an act of overdue revenge (which is probably satisfying enough in itself). And the final statement—"Daddy, daddy, you bastard, I'm through"—is disconcertingly ambiguous, particularly if we know (as we all do) that this was written within about four months of Plath's suicide.

The "solution" (if solution there can be at this stage) is not *in* the poem then: it *is* the poem. That is, the language structure which is the vehicle for the diagnosis of patriarchal silencing itself helps to break that silence. Trapped in a language (as well as in her life and times), Plath attempts to break out, to find herself alternatives. Not content like, say, the Movement to reiterate the established (and Established) linguistic gestures—in the conservation of which they, of course, have a vested interest as she does *not*—Plath strikes out "Beyond" them in an attempt to initiate The New Poetry, though her efforts were to be cut short, as we know, by her untimely death.

৯৮    ৯৮    ৯৮    ৯৮    ৯৮

Plath died in 1963 and yet, like her "Lady Lazarus," has somehow refused to stay buried, although her "part" in the drama has of necessity been played, and her voice supplied, by others. In the almost forty years since her suicide, her life and work have been fought over by generations of critics and commentators. Much of the friction in this process has been caused by the fact that Ted Hughes, who was still legally Plath's husband at the time of her death, became therefore her literary executor and had executive power over her *corpus* until his own death in 1998. This circumstance *might* have passed with relatively little adverse criticism were it not for the high profile and the symbolic significance of the players involved, as I've suggested elsewhere.[10] That is, Plath was to become for many years one of the best-known woman poets writing in English, a clear and urgent voice promoting concerns that were at the time, in adjacent fields, being articulated as the vanguard of a powerful feminism. Quite on the other hand Hughes, particularly after his subsequent elevation to the prestigious Establishment role of Poet Laureate, became—at least from one perspective—part of an entrenched official literary *patriarchy* assuming control over the Plath canon. In this office, he was able to select, suppress and prohibit as he saw fit, effectively performing the function that feminists have consistently argued male canon-makers and editors exercise throughout literary history—that of silencing the female other. The situation becomes doubly ironic given that a great deal of Plath's poetic energies were spent precisely dramatizing and articulating the female voice struggling on the edge of passivity and silence, to which she was being consigned by her "Daddy," and surrogate-Daddy (that is, Hughes himself), and by societal and cultural patriarchal notions of the woman's role. In fact, my motive in raising this issue at all here is that the Plath/Hughes (literary) relationship provides an excellent (if painful) illustration of a subversive voice breaking its way into its own form of English across geographical and gender boundaries, and then being counter-subverted (*re*-silenced?) when circumstances allow, so that the power over the language is once more taken out of the originator's hands.

The heated discussion of gender-political upheaval in Plath's literary estate occupied rather more than a decade, and came to a kind of head in the late-1980s with the publication of a number of "unauthorized" books on Plath, and notably Linda Wagner-Martin's *Sylvia*

*Plath: a Biography* (1988). Therein, and elsewhere, the accusations leveled against Hughes were that his selection for Plath's first posthumous collection of poems, *Ariel,* manipulated the final text in such a way as to foregound the "Mad Girl" poems[11] and minimize the record of her "belief system . . . developed from contacts with other women" and her "pleasure in her role as mother" (Wagner-Martin, 228). As well, parts of the written material disappeared into the silence altogether—two whole notebooks, the draft of a novel, and bits of the *Journals* (often, suspiciously, at points when some vitriolic criticism of Hughes himself seems imminent).

Another decade on, and the most recent datum in the controversy (and hopefully the last, now that the main parties in the situation are both dead) was the publication in 1998 of Hughes's *Birthday Letters,* which seems to raise all these issues again, rather than settling them once and for all. It also provides the amusing (if far from edifying) spectacle of the literary media tooling up for another bout of street-fighting.

On the one hand is the Establishment adulation of what under the circumstances might (literally) be described as a *master*piece, by the Official Poet. Typical of such reactions is that of *The Times,* as reported by "J. C." in the "NB" column of the *Times Literary Supplement,* who notes with scarcely-restrained glee the hyperbole generated for the occasion—"'the greatest book by our greatest living writer,'" "'a mystical humanism,'" and "'classical tragedy.'" Names of (male) literary giants thrown into the ring for appropriate comparison include Blake, Keats, Lawrence, and Auden (*TLS,* 23 January 1998, 16).

About as soberly, the literary editor of the *Guardian* describes the publication as "The 'literary scoop' of the decade, the century, the millennium" (20 January 1998, 2). Elsewhere in the same newspaper the sensationalist headline-making goes on with blithe abandon: "Plath: the first meeting"; "The blood of poetry"; "Sylvia Plath: the reckoning." And if all of this seems rather Hollywood, then so be it: as we're told in Stephen Moss's article, "Private Lines," rumors abound that Plath's life is to be the subject of a big-budget movie (11). Presumably, the reasoning was that if it could be done with such an unlikely duo as Tom and Viv, then why not Ted and Sylv? And "J. C." (again) in the *Times Literary Supplement* raises the stakes still higher by alluding to "Dianamania, Part II."

So much for wild celebration; but on the other hand it's entirely understandable that somebody would want to spoil the party!

Jacqueline Rose, for instance, author of *The Haunting of Sylvia Plath*, wrote a long and hostile article in the *Observer* (1 February 1998). Katherine Viner in the *Guardian* of 20 January 1998 wrote a briefer one entitled combatively, "The Blood of Poetry: on Plath as Feminist Heroine" (2–3), in which she points out Hughes's role as "feminist enemy," an approach clearly indicating that all is *not* forgiven.

As for the *Birthday Letters* themselves, perhaps predictably, one of the most intriguing aspects is their relationship with *Plath's* work—a relationship that I prefer to scrutinize in the area of poetic technique rather than of interpersonal skills. Hughes's poems here constantly echo phrasing, symbolism, and key referents from his wife's work. Whether one interprets this phenomenon as (say) homage, theft, atonement, infiltration, exorcism, or appeasement presumably depends on one's literary-political persuasions. But if his language appears somewhat "borrowed," the message is rather different from that of the Plath original. In *Ariel*, Hughes is presented most often as the active, hostile agent, the vampire, the Daddy behind the Daddy, waiting in the patriarchal line; but in *Birthday Letters* that all changes. So, for instance, in the poem "Visit" (7), Hughes portrays himself as the passive element in the situation, waiting patiently to be "auditioned/ For the male lead in your drama," to be fitted into a prescription Plath herself will presumably be writing. To emphasize his helplessness he compounds this role-playing with images of "a puppet" being manipulated "on its strings," and a laboratory specimen being experimented on: "a dead frog's legs touched by electrodes." The writer and the written seem to have been reversed here.

A few pages later, in the ambiguously-titled poem "The Shot" (16–17), Plath is dramatized not as the victim (who *gets* shot—as a reader of *her* poetry would normally expect), but as the bullet itself. The metaphor is supported by references to Plath's "cheek-scar" as "a rifling groove," and to the (regrettably) inevitable Freudian sexual guns. This is all more or less par for the phallogocentric course, except that on this occasion (as too in "Visit") Hughes and his fellow suitors become victims rather than *hommes fatales*. Plath's earlier boyfriends have failed to survive, and by the end of the poem Hughes himself appears passive, weak, almost discarded among the bedroom debris, certainly not in control. As well, he's at pains to separate himself from the Daddy-God in the poem (whereas, of course, in Plath's own version he's *identified* with that character). In "Daddy" Plath has him standing in line as son-in-law, waiting to inherit from the father direct power over the female; but in "The Shot" Hughes becomes a (presumably innocent) human shield behind which the "Daddy," the "real target" hides as the daughter (presumably) takes charge of the phallic weapon to seek appropriate revenge.

Again, in the "marriage poem" in *Birthday Letters*, "A Pink Wool Knitted Dress" (34–35), Plath seems to assume control: she is the strong, brightly-colored one, while Hughes is (like his clothes) faded and tired. It appears to be *her* wedding, at which *he* is nothing more than a bit-player, part of the supporting cast. In the epiphany toward the end of the poem, *she* is transported, and *he* merely goes along for the ride: "Levitated beside you, I stood subjected / To a strange tense." One notices that the words Hughes associates with himself here—"Levitated," "subjected," "stood"—are either passive or static; and one imagines that the "strange tense" of the future is to be written by Plath (Hughes in the poem being no more than a volitionless subject, hierarchically inferior to the royal presence of the woman in her formal attire, a male attendant at the mercy of outcomes he doesn't control). He seems, in fact, (here and elsewhere in *Birthday Letters*) to be virtually a helpless bystander at his own ceremony. In the volume, in fact, Hughes has written the relationship so that he appears somehow diminished, without willpower or effective strength —a tactic that is an interesting reversal in the norm of the Plath/ Hughes axis, where he usually plays the large patriarchal figure to Plath in her complementary role as little girl.

Most often, according to all the copious mountains of anecdotal evidence, he is Ted *Huge*—a name (according to Tim Kendall in his review of the significantly-titled *The Epic Poise: a Celebration of Ted Hughes*) bestowed by Plath and her friends as a token of his "larger-than-life status" ("The Salmon," *Times Literary Supplement*, 16 July 1999, 26). Or, wearing the distinction with an Italian difference, he becomes (in the mouth of Anthony Thwaite) "Taddeo Grande" ("Commentary," *Times Literary Supplement*, 13 November 1998, 16). Plath herself had bought into the myth early in the piece: in an entry in her *Journals* she notes that, at the party at which they met, Hughes was "the only one there *huge* enough for me" (111, my italics). And D. D. Bradley, charged with writing the Poet-Laureate's obituary for *Pembroke College Cambridge Society Annual Gazette* (no. 73 [September 1999]: 22–30) wrote that even as an undergraduate Hughes seemed "taller than his six feet."

Whether the motive of the diminution in authorial size in *Birthday Letters* is Hughes's way of deferring to Plath's memory, or his way of denying responsibility, is something that rival gender-political camps will presumably continue to argue. Suffice it to say here that, on the evidence of the text, the extraordinary outpouring of critical approval cataloged earlier seems out of all proportion (too huge) compared to the work itself. The tide of high compliments is occasioned, I suspect, by a veritable orgy of Establishment relief, of slightly hysterical guilt finally absolved, of an accommodation whereby, thirty five years on from a much-debated death, it's come out all right in the end (though Plath's perspective might have been rather different, had she been allowed one by the circumstances). The State's official poet is redeemed, exorcized, recanonized: the "white-wash" job begun by the poet himself is conveniently finished off by the journalistic Establishment. And if the rewritten world of *Birthday Letters* doesn't quite (re)constitute "gentility," then it gets close to it, with a somewhat souped-up and sexed-up version thereof.

An even more hostile perspective on the *Birthday Letters* affair might view the book as a final attempt at *silencing*—by speaking in Plath's place since she can no longer speak for herself (even in the work she left behind, which has until recently remained in the control of her literary-executor/ husband). Katherine Viner makes the point sharply in her remarks in the *Guardian* (20 January 1998, 3), noting that Hughes has "the last word" since Plath inevitably "cannot speak." And Ian Hamilton—who clearly isn't impressed with the technical quality of *Birthday Letters*, criticizing them as "lumpishly composed" and "Chopped-up"—describes the book (in his newspaper article entitled "A Mismatched Marriage") as being no more than "for the record," going on to ask rather uncomfortably *whose* particular record is involved, "his or hers?" (*Sunday Telegraph*, 25 January 1998, 7). Seen in this context, the volume might be regarded as an instrument of cultural and literary appropriation, or recolonization—of re-subsuming the aberrant American New World colonial into the Old World native English, dis-enabling the "other" (female) voice and pressing it back into the dominant patriarchal discourse. Perhaps this is to overread the significance of the text—but one thing seems obvious: *Birthday Letters* is a publication destined to be *overread*, one way or another. Certainly it provides a focus, a rallying-point for all the fin-de-siècle hype from *The Times*, the *Guardian*, et al., which attempts to convince us that Hughes—and through the

Poet-Laureate his patrons, the Royal Family, and through them the whole nation—is on the side of Good and Decency as we enter a new millennium. This reminds us that "English" may not after all be as "broken" as we might think, that its powers of healing and recovery and resistance remain redoubtable: as large, in fact, as the Hughes celebrated in the cultural mythmaking that surrounded his life and (inevitably) his recent death.

༄    ༄    ༄    ༄    ༄

## ADRIENNE RICH *DIVING INTO THE WRECK*

Irrespective of personal relationships, Plath's struggles not to be "written off" and "written out" may be construed as enabling strategies for other women writers faced with the might of the male literary Establishment and its remarkable ability to close ranks when necessary. One such poet, an exact contemporary of Plath's, who drew inspiration from her and has carried on the struggle more openly to break the patriarchal hegemony of language, is Adrienne Rich. Plath early in her career evidently saw Rich as some sort of rival,[12] but Rich quickly became aware of Plath as an ally in a common cause.[13] Always more overtly politically motivated than Plath, and committed to an increasingly radical feminism, Rich is absolutely central to any study of the breaking of "English," if only because the topic of an appropriate female discourse has been such a key concern in her work, articulated with such power and clarity that she has become an essential source of wisdom and inspiration for so many women writers in English in the last quarter of the twentieth century. Liz Yorke in her book *Adrienne Rich: Passion, Politics and the Body* (1997) may not be exaggerating the case *very* much when she claims that Rich's

> powerful critical assessment was to inspire the new field of Feminist Literary Studies, and lent force to the creation of a new model for critical enquiry which was to bring race, gender, class and feminism from the margins to the center of literary endeavour: Rich was to inspire feminist critics to redraw the boundaries of the discipline. (8)

The high profile Rich gives to her politico-cultural agenda is reflected in the polemically transparent titles of many of her books of poems and essays: *A Change of World; The Will to Change;* "Writing as

Re-Vision"; *On Lies, Secrets, and Silence* (the "Lies" and "Secrets" being the property of the patriarchy while the "Silence" is that to which women are consigned in the texts of the phallocracy, forced as they are to operate in the interstices of the male language). Not concerned with conservative notions of "gentility" (except perhaps in the formalism of some of her very early poems), she seeks (like Plath) a new poetry to articulate her "Re-Vision," and *The Dream of a Common Language* which will permit her to speak in an undamaged and uncompromised voice. Not believing in the sort of "Purity of Diction" propagandized by the Movement, she sees only a spoiled discourse which needs to be re-purified or cleansed before it can be of significant use (to her), a world and a language which must be *changed.*

There's hope for such change because history, in spite of being *partially* written (in every sense of that term), nevertheless offers individual role models who have already stood against orthodoxy, and somehow survived suppression—Whitman and W. C. Williams being significant to Rich, along with the even more notable Emily Dickinson. In the 1975 essay "Vesuvius at Home: The Power of Emily Dickinson," Rich employs a "lesbian/feminist criticism" as an act of "Re-Vision" to offer an alternative to the "male/mainstream perspective."[14] Under this new scrutiny, Dickinson is transformed from a withdrawn New England spinster into a daring innovator whose role is to "retranslate her own unorthodox, subversive, sometimes volcanic propensities into a dialect called metaphor" (*P and P*, 180) that will tell her truth (in Dickinson's famous formulation) "Slant" rather than by the direct male route. So, as Rich tells us in the poem "I Am in Danger—Sir—" (*P and P*, 26–27), Dickinson, although labeled by the presiding nineteenth-century patriarchy as "Half-cracked," is in fact a culture pioneer and heroine who is prepared to commit the "Perjury" of taking on the dominant discourse in an atmosphere of "air buzzing with spoiled language" so as "to have it out at last / on . . . [her] own premises." The pun here is a strategic one: traditional critics have usually pointed to Dickinson's agoraphobia, her self-seclusion in her own room (premises), as an indicator of mental imbalance; whereas Rich plays with the phenomenon as an act of self-assertion, of Dickinson's setting her own rules (premises) for linguistic combat with the phallogocentric discourse.

Her reading of more recent female writers who have tended to be marginalized by the mainstream orthodoxy on the grounds of psychological disorder is somewhat similar—particularly in the case of

Plath. Rich turns to Plath not as an example of the kind of hysteria that is somehow regarded as unseemly and offending the principle of gentility, but as a language pioneer out to clear away the inherited "spoiled language" and the culture that it articulates. Claire Keyes, quoting from p. xii of the Gelpi-edited original Norton anthology of *Adrienne Rich's Poetry* (1975) writes that "Plath's words and phrases appeal to Rich, mainly in their cleansing power in which 'a subjective, personal rage blazes forth, never before seen in women's poetry'" (86). She goes on to assert that Rich, inspired by this example, begins "transforming her own silences—her unsaid words" (88).

Rich's attitude to Plath is presumably very similar to her attitude to Anne Sexton, whose life is celebrated in the essay "Anne Sexton: 1928–1974" collected in *On Lies, Secrets, and Silence: Selected Prose 1966–78* (1979). Rich speaks of Sexton (who had at that time just committed suicide) as a woman who, while not necessarily regarding herself as a feminist, had nevertheless done "some things ahead of the rebirth of the feminist movement," particularly by writing of certain previously taboo subjects (abortion, masturbation, menopause) in spite of being subject to the unsympathetic "scrutiny of the male literary establishment" (121). Rich concludes with an assessment of what is to be gained from Sexton's (and again, presumably, Plath's) case, arguing that "her poetry is a guide to the ruins, from which we learn what women have lived and what we refuse to live any longer." This is the start of the process of liberating oneself from "the grip of a policeman who tells us we are guilty of being female, and powerless" (123).

While Rich's concerns here (and she's clearly already offering herself at this point as a spokesperson for women in general) go far beyond the merely literary, nevertheless her remarks seem to center in language, which she sees as of crucial strategic importance. In an essay of 1972 (also collected in *On Lies, Secrets, and Silence*) she states:

> At the bedrock level of my thinking . . . is a sense that language is power, and that, as Simone Weil says, those who suffer from injustice most are the least able to articulate their suffering; and that the silent majority, if released into language, would not be content with a perpetuation of the conditions which have betrayed them. But this notion hangs on a special conception of what it means to be released into language: not simply learning the jargon of an elite, fitting unexceptionably into the status quo, but learning that language can be used as a means of changing reality. (67)

If language really *is* power, then it needs to be nurtured. At the level of the text it will be an inadequate response simply to mimic the "jargon" of the governing "elite" (except, perhaps, for satirical purposes)[15] or to assent to the status quo: instead, reality must be changed just as the means of its expression—language—is changed. As Rich put it in the title of her well-known essay of 1971, "When We Dead Awaken: Writing as Re-Vision," women must awaken from the textual and cultural "death" (silence, passivity, impotence) to which they have been assigned by the patriarchy, and make their writing an act not merely of vision but of *re*-vision—re-seeing, redefining, restating themselves and their role in the culture. In the preamble to the 1978 essay, "Disloyal to Civilization: Feminism, Racism, Gynephobia," Rich quotes an extraordinary article from the *New York Herald* of 1852, as follows: "How did woman first become subject to man, as she now is all over the world? By her nature, her sex, just as the negro is and always will be to the end of time, inferior to the white race, and, therefore, doomed to subjection; but she is happier than she would be in any other condition, just because it is the law of her nature" (in *On Lies, Secrets, and Silence*, 277). If this really was the "law" of women's "nature," then that law needs to be challenged; if this really was the true story of the existing "Civilization," then it's important to be "Disloyal" to it as a subversive act; if this really is a legitimate view afforded by the *his*tory of the culture, then it's time for *her*story to take over instead. As Rich says in her foreword to *On Lies, Secrets, and Silence*, such a reorientation is predicated on "our need for real literacy, for our own history, more searchingly aware of the lies and distortions of the culture men have devised" (12).

This "real literacy" will involve not simply the ability to read and write, but the ability for a woman to read and write *herself*, however hostile conditions may be. That is, a woman must re-view herself in a changing reality, particularly since, as we're told in "When We Dead Awaken" (1971), "The creative energy of patriarchy is fast running out; what remains is its self-generating energy for destruction. As women, we have our work cut out for us."[16] So the scenario of "academicians rehearsing their numb canons in sessions dedicated to the literature of white males" (*P and P*, 166) is to be challenged, Rich's assertions and language here (as virtually throughout) alerting us to the fact that a dynamic counterargument is being mounted, a battle generally more equal and hopeful than that in (say) Plath's texts. We sense, as Rich in fact says (*P and P*, 167), that "It's exhilarating to be alive in a time of awakening consciousness;" and that "it is no longer such a lonely thing to open one's eyes"—a far cry from the tortured eye/I in Plath's "Tulips" (though Rich goes on [*P and P*, 168] to pay tribute to the "dynamic charge," the "rhythms of struggle, need, will, and female energy" to be found in Plath's work).

The language drama enacted in Rich's work, then, involves an ongoing process not of affirming a male-oriented status quo, not even of "a fascination and a terror" when faced with "Man's power" (as she perceives in Plath's writing), but rather a *re*-placement of Woman linguistically and culturally, and the formulation of an "English" that will be able to articulate a change in the balance of power (since "language" after all is "power"). Once more Rich was inspired in this project by the prior example of one of her culture heroines, the "Vesuvius at Home," Emily Dickinson (whose "Power" she paid tribute to in her 1975 essay of that title). Dickinson is credited with "inventing a language more varied, more compressed, more dense with implications, more complex of syntax, than any American poetic language to date" (*P and P*, 182).

As early as "Snapshots of a Daughter-in-Law" of 1960 (*P and P*, 9–13) Rich herself was following in these inventive footsteps, creating a poetry of intertextual detail in which a pantheon of canonical male poets (in this case Yeats, Baudelaire, T. S. Eliot, Catullus, Shakespeare) were appropriated alongside key female writers ([inevitably] Dickinson, and Mary Wollstonecraft) whose work became enshrined and iconized in Rich's poem. The surface of the text (and the title) may point to the patriarchal "Law" that enforces the ownership of women by men through fathering (and daughtering), and through male "giving" of women in marriage; but the writerly tactics tell a different story, written against the grain of male possession and female submission. The "belle" in the poem may be (predictably) merely an object of the male gaze, with her formal "dresses" and showy "wedding-cake"; but the daughter who "wipes the teaspoons" in an ostensibly repetitive and futile act of traditional female nurturing/cleansing is in fact already rebelling, "glowering" at the task imposed on her, and "Banging the coffee-pot into the sink." And in her head are subversive voices with messages suggesting conduct radically different from that associated with the conventionally female role of caregiving, or the "virtues" of patience, modesty, and self-sacrifice: "*Have no patience,*" "*Be insatiable,*" "*Save yourself; others you cannot save.*" The promise of this subversion is partly realized in the vision at the end of the poem of a sort of overdue female second coming, in which the flapping swan wings of Zeus raping Leda (appropriated from Yeats in section 3 of the poem) are transformed into the rotors of a helicopter (borrowed from Simone de Beauvoir's *The Second Sex*)[17] as the feminist protagonist delivers "her cargo" which is no longer merely a "promise" but finally "palpable/ours."

Bizarre as this clutter of referents appears, the underlying tactic is clear enough: the appropriation and over-writing of male-centered mythologies from a new perspective. The language may still be "English," but it's English worn with a significant difference—if not broken, then at least radically modified. However, there are significant problems here. Rich seems to be undermining the primacy of phallogocentrism, dismantling the dominance of the dominant discourse, in order to achieve a subsequent new accommodation. The ideal at this stage for Rich appears to be movement towards some kind of shared (common) language such as that dreamed of in the poem "A Marriage in the 'Sixties" (*P and P*, 14–15)—"the perfect hour of talk / that language aches for" in an imagined *linguistic* marriage of equals. But reality suggests otherwise, and instead of a shared communication we still end up with "two minds, two messages."

Furthermore, the relationship between the two voices underpins the power structures of the culture, so that Rich (like any other feminist writer, in fact) is caught in a double bind in her necessary dealings with the dominant discourse: as she says in "The Burning of Paper Instead of Children" (*P and P*, 40–43), "this is the oppressor's language/ yet I need it to talk to you." Under these circumstances, in spite of what's spoken, the "language" will remain "a map of our failures." To be privy to the burning in the poem may be to participate in an appealingly iconoclastic act of incendiary rebellion—to side with Antonin Artaud's urging us to "*burn the texts*" (which a footnote tells us is tantamount to calling for "the destruction of the values and structures that inform Western culture," the hegemony of the Patriarchy). But at the same time it may be to assent implicitly to other burnings referred to in the text—Hitler's incineration of the Jews, the burning of Joan of Arc as a witch (whose sisters were later to be burned in Puritan New England), the napalming of villages during the Vietnam war. To become implicated in the dominant discourse is to become implicated in all of this too. At the end of the poem, Rich presents herself as artistically helpless, tortured, and estranged—a long way, in fact, from any notion of sharing a viable "common language": "The typewriter is overheated, my mouth is burning, I cannot touch you and this is the oppressor's language."

The oppressor's language becomes a recurring motif at this stage of Rich's writing career. In "Our Whole Life" (*P and P*, 43–44), for instance, she notes how "Our whole life is a translation" which is "rendered into the oppressor's language," thus appropriating that life and silencing the "cloud of pain" that the marginalized protagonist (in this case a colonized male rather than female) experiences and for which "there are no words" in metropolitan English. And in "A Valediction Forbidding Mourning" (*P and P*, 44) the situation gets even uglier: in the very act of trying to appropriate a male canonical text (John Donne's famous poem of the same name), to get a footing in the phallocentric literary stronghold, Rich is confronted by a hostile dominant discourse not designed to accommodate a woman's voice, and wishing to push her back into the silence: "The grammar turned and attacked me." In the face of this hostility, she imagines a language (which here has a strong echo of Sylvia Plath in it) in which she will be able to say things not permissible in the bloodless male discourse: "*my bleeding is under control*" and "A red plant in a cemetery of plastic wreaths." Thus, she may in the end come (rather like Emily Dickinson in Rich's poem "'I Am in Danger—Sir—'") "To do something very common, in my own way"—*but not yet.*

In the interim, women may need alternative strategies, shielding themselves from oppression. To begin with, what Robert Lowell called "the tranquillized Fifties" must not be allowed to hang over into the later decades: the (literally and symbolically) drugged or anesthetized state that Plath describes so regularly must be resisted. In a sinister line from (her version of) "A Valediction Forbidding Mourning" Rich claims that "They gave me a drug that slowed the healing of wounds": it's clearly in the patriarchy's best interests to keep women in the passively suffering posture, to keep them wounded. So the would-be victims must combat the strategy: as Rich urges in another poem, "5.30 A.M." (*P and P*, 33–34):

> They've supplied us with pills
> for bleeding, pills for panic.
> Wash them down the sink.

While working towards the dawning new era, until the savior from the helicopter actually arrives, a drug-free clarity and energy will be required in dealing with reality since this remains—in a highly resonant pronouncement in the poem "From an Old House in America"—a "savagely fathered and unmothered world" (*P and P*, 65). Like Plath, Rich's relationship with her father becomes significant in the poetry itself, particularly in the sequence (of 1981–82), "Sources" (*P and P*, 101–14). Here he takes on symbolic as well as personal significance: "After your death I met you again as the face of the patriarchy, could name at last precisely the principle you embodied, there was an ideology at last which let me dispose of you, identify the suffering you caused, hate you righteously as part of a system, the kingdom of the fathers" (*P and P*, 104). Such an act of naming, of taking control, of exorcism is clearly essential to liberate the "Daughter" from the "Law" of the Father. Otherwise her "imagination" will stay "hooked into" unhealthy familial "Sources"[18]—including "the 'New' Englanders who hung on/ here in this stringent place" (*P and P*, 105). Breaking free from founding fathers is presumably necessary for *all* daughters, at least symbolically, and not just personally or autobiographically for Rich. Certainly, faced with the culture of the "savagely fathered . . . world" in which she finds herself, Rich (perhaps unlike Plath) feels enabled "to go on from here" (*P and P*, 81).

Part of the process of going onwards involves *Diving into the Wreck*. Of this 1972 publication Margaret Atwood writes: "her book is not a manifesto, though it subsumes manifestoes; nor is it a proclamation, though it makes proclamations. It is instead a book of explorations, of travels. The wreck she is diving into . . . is the wreck of obsolete myths, particularly myths about men and women" (in *P and P*, 280). Here, then, Rich is appropriating the male adventure/treasure-hunting mode, becoming a sort of feminist Jacques Cousteau (if such a thing can be imagined), though—as she is at pains to explain in the title poem (*P and P*, 53–55)—he would have "his / assiduous team" of assistants backed by all the resources of the patriarchal media, whereas she is "alone." The opening few lines of the text read almost like a parody of the tradition of ceremonial preparation for combat as she dons her battlegear (much as her "Knight" did in an earlier poem, though *his* armor turns out to be—like the male Establishment he represents—showy and empty, while *hers* is strictly functional).[19] Again the conventions being appropriated are male (with a few notable exceptions—such as Joan of Arc, one of Rich's culture heroines). Rachel Blau Duplessis emphasizes this when she writes,

"In this poem of journey and transformation Rich is tapping the energies and plots of myth, while re-envisioning the content" (in *Shakespeare's Sisters*, quoted in *P and P*, 404).

That is, the traditional quest hero is here written female; and the
goal is not (at least literally) some fabulous treasure trove, but self-
knowledge and awareness. The master-narrative has been recast in
Rich's own "language," the "dialect called metaphor"; and "the edge
of her knife-blade" (again intertextually echoing Plath, though with
different implications here) will be used not as a weapon whose "sudden slash" might release the blood, but as an instrument of criticism,
of dissection, symbolically of "re-envisioning." The "wreck" must be
examined before being written off completely. So the female protagonist, who interestingly assumes more power the deeper she de-
scends ("my mask is powerful / it pumps my blood with power"), is
performing an act of de-mythologizing—scrutinizing "the wreck and
not the story of the wreck / the thing itself and not the myth," in an
effort to see *both* "the damage that was done / and the treasures that
prevail." Among the latter perhaps there will be a salvageable language of self, even though at this stage the poem/dive ends only
with "a book of myths / in which / our names do not appear."

Certainly, it seems subsequently that the very fact of the "dive"
(like the chronologically later confrontation of the father in
"Sources," which we examined above) performs some kind of cathar-
tic function, even purgative clarification, permitting the language
exploration to continue. In an interview with Adrienne Rich in 1991,
David Montenegro argues as much when he suggests to her that:

> in the late 1960s, you broke the language down, you *let* it break down.
> And then you dove into the wreck—to use your title—and came out
> the other side with *The Dream of a Common Language*. In this book, it
> seems, the language is fulfilled. It's wearing its own skin, in a sense. Do
> you feel that you had to go through that period of destruction of tra-
> ditional order to go on with your work? (*P and P*, 269)

Rich concurs with this résumé, and proceeds (on 269–71) to item-
ise some of the data/texts involved in her process of "going on" from
the wreckage of the patriarchal discourse, her act of cultural salvage.
Among these she includes a series of "sprung sonnets" by the West
Indian poet Derek Walcott (who comes into my argument in the
next chapter), entitled *Midsummer*. Of the poem sequence she says:

It gives me a great rush, and I think I know why. It's because he is pulling on this contemporary, immediate, and historically powerful image of the riots in Brixton, as a West Indian, with everything that lies behind that—the British colonization of his own country, his own internal colonization. . . . And underlying the whole is the pulling-together of a consciousness split by colonization and diaspora, through an integrative kind of anger. And it seems to me that that's genuinely *new*. Nobody had done just that, in poetry, until the West Indians did it.

The sympathy evident in Rich's remarks here between the (marginalized) feminist voice and the (marginalized) ethnic minority voice(s) is a motif that has become common in recent attempts at "breaking English," as we shall see later, since both have been subjected to a similar kind of colonization at the hands of the metropolitan center. Rich herself had had some contact with the phenomenon of this colonization at the level of the (English) language during her time working in what she describes (in the essay "Blood, Bread, and Poetry" [*P and P*, 239 ff.]) as "an urban subway college, in a program intended to compensate ghetto students for the inadequacy of the city's public schools." She writes: "Among staff and students, and in the larger academic community, there were continual debates over the worth and even the linguistic existence of Black English, the expressive limits and social uses of Standard English—the politics of language." As a result of this experience, Rich "felt more and more urgently the dynamic between poetry as language and poetry as a kind of action, probing, burning, stripping, placing itself in dialogue with others out beyond the individual self." (*P and P*, 248) The "dialogue . . . beyond the individual self" here seems to point the way (again) towards the dream of a common language, held together perhaps by "an integrative kind of anger" of the kind she perceives in Walcott's example. But it's important to note that in Rich's case, certainly, "common" isn't synonymous with "universal." That is, at least at this stage, her programme doesn't include everybody: the language that David Montenegro describes as "wearing its own skin" doesn't quite come in one size for all. Politically, for instance, it's hard to see how there could be a meaningful dialogue between a teacher from a "subway" college and (say) the Oxford-oriented Movement writers: one imagines that Rich and Larkin would constitute an eminently uncomfortable juxtaposition sharing the same stage. Rich's "dream" certainly goes beyond herself—but only as far

as other women, since the male world continues to be viewed as destructive, contaminated (and contaminating), and sterile.

Olga Broumas points out that, in *The Dream of a Common Language*,
rather than "addressing men in the name of women" Rich now
chooses to address a "you [who] is almost always female" (in *P and P*,
322). Nowhere is this more evident than in the center-piece of the
book, "Twenty-One Love Poems" (*P and P*, 77 ff.), in which both ad-
dresser and addressee are female, rendering the male perspective irrelevant.[20] The situation provides at least a partial way out of the
awkward problem of having to share the phallogocentric discourse,
as Joanne Feit Diehl explains:

> women, in order to speak at all, either must subvert their own speech
> by using the patriarchal tongue or seek for themselves experiences
> available only to women—what it means to be a daughter, the emo-
> tions of a lesbian relationship, the process of childbirth—experiences
> that would serve to free women poets through their choice of subject
> from the history of patriarchal associations. (in *P and P*, 406)

So, as Rich puts it, speaking to her lover in the first poem in the series, "No one has imagined us" (*P and P*, 77): that is, they haven't
been constructed by (for instance) a male gaze, but instead take responsibility for creating *themselves*. The "civilization" in which they
participate may remain (as a result of the aftermath of the history of
the patriarchy) basically a "still unexcavated hole," an "absence" that
women "still have to stare into," seeing only "centuries of books un-
written piled behind these shelves" (ibid., 79). But essentially the act
of liberation has been made, as we discover in the beautiful "Tran-
scendental Etude":

> . . . We cut the wires,
> find ourselves in free-fall . . . .
> . . . . . . . . . . . . . . . . . . . . . . .
>
> No one who survives to speak
> new language, has avoided this:
> the cutting away of an old force that held her
> rooted to an old ground . . . .
>
> (*P and P*, 89)

The ultimate reward for this cutting away is "a whole new poetry
beginning here," an antidote to the sterility of the patriarchal order,

and firmly re-anchored into a substantial reality: "now the stone foundation, rockshelf further / forming underneath everything that grows" (ibid., 90).

In these poems, then, it seems that Rich finds a way out of sharing the phallogocentric discourse, evolving a tactic of liberation which frees her to "imagine" herself and her female lover, thus excluding or bypassing the male world altogether in an urge towards "a whole new poetry" that will share the "common language" women can speak to each other. And yet at this point, paradoxically, a male name appears to intrude—and one that has already occurred at a number of strategic places in my own overall argument: Robert Lowell. I've presented Lowell as a language pioneer in the ongoing process of "breaking English," and so it's appropriate (on one level at least) that he should function as some sort of source or model for Rich's project of breaking or discarding the "spoiled language" of the past. That he does so has been noted by so many commentators that it's become something of a critical commonplace which it's unnecessary for me to rehearse in detail here. But as Maggie Humm points out in her chapter on Rich—"Occupied Territories"—in *Border Traffic*, it's clear that "Twenty-One Love Poems" draw "most freely on Lowell's imagery and on his topics particularly on the poems in Lowell's *Notebook*" (175).[21]

What Rich is presumably doing here (following a strategy used throughout her career, of course) is performing an act of appropriation: as Humm suggests, "What Rich proposes . . . is Lowell's *Notebooks* revisioned and demisogynised" (178). This is necessary because, as Rich had argued in an article in *American Poetry Review* in 1973 (immediately before she embarked on "Twenty-One Love Poems"), she perceives in Lowell "a kind of aggrandized and merciless masculinity at work" (quoted in Humm, 175)—obviously grotesquely inappropriate in a lesbian text. Consequently Rich works, as Humm again points out, towards "a means to combat male aggression without diminishing her verbal capacity" (181). So (like Plath) she enables herself to be inspired by and take advantage of the subversive or countercultural energies of Lowell's work; and yet at the same time she contrives to avoid contamination by those parts of the appropriated text to which her gender politics won't permit her to assent.

This reminds us, usefully, that efforts at what I've called "breaking English" are categorically *not* all part of a single continuity, an integrated process. Rather, they constitute a series of more or less discrete processes sometimes, admittedly, working in parallel, sometimes using the same kind of textual tactics, and often sharing political sympathies (though not, obviously, in the case of Rich and Lowell!). In the end, then, Rich's "new poetry" may not be, for instance, quite what Alfred Alvarez envisaged when he used the same term, but it clearly operates in the same spectrum of response, setting itself against a conservative male-dominated dispensation, a Movement that is in fact unmoving and seemingly virtually immovable.

One might argue that Rich in the literary-cultural aspect of her work is merely substituting one notion of "purity" for another—setting up an exclusive poetic-diction-club for women rather than for eighteenth-century minor English male poets. Perhaps her anger, every bit as powerful and negative as the misogeny of Larkin or Amis, prompts her to construct a philosophy based to some degree on rejection—which in a sense, by finally ignoring men altogether, shirks some of the key problems. But it seems to me that her attack, the urge to "go on from here" irrespective of the power of the opposition (and the dominant nature of their language, which is also power), signals an unstoppable desire and an ability to break the impasse of the status quo, to break "English" (on whichever side of the Atlantic it happens to be spoken), and to offer a different path, whether it be mainly political, literary, or both. From the "wreck" of the patriarchal culture (the "breaking" of "English"), then, fresh alternatives may emerge.

ক্ট    ক্ট    ক্ট    ক্ট    ক্ট

## CAROL ANN DUFFY ON BEING "FOREIGN"

The "here" from which Rich intends to "go on" in her "Twenty-One Love Poems" (and subsequently) is not, of course, geographically located, or for that matter nationally-specific. Rather than being a physical place it expresses itself as a *gendered* space, much in the way that Mary Daly stated in a passage that Rich cites twice in the essay "When We Dead Awaken." Daly—in her book *Beyond God the Father: Towards a Philosophy of Women's Liberation* (1973)—spoke of exploiting "the boundaries of [the] . . . patriarchal space" (quoted in *P and P*, 166), and moving outwards towards "the 'new space' on the boundaries of patriarchy" (in ibid., 176). So we're dealing not with a *literally* mappable phenomenon, but with what becomes part (in Rich's own words this time) "of a whole new psychic geography" (*P and P*, 168).

In helping to open up this area, to decolonize the frontier, as it were, Rich's influence as feminist polemicist, and her popularity as spokesperson has not been restricted to the western side of the Atlantic, and has spread (in more conventionally geographic terms) to Britain as well as to many other English-speaking countries. Liz Yorke, for instance, has written enthusiastically about this in her book, *Adrienne Rich: Passion, Politics and the Body*. And Gillian Allnutt notes, in her introductory statement to the "Quote Feminist Unquote Poetry" section of the Paladin anthology *The New British Poetry* (1988) that she relies "for guidance" in her methods of selection on "Adrienne Rich's resounding declaration that 'the daughter of the fathers is a literary hack'" (77). Allnutt's definition of "a successful feminist poem" as "one that is written by a woman with respect not only for her own 'truth,' her own way of seeing and feeling the world, but also for the language" clearly owes a significant debt to Rich.

One of the poets selected by Allnutt from the younger generation who seems to "go on" from Rich (and to some degree from Plath) and has also developed a significant following of her own is Carol Ann Duffy. On the face of it, Duffy's work may not appear to be as overtly militant as Rich's, but it is ultimately, nevertheless, just as engaged, as the editors of the Bloodaxe *The New Poetry* suggest when they claim that the strength of her writing is "located in a tension between ironic social naturalism and confrontational political work." They go on to affirm that among her peers in contemporary British verse, "Duffy has been exemplary in re-energizing a feminist, public voice in poetry" (17). And the editors of *The Penguin Book of Poetry from Britain and Ireland since 1945* ([henceforth *PBPBI*] Simon Armitage and Robert Crawford, 1998) concur, seeing Duffy as part of "an increasingly confident generation of women writers [who] . . . incorporate into their work a strategic and imaginative awareness of issues of gender" (xxviii).

Duffy's starting point seems to be an awareness that women are strategically *foreigners* in the phallogocentric dispensation, an observation that may have been strengthened circumstantially (geographically) by the fact that she was born in Glasgow before moving to the north of England and finally gravitating south to live in London. The ambience of her poem "Foreign,"[22] though, indicates a foreignness more than the merely Scottish, since the poem is set in an ominous unspecified metropolis that may well be part of what Rich called "psychic geography." From the outset, the foreignness is marked most noticeably through language, the linguistic environment creating an estrangement and bifurcation in the narrator's consciousness, who talks in the local language but thinks in her own. This situation might most obviously seem to be that of an *immigrant* (probably from an ethnic minority, given the racism lurking in the milieu evoked) but—as so often in writing of this kind—it might apply just as much to the gendered *other* as to the geographically *other.*

In the second stanza of the poem, Duffy introduces the idea of "writing home"—a language act which allows the protagonist to reestablish comforting contact with both a matriarchal figure and a mother tongue: "the sound of your mother singing." This comfort is rapidly dissipated, however, when the "you" of the poem ventures outside into the alien city and finds a written identity of a very different sort waiting for her—an obscene name spraypainted on a wall. Under other circumstances the act of naming might be a positive indicator of identity; but here the violence and anger of the graffiti artist (whose highly informal text is "Red like blood") merely inscribe on the victim a generic term of abuse such as "Coon" or "Cunt" (though neither is actually specified in the poem itself). Either way, the offensive four-letter-word mentality underlines the hostility which will keep the protagonist *outside* the walled boundary of the xenophobic patriarchy, exiled in the land of the "impure." Even the (literal) currency of this capital/Capital—which might otherwise help to buy time (or a space)—is of no avail since, in a momentary lapse of concentration, and perhaps remembering her own local coinage, the protagonist is unable to make the money in her hand "translate." And finally, carrying on more literally this failure to translate, she lapses into a kind of pidgin, emphasizing her foreignness that essentially disbars her from the knowledge and meaning of the metropolitan center. The "broken English" involved at this stage of proceedings only has negative connotations.

The poem, like most of Duffy's work, seems simple on its surface, but is subtly packed with politico-cultural comment. The final ironic gesture in "Foreign" is the strategic use of the word "Imagine," which occurs right at the beginning and right at the end of the text, and is repeated in between. Clearly the word denotes the stock-in-trade of a poet/fiction writer: the irony arises, though, from the fact that the protagonist in the poem, whom the poet urges to "Imagine" this and that, doesn't *need* to imagine any of the violence, prejudice, or hatred alluded to, because it's all *real* in her everyday world. In another poem in the same collection (*Selling Manhattan* of 1987), Duffy offers us a different imaginative perspective (an allegorical one) on essentially the same data, though the patriarchal trap in which the women find themselves this time is a fish tank rather than a "dark city." The text in question is "The Dolphins" (*The New British Poetry*, 91; *SP*, 25–26).

The poem begins with Duffy's characteristic clarity and directness as the dolphins swim and dance in what appears to be their own world. However, immediately we realize that it *isn't* quite that simple, at least under the conditions that pertain in the poem, because the protagonists aren't as free as we might want to think. They may be in their "element," and have an almost telepathic rapport with each other; but the sisterhood of dolphins is compromised by the intrusion of demands from the world of the patriarchy: "There is a man" who will make them go through "hoops" and who will load them down with "guilt." Like Plath's "Lady Lazarus," they must perform their tricks for the gawking male gaze; but however often they perform they can find no meaning and no escape.

They try "to translate" their experience of having once swum free into the terms of this other (circumscribed) environment; but the translation doesn't transform or redeem the situation. The pool in which they live is a male-constructed and male-dominated space, governed by a patriarchal hierarchy in which they're at the bottom (with the man in position above them). They may continue to perform faithfully, but nothing alters, except that the moon somehow disappears, and the dolphins are left to sing their lament, the "Music of loss forever." Effectively, male power—by imposing a routine which in other circumstances might be tagged "domestic"—has cut them off from the strength of the female moon goddess, the tidal rhythms of the natural world with which they were in tune now perceived as an absence. Their sisterhood of mutual sympathy/empathy is only experienced in a debilitating "loss," for which the male world substitutes merely a series of tricks for them to amuse themselves (and others) with. Like Pavlov's dog (or children in school, perhaps), the dolphins are programed or conditioned to respond to basic signals on a "whistle" blown by the man, who continues to loom over them on the other side of the meniscus/boundary that they may only cross at his command. The dolphins may essentially share a single consciousness, but all that the mind in the poem can perceive is emptiness, obliteration.

So, at this stage, the dolphin's song/language code (as well as the woman's poem) can only communicate a plangent grief under the surface of a male linguistic structure that brings death. The notion of the male-principle as death-principle, constructed in a dead language of phallogocentric cliché, is further explored in another of Duffy's poems, uncompromisingly entitled "Psychopath" (*The New Poetry*, 226–27; *SP*, 43–46). This is a dramatic monologue—a highly appropriate medium, after all, for a male voice that doesn't countenance dialogue—in which the protagonist is an itinerant circus-worker and gynecide. The most chilling aspect of the poem is the cool tone in which the perpetrator discusses his crime, as if it weren't really a crime—or anything of great importance—at all. This notion is amplified by the way Duffy juxtaposes fragments of monologue about the murder with details from pop songs and Hollywood movies, as if all share the same level of significance—which for the psychopath of the title is probably accurate enough.

The speaker, and the text itself, are constructions of popular culture, mirror images taken from various branches of late-1950s media. The distance between these received images and reality is underlined right at the beginning of the poem when the speaker watches himself "pose" his "reflection between dummies in the window" of a men's-wear shop. The language here—"pose," "reflection," "dummies"—seems to suggest at least a threefold removal from the real; but the irony is that the "Psychopath" actually buys into the shopwindow culture and perceives no distance at all between the invented and the actual, so that later his macho violence (and the murder) appear to be no more than part of a film in which he features, along with his screen idols—James Dean, Marlon Brando, and Elvis Presley. Duffy underlines the point by quoting a telling phrase made famous by another macho hero, Humphrey Bogart: "Here's / looking at you"—a reminder of the male gaze, but here reflected or turned inward to apply to the protagonist (and perhaps to contemporary male readers of the text?).

For the psychopath, there's no hint that "looking at" him might be somewhat accusatory, of course: by *his* standards (and those of aggressive Hollywood male leads), he's done nothing more than star in his own movie. He perceives his actions as being as innocent as the plethora of male clichés with which he bolsters up his position: "Here we go, old son"; "giving her everything I had"; "Jack the Lad"; "Ladies Man"; "the world's your fucking oyster." And horribly counterpointed with these, like a ghastly illustration of cause and effect, is the reiterated flat statement "She is in the canal." She may have said "*No . . . , Don't,* like they always do," but she went for a ride on his merry-go-round, said "*Thank you*" to his "toffee-apple," "teddy-bear," and "gold-fish"; and the verbal contract ends with an echo of T.S.Eliot's *The Waste Land,* "down by the dull canal." Or, to be more accurate, the text itself ends with the psychopath's rendition of Little Richard's chorus from the rock-song "Tutti Frutti": "Awopbopaloobop alop-bimbam" (which itself grotesquely and uncomfortably echoes the "Wham bam, thank you mam" of more recent itinerant male sexual predators).

Is this the "moral" our culture gleans from the exceptionally unpleasant monologue we've just heard—a (virtually) meaningless chorus phrase, far cruder than the "Music of loss" we listened to in "The Dolphins"? Surely there must be more to it than this? Possibly by way of some accounting for the psychopath's actions, Duffy provides a series of flashbacks of the speaker's boyhood sexual abuse and humiliation at the hands of women. So she sets up a machinery of explanation, but nothing *really* gets explained, and the protagonist wanders off the page, whistling the hit parade. To me, the message from Duffy is precisely in the casualness of the whole deal, in the way the language of the poem is constructed in such a way that fragments of "harmless" male discourse turn out to be far from harmless. If phall-ogocentrism facilitates (even encourages) male self-images such as that of the psychopath, then the language *itself* is virtually psychopathic, or at the very least morally bankrupt. If this is the "English" with which female writers are faced, then it needs—as an act of survival—to be broken.

Language atrocities of a somewhat less lethal (but still highly significant) sort form the subject—and make up the text—of Duffy's "Poet for Our Times" (*The New Poetry,* 229; *SP,* 70–71). The monologist this time is a headline writer for a daily paper, debasing the language not with wornout macho clichés of the kind we experience in "Psychopath," but with new slogans of a similar nature. However, it must be admitted that the collage of sexism and xenophobia produced, while cheapening the poetic discourse, nevertheless has a certain rough linguistic energy to it, far removed from the flattened genteel tone of, for instance, "The Movement." And there's certainly a subversive quality in some of the poem's startling collocations— such as ex-Prime Minister of Britain, "MAGGIE [Thatcher]" and the "PAGE 3" pinup girl; or Martin Luther King's inspirational "I have a dream" and the bar-room slang of "*Stuff 'em! Gotcha!*" While Duffy is presumably not advocating quite the kind of sensationalist language we encounter in her text here, nevertheless she may be implicitly promoting the cause of a dynamic and eye-catching verbal structure, a diction not bound up in notions of purity and gentility but closely in touch with everyday reality.

Certainly, it seems—as we discover in "The Captain of the 1964 *Top of the Form* Team" (*The New Poetry*, 228; *SP*, 93–94)—the existing dispensation is in need of some re-invigoration. Duffy's emphasis (and tactics) appear to be changing, and the spokesman for the phallocracy is no longer all-powerful or menacing, but instead comical or even rather pathetic. As with other poems of Duffy's which we've looked at (particulary "Psychopath" and "Poet for Our Times"), the surface of the text is scattered with odd bits and pieces of language, perhaps indicating a discourse in the process of breakdown. Here we've got pop song titles, quotes from canonical poets (in this case, W. B. Yeats), quiz questions, and declensions of a Latin noun— declension again being an appropriate motif for a language in decline if not quite (like Latin) dead.

Our "Captain" on this occasion is only a captain in nostalgic retrospect, still competitively driven perhaps by the ambition to be "Top," still bound up in the masculist construction of hierarchies (even if only the "Top Ten" pop songs for October 1964), but somehow not fulfilling the promise of his youth. The school system—a favorite target of Duffy's, and a significant arm of the Establishment—in this poem educates only by the accumulation of useless bits of information which, however, underpin metropolitan certainties and rank: capital cities, and British kings and queens. The classroom works in a regulated, militaristic way, so that when the star pupil raises his hand to offer the unambiguously right answer, his waving arm performs a salute. Clearly we're in a world of winners (and losers), a world where we're expected to learn an appropriate vocabulary parrot-fashion ("*dominus, domine, dominum*")—a vocabulary, moreover, which lets us know who's the master ("dominus").

After school, the Captain can make his mark on the landscape, writing his identity into the mud with his "prize shoes," and claiming

"My country." All this is encouraged by the system, and backed by *Children's Hour* on TV so that the spirit of emulation becomes nationwide. Regrettably, though, the boy grows up and accumulates a "stale wife," a "Boss" and some "thick kids"—a situation from which his schooling won't be able to extricate him. His uniform ("The blazer. / The badge. The tie") no longer fits, though he may still believe in uniformity. He can still tell us the Prime Minister of Rhodesia, even though the imperial rule's gone now and British Empire Rhodesia has become independent Zimbabwe. He can still tell us the number of florins in a pound sterling, even though the florin doesn't exist any more and the pound's become decimalized. So, as this latter reference to currency tells us, his information's no longer current: the order he subscribes to is old-fashioned, a thing of the past. All in all, just as time has stolen the British empire, so too on a smaller scale it's taken his once seemingly unassailable (gendered) space at the top of the scheme of things, leaving him displaced so that he can only desperately yearn to go back to the time when his methods actually seemed to work. He wants still to be in charge, to have "all the answers"; but this one-time spokesman for the team has nothing (constructive) left to say: knowledge (or in this case, mere information) may, like language, be *power*—but at this point it's *gone*. One can imagine Adrienne Rich (or for that matter Duffy herself) warming up in the wings, ready to take over.

The image of a failed patriarchal hero, outdated and unwanted, is further explored later—and given Biblical status—by Duffy in her poem "Mrs. Lazarus" (*PBPBI*, 384–85; *SP*, 135–36). Not quite as spectacular as Plath's "Lady Lazarus," Mrs. Lazarus at the beginning of the poem has gone through the forms of traditional widowhood at her husband's death. The power of the male head of the house lingers for a while, his name being a kind of "spell" that fades until it reduces to "legend, language" and finally merely "memory." Mrs. Lazarus prepares to move on, only (we already know, of course) to be confronted by the resurrected man of the family, who doesn't really fit into her new plans. The male miracle, then, sanctified by God and His Son, is rather unwelcome, and lacks the air of spectacular triumph one reads about in the original: in Duffy's version the poem ends with Mr. Lazarus "cuckhold," "disinherited," and "out of his time"—rather miserable circumstances all round, one imagines! As an allegory, the poem is not unlike "The Captain . . ." in intent, since both male champions end up out of touch and essentially redundant—much as does the phallocracy as far as Duffy is concerned: certainly in "Mrs. Lazarus" her attitude seems to be, why bother to resurrect what can be replaced?

The superannuation of the patriarchy, and the subversion of the phallogocentric discourse, continue more recently as themes in Duffy's work. Language, in particular, often seems a fragile phenomenon —as, for instance in the poem "Adultery" (*The New Poetry*, 230–31; *SP*, 119–20), where it "unpeels to a lost cry." And communication, as one system breaks down and another vies to supersede it, continues to be a somewhat hit-and-miss affair, as the snowman-thief realizes at the end of the poem "Stealing" (*The New Poetry*, 231–32; *SP*, 49–50) with the assertion, "You don't understand a word I'm saying, do you?" The codes and rituals on which so much language is founded don't always appear to work properly (like the mourning ceremony at the beginning of "Mrs. Lazarus," or the "Prayer" in the poem of that name [*PBPBI*, 384]). In the latter case, the "Music of loss" from "The Dolphins" becomes the "Grade I piano scales" that are the only consolation for the boarder "looking out across / a Midlands town." The echo of the situation of Larkin's Mr. Bleaney here presumably acts as an intensifier of the sense of emptiness, the "loss" and loneliness we experience when the neighbors (who obviously aren't alone) call out to their children at teatime. Under the circumstances, we're not in the least surprised to discover that in this environment "the radio's prayer" turns out to be not some transcendent redemption or call for divine intercession, but the marine weather forecast: "Rockall. Malin. Dogger. Finisterre." The message conveyed by this language isn't really what we need to hear.

❧    ❧    ❧    ❧    ❧

Duffy may not have yet formulated a suitable "common language" of the kind about which Adrienne Rich "dream(s)," then; but her work is full of an awareness of the progressive inoperancy of the phallogocentric discourse from across the gender border, a conviction that masculist English is broken and needs to be replaced by a more sensitized language structure or structures. Of course, replacement may be easier said than done, as Wendy Mulford warns us in her "Notes on Writing: a Marxist/Feminist Viewpoint" in Michelene Wandor's essay compilation, *On Gender and Writing* (1983). Mulford says:

> Yes, we must break through our silence. But we cannot *create* a language. We can make a lexical selection, designed to exclude, for ex-

ample, the obvious phallic metaphors of penetration, thrust, etc. for forceful action, for energy and desire. Such a lexical pruning and substitution of new items (such as chairperson) is part of the process of *thinking* our language, realizing its subtle articulations of male dominance, making some redress and calling the female into presence in verbs, qualifiers, substantives and pronouns. (34)

These things can be done, but (as Mulford goes on) they're only part of "a small linguistic process," which doesn't begin to address the wider issues. Prime among these is the notion of history (on both the personal and larger scales). Young girls have their individual and social roles prescribed for them from early on, so their own history is written for them by the rule of the father. Further, as adults, if they choose to write they do so from an inherited body of work which is heavily male-oriented; and their relationship to this material is, therefore (as Mulford emphasizes), "colonial," since the canon has been generated from "a differently gendered place" in which women don't comfortably fit (34–35).

By Rich's standards, this might well be perceived as an *under*statement of the case, but clearly the issue of possessing a suitable gendered space from which to write, which will "fit," is a key requisite. Rich herself (we may remember) in "When We Dead Awaken" used Mary Daly as authority for opening up discussion of this topic.[23] In the section entitled "*New Space: New Time*" in her volume *Beyond God the Father,* Daly had argued for "creation of new space, in which women are free to become who we are, in which there are real and significant alternatives to the prefabricated identities provided within the enclosed spaces of patriarchal institutions" (40). One such "patriarchal institution" is that which primarily concerns us here—language, and particularly literary language. Maggie Humm in *Border Traffic* (an important document in this discussion) paraphrases Alice Jardine as saying in *Gynesis* that "the 'spaces' in master narratives over which these narratives have lost control *are* women, that is to say these are spaces with feminine connotations" (13). So on the borders of the patriarchal discourse there are evidently areas which are at least contestable. Daly (again) affirms that "The new space is located always 'on the boundary'" (40). She adds the warning, though, that "life in the new space may be 'dangerous' in that it means living without the securities offered by the patriarchal system for docility to its rules" (41). However, the risk may well be worth it since, seen from another direction, being on the boundary permits

one to be simultaneously "in and out of 'the system'" (43). Humm
puts it slightly differently when she argues that women are circumstantially ideally suited for survival in this margin(alized) area, because

> it is women with our long-term history of crossing between received
> languages and undervalued ways of speaking who can be said to have
> a poetics of displacement. For women, the condition of patriarchy
> presupposes the reality of borders, even if, for some women, these
> are often internalized borders experienced as exclusion. (*Border Traf-
> fic*, 1)

So, if they're to claim a voice at all, women are obliged to become
adept at what Humm calls a "complex criss-crossing of the margins
of identity and writing possibilities" (1–2)—tactics which mean that
they "do not privilege one 'pure' style but make many moves out of
the checkmate of representation" (9). This versatility and flexibility
(so different, it need hardly be added, from the masculist Movement) will help to undermine or subvert the patriarchy's efforts to
impose its absolute rule (and rules) over the language women are
(grudgingly) permitted to use, and the space they're permitted to
occupy—a phenomenon on which Humm remarks in the colonial
context of Jean Rhys's *Wide Sargasso Sea*, though what she says might
equally be applied more universally: she notes that "To impose English customs and language is a normalizing act whose work is to
codify difference, to fix the Other . . . outside the boundary of the
civilized" (73). As we'll see in subsequent chapters, this act of colonizing arrogance has to be combatted not only by women (viewed by
the metropolitan patriarchal culture as gender barbarians), but also
by ethnic minorities (racial barbarians), ex-members of the Empire
(colonial barbarians), and even non-centrist British male poets
(provincial barbarians or as one of them prefers, "rhubarbarians").[24]
Certainly, back in the feminist context for the time being, there are
vociferous opponents showing up the dangers of such a "normalizing act," as we've seen. One of the heroines Humm chooses as exemplary in the transgressive act of boundary crossing is (almost
inevitably) Adrienne Rich, who is accorded a whole chapter of *Border
Traffic* (chapter 5, 160–84). At various points therein, Humm credits
her with crossing the border between "a masculine past and the feminist future" (164), or between "history and herstory" (180), noting
that for Rich the past is "identified as a collective patriarchal mes-

sage" (168). As well, Humm explains that Rich is concerned with the project of "vault[ing] over" the "border between art and life" (169); and with writing in a way which will "help women to cross the boundary of institutionalized misogyny" (165).

Obviously Rich occupies a significant space in the recent history/herstory of the "English" with which women are obliged to deal, and which they seek to modify (however radically) to their purposes. As we've seen in this chapter, she shares the preoccupation with a number of other committed female writers in English, not least Sylvia Plath and Carol Ann Duffy. But before we leave the arena of women's writing in the contemporary period there's one more part of that space we need at least to mention in passing: the area of the *marketplace*, that is of *publishing*.[25] It goes almost without saying that if women need a language to write themselves, that writing also requires public outlets—the most obvious of which (though of course by no means the only one) is formal publication. But if the patriarchy has been generally churlish in the face of women's attempts to formulate their own kind of "English," it's been at least as stingy in offering them space in its publications—as can be seen from a casual glance at any Establishment publisher's general poetry anthology one happens to have to hand.

The obvious answer to this problem is for women to take over the publishing endeavor themselves: just as the patriarchy can't be relied on to be fair in writing women, so it can't be relied on to be fair in publishing them either. Since the written language is only viable when it's available to be read, for the feminist literary project to succeed women must assume responsibility for the means of distribution as well as of production. As the editors of the significantly-titled Onlywomen Press declare on the copyright page of their anthology of British feminist poetry, *One Foot on the Mountain* (1979): "Onlywomen Press believes it is necessary to create a women's communication system. At the very least, this would mean we could and would print our own books on our own machines with our own hands." Over the last twenty or so years, more and more independent publishing houses specializing in women's literature have appeared, from the small-scale (like Onlywomen) to the much-larger concerns such as Virago, which has gone a long way towards filling the historical gaps in available literature by women. And non-Establishmentarian broader-spectrum presses, such as Bloodaxe, have also significantly increased the marketspace for women's writing.

All in all, it seems that Adrienne Rich's desire "to go on from here" is an increasingly practicable one, as suitable language(s) and systems of distribution evolve—certainly not smoothly, but at least progressively. In the next chapter we go on to look at another group of feminist writers—those whose case is complicated by their ethnic origins—and also at their male counterparts.

# 4

# Ethnic Spaces
# in the Empire of Words

IN THE PREVIOUS CHAPTER WE LOOKED AT CAROL ANN DUFFY'S POEM, "Foreign," and I suggested that the title might refer to Duffy herself either as a Scot living in England, or as a woman living in a male-constructed world. The most obvious reading of "foreignness" in that text, though—and one that is supported by the deliberately awkward and obtrusive pidgin towards the end of the poem—is that of ethnic minorities living on the margins (geographical or cultural) of the metropolitan center. It's the situation of these "foreigners" that I want to explore in this present chapter, centering my attentions in the main on some of the Westindian-British poets working in England over the last part of the twentieth century.[1]

Duffy's poem, as we saw, revolves around a "foreign accent" and a "local dialect" that seem distinctly *other* to the eminently inhospitable culture in which they "echo" emptily. Such a sense of estrangement centered on language is, perhaps not surprisingly, a theme, too, in Black British poetry. Gabriel Gbadamosi, for instance, in the poem sequence "No Blacks, No Irish" (an ironic title, given that the poet himself is *both*) writes of traveling by sea to England and arriving to find the place shrouded in snow, a cold welcome in which "No-one spoke" and "Our breath frosted" (in Allnutt et al. *The New British Poetry*, 36–37). The country seems as hostile as the climate, and the poem extends the meteorological into the temperamental, so that the "frost" that causes the speech act to freeze in the mouth is more than merely a consequence of the thermometer—climate and national character after all often being traditionally related to each other. Andrew Salkey evidently thinks this is the case in his "A Song

111

for England," in which, having watched the horrid pageant of the English weather unfold, he finally sees the reason for the "misery" of the local populace (in Brown and McDonald, comps., *The Heinemann Book of Caribbean Poetry* [1992], 193). And John Agard might agree as a result of the experience recounted in "Finders Keepers" when, on a commuter train to Charing Cross, he finds a "stiff upper lip" in a railway carriage and decides that it needs to "thaw off" by being taken "to the Third World" (in Horovitz, ed., *Grandchildren of Albion* [1992], 29).

So the culture of the "Third World" (or some excolonial equivalent) may be needed to raise the temperature of the metropolitan culture, to bring a smile or a kind word to that gelid stiff upper lip: that is—to change the metaphor somewhat—in a reversal of what happened historically during the colonizing period, the margin may be called on to transform the center. This may not be quite as implausible as one might think, since the hitherto *de*-privileged, the "foreigners" held so coldly at bay by Movement-style xenophobia, may be in a unique position to alter the cultural status quo—particularly through the medium of *language*. A monoglossic culture accustomed to a single dominating discourse, to (for instance) a notion of "purity" such as that put forward by Donald Davie in 1950s England, may have great imperial power; but it may pay for that with a lack of flexibility. "Foreigners" coming into this dispensation, on the other hand, bringing their own language or language variant with them into this discourse, for survival are obliged to be (at least) bilingual.

The downside of the situation is that their "foreign" (lack of) status may be underlined in their speaking voice—as it is in Duffy's poem; or as Maggie Humm puts it in *Border Traffic*, "The bilingual writer lives in countries of contradiction because, of course, language is the key instrument in the construction of national as well as individual entities." There's an advantage, though, which may be gained from this ambiguous or contradictory situation: Humm goes on to assert that "bilingualism is a creative process because it talks of differences and living transformations. It is the epitome of border crossings" (94). The need "To translate from one set of meanings into another," then, is actively creative, and prevents the cultural system from being closed, from stagnating or *going cold*.

The editors of the anthology *Watchers and Seekers: Creative Writing by Black Women in Britain* (Cobham and Collins, 1987) evidently concur with Humm's positive view of cultural border crossings, seeing it as a significant virtue that several of their contributors "have lived between societies: Africa and the Caribbean; Africa and England; the Caribbean and England; India/Pakistan and England; China, the Caribbean and England" (5). Such combinations become more common as immigration, and in fact global travel in general, increase. A pioneer whom the editors single out as a key figure is Una Marson, whose immigration to England from Jamaica created in her a "new sense of a racial identity" in the new community in which she found herself in the United Kingdom (4). To articulate this new sense, Marson saw that she needed a new language, a literary vehicle that would give a voice to her otherwise silenced "foremothers," as well as simultaneously reflecting the contemporary world. What she came up with was a mixture of Jamaican Patwah combined with the beat of "Afro-American Blues" (7).

With Marson, we seem to be approaching the notion of a "Black English" set up in the cultural spaces on the borders of "standard English" which Adrienne Rich (as we saw in the previous chapter) recognized and admired in the work of Derek Walcott.[2] Certainly Caribbean writers seem, as Paula Burnett argues in the introduction to *The Penguin Book of Caribbean Verse in English* (1986), to be in a strategic position to formulate an "English" to contest "English": She writes, "The English-speaking Caribbean is uniquely placed, both geographically and historically, at the meeting-point between three continents—Europe, Africa and America—and between three poetic traditions—the British, the West African and the North American" (xxiii). Furthermore, she goes on, "Over the last fifty years" the literary-cultural orientation has shifted from dominance by the (various) colonizing powers—that is, for instance, away from a monoglossic standard English—"to a mode which is closer to the vernacular, influenced by the oral traditions of Africa" and also by aspects of "the American tradition" (xxiii). Grace Nichols adds her voice to the discussion, seeing this reorientation as an act of reclamation of the history of colonization: in the face of the imposed colonizing language, she asserts, many West Indian writers have reaffirmed "a language our foremothers and forefathers struggled to create after losing their own languages on the plantations and we are saying it's a valid, vibrant language." This is *not*, she asserts, a simple dialectal variant of English, even if many of the words themselves "are English-based": set against (or with) the anglophone elements are the "structure, rhythm, and intonation [which] are an influence of West African speech" (in *Six Women Poets,* ed. Judith Kinsman [1992], 31).

James Berry amplifies this somewhat in his essay on "Westindian-British Poetry" in *Poetry Review* (June 1983), suggesting that "In their obsession to establish a firm identity and security, to feel a wholeness, Westindian poets have had to claim the language most natural to them to express their poetry. Caribbean Creole was an African response to language and changes standard English into simpler and speedier communication." So this new "English" is enhanced "with emotional tones inherited from Africa and colored by the Caribbean experience" (6). In fact, as the authors of *The Empire Writes Back* tell us,[3] the result linguistically is a very potent mix indeed, involving (as the Caribbean begins to "Write Back" to English) not one but a number of related voices which theorists have subsequently grouped together in what is known as the Creole continuum. Of the distinctive linguistic culture of the Caribbean, Ashcroft et al. write: "the Creole complex of the region is not simply an aggregation of discrete dialect forms but an overlapping of ways of speaking between which individual speakers may move with considerable ease" (45). That is, the language matrix of the area is fluid and flexible, destabilizing any possible assertion of "a standard code in the language and any monocentric view of human experience." These latter are discarded in favor of a recognition of "the syncretic and hybridized nature of post-colonial experience" (41), for the articulation of which a concentric model of Standard English becomes inappropriate. The implications of this are significant and quite widespread, since the process involves "not a subversion of language alone, but of the entire system of cultural assumptions on which the texts of the English canon are based and the whole discourse of metropolitan control within which they were able to be imposed" (48).

The "subverted" metropolitan English, then, can be substituted by a new "English" (or englishes) solidly founded on a Creole continuum which is polyglossic and multivalent. These qualities, added to the characteristics mentioned in passing by Nichols and Berry above —"vibrant," "natural," "simpler," "speedier," "emotional"—seem to guarantee a Caribbean literary English significantly different from that prioritized by any retrogressive notion of purity of diction in English verse. Above all, it will have the energy of the *new,* the aggression and assertiveness of a voice breaking through a previously enforced silence and passivity. It will have more in common with

Walt Whitman's slang than with the Movement's gentility, more to do with an emergent provisional diction than with a stable canonical (and canonized) one, as David Dabydeen suggests in a powerful essay entitled "On Not Being Milton: Nigger Talk in England Today" (in *The State of the Language*, Ricks and Michaels, ed. [1990], 3–14). He writes:

> Words are spat out from the mouth like live squibs, not pronounced with elocution. English diction is cut up, and this adds to the abruptness of the language: *what* for instance becomes *wha* (as in *whack*), the splintering making the language more barbaric. . . . The creole language is angry, crude, energetic. The canecutter chopping away at the crop bursts out into a spate of obscene words, a natural gush from the gut. (3)

This "Nigger Talk,"[4] this Caribbean barbaric yawp, conveys, Dabydeen argues, "sheer naked energy and brutality," a "quality of lawlessness" amplified by its "primarily oral form" (4). Interestingly, these phrases are used not initially of the creole itself, but of a parallel case which Dabydeen surprisingly draws in the essay—the northern dialect Middle English of *Sir Gawain and the Green Knight*. He makes a fascinating comparison (which we will come back to in a different context in the final chapter), in which the north/south divide between the dynamic local diction of the Gawain-poet and the more regulated conventional iambic pentameters of the London-based Chaucer is seen as a kind of historic parallel to the divide between "the so-called Caribbean periphery and the metropolitan center of London" (4).

It seems that the arrogant imposition of the category of provincialism as an indicator of supposed inferiority has been around for a long time, then—from the fourteenth century, at least! To bring the discussion back up-to-date, Dabydeen's singling out of the iambic pentameter here as suggestive of a suave, educated literary metropolitanism against which the "barbaric" Gawain-poet vies is interesting because the pentameter becomes the target in the work of another prominent speaker on behalf of things Caribbean, Edward Kamau Brathwaite. Brathwaite in his study, *History of the Voice: the Development of Nation Language in Anglophone Caribbean Poetry* (1984),[5] draws attention to the divergence from colonial models of what he calls the "software" of the "emergent language in the Caribbean," pointing out that "What English has given us as a model for poetry

... is the pentameter" (9). The regularized and measured line produced by adherence to the iambic pentameter may be all very well
for the English; but for the more adventurous it becomes an alien
stricture. The first effort to break the dominance of the pentameter
came—as we saw much earlier—from the United States: Brathwaite
notes that "Over in the New World the Americans—Walt Whitman—
tried to bridge or to break the pentameter through a cosmic movement, a large movement of sound" (10). Carrying on this pioneering work from a slightly different geographical location, the
Caribbean writers have followed suit: as Brathwaite puts it, "It is *nation language* in the Caribbean that, in fact, largely ignores the pentameter. Nation language is the language which is influenced very
strongly by the African model, the African aspect of our New World/
Caribbean heritage." He goes on to say that Caribbean texts may appear to be in English, but often "It is in English which is like a howl,
or a shout or a machine-gun or the wind or a wave. It is also like the
blues. And sometimes it is English and American at the same time"
(13). He clinches his argument (his Ginsbergian howl) against the
pure and chaste English pentameter by confronting it with an alternative prosodic phenomenon of distinctly Caribbean pedigree: "In
order to break down the pentameter, we discovered an ancient form
which was always there, the calypso [*kaiso*]. This is a form that I think
nearly everyone knows about. It does not employ the iambic pentameter. It employs dactyls" (17). The Creole continuum, then,
provides ample technical tools for literary iconoclasm among the
Caribbean poets, whether it be through Brathwaite's calypsoes or
Dabydeen's "Nigger Talk." That such oppositional gestures continue
to be necessary in the postcolonial situation is emphasized in Mervyn Morris's poem, "Literary Evening, Jamaica" (in Markham, ed.,
*Hinterland* [1989], 165–56), a tale of latter-day cultural colonization
in which the presenter reads out poems by Larkin and D. J. Enright
for his West Indian audience. No false claims are made for this
poetry, which is described by the compère as "anti-gesture, anti-
flatulence" and as dealing with "quiet honesties without pretence."
Harmless enough, one might think—except that "Dull-mannered,
scared, regressive Phil" [Larkin, that is!] is occupying space that
could be given to a local (ethnic) voice that may be "coarse," "wild,"
"violent," "Screaming hot curses anti-slavery," and so on, but is at
least dynamic and appropriate to the immediate situation. The
poem concludes with the narrator questioning how relevant Move-

ment-style "bland negation" is to a turbulent and boisterous Caribbean nation.

The collocation of "Nigger Talk" and Movement poetry in Morris's poem is matched by a similar juxtaposition towards the end of Dabydeen's essay "On Not Being Milton" when he claims that

> [Linton Kwesi] Johnson, [John] Agard, and others are reacting against the "rational structure and comprehensible language" which Robert Conquest saw as a distinguishing feature of the Movement poets and which still afflicts contemporary English verse. The charge that Alvarez leveled against the Movement—the disease of gentility— is still relevant today. (10–11)

୬  ୬  ୬  ୬  ୬

For West Indian poets, then (just as—in a somewhat different context—for Adrienne Rich and, behind her, Emily Dickinson), metropolitan English continues to be "spoiled language" that needs to be handled with extreme caution, a "disease" that may still contaminate emergent fresh linguistic manifestations. Paula Burnett in the Penguin anthology of Caribbean poetry changes the metaphor somewhat, suggesting that an *evolutionary* step beyond the standard code is what is required in order to proceed in a healthy direction. Looking back, (like Whitman) she acknowledges the *historical* richness of English (at the same time, incidentally, undermining any notion of that language's "purity" by stressing its *hybrid* nature);[6] but looking forward, she promotes the Creole continuum as extending this linguistic wealth into the future: she writes, "Just as the richness of the English language is derived from its history as a hybrid, the process is carried further with the English of the Caribbean" (xxv). The assertion here carries with it the message of cultural Darwinism of the kind we saw much earlier in Whitman's remarks on English: that is, the newer language (whether it be American English or Caribbean Creole) while perhaps continuous with the older one, effectively *supersedes* it as the fitter to survive (in Burnett's terms, "carrying it further"). Seen in this way, the new speech, then, like Grace Nichols's "Sugar Cane" in the poem of that name (in Markham, *Hinterland*, 301–3), represents an undiseased shoot, a (sweet) linguistic bud to provide a fresh crop springing out of the unpromising context of colonial dispossession and loss. As Nichols puts it, having "crossed an ocean" and lost her old "tongue," she finds that a "new one" grows in its place.

Regrettably, though, there may be a problem here: to continue
Nichols' reference, and my own earlier metaphor, the climate in
England may not be (definitely *isn't*) as conducive to the transplan-
tation and flourishing of sugar cane as is that of the Caribbean.
James Berry notes that while calypso and folk poetry may flourish in
the West Indies, "a different place, Britain, . . . with new circumstances, makes its new demands" ("Westindian," 5). Up to this point,
the discussion has been occupied in the main with the *Caribbean* language situation—that of the colonized becoming the postcolonized
on home soil. But when the West Indian becomes the Westindian-
British, the rules change somewhat. In the metropolitan center itself,
notions of a single dominating discourse, of standardization and purity essentially inimical to the immigration of Creole (or any kriols
for that matter), may persist. That is, the spirit of "regressive Phil"
may live on, and enjoy more power in England than abroad; and the
unacceptable *otherness* of the "foreign" may generate significant resistance.

Merle Collins in her poem "No Dialects Please" in the anthology
*Fire the Sun* (Healy, ed., 1989) takes the situation quite lightly, mocking the English for their defensive attitude towards their own language. The stricture in her title against dialects (actually part of the
rules for a local poetry competition) puzzles her since she sees English itself as no more than an agglomeration (or hybrid) of dialects,
a "language-elect" maybe, but created out of "de dialect of de Nor-
mans and de Saxons / dat combine an reformulate" (7). In this case,
linguistic restrictions, rules and prohibitions (she seems to think)
can only be motivated by fear, by a protectionism seeking to hide the
inherent "impurity" and *weakness* of a language which she knows "we
could wrap roun we little finger" (9).

The poem may be amusing in tone, but the basic (polite yet insistent) prescription in the title is really no laughing matter, and the
desire to project and protect a dialect-free (pure) metropolitan discourse, standardized and uniform, has profound implications—not
only literary ones—for the ethnic minority population at large, including the Westindian-British. John Honey explores some of these
implications in his books, *Does Accent Matter?*[7] and *Language is Power*,
in the latter of which he points out that "the whole of our educational system, as it is at present constituted, presupposes the ability to
handle standard English"—to such a degree, in fact, that "there is a
long-standing and now overwhelming association, right across Brit-

ish society, between the use of grammar, vocabulary and idioms of standard English, and the concept of 'educatedness'" (39). This doesn't seem to leave much space in the language or learning process for ethnic voices (or what Collins in her poem satirically calls "dialects"), which will therefore be excluded from the structure. Consequently, the situation necessitates the vigorous and vocal advocacy of *difference*, which may otherwise be swallowed up by the normalizing impetus of the system. This is the gist of an anonymous article (based on Joan Baratz's report, "Bi-Dialectical Test for Determining Language Proficiency in Economically Disadvantaged Negro Children") to be found in the publication *Race Today* (vol. 1, no. 7 [November 1969]: 222–23), and entitled "Deficient—or Different?" The writer argues that many negro children are labeled "deficient" when in fact they haven't exactly *failed* to learn the rules of the standard linguistic system, but are instead operating by a different set of rules, structured on a (secondary) code of nonstandard English that in the individual instance supersedes the primary or dominant code.

Appreciation of this situation requires a far more flexible attitude towards language (and towards the categories of "right" and "wrong" in that context) than perhaps the English education system is prepared for. Of course, in the end, whether the linguistic behavior is tagged "deficient" or "different" will remain a matter of viewpoint, of (in)tolerance, the degree to which the "foreign" is countenanced. Terry Eagleton, for one, clearly doesn't hold out too much hope for accommodation between Establishment and ethnic minority in this area. In his article "New Word Train" in *Poetry Review* (57–59) he rather grimly describes the poetry produced by Westindian-British writers as "rife with a painful rootlessness, seared by an eloquent protest against the British imperialism which, having systematically dismantled Westindian identity in the Caribbean, then runs through the process again on its own home territory" (59). The dismantling of identity (an identity, of course, closely bound up with the language one uses to write and speak oneself) needs to be resisted at all costs, then. Dennis Scott in an interview in the anthology *Hinterland* underlines this fact (again with a hint of cultural Darwinistic New World/Old World opposition), warning against the seductions of the metropolitan center. He says that "every time a New World man has chosen to swallow the value systems, the culture, wholesale of the Old World, we've gone amiss" (139): evidently in this case swallowing amounts to *being* swallowed.

One of the primary data that becomes highly significant in the Westindian-British resistance to being assimilated by the "Old" home culture, in the continued affirmation of *other*, non-colonized identity, is the Jamaican-based religion of Rastafarianism. Rastafarianism emphasizes the African element and influences in Caribbean identity, its primary focus being the Emperor of Ethiopia, Haile Selassie, who—as Jah Rastafari—was worshipped as a Messianic figure, even God on earth[8] (and for whom, incidentally, one of the West Indian literary-cultural pioneers—Una Marson—worked as personal secretary). The strictly religious elements don't concern us as much here as the broader, popularized black-consciousness-raising aspects of the movement. James Berry argues this case in *News for Babylon* when he emphasizes "the importance of Rastafarianism as the expression of a new black aesthetic," a pride in black origins. One superficial manifestation of this pride is the adoption by certain writers of personal names reflecting "African cultural roots"—the examples Berry cites being Edward Brathwaite's adoption of Kamau as a middle name, and Linton Johnson's adoption of Kwesi as his (xxv).

And perhaps this tactic isn't so superficial after all, at least by implication, since naming oneself (as opposed to having a name *imposed*) is a positive act of taking control, a personal decolonizing gesture of a kind duplicated in the recent history of many excolonized cultures—including, as we'll see later, that of the Aboriginal peoples in Australia (who, a very long way from the Caribbean or Africa, have been influenced by the example of Rastafarianism in their own consciousness-raising).[9] Just as naming oneself is predicated on how one sees oneself, and how one constructs oneself culturally, so Rastafarianism promotes for the Caribbean community (and, more specifically to our present discussion, for Westindian-British poets) a way of (black) seeing preparatory to a way of (black) writing. Dennis Scott (again) admits to being particularly impressed by "the kind of strategies—linguistic strategies—that [Rastas] . . . have used to redefine themselves in the world," seeing these tactics as instrumental in the attempt to "specify" an independent "self" (in *Hinterland*, 139).

One of the tactics involves manipulation and variation of the highly-significant first person pronoun (that most obvious indicator of identity). Joseph Owens in his study, *Dread: the Rastafarians of Jamaica*, explains as follows: "The pronoun 'I' has a special importance to Rastas and is expressly opposed to the servile 'me.' Whether the singular ('I') or the plural ('I and I' or briefly: 'I-n-I') or the reflexive

('I-sel,' 'I-n-I self') the use of this pronoun identifies the Rasta as an individual. . . . Even the possessive 'my' and the objective 'me' are replaced by 'I'" 65–66). The reason for eschewing or replacing parts of speech such as "me" and "my" is that as grammatical objects governed by the subject of the sentence, they are considered to be "servile," the syntactic relationship reflecting the subjection of African slaves by white European colonists. This amounts to the cultural rewriting or dismantling of negative historical connotations inherited in the standard code of English.

The primacy of "I" isn't restricted to first person pronouns, however, but gets extended into other parts of the Rasta vocabulary. Several words in Dread Talk have their first syllables replaced by the letter "I" so that, for instance, "ancient" becomes "I-cient"; "equality" becomes "I-quality," and so on.[10] The fixation with "I" carries over into many West Indian poems, Jean Binta Breeze's "Red Rebel Song," for example, ending with a positive plethora of first person pronouns: having paid her respects to Rastafarianism as a free Christian who knows "Jah," the protagonist writes:

> I jus a come
>  I I I own rainbow
>  I I I own song
>
> (in *Spring Cleaning*, 6)

This is clearly the work of a writer who describes herself (in a poem of that title in her collection *Spring Cleaning*) as "I Poet" (88–89). Velma Pollard continues the "I" theme by disclosing the obvious I = eye pun in Rastafarian English (or, as it's known more colloquially, "Dread Talk"). In her article "Dread Talk—the Speech of Rastafari in Modern Jamaican Poetry" in Anna Rutherford's compilation *From Commonwealth to Post-Colonial* (1992) Pollard uses Mervyn Alleyne to explain, as follows:

Alleyne, commenting on the Rastafarian division of the world into positive and negative forces, says with regard to seeing: "The most positive force is perception physically realized through the eye by means of the sense of sight and leading to the metaphysical realization of the self, the ego, the 'I.'" And the Rasta man himself, comparing his ability to perceive with that of the non-Rasta man ("Babylon" in the code of Rasta), says, "Eyes have they and see not, only Fari could see." Note the pun on "fari" which becomes both part of Rastafari and "Far eye" suggesting "far-seeing eye." (219)

Dread Talk, then, contributes significantly—in the way it sees and the way it says—to the postcolonized West Indian i-dentity. In Rastafarianism's Caribbean base of Jamaica, as Pollard notes, "DT" [Dread Talk] contributes to the local branch of the Creole continuum by interacting "with SJE [Standard Jamaican English] or with JC [Jamaican Creole] or with both" (221), all part of a fluid intermixture of "Englishes" (since "All language within the Jamaican speech community may be described as 'English related.'" [216]). Because of DT's culturally-significant promotion of the first person pronoun, Jean Binta Breeze can celebrate enthusiastically the existence of "Ilands" (*Spring Cleaning*, 77–85)—that is, I-lands (spaces for the individual self) and Islands (separate uncolonized communities): she writes of Jamaica, where the poem starts; "Haiti" (in part 3); "St[a] Lucia" (in part 4); "Trinidad" (in part 5); "Guyana" (in part 6); "Grenada" (in part 7); "Barbados" (in part 8); and "Antigua" (in part 9).

One set of islands not mentioned here (and which may not, after all, be I-lands in the Caribbean sense of the term), but which the Rastafarian i-dentity must deal with (even attempt to colonize) is, inevitably, the *British* Isles—the seat of *Empire* to which the colonized must now *Write Back*, the one-time "center" where the history of imperialism must be rewritten.[11] Breeze herself, like a number of other Westindian-British poets, has been virtually a commuter between the island groups on opposite sides of the Atlantic, and her contact with the colonizing and patriarchal dispensations hasn't always been —predictably enough—as ecstatic as the experience written in "Ilands." The editors of the important collection, *A Double Colonization: Colonial and Post-Colonial Women's Writing*[12] warn that (as a West Indian and a woman) she may well be subject to *at least* a double form of colonization in the metropolitan culture. They argue that Caribbean women writers are at the mercy of "a double set of myths which seek to deny their creative existence" and are therefore struggling desperately for "visibility," the difficulty being exacerbated by "problems of racism and immigrant status" (Petersen and Rutherford, eds., 9).

Certainly in her best-known poem to date, "Riddym Ravings (The Mad Woman's Poem),"[13] Breeze dramatizes a female protagonist struggling not to have her existence denied, her power "switched off" by the male Establishment. The poem is a dramatic monologue spoken by a woman who is from the outset culturally disoriented by the shift from country to town (which may also be read, it seems to me, on the larger scale as the migration from "colony" to "Imperial center," from a mango-rich environment to a mango-deficient climate!).[14] Whatever the context, the woman is labeled (like so many literary female speakers before her) as "Mad"—though from her perspective, of course, it's the "Town" that's mad (Gordon Rohlehr suggesting appealingly in his introduction to the anthology *Voiceprint* that the poem presents us with "kaleidoscopes of the city's derangement" [Brown, Morris, and Rohlehr, eds., 15]). One way or another, though, she's certainly depicted in the text as *other*, marked (by her accent and actions) as *foreign*. Faced with her unorthodoxy, the Establishment (Jamaican, or English, or both), symbolized by the doctor and the landlord who represent the male power structure in the poem, seeks to neutralize her. The bizarre metaphor Breeze uses for this action is the Mad Woman's enforced disconnection from the radio in her head—presumably a fictionalized rendition of the kind of electric shock "therapy" that Sylvia Plath underwent, or of the lobotomy suffered by Lepke Buchalter in Robert Lowell's "Memories of West Street and Lepke" which left the victim "hanging . . . in his air / of lost connections."[15] Breeze's persona, though, subverts the process by resisting the loss of connection and persistently plugging back in: as Rohlehr puts it, "she clings to the lifeline of her radio, her story" in spite of the efforts by the powerful men in the poem to separate her therefrom (16).

The radio is a key cultural referent in several ways, and not just in Breeze's poem. Until the advent of the internet, at least, it was probably the least *censorable* of the media, and so in some ways the most potentially subversive.[16] As well, like performance poetry (as opposed to printed texts), and like the literature of many West Indians' African origins, it prioritizes the oral. In addition, it performs a significant function in making available across national boundaries music which (as we'll see presently) operates across cultural boundaries as well, creating space for ethnic voices to be heard. In Breeze's poem, the radio acts primarily as a kind of counterforce to the power of the male Establishment which seeks to hospitalize or otherwise encarcerate what is interpreted as the hysteria of the female. On the one hand, the representatives of patriarchal power seek to isolate and victimize the woman, silencing her and giving her cancer. But on the other hand "de D. J. fly up eena mi head," providing a kind of rhythmic antidote. Nevertheless, in real time the Mad Woman inhabits a world of alienation and displacement, and feels unable to settle in town. She falls prey to unrequited longing and homesick-ness ("*mi waan go a country go look mango*"): in reality it may be a long time before she enjoys the total experience of mango again—soft, squashy, aromatic, sensual, such an ungenteel, *unEnglish* fruit. In the meantime, though, the radio helps her to cling to a sense of belong-ing, however humble: when she tries to get on the bus, for instance, she realizes that "di riddym eena mi head" is the "same as de tape weh de bus driva a play." More significantly, it even allows her to keep in touch with the continuities of her innermost "Riddym," as is graphically enacted towards the end of the poem in a (literally) preg-nant gesture that happily escapes the attention of the governing dis-pensation:

> mi tek di radio
> an mi push i up eena mi belly
> fi keep de baby company
> fah even if mi nuh mek i
> me waan my baby know dis yah riddym yah
> fram before she bawn
> hear de D. J. a play. . . .

Admittedly the dominant discourse may apparently ultimately tri-umph in the text, when the woman isn't allowed onto the bus, and the doctor and landlord once more resort to electric shock treat-ment of their victim; but the so-called Mad Woman at least keeps her soul (musical or otherwise) intact. Or, to put it another way, at least she's able to pass on her "Riddym" to her descendant(s), in much the same way as Grace Nichols's "Sugar Cane" will continue to put out fresh shoots when the old growth is cut down.

And, unavoidably, there's as well the "Riddym" of the actual utter-ance here, and in fact the whole shape of the language used in the poem—so "foreign" if judged by the norms of standard English. The Mad Woman may certainly be oppressed, marginalized by the cul-ture in which she finds herself; and yet this is undeniably *her* poem: it couldn't be mistaken for something by "regressive Phil" or his friend Kingsley Amis. Breeze's monologue form underlines the fact that the woman is saying and writing *herself*: it's *her* voice that we hear, *her* rhythms that govern our reading/listening, and finally *her* baby that will be born to inherit the future (perhaps). Mad or not, the woman is certainly alive, as the liveliness of her language amply attests: it may be Jamaican Creole more than Dread Talk (using the "me" form ["mi"] rather than the "I"), but like the voice of Rastafarianism it has a kind of I-ntegrity, an assertion of selfhood if not triumphant then at least determined to endure even against the odds.

In the *Caribbean* context this selfhood, this linguistic self-affirmation, may receive—as we've seen—strong cultural support from such phenomena as the Rastafarian emphasis on "I," on a strong statement of individual identity unbowed by (syntactic) slavery, and freed or redeemed from the negative connotations of the erstwhile colonizer's language code. But unambiguously on the other side of the Atlantic—at least as Jackie Kay reads it—the situation's different: in the poem "Prizes" (*Angels of Fire: an Anthology of Radical Poetry in the '80s* [Sylvia Paskin, et al., eds., 1986], 63–64) she says "the old slave-holder philosophy" still pertains and "England has not changed." For Kay, "I" doesn't imply a position of unique subjectivity, an ethnic freedom from oppression, but instead functions as the selfish and overbearing imperative of (continued) colonial exploitation: "The colonizer still constant in the vowel I / the Imperialist wish, the unfinished business."

In section 7 of her long sequence, *The Adoption Papers* (1991), she traces this ominous-sounding "unfinished business" further—through the *education* system. Given the strategic position of education (or what Dread Talk labels "head-decay-shun")[17] in British imperial history as regards maintaining the dominant discourse, the system is perhaps predictable enough as a target—though in this case Kay actually deals with education in Britain itself rather than some (other) colony, scrutinizing the ongoing arrogant prejudice she herself faced as a black school pupil. In this section of the sequence, subtitled "Black Bottom" (a term indicating in this case, one feels, a site of chastisement as much as a 1920s dance fad that Kay is trying to learn) she dramatizes a playground confrontation with a budding member of the National Front, and its aftermath.[18]

The title *The Adoption Papers* suggests not only Kay's own adoption, but the process of adoption on a wider scale—adopting a culture, adopting a language: perhaps adoption is a suitable metaphor for the immigrant situation, that of the ethnic minority, the "foreign" at large. Certainly the problems the protagonist experiences at school to some degree stem from her visible difference, the *otherness* of "her being black" (as her adoptive mother puts it), since "color matters to the nutters" (297). The "wee shite" who calls her "*Sambo, sambo*" gets his just desserts, but not before one of the teachers notices. The appalling (but probably not surprising) truth of the matter is that the blatant color-prejudice of the young blond boy is echoed in the more subtle prejudice voiced by the school Establishment (the form teacher, the headmaster). The teacher labels the young black woman as "a juvenile delinquent" in the making, and orders her:

> Look it up in the dictionary.
> She spells each letter with slow pleasure.
> Read it out to the class.
> Thug. Vandal. Hooligan. Speak up. Have you lost your tongue?
>
> (298)

The irony of the rhetorical question here is, of course, that *yes* she has lost her tongue—either through having an immigrant language replaced by a standard one (a situation which *doesn't* pertain to Kay biographically here), or by having the teacher (and the dictionary) bully her and write her into negative categories.

Later the same pedagogue is guilty of another act of color-discrimination, when she tries to persuade the protagonist to do the famous "Black Bottom":

> . . . Come on, show
>
>> us what you can do I thought
>> you people had it in your blood.
>> My skin is hot as burning coal
>> like that time she said Darkies are like coal
>> in front of the whole class—my blood
>> what does she mean?
>
> (298)

The first part of the statement might superficially appear to be a compliment; but in fact it's another way of marking difference or otherness, thus enforcing a binary reductionism or typecasting which denies individual identity. And the second part of the statement has no excuse at all. The result is that the pupil goes home from school embarrassed by color-prejudice, *and* wondering what's wrong with her blood. Having been named "*Sambo*" and "delinquent" and "Darkie" by the dominant discourse, she looks in the mirror to try to establish some sense of her own identity, but can only come up with saying to herself, "*Do you really look like this?* / as if I'm somebody else" (300).

Such, presumably, is the plight of the "adopted" (and the colonized). However, the form of the poem perhaps offers some hope after all. Kay has written the sequence as an interacting drama of three voices—the Daughter; the Adoptive Mother; and the Birth Mother (each indicated in the text by a separate typeface). So, in a tactic very different from Breeze's, we get three perspectives rather than a single one; and the protagonist's identity and cultural definition aren't established by a single (biased) speech, such as the teacher's or the dictionary's, but are formulated from a combination of (sympathetic) voices, creating a multifaceted persona rather than a stereotypical one. As Ian Gregson says in *Contemporary Poetry and Postmodernism: Dialogue and Estrangement* (1996), the women's various perspectives and statements "multiply each other through juxtaposition and inter-penetration: terminus, the masculine god of boundaries, is very much opposed in this feminine polyphony where boundaries are crossed and re-crossed" (244). This may not entirely negate the prejudice in the discourse, or the rigidity in dictionary definitions insisted on by unsympathetic schooling; but at least it puts the system into a context in which its authority isn't absolute.

Another Westindian-British poet who writes of difficulties with the power structure immanent in the British education system—though this time at the tertiary level, is John Agard. Agard's well-known "Listen Mr. Oxford Don" takes pride of place as the first poem in Fred D'Aguiar's selection of "Black British Poetry" in the Paladin anthology, *The New British Poetry* (5–6).[19] In the poem, Agard demands the attention of an academic from a key center of cultural and educational power in the English-speaking world. Oxford is, of course, home base of the prestigious Oxford University Press, which, as we've already seen, has produced a series of canon-forming anthologies of verse in English—including Philip Larkin's significant *The Oxford Book of Twentieth-Century English Verse*, in which he tried to establish as normative his own "little England" taste, and to exclude or play down texts that he regarded as in some way unEnglish. As well, Oxford University was the alma mater of most of the members of The Movement, who engaged in Larkin's project to a greater or lesser degree. And, most significantly for Agard in his poem, the OUP is responsible for the famous range of dictionaries grouped around *The Oxford English Dictionary* that historically has done so much to Establish a standard vocabulary and usage of the English language.

The Oxfordness of the "Don," then, is symbolic of an élite structure of which Agard is emphatically not part, as he defiantly tells us
at the outset, both in the substance of the statement and in the language in which that statement is couched: "Me not no Oxford don."
He doesn't even have any affinities with Oxford *Circus*, since he
comes from Clapham Common. Instead of being a part of the Establishment, then, he's clearly an outsider, an immigrant rather than
member of a college. Nevertheless he compels our attention, demanding a space from which to speak and be heard, confronting us
as a desperado for whom "mugging de Queen's English" has become
part of his proactive tactics. The introduction of the notions of violence and criminality into the poem at this point is part of a recur-
rent satirical reference throughout the text: just as Sylvia Plath would
sometimes, as an act of subversion, adopt the tactic of dramatizing
herself as a little girl since that was what the patriarchy expected of
her, so Agard does the same as the black man accosting a respectable
white upper-middle-class citizen.[20]

The linguistic mugger, then, before our very eyes runs riot over
the standard codes—of genteel behavior as well as of language. He
may not have any actual weapons other than his own voice—but that
could be enough as he sets about creating mayhem, challenging the
*OED* on its home turf and giving the metropolitan language a taste
of Creolization. By the end of the poem his ambitions have grown
still further as he plans to make "de Queen's English accessory / to
my offence." This final statement is important because it amounts to
the most serious subversion in the text of the Establishment's Law
(judicial or linguistic): it constitutes a reversal in which the primary
code becomes secondary ("accessory") and vice versa.

The humor here (a characteristic of much of Agard's writing, as
well as of many other Westindian-British poets) shouldn't deflect us
as readers from the fact that important business is going on—the
"unfinished business," which Jackie Kay talked about in "Prizes," of
the continuing negotiation between "Imperialist . . . colonizer" and
colonized ethnic minority. In Agard's poem, of course, the topic is
seen from a different angle, with the immigrant effectively exploiting the colonizer, and given the textual power of a voice whose Creole energy seems (at least temporarily) to undermine the authority
of the "Queen." This is all accomplished in a chirpy near-doggerel,
and with a series of outrageous rhymes and puns which are (to carry
on the poem's own reference system) disarming. But sometimes the

mood can't be quite as bright: politically, that is, ethnic minorities are unlikely to be able to laugh their way into a significant share of the metropolitan power. So, for instance, in the title of his selected poems of 1984, Agard sees that there may need to be *Mangoes & Bullets*[21]—not only Breeze's Mad Woman's ethnic fruitiness, but something more violent. Practical necessity, then, may compel not only a cultural assertion of ethnic minority rights (the mango being, as Gordon Rohlehr notes, part of a symbolism of "endless fruit . . . which is a recurring theme in Jamaican literature" [Brown, Stewart, and Rohlehr, *Voiceprints*, 16]) but also a *physical* assertion in which the speaker in "Listen Mr. Oxford Don" may actually need to take up literal weapons. As Agard warns in his poem "Pan Recipe" (in Brown and McDonald, *The Heinemann Book of Caribbean Poetry*, 5–6), colonization may be a recipe for disaster if the Imperial power is content to "rape a people" and to let them "simmer for centuries." The result is virtually inevitable: the mix is likely to "explode."

And explosions have, regrettably, occurred—notably in the late 1970s and early 1980s, in Bristol and Brixton, Southall and Toxteth (to mention only a few sites of confrontation). Even such traditionally conservative Caribbean writers as Derek Walcott have felt impelled to address these events in their work. Earlier I mentioned that Adrienne Rich found some of Walcott's work inspiring in her own battle against the coercions of the centrist culture (for her, of course, the target being the sexist tyrannies of the patriarchy, which significantly parallel the colonial impositions of the Imperium). The specific text that she cites is poem 23 of his sequence *Midsummer*, which deals with the Brixton riot of April 1981.[22]

What Rich particularly admires in the poem is the way that Walcott uses "an integrative kind of anger" to combine the various elements in the text, the rioters and burning tenements with "Caedmon and Shakespeare and Turner" (*Adrienne Rich's Poetry and Prose*, 270–71).[23] Certainly, as always in Walcott, the text is a consummately realized artefact; and in the case of poem 23, the narrative is perfectly balanced between images of high culture and low destructiveness, providing an effective counterpoint for each other, a powerful contrast of "civilized" and "uncivilized." Yet for me, at least, the "anger" seems, under the special historical circumstances being engaged in the text, almost *too well* controlled. Another Westindian-British writer whose "integrative anger" strikes me as *more* effective in this context, and whose language is more suited to the occasion, is Linton Kwesi

Johnson. The integration *he* achieves is not between the last days of empire and the British artistic canon, but between street fighting in London and radical Caribbean-inspired music, creating a distinctive voice, a "Riddym"—angry and violent—more fitting than Walcott's carefully measured tones. To me, that is, Johnson's use of Creole is in this case more effective than Walcott's use of standard English, since "breaking English" is a necessary element in the process being described and enacted.

Before we look at Johnson's "Di Great Insohreckshan" or "Five Nights of Bleeding," though, it might be best, in order to provide a suitable context, briefly to develop my earlier remarks on Rastafarianism. By no means all Westindian-British writers are interested in Rastafarianism per se, and by no means all of them have anything to do with "Dread Talk." But Rastafarianism is nevertheless influential as a device for consciousness-raising, particularly as regards its African orientation, and particularly in the embattled territory of Caribbean-origined writers who have immigrated to Britain. This influence tends to be mediated not specifically through "Dread Talk"—though of course the creation of a local language that rivals or undermines or breaks standard English is an interesting phenomenon in itself for linguistically-marginalized writers—but through *music*, through the medium with which Breeze's Mad Woman persists in connecting.

I don't want to fall here into the error of Jackie Kay's school teacher and say that "it's in the blood"; but undoubtedly various forms of music play a large part in the Caribbean culture (just as they do in the related Afro-American culture). We saw earlier in this chapter that Una Marson was keen to introduce the rhythms of "Afro-American Blues" into her work (Cobham and Collins, *Watchers and Seekers*, 7). And Edward Kamau Brathwaite likened "*nation language*" to "the blues," and credited the ancient West Indian song form of "the calypso" with helping to break the tyranny of the imported English pentameter (*History of the Voice*, 13, 17). But the musical form with which Rastafarianism is most closely identified is Jamaican reggae, whose best-known exponents—Bob Marley and the Wailers—conveyed the news of Ras Tafari to a huge worldwide audience of the kind that only popular music can reach, in the process elevating the profile of the West Indies to heady new heights. Joseph Owens in his study, *Dread*, describes how, shortly after the death of the Rasta Messiah God-King, Haile Selassie (or, in Dread Talk, "Haile-I Selassie-I"), "the prince of Rasta reggae, Bob Marley, stood before many thousands of Jamaicans in the National Stadium, where he was performing along with Stevie Wonder. With lights flashing and locks flying and drums thundering, Marley intoned an anthem" beginning *"Jah live, children, yeah! / Jah-jah live, children yeah!"* (279). We seem to have come a long way here from the stiff-upper-lipped restraints of "the gentility principle." Above the infectious rhythms ("Riddym"), as Laurence A. Breiner puts it in *An Introduction to West Indian Poetry* (1998), reggae lyrics often offer (among other things) a "millenarian view of Africa as a realm from which one is absent but in which one's place is kept available" (159)—essentially the message of what Aimé Césaire had termed *"négritude,"* a decolonizing strategy in which Africans and Afro-Americans become central, and white people become (therefore) marginal (or irrelevant).[24]

Out of reggae was subsequently to grow the cultural phenomenon with which Johnson is associated, that of "dub poetry." As James Berry puts it in his introduction to *News for Babylon*: "The 'roots' quality of Bob Marley's reggae music claimed new ground. Its expanded folk consciousness influenced Linton Kwesi Johnson and fellow Jamaican Oku Onuora to become known as 'Dub Poets'—poets who, in culture-style, dance their memorized poetry to a backing music" (xxv). Gordon Rohlehr in *Voiceprint* concurs with this, adding some extra "roots" and shoots, saying:

> The Dub poems . . . have grown directly out of the speech and music rhythms of reggae and Rastafari. They represent an extension of the much older toaster tradition, which in Jamaica involved the DJ talking smart, slick and often silly jingles into the microphone. . . .
>
> Technological change in the mixing of music, the advent of the 16-track tape and easy over-dubbing, the development of the synthesiser, intensified the DJ's role as a manipulator of sound. . . . (Brown, Morris, and Rohlehr, 17)

And David Dabydeen, definitely on this occasion "Not Being Milton," adds some theoretical and political niceties to the subject of (less formal) "Technological change" in dub. He argues with great ingenuity:

> "Sound systems," essential to "dub-poetry," are often homemade contraptions, cannibalized parts of diverse machines reordered for black expression. This de/reconstruction is in itself an assertive statement. . . . The mass-produced technology is remade for self-use in

the way that the patois is a "private" reordering of "standard" English. . . . Caliban is tearing up the pages of Prospero's magic book and repasting it in his own order, by his own method, and for his own purpose. ("On Not Being Milton," 9)

The tearing metaphor underlines the subversive or iconoclastic character of dub, as another form of "English" (Prospero's) gets dumped, and an alternative means of cultural delivery offers itself. The Oxford editor fades into the background and the DJ/poet moves center-stage. As Rohlehr puts it, getting rather carried away by the excitement of the whole situation: "The DJ became high priest in the cathedral of canned sound, fragmented discotheque image projections, broken lights, and youth seeking lost rituals amid the smoke of amnesia" (17). This all sounds far more exciting than a Movement poetry recital: no wonder Breeze's Mad Woman was prepared to fight for her radio to stay in touch with the DJ! Certainly Breeze herelf is usually described both in Britain and in the Caribbean as a "dub poet," though there seems to be some small controversy over the origins of the actual term. J. Edward Chamberlin, for instance, claims that Oku Onuora "popularized" the label "to characterize the work that he and other Jamaicans . . . were performing in public." However, Chamberlin also finds Brathwaite of importance in this context for being a sixties pioneer of "bringing the indigenous rhythms of African and West Indian drumming and of jazz into his poetry and performances." (*Come Back to Me,* 235) And Rohlehr soberly agrees, mentioning Brathwaite's being influenced by "Akan traditional drum-poets, . . . Afro-American musicians and poets, and the Beat poets" (Brown, Morris, and Rohlehr, *Voicepoint,* 2)—as "ungenteel" and unEnglish a mix as one might wish.

Irrespective of Brathwaite's and Onuora's position on the genealogical tree of dub, though, Johnson claims that it was *he* who actually invented the name. He says, in an interview in *Hinterland* that he "coined the phrase 'dub poetry' . . . as early as 1974," associating the performance of the reggae DJs with "traditional African poetry in so far as it was spontaneous, improvisatory and had a musical base" (Markham, 255–56). Certainly Johnson's own career has kept in close touch with the DJs, since he clearly sees pop music as an undifferentiated part of the "literary" world. In fact his poem "All Wi Doin Is Defending" came out as a single from Virgin Records (for whom he worked as a freelance copywriter while at college) in 1977. Johnson is on record as describing the demo as "very poorly recorded" and sounding "awful"; but Virgin were obviously impressed, and quickly followed up with the LP *Dread Beat an' Blood.*[25] As Brathwaite tells us, moreover, this and the subsequent LP (*Bass Culture*, 1980) enjoyed significant commercial success, both making it into the reggae charts in the United Kingdom, *Bass Culture* getting as high as number three in mid-1980 (*History of the Voice*, 45 n. 58).

We're obviously dealing here with a radically *different* definition or notion of literary text and genre, as well as of the English language; and "purity of diction" clearly isn't one of the governing criteria. It seems certain, to speculate for a moment, that—faced with Johnson's work—Philip Larkin in his capacity as editor of *The Oxford Book of Twentieth-Century English Verse* would have denied its validity as poetry, and as being in "English." And yet we shouldn't allow any high culture prejudice against the reggae content or label to mislead our reading or judgement. Johnson's contribution to *The New British Poetry*, for instance—"Reggae Fi Dada" (Allnutt et al., 49–51)—is a fine lament of personal and cultural loss, unexpectedly delicate compared to his more overtly militant work: as Chamberlin puts it, the text shows that the poet's mode is "capable of extraordinary power and sensitivity," his language a fascinating "fusion of traditions, and of private and public witness" (264). And "Reggae for Radni" (Brown, Morris, and Rohlehr, *Voiceprint*, 82–83), occasioned by the assassination of controversial Guyanese black power advocate Walter Rodney, is (in Gordon Rohlehr's words) a "beautiful . . . [lament] for the failure of some great moment," a text which "explore[s] every register along the speech continuum" (ibid., 17) with its haunting echoes and repetitions, its visions and dreams, its commemoration of a hero "blown to smidahreen / inna di miggle a di dream" which is simultanously Rodney's dream and also that of the poet.

In spite of such poems, though, it's probably true to say that as a vehicle (or weapon), Johnson's reggae dub is best suited to the task of bearing what Chamberlin calls "public witness," telling the dramas of racial conflict that he sees in the streets around him. Nicholas Axarlis in the British inter-cultural arts magazine *ARTRAGE* (Rodrigues, et al., 2) argues that changed social conditions emerging in Britain, of which the inner city riots of the period are a symptom, require (among other things) "new artistic practices," and it's here that dub comes into its own, carrying an immediate and urgent culturo-political message in an ethnic minority language to a mass audience

through the medium/mediation of what might be popularly regarded on one level as simply dance music. The full impact of this
combination is really only available in performance, either in live act
or in oral recording; but even in the more conventional medium of
written literary text, it's still possible to gain some idea of the power,
the high voltage of the presentation.

One of the consequences of the Creolization of the standard code
of English (apart from the obvious surface differences of spelling,
punctuation and—to a lesser degree—lexicon) is a dramatic transformation of the speech rhythm. As Johnson himself puts it in "Bass
Culture" (*Dread Beat and Blood*, 57–59; Hulse, Kennedy, and Morley,
*The New Poetry*, 185–86):

> and the beat will shiff
> as the culture allta
> when oppression scatta.

In traditional calypso, as Edward Kamau Brathwaite noted above,
the "normal" and normative rhythm of English iambic pentameter
tends to be superseded by dactylic feet (*History of the Voice*, 17), thus
effectively *decolonizing* the native Caribbean rhythm. Laurence A.
Breiner notes the same shift away from the iamb in Johnson's work:
analysing "Dread Beat an Blood" (though the comment holds good
for many Johnson texts) he points out a system of "very emphatic
trochees and dactyls" (190), which subvert the iamb [ ˘ ´ ] by reversing the stress pattern or beat (the trochee [ ´ ˘ ]) or introducing an
extra unstressed syllable (the dactyl [ ´ ˘ ˘ ]) which syncopates the
basic foot. This syncopation is magnified by the frequency of present
participles (there being thirty-one in the twenty-two line "Dread Beat
an Blood"), which in addition to supplying a framework of polysylla-
bles also have the dramatic effect (as we saw much earlier, in Dylan
Thomas's work) of creating a dynamic ongoing "presentness" to the
narration.[26]

Johnson's "Di Great Insohreckshan,"[27] while exhibiting some of
these features, actually contrasts this narrative presentness with a retrospective telling at the beginning of the poem of the Brixton riots.
The tactic of using a past tense has a particular point in this text,
since Johnson wishes to emphasize that the ethnic minority population in "babylan"[28] is in the process of (as he puts it in the title of
another poem) "Mekkin Histri."[29] This "histri," this affirmation of
having local roots and a group identity to celebrate, involves the

rewriting of the standard or official versions (as purveyed by the British media) and taking responsibility for the telling of one's own "I." In his *Hinterland* interview with Mervyn Morris, Johnson says of the poem that "'Making History' simply says, well, it's not no great mystery, you know, we just simply making history—we making history in Britain now" (Markham, 259–60).

This theme, the accumulation of what amounts almost to black urban myth as instances of resistance to oppression pile up in the memory, is reiterated in "Di Great Insohreckshan": of the Brixton experience Johnson writes "it woz a truly an historical okayjan." He wasn't present personally, but found out the details not from TV or the papers (which are in the service of "babylan") but from "di ghetto grapevine," an underground or alternative news medium. So in spite of not being there, he was able to share in the experience as a kind of collective act, since "evry rebel jussa revel in dem story." And as the stories accumulate, they facilitate a (self-)belief system which overrides (and over-writes) that previously imposed by the Imperialist Establishment, whose slogans the rebels now appropriate for their own use: "dem a taak bout di powah an di glory."[30]

"Five Nights of Bleeding" (*Dread Beat and Blood*, 15–17; Markham, *Hinterland*, 264–66) also centers on the Brixton area, though it's harder for Johnson to "revel" in this "story" because not all of the violence is "righteous": that is, some of it involves confrontations between rival black gangs rather than with the forces of colonial and racist oppression. The poem deals with (enacts) the hard-bitten reality of black youth in the dancehalls and streets of Babylon's capital city, the frustration of being marginalized, disempowered—the "recipe" (as John Agard put it in "Pan Recipe") for disaster, for an explosion. Right from the start there's "madness" in the air, a madness, though, far more ominous and threatening than that of Breeze's protagonist. It's repeated three times in the first line and a half of poem 1, and overall occurs no less than thirteen times in only some seventy-five lines in total. Performed, the word—and the text as a whole—becomes a rhythmic chant, insistent and unrelieved right up to the last gasp of "war." Trigger words such as "bleeding" and "blood" are also repeated (eight times), a tactic Johnson employs often throughout his work: in "Dread Beat an Blood," for instance, the three key words of the title are constantly reiterated in the text, along with the word "fire." And the poems *are* fiery, *and* bloody—the absolute antithesis of the fireless, bloodless Movement;

and very different, too, from Walcott's brilliantly conceived simile of "Brixton, burning like Turner's ships."

The long lines of the poem are punctuated by sudden short ones, which echo, and alter the rhythm; and the punctuation itself breaks lines down into sudden short thrusts of language. Very basic sense impressions and consequences are conveyed immediately ("hot. hot heads."); and an extraordinarily economical compression highlights and dramatizes key elements ("blues dance / broke glass"). Reggae rhythms occupy the foreground, but something sharper and colder lurks in the background, "a jab and a stab."

The "Five Nights" of the poem in question find the narrator cruising various hot spots, districts, pubs and nightclubs all named in capital letters: "BRIXTON"; "RAILTON ROAD"; "SHEPHERD'S"; "THE RAINBOW"; the "TELEGRAPH." The names are important because, however negative the experience may be, they're all part of the "histri" in the "Mekkin," virtually amounting to documentary evidence. And they need to be named here, in a sympathetic (con)text because they'll certainly be named in the Establishment media (which will magnify or suppress as their prejudices require). So they're (literally) writ large so that they can't be readily subverted. Effectively, the metropolis is being redrawn before our very eyes, the map of Babylon rewritten. Attention is being attracted to the underprivileged, normally hidden or unspoken areas that casual tourists don't see or hear about in the course of their visits to the Capital's Establishment shrines which celebrate the history of white power and colonialism. It's as if Johnson is saying, "This is what it's really like to live here: feel it." As an indicator of authenticity, he even names in his text the "SOFRANO B sound system" being used in Brixton: after all, it's a significant actor in the proceedings (as David Dabydeen realized), an important element in the local culture.

That culture may be embattled (the word "war" is repeated eleven times in "Five Nights of Bleeding" and, together with "madness" forms a kind of chorus at the end of each section); and yet there's hope because the recent "histri" being written records that the ethnic minorities are "winnin victri," and that the Establishment's "racist pallyticks" can be challenged (Hulse, Kennedy, and Morley, *The New Poetry*, 183). So in "All Wi Doin Is Defendin" (*Dread Beat and Blood*, 26–27; *Tings an Times*, 19–20), the poet is prepared to go "grievous blow fe blow" to protect a "freedom" that "is a very firm thing"; and as poet/performer he's prepared to sing "songs of fire." Johnson's work, then, offers significant opposition to "Babylon." It shows that the Imperialist forces of the English Establishment (*still* Imperialist in mind and spirit, even though the Empire itself is long gone) can be resisted—on the streets, in the language, and through alternative artistic media. "Inglan," in his famous formulation, may be "a Bitch," but it can be survived; and after survival, who knows?:

> Inglan is a bitch
> dere's no escapin' it
> Inglan is a bitch fi true
> is whey wi a goh dhu 'bout it?
> ("Inglan Is a Bitch," Hulse, Kennedy, and Morley,
> *The New Poetry*, 187–88)

అ  అ  అ  అ  అ

Fred D'Aguiar in his introductory remarks to the "Black British Poetry" section of *The New British Poetry* coins a very useful phrase when he suggests that the poets chosen, as well as sharing ethnic origins also share "a strong sense of being 'other' than what is lauded as indigenous and capitally British." (Allnutt et al., 3) The term "capitally British" covers a number of facets of the prejudice against which Caribbean writers are reacting—"capital" in the sense of being capital-city- (London) oriented, privileging a metropolitan (and colonizing) center; "capital" in the obsolete upperclass English sense of being "excellent" (since British is obviously best); and "capital" in the sense of embracing the dictates of western capitalism, since *money* (along with language perhaps) is power, and relative affluence is used as a hierarchizing device both in society on the smaller scale, and in the global community on the larger scale. Westindian-British writers, it need scarcely be added, seem to come out on the wrong side of each of these meanings.

Not surprisingly, therefore, such writers tend to choose other metaphors to distinguish their position(s), putting themselves in a better light—or, rather, better climate. One of the ways in which they convey the difference between their "otherness" and the metropolitan norm is through reference to heat and coldness, terms that (as we saw earlier) go beyond mere temperature difference. Grace Nichols's celebrated persona of the "fat black woman," for instance, in the poem "Tropical Death" (Hulse, Kennedy, and Morley, *The New Poetry*, 155–56) goes as far as to opt—when the time comes—for "a brilliant tropical death," a genuine and exuberant celebration, an act of affirmation rather than a Northern European ceremonial governed by coolness (and gentility).

Further from the grave, other writers emphasize their positive cultural difference by reference to what in England would be regarded as exotic flora. We've already seen that Dabydeen chose the sugar cane harvest (the canecutter's vigorous chopping) as a metaphor for the "angry, crude, energetic" elements of "creole language" ("On Not Being Milton," 3); and that Nichols, actually using the cane as her poetic persona in "Sugar Cane" (Markham, *Hinterland*, 301–3) saw it as embodying the spirit of her people who have "crossed the ocean" in the hope that a "new . . . tongue" will shoot up to take the place of the old. As well, we saw that both Agard and Breeze use the mango as an indicator of cultural warmth, sweetness, even sensuality—a fruit symbolically (as well as literally) absent from the metropolitan environment. And D'Aguiar, in one of his well-known "Letter[s] from Mama Dot" (Hulse, Kennedy, and Morley, *The New Poetry*, 286) employs the sunflower (whose name, of course, combines climatic and floral referents) for his poetic purposes.

In this latter instance, the sunflower seeds (an appropriate metaphor for the African diaspora), coming from what the metropolitan center would regard as an obscure place with a name which the English "can't pronounce," end up in the garden of a terraced house in a cooler climate more fitted to the cultivation of begonias. The fact of the "sun falling" on the nonexotic side of the fence is typical, but ambiguous. One reading would suggest that the Caribbean is de-privileged, and the English side conversely privileged by the sun illuminating it—after all, the popular boast during the heyday of Imperialism was that the British had an empire on which the sun never sets. However, if one reads "falling" as "setting" rather than "shining on," then the metaphor switches entirely, and becomes indicative of the *end* of the empire's day. The encroachment of the sunflowers "craning over" thus becomes metaphoric of the proliferation of West Indian immigration, of the colonizing of the erstwhile Imperial center. The mutual embrace of begonia and sunflower, "the roots of both intermingling," might seem hopeful of future peaceful cohabitation; but the hope seems undermined by the grudging and combative tone of the writing, and by the fact that when the people living adjacent "bare [their] teeth" this looks more like a grimace or snarl than a smile.

Whatever interpretation(s) one imposes on D'Aguiar's poem, though, the accommodations between tropical and nontropical seem rather uncomfortable and ambiguous. As regards the Westindian-British poets, they gain strength in this situation by constantly reminding themselves (and the English) of not just their sugar canes and mangoes and sunflowers but, to carry on the organic reference, their *roots*. In John Agard's case, in his "Memo to Crusoe" (Horowitz, *Grandchildren of Albion*, 24), this involves Tobago, and the reopening of a dialogue with the colonizing ethos. In the poem the colonizer (Robinson Crusoe) is *not* the first articulate inhabitant of the island (though the canonical text bearing his name might want to assert that he was). Long before Crusoe's arrival the indigenous Man Friday was in residence, even keeping a record of the fact—a kind of "diary" using the local cultural medium "called calypso."

This circumstance is a reminder to the Imperial intruder coming to impose an alien written tradition on the local voice, that the speech-acts of first colonial contact are significantly predated by an indigenous oral culture (as is of course the case in all colonial territories, and as we shall see later with specific reference to the Aboriginal peoples in Australia). Acknowledgment of this case will involve a *re-viewing* of the standard histories so that the inappropriate and biased attitudes towards the various Men Friday scattered over the map can be set aside. To combat the historical wrong, the black writer must no longer be constructed by the white gaze, but assume responsibility for seeing (and writing) him- or her-self.

Agard's Man Friday's "Memo" points the way, affirming (re-memorising) the *calypso* which has been an influential medium in subverting Establishment discourse in the Caribbean. We've already heard how Brathwaite in *History of the Voice* considers the calypso instrumental in undermining the primacy of the imported English iambic pentameter (17). And Laurence A. Breiner adds his voice to the discussion, telling us that calypso affords a "powerful model" here, in the way it can articulate "topical political and social commentary directly to a live audience." (*Introduction*, 10) Moreover, it's an ancient form that's been in the ascendant more recently (particularly in the second half of the twentieth century) for an odd—and highly nonliterary—reason. Breiner explains that, as a result of World War II, "surplus oil drums led to the creation of the steelband as a powerful adjunct to calypso performance and to the culture from which it arises." (ibid., 74) Agard's own poem sequence *Man to Pan* (Havana:

Ediciones Casa de las Américas, 1982) was actually designed, as the subtitle of the book tells us, "to be performed with drums and steel-pans."

The sequence constitutes a dialogue between the poet/drummer and the drum (or "Pan") which is his medium, his calypso voice; and several of the poems take the form of rhythmic and audiovisual experiments mimetic of drum beats. As well the text is, at least in part, an act of angry exorcism as the author "beat[s] out the fury / of a history" (40) that is his own even if he hasn't hitherto been able to write it himself. Now he has the chance, though, to alter that previous textual silence, a circumstance indicated by Agard's "black" appropriation of the Greek god Pan, who—in a bicultural pun with "steel-*pan*"—gets completely recontextualized and rewritten here (a subversive colonizing tactic on the part of the hitherto colonized which, as we'll see in chapter 6, has been used by Australian poets too).[31]

The colonial Church may once have banned the Shango drums in some parts of the West Indies as an act of religio-cultural control or dispossession ("to licence we tongue," as Agard puts it [18]), but now *négritude* takes over and the spirit of the steel drum (pan) is reborn in the poet's emphatic act of baptism, naming and invocation:

> we name you
> PAN
> (24)

The alien music of colonization (in which "octave / is a word dat rhyme with slave" [67]) gets set aside, and the thundering drum god leads his acolytes in the "bacchanal" (50, 51) of "Carnival" (45). Clearly, Agard is tapping into a language of ancient ethnic rhythms, evolving a distinctive voice, exploring a mode in which to speak and a space from which to speak. This is crucial because of the *empowerment* it implies: in *Dread*, his study of Rastafarianism, Joseph Owens gives us the Rasta "take" on the situation:

> The brethren ask themselves the question: "Why are the Chinese and the Indians so well off here [in Jamaica] compared to the Africans?" and they answer: "It is because they still have their own language! . . ." Language is an incarnation of God for the Rastafarians, so that a man should not easily tamper with it. The white slave-master knew what he was doing when he deprived the African slaves of their native tongue, for the slave then had to accept the language . . . of the master. (182)

Agard's Man Friday, then, was silent/silenced in the presence of Crusoe—*was*, but in a new world needs to be no longer. All that's required (and it's no small thing, of course) is for the Caribbean culture to reverse the thrust of colonial invasion, to subvert the master narrative, and to write Man Friday not as victim/slave but as hero.

The primary cultural tool in all of this will be, as the Rastafarians (and others) noted, *language*—not the tongue of the Amerindian Arawaks, who have long slipped away into Jamaican history; not the Ethiopian Amharic of the Rastas' distant African origins (though there are a few loan terms from it in Dread Talk); but also emphatically *not* pure standard English. What offers itself instead is what Brathwaite calls "*nation language*," a linguistic medium that literary pioneer Louise Bennett describes as "very adaptable" when "used by the people to express their feelings": she claims, "You can twist it, you can express yourself so much more strongly and vividly than in standard English" (in *Hinterland*, 45). The strength and flexibility come to some degree from being part of what linguists call the "Creole continuum," itself a phenomenon which "overturns 'concentric' notions of language which regard 'Standard' English as a 'core'" (*The Empire Writes Back*, 47), and instead sees "The world language called english" as "a continuum of 'intersections' in which the speaking habits in various communities have intervened to reconstruct the language" (ibid., 39–40). Gordon Rohlehr explores the case from a slightly different angle in his introduction to *Voiceprint*, saying that "The Either / Or approach of the colonial era which had promoted English styled poetry and put down Caribbean orality was gradually replaced by the Both/ And approach in which, as the situation demanded, writers varied freely along the continua between Folk and Modernist, Creole and Standard, Oral and Scribal" (Brown, Morris, and Rohlehr, 11–12). As well, strength and flexibility come from what one might call the cultural geographic context—the Caribbean accustomization to polyglossia and border crossing, the region's unique position at the meeting point of the spheres of influence of Africa, Europe, and America. This location facilitates cultural cross-fertilization, offering a wider literary gene pool on which to draw than was available to, say, the Movement (suggesting that perhaps Darwin was right after all!). The *mobility* of the West Indian cultural community is also a factor, to be set against the relatively static and rigid metropolitan Establishment in England: many Caribbean writers and performance artists have moved regularly to and from Britain, and those born in Britain have looked back to their Caribbean or African cultural heritage to inform their British practice. This "travel" provides a means of enrichment to be set in the scales against English literary exclusionism and xenophobia.

These writers seem to have claimed their own ethnic space(s) from which to speak, then. Like the Rastafarians they've asserted a decolonized voice, an "I" that sees and writes itself; and they've found a viable language to facilitate articulation of this identity (i-dentity). That may be all very well, but to *enable* that identity in the public forum (as we saw feminist writers realize in the previous chapter), a cultural *means of delivery* is necessary. It's here that Westindian-British poets have shown themselves to be remarkably versatile. Traditionally, access to the public has involved publication in book form, and certainly this has remained at least one of the paths to the marketplace for Westindian-British writers. As was the case with women's writing, where mainstream publishing houses have been somewhat reluctant to open their doors to the *other*, then the *other* has taken matters into its own hands, forming small independent publishing houses of its own (both in the Caribbean and in Britain)—such as the Savacou Collective, and Bogle-L'Ouverture. It might be added, too, that inclusion in a number of popular anthologies of Caribbean poetry (many of which have been cited in this chapter) has resulted in a finite but significant body of work being available from larger international publishers.[32]

In addition to Caribbean-oriented publishing initiatives, a number of other cultural support systems and publicity ventures were being put in place from as early as the mid-1960s. John La Rose, Edward Kamau Brathwaite, and Andrew Salkey, for instance, started CAM (the Caribbean Artists Movement) in 1966. Then, in the 1970s, there was RAPP (Radical Alliance of Poets and Players), which described itself as "a coalition of community artists" (in Berry, ed., *News for Babylon*, xxvi). And later, and perhaps most significant of all, was MAAS (the Minority Arts Advisory Service), sponsoring "Ethnic minority arts" and seeking to alter the situation in which "Britain's racial minorities" have been "deprived of money and facilities necessary to organize and stage cultural events" (Rodrigues, et al., AR-TRAGE, 1). As part of this project, MAAS published two magazines to provide an appropriate forum for ethnic minority discussion—first *ECHO* and then *ARTRAGE: Inter-Cultural Arts Magazine*.

But the most spectacularly successful outlet for Westindian-British poetry has been negotiated through the world of music—not just Agard's Trinidadian calypso, but on a larger scale the performance work of the dub poets. Rohlehr notes that "Music, because it has been the means of preserving linkages between the Caribbean and non European sensibility, has become the container of a wealth of alternative rhythms" (Brown, Morris, and Rohlehr, *Voiceprint*, 3). And well-known dub poet Benjamin Zephaniah adds his assent to this suggestion, noting too in "Dis Poetry" (*PBPBI*, 395–97) that while it exists spectacularly in the oral arena, as well

> Dis poetry is not afraid of going ina book
> Still dis poetry need ears fe hear an eyes fe hav a look
> Dis poetry is Verbal Riddim. . . .

More than that, though, the rhythm of what Linton Kwesi Johnson calls this "Bass Culture" (*Dread Beat and Blood*, 57–59; Hulse, Kennedy, and Morley, *The New Poetry*, 185–86) has provided unprecedented access to a mass popular market, as is evident from the success of Johnson's own dub recordings and concert performances. That bass line, inherited from reggae (which, Rohlehr points out, by its very "nature" has a "heavy bass-line and space between voice and 'riddim'" [Brown, Morris, and Rohlehr, *Voiceprint*, 18]) runs directly counter to the *New Lines* prescriptions of the earlier-generation British literary imperium: Robert Conquest had warned against "giving the Id, a sound player on the percussion side under a strict conductor, too much of a say in the doings of the orchestra as a whole"—a situation that had occurred in the 1940s with the New Apocalypse movement (*New Lines*, xi). What Conquest has made of the subsequent "percussion side" of reggae and dub and the steel drums of calypso bands is anybody's guess—though one imagines that he certainly sees it as "base" if not "bass." But, without wishing to overplay the pun, that "bass" forms the "base" of Johnson's (and Breeze's) operations, their iconoclastic assault on the status quo at the heart of literary "English."

So successful has this been that Caribbean English has even been granted a dictionary of its own (though, in view of the earlier history of dictionaries, that may not be a totally positive circumstance). Brathwaite, always an enthusiastic proponent of things West Indian, and of "*nation language*," writes of this most recent chapter in the *His-*

*tory of the Voice*: "The detonations within Caribbean sound poetry have imploded us into new shapes and consciousness of ourselves, so that suddenly a *Dictionary of Caribbean English* is no longer [merely publisher's] list but [actual] life. Bob Marley and Oku [Onuora]'s riddmic words become Authorities for linguists" (49). And a page later he voices the slogan (of which Walt Whitman would have been proud), "new world makes new words" (50).

In the next chapter we move on to look at the "new words" made in English in the Gaelic world.

# 5

## "English" across the Gaelic Frontiers

IN THE PREVIOUS CHAPTER WE SAW (AMONG OTHER THINGS) THE response of some West Indian poets to the impositions of standard English on their local tongues, the ways Caribbean-origined writers resist cultural and linguistic colonization in the historical aftermath of empire. In this chapter we shall be looking at somewhat related cases closer to the Metropolitan center, beginning with Ireland and the work of Seamus Heaney.

One of the ways in which the cases may be related is suggested in the title of an essay Heaney wrote about Derek Walcott, "The Language of Exile."[1] Heaney associates Walcott's Caribbean "language of exile" with that of J. M. Synge (and therefore, presumably, his own), suggesting that Walcott has evolved in the West Indian context (as did Synge in the Irish), a linguistic mode "woven out of dialect and literature, neither folksy nor condescending . . . that allows an older life to exult in itself yet at the same time keeps the cool of 'the new.'" (in *Government*, 23).

It appears that the Creole continuum may stretch, ideologically rather than linguistically, of course, further than one might otherwise suspect. Heaney goes on to point out that Walcott's endeavors don't ghettoize the literary language on the margins of metropolitan English, but on the contrary lead to the very essence of the center (in an act of cultural and linguistic appropriation, of *de*-exile, as it were). He praises Walcott's artistic expertise, saying that "his fidelity to West Indian speech now leads him not away from but right into the genius of English" (25), concluding that in this work the old notion of Commonwealth Literature (perhaps perceived in the metropolitan culture as secondary, even inferior) is superseded, since "Walcott possesses English more deeply and sonorously than most of the

English themselves" (26). "The Language of Exile" closes with a quotation from Walcott's 1979 poem sequence, "The Schooner *Flight*" which—like so much of the essay—might apply equally to the Caribbean or the Hibernian situation: "that's all them bastards have left us: words. . . ."[2] The sourness of this note on which Heaney leaves his topic doesn't quite tell the whole story, though. The above quotation occurs in Walcott's poem immediately after a highly unsatisfactory and humiliating meeting between "History" and the protagonist (described as a "parchment Creole")—the "nigger" whom History at first doesn't recognize, and then spits on. However the tone of Walcott's "The Schooner *Flight*" is dramatically modified later in the poem when, in a lyric-elegiac section entitled "After the Storm," the voyager's attitude undergoes a sea change of which Heaney would surely approve. Sabine, the "nigger" in question, says with wonder— and what I would read as a mixture of national pride and assertion of independent identity after the spat-upon slave state—"There are so many islands!/ As many islands as the stars at night" (*Collected Poems*, 361). As we saw in chapter 4, the word play *island / i-land* is a key referent in the Caribbean consciousness, and by a small extension becomes significant in the context of this present chapter. That is, Walcott's "islands" are equivalent (we already know) to Jean Binta Breeze's "i-lands," which in turn have much in common with (say) Synge's and Heaney's "I[re]lands"—all united in seeking to formulate postcolonial cultures beyond the notion of Commonwealth literature with the "words" that the colonizing "bastards" have left behind as their only legacy.

If my suggestion seems to be stretching cultural geography too far, then it's certainly a stretch that Walcott himself makes on at least one occasion. In poem 52 of *Midsummer* (the sequence that, we remember, so impressed Adrienne Rich) he juxtaposes his own West Indian setting, the physical remnants of colonization—"the broken stones of the barracks of Brimstone Hill"—with "the gaping brick of Belfast" (n. p.). The collocation occurs in the context of a vision (or *audition*, since the primary reference is oral) of a colonizing discourse enslaving the local. The poet imagines he hears two groups marching into history—the invading force of "redcoats," herding along a band of "black, barefooted" people whose syntax gets "trampled to mud." Faced with this circumstance, Walcott worries that even writing about it may be aiding and abetting, inadvertently assenting to the situation. He's painfully aware that "no language is neutral" and that he may therefore be accused (since he's here using the dominant discourse) of changing sides, of locating himself in the settler diction rather than the indigenous *kriol.*

Similar questions have been raised in the politically highly-charged atmosphere of the *Irish* border, of course; and Heaney's motives in the early 1970s in crossing it, and the degree to which he has struggled to make his "language . . . neutral" have been the subject of considerable (sectarian) discussion. Walcott, then, might easily be writing about Heaney here; just as Heaney, in "The Language of Exile," might easily be writing about Heaney too!

ↄ   ↄ   ↄ   ↄ   ↄ

## Seamus Heaney and the "scop's / twang"

Border crossings aside for the moment, it's necessary to begin any discussion of Irish variants of English in contemporary poetry with a look at some of Heaney's work, not only because Heaney himself invites and engages in such a discussion, but also because—as was the case earlier with Rich—the profile of the topic has been raised so high by commentators as to make it virtually unavoidable. Heaney's *corpus* has been dug over enthusiastically by a whole generation of commentators and, one fears, a whole *new* one waits in the wings to carry on: outstripping "The Tollund Man" and "The Grauballe Man," he remains the most celebrated exhumee from the peat of his own pronouncements. For my own purposes in the current case, I don't intend a general survey of what the poet digs from the linguistic bog, since Bernard O'Donoghue has already made one available to readers of *Seamus Heaney and the Language of Poetry* (1994). Rather, I shall confine myself in the main to the earlier work where the comments on and experiments with literary English are most evident: after all, there's a certain integrity to this selection since, as Heaney himself said in interview, "I'm certain that up to *North,* that that was one book; in a way it grows together and goes together."[3]

That Heaney concerns himself significantly with the language available to him as a Northern Irish poet is evident in the way that—as O'Donoghue notes—a number of his early volumes begin with "a poem which considers linguistic issues expressly in a kind of manifesto" (110). From the outset (the first poem, that is, in *Death of a Naturalist* [1966]) Heaney chooses as his weapon the "squat pen" which is "snug as a gun" in his hand.[4] Where his father and grandfather engaged in the archetypal Irish occupations of digging potatoes and peat respectively, the poet will involve himself instead with textual and linguistic "digging."

The gun-pen may be used iconoclastically to assert Irish (cultural) rights in the face of imposed English norms. As Heaney says of *North* (1975) in an interview with Frank Kinahan in *Critical Inquiry*, after working on that collection's "little narrow lines" which cause a "sense of constriction" lending itself to the "tension" appropriate to the subject, he felt that by contrast "the melodious grace of the English iambic line . . . was some kind of affront, that it needed to be wrecked."[5] Here he takes on a target which, in a variety of cultural times and circumstances (as we've seen) has formed the strategic object also of attacks by, for instance, Walt Whitman, William Carlos Williams (particularly in his campaign against the "'fascist' sonnet form"), Ezra Pound (for whom "To break the pentameter . . . was the first heave" in his effort to "MAKE IT NEW"), and—on non-American soil—Edward Kamau Brathwaite (whose assertion of the dactyls used in *kaiso* [calypso] undermined the literary rule of the iamb in the Caribbean).[6]

Heaney reiterates the latter part of this genealogy of iconoclasts in the first part of his lecture, "The Redress of Poetry," when he urges us, in the face of English linguistic colonization, to

> think of black Caribbean poets like Edward Kamau Brathwaite and Derek Walcott, who would retrieve an Afro-consciousness through an Anglo-idiom; or consider an American feminist poet like Adrienne Rich; or contemporary rap and rasta poets like Benjamin Zephaniah. . . . All of these experience a pressure to refuse the exclusive civilities of established canonical English literature, to alter if not deform the modes and decorums of poetry as they are understood by the education system and the influential cultural media. (*The Redress of Poetry*, 1990, 7)

However, if Heaney is associating himself with such writers here, one notes that the tone is very different from what might be expected in (say) Pound or Rich—far less hostile or aggressive (in spite of Heaney's early on grasping his pen as if it was a gun). Iconoclasm seems to be a tactic he generally prefers to avoid, or at least minimize: as O'Donoghue (again) says of Heaney, "Even the Poundean urge to go against 'the tyranny of the iamb' was not natural to him, and was not sustained." (153) Instead of the combative posture, then, Heaney clearly favors something more like an integrative (if not quite conciliatory) one. So, as he goes on to explain,

> as an Irish writer whose education was undergone in Northern Ireland, on the crest of the 1947 Education Act (a definite British benefit) and in the wake of the Irish Literary Revival, I am sensitive to the claims and counter-claims exerted by the terms "English Literature" and "Irish" or "Anglo-Irish Literature." And I am well aware of the complications which English-language poetries must encounter as they attempt fission from the central English canon and seek redefinition within a new historical, geographical, and political framework. (8–9)

He follows this up by noting that even great Irish "revolutionary" writers (such as Thomas McDonagh and James Joyce) didn't find it necessary "to proscribe within . . . [their] own reader's memory the riches of the imperial culture" in spite of the fact that they were themselves "intent on displacing within the general consciousness" the "imprint" of that culture. This is an important point for Heaney because the poet Sean O'Riordain (whose work he has translated) *does* seem to be making such a proscription, to which Heaney is categorically unwilling to subscribe. In his essay/lecture *Among School Children* (1983) he quotes O'Riordain's instructions to Irish writers to

> Unshackle your mind
> Of its civil English tackling,
> Shelley, Keats and Shakespeare.
> Get back to what is your own.
>
> (12)

Following such alien models as Shelley or Shakespeare needs to be avoided, evidently, since it results in the writer getting "out of step" with him- or herself. What O'Riordain seems to want amounts to a purity of diction in *Irish* verse, and Heaney isn't to be taken in: when it comes to getting "back to what is your own," Heaney would obviously rather decide for himself what that may be, rather than having the decision imposed on him (albeit by a fellow Irishman). He asserts, "As somebody whose sense of poetic form derived not only from Yeats and Patrick Kavanagh, but also from Keats and Shakespeare, I found the advice to ditch all that impossible, since I do not find the syntax of my speech puts me out of touch with myself" (12). He ends his dispute with the Irish literary elder as follows:

> That Irish is a fortification and an enrichment I hope I have made clear, but I also hope I have made clear that as a teacher and writer, I do not yield to the notion that my identity is disabled and falsified and somehow slightly traitorous if I conduct my casual and imaginative transactions in the speech I was born to. Both languages are part of the landscape. . . . (12)

Obviously, then, Heaney feels able to operate on both sides of the (language) border, not wishing to break English (which would be partly *self*-destructive) as much as to achieve "an enrichment" of it.

And linguistically what's available to him, while not in the least "pure," is certainly rich. Loreto Todd in her book *Green English: Ireland's Influence on the English Language* (1999), affirms that the differences between what she calls "Green" and standard (RP) English are far more than "merely those of accent," and have been incubated over "a long period of bilingualism, during which English was assimilated to Irish speech habits" (24). The downside of this "bilingualism" is that historically it's been open to *sectarian* readings, employing metaphors of division, so that (for instance) Morris Fraser, a Belfast doctor, can say that "Ulster's problem is a racial one, a conflict of cultures and ideals between two ethnic groups as distinct as are Blacks and Whites in the United States or Southern Africa" (quoted in *Green English,* 74).

Todd prefers to put the situation in a somewhat less "racist" manner, suggesting that "Irish Gaelic has affected the speech of the original natives of Ireland in much the same way that African languages have influenced the English of Creole-speaking West Indians" (91). The parallel drawn here between Ireland and the Caribbean (which we've already encountered above through the Walcott/Heaney connection) is valorized through colonial history by no less a figure than Oliver Cromwell who, fresh from the bloodbath at Drogheda in 1649, shipped the remains of the defeated Irish garrison to Barbadoes. This ploy was to be followed up by the British Council of State six year later when, because the original English immigrants to Jamaica found conditions too arduous for their liking, "1,000 Irish girls and 1,000 Irish youths of fourteen years and under were sent" (*Green English,* 110) to suffer in their stead. No one doubts that the British, like all colonizers, could be—to say the very least—hard taskmasters (slave-owners), whether the experience occurred geographically in Ireland or the West Indies; and yet linguistically there may be positives to be gained. One such benefit is, as Todd tells us, "the grafted English that allowed the Irish to communicate with their colonizers and yet still keep alive their Gaelic world view" (ibid., 139). In a case that to some degree seems to echo that of the Creole continuum, "The spectrum of Englishes in Ireland was forged into Green English, a unique amalgam" amounting almost to *triligualism* (and that's for the moment not counting *Gaelic* itself), consisting of the "three varieties of English in Ireland, Anglo-Irish, Ulster Scots and Hiberno-English" (139).

Heaney is aware of the potential sectarian fission in this language state, as an example (literally) close to home reminds him. In a well-known passage from the essay "Belfast" he speculates on the meaning and location of his cultural place by digging through the possible etymologies of the name of the family farm: he writes:

> Our farm was called Mossbawn. *Moss*, a Scots word probably carried to Ulster by the Planters, and *bawn*, the name the English colonists gave to their fortified farmhouses. Mossbawn, the planter's house on the bog. Yet in spite of this Ordnance Survey spelling, we pronounced it Moss bann, and *bán* is the Gaelic word for white. So might not the thing mean the white moss, the moss of bog-cotton? In the syllables of my home I see a metaphor of the split culture of Ulster. (in *Preoccupations*, 35)[7]

This "metaphor" is not to suggest any confusion on Heaney's part: he seems quite clear about his own position in the "split culture." He won't automatically accept the dominant discourse (with its official, Establishmentarian "Ordnance Survey" map) as *sole* authority, any more than he would be prepared to follow exclusively the dictates of Sean O'Riordain. Rather, given his essentially noncombative cast of mind, Heaney tends to minimize the divisive possibilites in Green English and, as O'Donoghue notes, he "sees its potential, as in all verbal effects, of positive application." That is, Heaney is aware that "Linguistic difference can achieve alliance as well as hostility" (113), fusion instead of fission, enrichment instead of destruction. After all, as he notes in the paragraph immediately before the one I quoted above, his schooling involved Gaelic *and* English literatures, *both* of which contributed to the essential "notion of myself" that he evolved (*Preoccupations*, 35).

The positive application of this situation, the integrative rather than divisive attitude, is manifested in another personal and local eytmology teased out by the poet, in the poem "Broagh" (*NSP*, 25). Heaney writes that while the title-word is derived from the Irish *Bruach* (the bank of a river), other elements in the local linguistic landscape come from "old English" ("docken") and "Scottish" ("rigs"), the total mix amounting to a celebration of "all the elements of heritage in my natural speech" (*Among School Children*, 9).

Here Heaney is using the act of digging with his pen to unearth strategic etymologies, to uncover and do justice to his whole linguistic "heritage" as part of a single poetic structure, essentially creating a new English with which to write, not absolutely denying standard English, but enriching it with local resonances. He amplifies this notion when talking about cultural and linguistic structures in an interview for the *Listener* on 8 November 1973, saying:

> If you're involved with poetry, you are involved with words, and words, for me, seem to have more nervous energy when they are touching territory that I know, that I live with. . . . I'm very interested in early Irish poetry. . . . On the other hand, I'm fascinated by Anglo-Saxon: the noises of the English language, the texture of it, the history of it, as stirring an element in my imagination as the Irish experience.(in Broadbridge, ed., *Seamus Heaney*, 54)

He goes on, in another famous (and ingenious) formulation, to suggest that the English influence on his poetic diction is equivalent to "a kind of consonant" while the Irish element acts as "a vowel," the combination of consonants and vowels adding up to a full voice, articulating "a harmony of some kind."

Harmony, then, is the ideal, a balance between English and Irish—but to put this in perspective it might be worth considering for a moment how *unlikely* harmony actually was in the context of Northern Ireland in the 1970s. John Montague, for instance, portrays a country and a language incapacitated (radically unbalanced) by the enforced political separation of North from South. In the poem "A Grafted Tongue" (the adjective here being used in a far less positive and optimistic way than Todd uses it in her formulation of "Green English") he sees only mutilation, the "severed / head" of the North rendered "Dumb, / bloodied" as it "chokes to / speak another language." Ritually maimed, literally disembodied, and thus symbolically disempowered, the head's tongue becomes engaged in a futile (inarticulate) effort to say itself, and is rendered dumb as it struggles with the "altered syllables" of its own name (in Fallon and Mahon, eds., *The Penguin Book of Contemporary Irish Poetry*, 46). Here the dominant discourse has colonized or invaded the local identity, effectively silencing it: there's no hint of balance or harmony of any kind.

Heaney implicitly acknowledges this case in an epigraph to his poem "Freedman" from *North* ([1975] 61), contemplating slavery and colonial domination (as opposed to some more equitable and balanced sociopolitical and cultural structure). He quotes R. H. Barrow's assertion in the book *The Romans* that being a slave might on one level offer actual benefits, allowing someone from "*a 'backward' race*" to be brought "*within the pale of civilization*" by being trained or educated in some useful occupation. Barrow's context for these remarks may be the *Roman* Empire, but it's clear that Heaney's interest here is more than purely historical, and embraces the *British* Empire's tactics of assimilation following enslavement (whether literal—as was the case in the West Indies—or metaphorical—as in Ireland). To indulge the etymological impulse again, the Irish link in the picture is hinted at in Heaney's use (via Barrow) of the term "the pale." *The Pale* was actually a series of fortifications and barriers set up by Henry II during the twelfth-century Norman conquest of Ireland to protect the "civilized" Norman English (within the pale) from the barbaric Irish (beyond the pale). Heaney is aware that some aspects of his own education were designed—precisely in the way Barrow suggests—to shift him from his "backward" Irishness to a point "within the pale" where he might be turned into a useful member of society—useful, that is, from the perspective of the imperial colonizer.

This appears to give a less positive slant on Heaney's schooling than he was sometimes inclined to use. Carrying on the negative theme, in the essay "Mossbawn" he criticizes the school system because in the classroom

> The literary language, the civilized utterance from the classic canon of English poetry, was a kind of force-feeding. It did not delight us by reflecting our experience; it did not re-echo our own speech in formal and surprising arrangements. Poetry lessons, in fact, were rather like catechism lessons: official inculcations of hallowed formulae that were somehow expected to stand us in good stead in the adult life that stretched out ahead. (*Preoccupations*, 26)

As a result, he tells us in an essay on Irish poetry entitled "The Poems of the Dispossessed Repossessed" (in *Government*, 32), outdated seventeenth- and eighteenth-century English poets—"bookish clergymen and witty lords"—are imposed "as the norm against which everything is measured." This might be admirable as far as Donald Davie is concerned; but from the other side of the pale it's clearly disempowering. In his essay "Feeling into Words" Heaney goes as far as to draw analogies with Solzhenitzyn's "prison camp" in the novel *The First Circle*—an ominous enough referential system to begin with! He complains that "one of the purposes of a literary education as I experienced it was to turn the student's ear into a poetic bugging device" for identifying verse.

This mechanical approach, which amounted to a "secret policing of English verse," tended to enforce norms and minimize the expression of individual literary identity, effectively suppressing "the core of a poet's speaking voice" and "his original accent" (in *Preoccupations*, 43). Obviously in such a system, only the "civilized" would survive— and Heaney appears to place himself *beyond* Barrow's "pale of civilization" in this instance (the term "civilized" and its variants always seeming to carry significantly *negative* connotations in his work—"the *exclusive* civilities of established English literature" [*Redress*, 7 (my emphasis)]; the mind shackled by "civil English tackling" [from his translation of O'Riordain, *Among School Children*, 12]; the coercive "civilized utterance from the classic canon" [*Preoccupations*, 26]; and so on).

We need to be as clear at this point of the discussion as Heaney himself is. Not *all* Eng. Lit. is being summarily dismissed, any more than *all* education is being disparaged: Heaney acknowledges generously on any number of occasions the benefits he's gained from English writers, and from his State education in Ulster. What he's objecting to is the authoritarian imposition of texts and values which create a dangerous cultural imbalance that inhibits his ideal of enrichment and harmony: he's talking, that is, essentially about the inequities and injustices of colonization. And the imbalances evident in the colonial situation, in imperialistic *droit de seigneur*, go far beyond the language or the literary text, of course, while at the same time being inextricably entwined with them. Heaney indicates as much in the poem "From the Frontier of Writing" (*NSP*, 216), where we discover that the gun sometimes really *is* a gun (rather than a pen), the frontier an actual fortified border (rather than a metaphor for Maggie Humm):

> The guns on tripods;
> the sergeant with his on-off mike repeating
>
> data about you. . . .

Under this kind of critical scrutiny—rather different from that of an F. R. Leavis or a Donald Davie—the poet remains "subjugated" (what other immediate choice is there?). Language gets reduced to the most basic (and uncomfortable) of functions; and the poetic persona shrinks to a coldly depersonalized set of data: even a neatly regulated rhyme scheme can't be guaranteed to get the writer through, and (unlike Philip Larkin) he can't merely look down on all this from the safety of his *High Windows*.[8] These circumstances don't, to say the least, seem very auspicious for the formulation of an alternative English, green or otherwise.

Heaney encounters another roadblock in another poem, "The Ministry of Fear" (*NSP*, 82–84), and is again forced into what amounts to the victim posture. Early on in the piece the poet potters around linguistically, looking to inject a little local color into the text and even to formulate an appropriate local diction (or at least accent) in which *"hushed and lulled"* become full rhymes for *"pushed and pulled."* In standard English these would be half-rhymes, of course; but here they're made to fit together perfectly, and form an interesting collocation. The first pair evokes the comforting and contemplative lyric world in which the poem begins, while the second pair adds the element of coercion and physical violence that is to interrupt that comfortable atmosphere. This accurately reflects the narrative trajectory of the poem. At one moment the poet is courting innocently enough in the back seat of his old car; but at the next that's all changed utterly as the policemen crowd round:

> black cattle, snuffing and pointing
> The muzzle of a sten gun in my eye:
> "What's your name, driver?"
>                         "Seamus . . . "
>                                 *Seamus?*

The brilliant enjambement of the innocent enough "pointing" followed by the absolutely unambiguous "muzzle of a sten gun" registers the shock of intruding mortality. The "muzzle" itself might be part of the farm animal ("black cattle") reference for two unstressed beats, but the two heavy stresses immediately following underline the menace indelibly. What we're witnessing is, in effect, a rape as the phallic gun offers to penetrate the eye; and as the "eye" is threatened with violation, so too (of course) is the "I." Given such enforcement, how does one retain an "eye" (a way of seeing) or an "I" (an independent individuation and way of saying)? Under interrogation, the writer names himself ("Seamus"), but rather than being an affirmation of self-hood, this act relegates him (in the policemen's eyes, at any rate) to an Irish Catholic margin, deprivileged, beyond the (imperial) pale, barbarian.

So he must suffer the draconian laws of the colonizer, but be denied its benefits:

> Ulster was British, but with no rights on
> The English lyric. . . .

The poem is, ultimately, a kind of conundrum, succeeding admirably in proving that such a poem as itself can't be written under these conditions. Heaney subverts the system of prohibition by anyway using the lyric mode which is proscribed. But only by maintaining a fine linguistic balance that displays neither a confessional of fear nor a rhetoric of propagandist anger, can the poet pull off the conjuring trick of the text, and preserve his identity from (cultural) rape.

The language, then, and the poetic form are put under unprecedented pressure by the circumstances of the writing. In Michael Longley's poem "Wounds" (in Frank Ormsby's anthology of *Poets from the North of Ireland*, 145–46), for instance, an assassin (actually no more than "a shivering boy") can think of nothing better to say than "Sorry Missus" to the victim's wife—scarcely adequate one might think as a speech act in this context (but then, what *would* be an adequate formula of words?). The point is underlined by the only rhyme in this passage of the poem, collocating the phrase "shot through the head" with "what he said": after all, what *do* you say when you've just killed somebody? Or, to put it in terms appropriate to the argument I've been developing here (not to mention to the politics of non-sectarian accommodation), how do you harmonize a gun shot?

In this world, violence strikes unannounced, puncturing the quotidian domestic comfort. The target in "Wounds" collapses "beside his carpet-slippers" and "the supper dishes." In a similar context, Derek Mahon draws attention to "spent / Cartridges" behind the "talk / Of fitted carpets"; or, a few lines earlier, uses the unsettling simile, "Harsh as a bombed bathroom."[9] There's obviously nowhere for the poem to seek comfort, to withdraw to—no "high windows" from which to look down as a god. Does the text, then, have to become itself a "terrorist" act, words lurking as lethal weapons like the "guns / Now snug in their oiled paper" beneath the floor in Tom Paulin's ironically titled "Settlers"? Unsettlement may be a common enough tactic of avant-garde artists and writers, but unsettlement by assassination is rather extreme. Yet the idea creeps in surreptitiously: I've argued elsewhere, apropos another Paulin poem, "Under the Eyes," that the "Time-switches" ripped from the street lamps and reused as triggering mechanisms for bombs ("clamped / To sticks of sweet, sweating explosive") are arguably symbolic of a poetic language turned from enlightenment to destruction.[10]

For an extremist, this might be suitable—but certainly not for Heaney, though he's aware of the *insidiousness* of the violence that can implicate an inhabitant unwittingly. In "Act of Union" (*NSP*, 74–75), for instance, Heaney lies with his pregnant wife in bed, pondering the relationship between male and female. Here, in spite of the potentially hopeful theme of pregnancy, the metaphor for the relationship changes from the positive one of [female] vowels and [male] consonants turning into a harmony of some kind:[11] now it becomes the relationship between [female] Ireland and [male] England, the colonizing power structure in which Heaney is obliged to write himself as male/aggressor/causer of pain and suffering. The "Act of Union" is of course simultaneously marriage, sexual intercourse, and (whether Heaney likes it or not) political act. While a new life may stir in the gynemorphic landscape of Ireland (leading ultimately to the "bog-burst" of birth), the poet remains cast in the negative role of "the tall kingdom over your shoulder" (a Britain that, as a glance at the map will tell us, reaches out physically to grasp Ireland), "imperially / Male," seeking to colonize.

Biology, as well as history, conspires to ensnare the writer in a cycle of violent oppression (as Adrienne Rich would no doubt agree): hence, rather than displaying the usual emphasis on the joys of impending birth, the poem is loaded with metaphors of the military— "battering ram," "fifth column," "cocked" weapons ("fists"). Even leaving aside the phallic implications of battering rams and cocks, the poet is in an unenviable (politically highly incorrect) position.

What I've been arguing for some time here is that Heaney may have an *ideal* of harmony and balance, but that the cultural, historical, and political circumstances militate against such notions. To speak at all—to claim a language and a space from which to speak— is itself an act against the odds, let alone attempting to harmonise, balance and articulate the "I." As much is suggested in some remarks Heaney makes in the essay "Belfast," discussing the British (cultural) colonization of Ireland in which he feels himself uncomfortably somehow complicit in "Act of Union." The "Gaelic music" of precol- onized days, he writes, echoes "that civilization whose demise was ef- fected by soldiers and administrators like Spenser and Davies, whose lifeline was bitten through when the squared-off walls of bawn and demesne dropped on the country like the jaws of a man-trap" (in *Preoccupations*, 36). The imperial power, then, sends out its soldiers and administrators (who happen, ironically, to be poets too) to make everything conform neatly to its preordained pattern ("squared-off walls"). This effectively imprisons the original inhabitants in a (cul- tural) "man-trap" which turns out to be a language trap too, since the "jaws" bite through the lifeline of the Gaelic music, basically si- lencing it. Even a non-Gaelic writer such as Heaney is severely inhib- ited by this circumstance, since it threatens to cut him off from a significant element in his heritage, disempowering one of the con- stituent parts of the "harmony" he seeks for his poetic voice.

We've already seen, in "The Ministry of Fear," though, that Heaney manages to maneuver his way past barriers, refusing to be silenced. So, predictably, he's prepared to consider various options to avoid the language "man-trap." In his essay "Tradition and an Individual Talent," for instance, he considers the experiments, in another Gaelic culture, of Hugh MacDiarmid (whose formulation of "Lal- lans" we'll no doubt revisit in the second half of this chapter). Hea- ney writes that MacDiarmid, aware of the damage done "by influ- ences from south of the Border," evolved the project "not so much to purify as to restore the language of the tribe" (in *Preoccupations*, 195).

The "Lallans" in question is "based on . . . the dialect of MacDi- armid's home district around Langholm in Dumfries-shire"; but, drawn from local reality though this base language may be, Heaney doesn't always find it particularly accessible: as he rather jocularly re- marks, "Dictionaries are necessary to his diction." (195) And he fol- lows up this comment a couple of pages later by suggesting that at times "MacDiarmid can write like a lunatic lexicographer." (197) Rather more circumspectly, and to the point for his own endeavors, he notes that there's an "uncertainty" to these linguistic experiments where the local language is at variance with the standard English code. Widening the perspective, he suggests that the situation applies not only in Scotland (and Ireland) but that "It can be a problem of style for Americans, West Indians, Indians, Scots and Irish. Joyce made a myth and a mode out of this self-consciousness, but he did so by taking on the English language itself and wrestling its genius with his bare hands" (196). While perhaps unwilling to tackle such a large opponent head on, Heaney realizes that at least some guerrilla action or sleight of hand may be required in overcoming the "uncertainty" and evolving an ideal medium which (like Joyce's—and MacDiarmid's at its very best) is "manifestly literate but opts for a local geography and idiom" (197). One such sleight of hand is Heaney's infiltration of key canonical English poets, notably William Wordsworth and Gerard Manley Hopkins. In his "manifestly literate" lecture "Feeling into Words," given at the Royal Society of Literature in October 1974, he begins with a quotation from *The Prelude*, and proceeds to drag it over into the icon of his own "local geography and idiom" by describing it in terms of "poetry as divination, poetry as revelation of the self to the self, as restoration of the culture to itself; poems as elements of continuity, with the aura and authenticity of archaeological finds" (in *Preoccupations*, 41). What concerns me here is not how true this is of Wordsworth, but how true of Heaney: he uses the work of the English canonical writer as an occasion to speak about *himself*—as is evident from the fact that by the start of the second paragraph of the lecture script he's contextualizing the poem, "Digging," the manifesto-text opening up the theme of "archaeological finds" so crucial to his own poetry (and language).

I'm not suggesting that there's anything illicit, or for that matter particularly uncommon, in this procedure—but it *is* interesting how often the English Lake District seems to become part of Ireland in Heaney's critical discussions. In his lecture on "The Makings of a Music," the cultural metamorphosis continues when his "Reflections on Wordsworth" (in *Preoccupations*, 61 ff.) lead him to a series of key similes and metaphors again linking him strategically with the English poet. Heaney picks out as significant to Wordsworth's method of composition the notion of "The poet as ploughman . . . and the suggestive etymology of the word 'verse' itself"—"verse" meaning a line of poetry and also a line of ploughed land—(65), something he follows up in his own poems "Follower" (*NSP*, 6) and particularly

"Glanmore Sonnets" 2 (*NSP*, 110). Then there are the "high moments of Wordsworth's poetry" described in terms of "a kind of sus-
pended motion . . . as a hanging bird," a "prolonged moment of
equilibrium" reminiscent of the birds in Heaney's own poem "Saint
Francis and the Birds" (in *Death of a Naturalist* [1966], 53) which, in
taking flight "like images" turn into "the best poem Francis made."
And, most striking of all, there's "the water metaphor": Heaney argues that "any account of Wordsworth's music must sooner or later
come to the river"—clearly the case, too, with his own poetry (as
we'll see presently).

In these examples, I'm trying to say *more* than simply that there
are ploughs, birds, and rivers in the Lake District, and also in Northern Ireland too (true though that statement may be!). I'm trying to
say more, too, than that Heaney merely buys into Wordsworth's
brand of Romanticism. What I'm suggesting is that Heaney, sited on
what might be regarded as the geographical and cultural "fringe" of
English, is using Wordsworth's prior example as a means of empowerment. It's as if, to overcome any lingering "uncertainty about language," the very fact of Wordsworth's texts (cited many times in the
*Heaney* corpus) gives the Irish poet added licence and authority to
continue—access and entitlement to a language which is, of course,
*his* native language as well as Wordsworth's.

Heaney's treatment of Hopkins is more straightforward, closer to
appropriation, almost turning Hopkins into a Northern Irelander. In
"Feeling into Words" he draws attention to the "connection . . . between the heavily accented consonantal noise of Hopkins's poetic
voice, and the peculiar regional characteristics of a Northern Ireland
accent" (in *Preoccupations*, 44). So it may not be entirely surprising
that, as Heaney puts it here, "when I first put pen to paper at university, what flowed out was . . . the bumpy alliterating music, the reporting sounds and ricochetting consonants typical of Hopkins's
verse." Given Hopkins's "Northern Irish" voice, this isn't slavish imitation of the colonizing culture (any more than is Heaney's reliance
on Wordsworth), but instead an assertion of local authenticity.

Mind you, Heaney is very careful in choosing the examples he
wishes to "borrow" (or appropriate, or even colonize), as is evident
in his lecture, "Englands of the Mind," given on "neutral" territory at
the University of California at Berkeley in 1976 (in *Preoccupations*,
150 ff.). The talk takes the attitude that in the world of contemporary poetry there's no single or pure England or English (as Donald

Davie may have wished), but instead a number of Englands of the mind. Heaney's particular focus is the "auditory imagination" evident in poetic language, and he distinguishes between three such Englands/Englishes—"northern deposits" of pagan Anglo-Saxon and Norse (as typified by the poetic language of Ted Hughes); a later Anglo-Saxon base, modified "by the vocabularies and values of the Mediterranean, by the early medieval Latin influence" (as manifested in the work of Geoffrey Hill); and finally "the English language . . . turned humanist, . . . and besomed clean of its inkhornisms and its irrational magics by the eighteenth century" (as evident in the work of Philip Larkin) (151).

We shall return to the Anglo-Saxon presently; but in terms of poetry in England since the advent of the Movement, it's the England of Philip Larkin's mind (and language) that has been undoubtedly the most widely-publicized and available—most prominent, but (for Heaney's taste and purposes at this point) also most characterless and colorless. In Larkin, he says (ironically adopting Movement-style negative statement), "what accrues in the language is not 'a golden and stinking blaze,' not the rank and fermenting composts of philology and history, but the bright senses of words worn clean in literate conversation" (164)—almost pure, perhaps, but almost sterile too (in every sense of the word). Heaney continues with the admission that, certainly, Larkin has "roots" as he himself does; but Larkin "puts inverted commas round his 'roots.'. . . His childhood, he says, was a forgotten bore. He sees England from train windows, fleeting past and away. He is urban modern man, the insular Englishman . . . and his voice is the not untrue, not unkind voice of post-war England" (167).[12] The problem is that such an England of the mind is predicated on an anachronistic belief in the continued stability of old imperial realities, and is consequently undermined—even rendered redundant or untenable—by what Heaney goes on to describe as "The loss of imperial power, the failure of economic nerve, the diminished influence of Britain inside Europe [and outside it too, one might add]" (169). He concludes (in a bon mot too good to resist) that these problems are symptomatic of the fact "that English poets are being forced to explore not just the matter of England, but what is the matter with England" (169).

If there's something the matter with Larkinian England, then Larkinian English is probably debilitated too, and certainly not an example for Heaney to follow. Instead, there's always W. B. Yeats who—*Anglo*-Irish though he was—set Ireland somewhat apart, as culturally different, and emphasized precisely the kind of "irrational magics" notably absent in Larkin's world. Heaney describes Yeats's project as "a conscious counter-culture act against the rationalism and materialism of late Victorian England" (in *Preoccupations*, 101). And in the well-known lecture "The Sense of Place" Heaney adds that Yeats is a viable literary role model for an Irish writer because his "sense of the otherness of his Sligo places led him to seek for a language and an imagery other than the ones which were available to him in the aesthetic modes of literary London."

As well, in Yeats's poetry at times Heaney perceives not just magic and local color but something more vigorous—more vigorous, that is, than late-nineteenth-century aestheticism, and more vigorous (as it happens) than mid-twentieth-century Larkinism. Heaney vividly describes in "The Makings of a Music" how "In Yeats, the voice muscles its way over the obstacle course of the form and flexes like an animated vine on the trellis of its metric and rhyme scheme" (in *Preoccupations*, 73–74). He goes on: "The words fly off . . . like stones in a riot; this is not a region to wander in but a combat zone where rhymes collide and assertions strike hard music off one another like quarter-staffs striking" (74). Obviously this is more in keeping with the tense, violent world of *North* than is the "melodious grace of the English iambic line" (which, of course, Yeats could do as well, if he so chose).

From what we've seen so far, it's clear that Heaney is eclectic in his choice of ingredients for the particular type of English he's trying to evolve: the language is a carefully balanced artefact constructed from many components—not pure or purified, but multifaceted and dynamic. One of the key strands we haven't yet looked at is Heaney's borrowing from the Gaelic. Heaney can read (and translate) the language, but doesn't write it: however, in his verse (particularly that up to and including *North*), he uses two significant elements unique to Gaelic poetry. These are *deibidhe* and *dinnséanchas*. *Deibidhe*, as Bernard O'Donoghue tells us, is a "form which rhymes monosyllables with the unstressed syllable of a two-syllabled word" (*Seamus Heaney*, 18), and works mainly in "seven-syllable structures" that are generally unfamiliar in English prosody (ibid., 90).[13] Difficult though it may be to import this form from Gaelic to English poetry, it does have what for Heaney is the positive and distinctive effect of destabilizing the regular English iambic pentameter, altering the authority of the stress pattern.

*Dinnséanchas* O'Donoghue describes as "poetry of locality, with its rootedness in Irish place-names" (ibid., 59). Heaney himself defines the term in his favored context of lexical roots, calling it a genre made up of "poems and tales which relate the original meanings of place names and constitute a form of mythological etymology" (*Pre-occupations*, 131): we've already seen this mechanism in operation to some degree in Heaney's discussion of the names "Mossbawn" and "Broagh." The cultivation of *dinnséanchas* is highly significant in the context of (Green) English writing in Ireland because original etymologies may have been obscured in the process of colonial renaming (a common phenomenon in territories once part of the British Empire), and therefore need to be reclaimed from the silence to which they have been consigned by the dominant discourse. In "Gifts of Rain" (*NSP*, 22–24) Heaney listens for an ancient name, an assertion of identity from the land, but seemingly in vain:

> I cock my ear
> at an absence. . . .

That absence, precipitated by the overbearing *presence* of English, needs to be redeemed: as Heaney puts it in "The Sense of Place," "We have to retrieve the underlay of Gaelic legend in order to read the full meaning of the name and to flesh out the topographical record with its human accretions. The whole of the Irish landscape, in John Montague's words, is a manuscript which we have lost the skill to read" (in *Preoccupations*, 132). Retrieving the underlay will necessitate, of course, Heaney's digging back with the pen (as he promised us at the outset): in the article "Belfast" he notes that his "quest for definition, while it may lead backward, is conducted in the living speech of the landscape I was born into" (in *Preoccupations*, 36–37). This living speech, in which the landscape asserts its own identity and makes its own music, is discovered in part 4 of "Gifts of Rain" (*NSP*, 24), where the river Moyola "spells itself" and "is its own score."

Through the magic of naming (of "spells"), place and language are reunited ("bedding the locale / in the utterance"). The resonant voice of the water in the reeds sounds like "an old chanter" (the finger pipe of a set of bagpipes) but—old though the instrument is—it may play what in another poem Heaney calls "A New Song." In "A New Song" itself (*NSP*, 27), in which the Moyola again features, *dinnséanchas* is once more significant, as the poet contemplates the

name "Derrygarve," a place redolent with fleeting excitement which
promises

> To flood, with vowelling embrace,
> Demesnes staked out in consonants.

In this mysterious textual moment we have a reiteration of the reference to the invader's "demesne" which (we remember) "dropped
on the country like the jaws of a man-trap" during the seventeenth
century (*Preoccupations*, 36). Here, "staked out in (English) consonants," it waits to be inundated by the local river's "tongues" (the
Irish vowels), so that the "forgotten Gaelic music" of a civilization
whose "lifeline was bitten through" (ibid.) may now be made new.

In "Anahorish" (*NSP*, 21), too, the old (and beautiful) music of
the place name is reanimated so that locale and language intersect
and become synonymous in the "soft gradient" of the "vowel-
meadow." The name's modernized version obscures its Gaelic origin
which, Heaney tells us in the essay "Belfast," is "*anach fhíor uisce . . .
the place of clear water*" (in *Preoccupations*, 36). For him it seems to
have a foundational, almost paradisal quality of sparkling spring
water and grassy riverbanks. As well, the *dinnséanchas* calls up for the
poet a vision of ancient ancestral "mound-dwellers," putting him in
touch with his deepest cultural roots.

"Mossbawn," too, is another place whose name resonates with
(among other etymologies) Gaelic music, celebrated on this occasion by Heaney in two ways—as the title of a two-part poem in *North*,
and as the title of an autobiographical essay in *Preoccupations*. In the
latter he gives us an extraordinary description of a boyhood adventure, in which the longing for contact with ancient roots became actually physical. Heaney's fascination with that most archetypal of
Irish locales, the peat bog, is well-known; but in this essay he goes as
far as to call the relationship a "betrothal." Moreover it becomes a
betrothal acted out "when another boy and myself stripped to the
white country skin and bathed in a moss-hole, treading the liver-
thick mud, unsettling a smoky muck off the bottom and coming out
smeared and weedy and darkened. We dressed again and went home
in our wet clothes, smelling of the ground and the standing pool,
somehow initiated" (in *Preoccupations*, 19).

I've suggested elsewhere that this initiation (which, as we'll see
presently is an initiation, among other things, into *language*) is more
like a baptism than a betrothal;[14] but either way a potent *rite de pas-*

*sage* is being enacted here. If we stay with Heaney's own suggestion of betrothal, and at the same time battle Freudianism into the background, then a passage from "Feeling into Words" becomes apposite, where the poet (taking his cue from P. V. Glob's study *The Bog People*) writes of the exhumees: "a number of these . . . were ritual sacrifices to the Mother Goddess, the goddess of the ground who needed new bridegrooms each winter to bed with her in her sacred place, in the bog, to ensure the renewal and fertility of the territory in the spring" (in *Preoccupations,* 57). Though the context here is superficially Danish, Heaney adduces an Irish connection by going on to claim that "Taken in relation to the tradition of Irish political martyrdom . . . this is more than an archaic barbarous rite: it is an archetypal pattern" (ibid.). So Heaney, by his literal ritual immersion, puts himself in contact with something far more than mere mud.

More often, though, it's not the poet's body that goes down into the peat of ancestral origins as much as his pen that penetrates the bog—the most obvious instances, of course, concerning the exhumed "bog people" of his texts (principally "The Tollund Man" [*NSP,* 31–32]; "Bog Queen" [*NSP,* 66–68]; "The Grauballe Man" [*NSP,* 69–70]; and the victim of "Punishment" [*NSP,* 71–72]). These are, as he puts it, "Kinned by hieroglyphic / peat" in the "bog" which is the "resting ground, / outback of my mind" ("Kinship," in *North,* 40–45). Such statements are important since the word "hieroglyphic" reminds us that we're dealing with language as well as archaeology here—the victims becoming written texts in which Heaney reads the past—and the "kinn[ing]" encompassing not only the objects of these poems, but the poet too, since it's not just the past in general but *his* past which he mediates in his own texts.

The bog is obviously much more than a topographical phenomenon, then. Like so much in Heaney at this stage it becomes highly symbolic: as he says in "The Sense of Place," it dramatizes "our sense of ourselves as inhabitants not just of a geographical country but of a country of the mind." In terms of "our *sensing* of place" the landscape was (and in these poems still is) "sacramental, instinct with signs, implying a system of reality beyond the visible realities" (in *Preoccupations,* 132). In the end, in fact, the bog for Heaney becomes mythic in its scope—as he admits in "Feeling into Words." In an interesting re-vision of the American frontier myth as a way of claiming a pioneering space (from which to speak) he explains:

"We have no prairies . . ."—but we have bogs.

At that time [the period of putting together the significantly titled collection *Door into the Dark* (1969)] I . . . had been reading about the frontier and the west as an important myth in the American consciousness, so I set up—or rather, laid down—the bog as an answering Irish myth. (in *Preoccupations*, 55)

And in the poem "Bogland" (*NSP*, 17–18) he reiterates this notion, contrasting the American expansion westwards into "a big sun at evening" with "Our pioneers [who] keep striking / Inwards and downwards."

Going inwards and downwards into his culture is highly important not only because of the *dinnséanchas* that it reveals, but because it puts Heaney in touch with a much wider concept of *North*—not just Northern Ireland but a large part of Northern Europe, as the bogland stretches across the map. From our present point of view, the significance of this is that it allows the poet to dig back into a language which *predates* the fact of British colonization, and which in fact itself colonized part of Britain in the shape of the Viking invaders. The Vikings (present in Heaney's text mainly in the poems "North" [*NSP*, 56–57] and "Viking Dublin: Trial Pieces" [*NSP*, 58–61]) sweep down "the long strand" on which the poet stands, facing "North." They're "fabulous raiders" out of the cold of Iceland and Greenland, bringing with them a tradition of violence, "revenges" and "hatreds" that *hasn't* been buried with them but survives in the *North* of Ireland today. Yet as well as this *un*civilized and *un*genteel history, the "longship's swimming tongue" has amassed a "word-hoard" set down in the "burrow" of the poet's "furrowed brain"—a cultural enrichment, a buried treasure that doesn't necessarily defray the barbarity of lifestyle, but at least shares its vigour and energy.

Earlier we saw that, in the "England of the mind" that Heaney associates with the (pre-Laureate) work of Ted Hughes, there's a reliance on "the northern deposits, the pagan Anglo-Saxon and Norse elements" (*Preoccupations*, 151). Now, via *North*, Heaney himself is able to tap back into this "hoard." As Nicholas McGuinn puts it his *Seamus Heaney: a Student's Guide* (1986), "he quarries more deeply than ever among the treasuries of Gaelic and Anglo-Saxon—the twin legacies of his divided cultural heritage—excavating such curiosities as 'pampooties', 'gombeen-men', 'pash', 'felloes', or 'crannog'"

(103). I'd suggest that the "divided cultural heritage" is in a way actually united as Heaney digs back—even if only in sharing the experience of having been colonized by the Vikings.

Certainly the archaeological perspective allows a different take on the (subsequently) dominant discourse of English, permitting Heaney to dismantle it as he works his way back (or down). In "Bone Dreams" [*NSP*, 62–65], finding himself in "the tongue's / old dungeons" he starts to "push back / through dictions" as he explores what might be regarded as the *impurities* in English—"Elizabethan canopies," "Norman devices," and sexy bits and pieces from mediaeval Provence. Finally, as he unearths "the coffered / riches of grammar / and declensions"—word gems such as "*ban-hus*"—he gets

> to the scop's
> twang, the iron
> flash of consonants
> cleaving the line.
>
> (*NSP*, 63)

Here, deeply embedded in the language he finds a dynamic poetic diction that he can use, a pungent bardic utterance not compromised by later English gentility, nor by an RP accent that might give him access to the British Civil Service (but not to the roots of the peat). This is the "Green English" equivalent of Whitman's "barbaric yawp," or (in its "iron" "twang") of John Agard's Caribbean steelband dialogue between "Man" and "Pan." It liberates the poet into his own voice, and unapologetically into an "Ulster accent" which, Heaney tells us in "Feeling into Words," "is generally a staccato consonantal one" in which "Our tongue strikes the tangent of the consonant rather more than it rolls the circle of the vowel" (in *Preoccupations*, 45).

It's important to emphasize at this point, without wishing to insult the reader's intelligence, that this English, while Irish and local, is nowhere near Gaelic. Other poets (in Scotland as well as Ireland) *do* choose to write in Gaelic, either with or without adjacent translation: a glance at the recent *Penguin Book of Poetry from Britain and Ireland since 1945* offers us the work, for instance, of Nuala Ní Dhomhnaill, as well as (from Scotland) Somhairle MacGill-Eain, Ruaraidh Mac-Thòmais, Iain Mac a'Ghobhainn, and Meg Bateman. But Heaney *doesn't* so choose (though if he did, it would take him beyond the scope of the present study, of course). Similarly, some writers have resisted or reversed the Anglicization of their names, but Heaney hasn't (finding it already culturally recognizable enough—as we saw in the confrontation described in "The Ministry of Fear"!). To do so would be to imbalance his case, to prevent harmony; it would be to suppress the "English" part of him which he sees as essential to his development (first at school and later as a writer).

As Loreto Todd tells us, "Irish Gaelic is officially sanctioned in the Republic of Ireland and is taught in all schools"; and as well as "the serious attempts being made to reinvigorate Gaelic in the Republic" there are moves "to reintroduce it as a mother tongue in the North" (*Green English*, 141). But, sympathetic as Heaney no doubt is to all of this, he stands somewhat apart from it. For him, becoming a "scop," a poetic spokesperson, and exercising the "twang" of his own accent is enough, particularly when it's resonating with his "country of the mind, whether that country of the mind takes its tone unconsciously from a shared oral inherited culture, or from a consciously savoured literary culture, or from both" (*Preoccupations*, 132). This doesn't entirely displace English, but it re-views what in the volume *The Government of the Tongue* Heaney describes as English's "hitherto world-defining poetic heritage" (40).

That may not be going far enough for all concerned. As Bernard O'Donoghue notes, Alfred Alvarez was suspicious when Heaney began to draw back from his experiments with *deibidhe* and *dinnséanchas*, accusing him of "recidivising into the 'gentility principle' that Alvarez himself . . . had seen as a deplorable feature of the Movement poets" (*Seamus Heaney*, 153). However, as O'Donoghue goes on to say, such an attitude is "particularly absurd" in the circumstances. True, Heaney is relatively moderate in his stance. He can, for instance, admire "all the pounce and irrefutability of a tiger lashing its tail" in Sylvia Plath's last poems—for which, presumably, Alvarez is grateful; but at the same time he sees it as an "extreme case" rather than a model to follow (in *Government of the Tongue*, 167). For Heaney, then, the "tongue" needs significant "government"—albeit not automatically *British* Government!

The imposition of a single, indivisible, immutable, colonizing English is something Heaney continues to resist. His history, and the history of his culture, persuade him that a fixed and static "pure" language of the kind Davie prescribed is, if not impossible, at least certainly undesirable. The tangible inheritance going back (literally) to the bone of the artefacts he describes in "Viking Dublin: Trial Pieces" convinces Heaney that though an "outline" may need to be "incised," providing "a cage / or trellis," this stable structure is not an end in itself, but simply a framework "to conjure in." So the bone texts in the museum are not the final word, but provisional "Trial Pieces" enabling an exploration of magic dictions, "the craft's mystery / improvised on bone." Inside formal appearances, "the line amazes itself," even "eluding the hand that fed it" and becoming (later in the poem) "a buoyant / migrant line" defying fixity.

For David Lloyd, scrutinizing *Anomalous States: Irish Writing and the Post-Colonial Moment* (1993), this is all too *aesthetic*. In his chapter entitled "Pap for the Dispossessed" (which turns that phrase [the last line of Heaney's poem "Hercules and Antaeus" (*NSP*, 76–77)] like a weapon back on the poet himself), Lloyd complains of Heaney's "innocent yet possessive relation to his objects," his "satisfaction in a merely aesthetic resolution," the way his verse projects "more fashionable swagger than [genuine] engagement" (21). What Heaney achieves, according to Lloyd, is a "purely aesthetic . . . performance, which evades the logic even of his own mythologies" (28); a lack (in the "solemnly voiced pursuit" of the "Glanmore Sonnets") of "intellectual strenuousness" in texts "reduced as they are to such highly strung aestheticism" (34). Lloyd's sharp eye (and tongue) pick out "an uneasy oscillation between local piety and universalist cultural claims" (4); the relocation of "an individual and racial identity through the reterritorialization of language and culture" (20). He goes on to argue that "The signs of difference that compose the language are underwritten by a language of containment and synthesis" (23); and that "This difference . . . is posed as the context for a resolution beyond conflict . . . which is at once pre-existent and integrating" (26). These latter remarks strike me as being entirely valid as regards Heaney's work, the only problem being the negative spin put on them by Lloyd, whose own agenda clearly demands something more iconoclastic.[15]

It seems to me that the harmony Heaney sets up as his ideal, and toward which he moves as he balances the various elements of the "Green English" available to him, is not quite as *soft* as Lloyd obviously believes. It *does* challenge the *droit de seigneur* of the colonizing discourse, and refuses to be dumped beyond the pale. It would be too oxymoronic to speak of a "militant harmony," perhaps; but at the same time it would be a mistake to read Heaney's attitude as overly passive or vapid: for him the harmony of the intermarriage of English consonants and Irish vowels is a dynamic and active phenomenon. If his cast of mind tends to lead him away from the iconoclastic, away from the urge to "break English" entirely, nevertheless the "Green English" that emerges in his early work constitutes a significant variation on the standard code.

જી   જી   જી   જી   જી

## "BARBARIANS" NORTH OF THE BORDER:
## SCOTLAND AND LANGUAGE INVASION

If in the 1970s and early 1980s Ireland was receiving a very large amount of literary attention and publicity, perhaps in the 1990s the focus shifted somewhat towards another Gaelic frontier—that of Scotland. One of the figures involved, W. N. Herbert, in the poem "Letterbomb" (in the collection *Contraflow on the Super Highway*, 46)[16] uses an unhappily appropriate incendiary metaphor to portray the (surprising) revelation of Scottish dissent going on behind the higher-profile Irish one. He creates a scenario in which shelves full of recent Irish poetry burst spontaneously into flame and reveal, stacked behind them, the equivalent Scottish product, waiting for readers. However, Scotland's voice, Herbert goes on with ironic self-deprecation, is less inflammatory since what it engages with is "anely aestheticism." So the bombs are only notional or abstract, the grievances long back in history, independence an illusion, and the colonization north of the Border a phenomenon in which the locals have been complicit—or *not*, as we shall see presently. True, the "bombs" in Scottish poetry are made of language rather than of Semtex; but perhaps, as John Agard warned us in "Listen Mr. Oxford Don," language—the human voice—can be a potent weapon too.

Certainly this would seem true of one of the key figures in the conflict, that old incendiarist, Hugh MacDiarmid (Christopher Murray Grieve). If Seamus Heaney was somewhat disparaging about Hugh MacDiarmid's experiments with "Lallans," raising a (legitimate) question of accessibility in complaining that his "diction" demanded "Dictionaries" (*Preoccupations*, 195), MacDiarmid's younger generation fellow Scots seem more sympathetic—both toward dictionaries (in the hands of either writers or readers) and towards MacDiarmid. David Kinloch, for instance, in his essay "The Apology of a Dictionary

Trawler," confesses that his Scottish dictionary is an aid to coming to terms with what Scots means to him, how it enables him to come to terms with "the language of my forbears"; and he adds that he feels "more alive in some of these [Scottish] words than in their English equivalents," sensing that "I 'knew' them and 'recognized' them as my own even as I came upon them for the first time" (in Crawford, et al., *Contraflow*, 5). So "dictionary trawling" is legitimated, however artificial it may appear to be as a literary tactic. In exhuming forgotten or discarded linguistic materials and inserting them into the contemporary text, Kinloch concludes, it's a question of "admitting the lost and unsayable into your poem and celebrating or at least articulating the loss and unsayability they bring with them" (6).

Various dictionaries, then, (though probably not the *OED*) may provide language hitherto marginalized, silenced, or otherwise not available in the standard code, offering access to what Richard Price describes as "Scotland's three languages: Gaelic, Scots, and Scottish English" (in Crawford, et al., *Contraflow*, viii). And particularly as regards the latter, Price supports his position by quoting Edwin Morgan's opinion that new Scottish poets are formulating a "linguistic approach which after all is in line with the nature of the country." So, as Morgan sees it, while these writers still use what (for want of a better word) might be labeled "English," "it is often an English which has many lexical, syntactic, and especially tonal departures from southern standard, if indeed any such standard can now honestly be said to hold sway, or hold water, or even hold out" (quoted in *Contraflow*, ix). The modern originator of this Scottish linguistic subversion, who sent everyone scurrying for their dictionaries, was of course MacDiarmid. Morgan, in an essay on "James Joyce and Hugh MacDiarmid" (in *Crossing the Border: Essays on Scottish Literature* [1990]) writes that for MacDiarmid:

> the language had to be fresh, surprising, unconventional. . . ; that was why Jamieson's dictionary was important to him. In these early poems he showed an extraordinary ability to mix convincingly together English words (to be spoken of course with a Scottish accent), Scottish forms of words which are still commonly heard and understood, and then suddenly the startling dictionary word given a new life in a new context. . . . (176)

Such a revivification was necessary (as far as both Joyce and MacDiarmid were concerned) on at least two grounds—because issues of nationality were at stake; and because the standard code had anyway become so pallid (while still remaining loaded with colonizing power). Morgan (again) commenting on MacDiarmid's *In Memoriam James Joyce* (1955) tells us:

> The fifth section is a satirical scherzo called "England Is Our Enemy" where MacDiarmid parades what in *Who's Who* he liked to define as his Anglophobia (a characteristic not unknown to Joyce either), attacking English literature and criticism for that very bland, anti-extremist insularity—"a stone-heap, a dead load of moral qualities"—which he and Joyce had been doing their best to discredit by bypassing Anglosaxondom. . . . (181)

If, as we saw earlier, Heaney's cultural nationalism is a moderately-stated one, then the same can obviously *not* be said of MacDiarmid: as Robert Crawford puts the case rather mildly in his essay "Scottish Literature and English Studies," the notion of writing developed by MacDiarmid "leads to the thorough questioning of Anglocentric standards in Scottish literature" (in *The Scottish Invention of English Literature* [1998], 232).

In the same essay Crawford extends his argument to show MacDiarmid's global, as well as local Scottish, significance as a linguistic pioneer and iconoclast. He claims:

> Given the way in which today the international English language remains strongly but vestigially linked to England, and across the English-speaking world from Australasia to Canada we see literature and the teaching of Literature frequently involving a wish to assert native voices and traditions in the face of Anglocentric norms, the works of . . . MacDiarmid, in addition to their importance within Scotland, are widely emblematic. MacDiarmid's fierce fighting for Scottish Literature in some ways anticipates the more moderate arguments in 1950s Australia, for instance, which led to poets and academics arguing about the relative status of Australian and English Literature. . . . (238)

And, closer to home, though MacDiarmid died in 1978, his influence lives on, Crawford arguing that Roderick Wilson's single-volume history entitled *The Literature of Scotland* (1985) and his subsequent anthology, *The Poetry of Scotland* (1995)—the first substantial collection to contain work "in Scots and Gaelic as well as English"—"follow the seminal . . . lead given by Hugh MacDiarmid" (239).

Clearly, then, MacDiarmid is an important pioneer, though the aggressiveness of his assertions doesn't suit everybody following in his footsteps. Douglas Dunn, for instance, in an interview with John Haffenden says: "I feel no affinity with MacDiarmid, though I have a lunatic respect for his work. He was a volcano, but his mind was totalitarian. He imposed rather than expressed" (Haffenden, *Viewpoints*, 33). So, though Dunn credits MacDiarmid with being Scotland's "only indisputable modern landmark" on the literary map, he admits that "What I've wanted is a release from the terms MacDiarmid laid down as the only ones for discussing Scottish history, politics and literature" (ibid., 28). And elsewhere he speaks of the need to "shift MacDiarmid a little, and make room for ourselves to breathe" (quoted in *Reading Douglas Dunn* [Crawford and Kinloch, eds., 1992], 176).

Perhaps this is what *has* happened, particularly since 1978. More moderate than MacDiarmid, but equally influential on the younger Scottish poets at the end of the twentieth century has been Edwin Morgan. W. N. Herbert lists him (along with MacDiarmid and John Davidson) as being one of the "three writers" whose work has "largely shaped" the new generation's "specific poetic agenda" (in Crawford, et al., *Contraflow*, xv). This agenda involves breaking down the old metropolitanism of the standard code, in what Morgan describes in the essay "The Resources of Scotland" as "a growing climate of opinion that favors de-Londonization as a general aim" (in *Crossing the Border*, 21). In such a climate, the linguistic issues raised will involve more than simply the local: so in the essay "Scottish Poetry in English" he suggests that "we now look round, with some uneasiness, at a large, different, more elusive territory, where we rub shoulders with Americans, and Australians, and West Indians, and Irishmen—the 'English' language(s)" (in ibid., 16).

So in Morgan's dictionary, the language on display is likely to be more expansive, even internationalist. Ian Gregson in *Contemporary Poetry and Postmodernism* (1996) describes it as a "more centrifugal poetic"; and goes on to draw the ingenious (postmodern) analogy that "Reading Edwin Morgan can seem less like reading and more like channel-hopping" (134). The stations involved will not only be beaming in from (in Morgan's own words) "the lunar mountains in Hugh MacDiarmid," but will also involve "the orbiting rocket in Anselm Hollo" and "the lobotomy in Allen Ginsberg" (quoted ibid., 136). This latter statement reveals that a high premium is obviously

placed, in the literary process of de-Londonization, on that original
pioneer of the political aspect of the phenomenon, America—something Morgan acknowledges extensively in an interview with Robert
Crawford published in *Talking Verse* (1995). He says:

> I think Whitman was probably the earliest American poet that I really
> enjoyed. . . . But also much later when the Beat writers came on the
> scene—Ginsberg, Corso, Ferlinghetti—I enjoyed them and I could
> understand what they were doing. . . . [I]t seemed to unlock some-
> thing in me that I could certainly use; and it also helped to get me
> into other kinds of American poetry which I hadn't liked before at
> all . . . ; I got into [William Carlos] Williams from them. (Crawford,
> 157–58)

Contemporary American poetry, then, and particularly Beat poetry, liberated Morgan into realizing "that there was nothing you
couldn't write about" and that it was appropriate to permit oneself
"certain kinds of spontaneity" (158) which the straitlaced metropolitan English culture wished to suppress. In an interview with W. N.
Herbert in the magazine *Gairfish* (Autumn 1998), Morgan singles
out Ginsberg for special mention, applauding his "freedom of spirit
and form": he adds, "I am thinking of *Howl* in particular, which was
the first poem of his I read. The long, swinging lines, the extraordinary juxtapositions of imagery, the sexual explicitness—all these ap-
pealed, not separately but as part of a new amalgam of liberation"
(quoted in *About Edwin Morgan* [Crawford and Whyte, eds., 1990],
33). In *Howl,* and in other "long American poems" such as Williams's
*Paterson,* Robyn Marsack claims, Morgan finds "an eagerness to embrace the new, poets leaning forward into the future instead of using
the past as prop and stay," and this allows him to achieve "A Declaration of Independence" for himself (in ibid., 34).

Whatever the source, though, the result has been kaleidoscopic, a
random glance at Morgan's extensive poetic output (the Carcanet
*Collected Poems* of 1990 stretching to just over six hundred pages)
showing all manner of delighted and delightful literary-linguistic ex-
perimentation from "Newspoems" (cut out of newspapers) to "An
Alphabet of Goddesses"; from "Science Fiction Poems" to concrete
poems; from "the Video Box" to "Sonnets from Scotland." As Roderick Watson puts it in "Edwin Morgan: Messages and Transformations," he has "explored a most fruitful fascination with changing
messages and messages of change" (in *British Poetry from the 1950s to*

*the 1990s* [Day and Docherty, eds., 1997], 191)—a sprightly variousness in significant contrast to Movement-style homogeneity and poetry of the status quo.

Robert Crawford's essay on Morgan, "to change / the unchange-
able" emphasizes this theme, underlining the point by quoting Morgan's version of the famous Ezra Pound dictum, "MAKE IT NEW."
Crawford writes:

> Prefacing his 1972 collection of *Essays*, Morgan declared punningly,
>
>> CHANGE RULES is the supreme graffito. Gathering up the shards
>> —performances, assortments, résumés—can hope perhaps to scat-
>> ter values through a reticulation that surprises thought rather than
>> traps it. (in Crawford and Whyte, *About Edwin Morgan*, 19)

One aspect of Morgan's work that particularly manifests the desire
for (and the act of) change, Crawford argues, is the process of translation, changing a text from one language into another. Morgan has
translated from a large suite of languages—including Old English,
Dutch, Spanish, Italian, French, German, Russian, and Hungarian—
and Crawford suggests that this penchant comes from the fact that
Morgan's "own attitude to poetry appears to be that it, like life, is
bound up with translation, with change. . . . Translation is a crossover, a change, a rite of passage into something other" (ibid., 17).
The thinking here is clearly more Poundian—with his notion of
translation as "blood brought to ghosts"[17]—than consonant with
Movement-style notions of purity, exclusivity, and downright xenophobia. So the pull for Morgan, again, is clearly away from England,
and away from narrow definitions of English into "something other":
as he says in interview with Robert Crawford, his "passport" may say
he's "UK or British," but, he emphasizes, "I don't feel British" and in
particular "I don't feel, certainly, English" (quoted in ibid., 25).[18] Little of promise, as far as Morgan's concerned, lies south of the border: Robyn Marsack reminds us that the poet's contemporaries in
England were the members of the Movement—writers "fixed in the
aspic of Kingsley Amis's ban on foreign cities, philosophy and art gal-
leries as fit subjects of poetry. Where were the ideas to come from,
where the sense of linguistic adventure?" (ibid., 27). One avenue
Marsack singles out in answer to this rhetorical question is concrete
poetry—an international phenomenon that received scant attention
in England but was given a significant profile in Scotland by such

writers as Ian Hamilton Finlay (in his own work and in the magazine *Poor. Old. Tired. Horse.*), and by Morgan himself. Marsack suggests that the whole theory of concrete poetry challenges "the mildly erotic, faintly speculative, conversational, 'witty,' metropolitan (or week-end rural) English poetry . . . produced in the 1950s and 1960s" (30).

Morgan tends to see his own experiments in the genre as tentative explorations, to see what would happen with the text under changed or unconventional circumstances. In an interview with Marshall Walker he muses:

> I think I wanted to see what concrete poetry was up to in relation to poetry in general. It wasn't that I just switched over to concrete poetry as a means of producing instantaneous images—that was part of it— but I think I also wanted to see if there was some kind of common ground between it and linear poetry. Quite a number of my poems are exploring that half-way house, not strictly concrete and not strictly linear but mixing the two forms. (Walker, *Edwin Morgan; an Interview* [1977], 3–4)

The tone here indicates an amazingly open mind (particularly in contrast to those contemporaneous closed ones down south), a willingness to range widely and tentatively—to such a degree, in fact, that Morgan can be lured into sci-fi to speculate that "It may be that there could be a simple, even perhaps romantic kind of poetry of space exploration" (ibid., 11).

Ultimately, though, extended and extensive as his experiments may seem, and de-Londonized as his literary and cultural ethics may be, there remains a center for Morgan's work—and it's, of course, close to home: Scotland itself. That is, the "space" he actually explores is that cultural one located north of the border. Even early on, and even when ostensibly examining the archaic, Morgan is directing his attention towards local and contemporary circumstances: so, when he reads the work of the so-called Scottish Chaucerians, notably Dunbar, his dominant interest is in these much older poets' "rapid, mercurial manifestation of change as energy," a phenomenon paralleled in his own poetry where "change is similarly displayed" (Crawford and Whyte, *About Edwin Morgan*, 17).

What he sees as distinctive in Scots is what he sees as distinctive in the *whittrick*, a Scottish word for the weasel. It forms the title of a long poem (Morgan, *Collected Poems* [1990], 79–116), the first part of which is a dialogue between James Joyce and Hugh MacDiarmid, or rather an intersection of their dictions, *Ulysses*-speak and *Lallans*. Crawford says that the poem "celebrates an elusive . . . essence imaged in Scots," the whittrick, "the spirit of creativity" (13). The whittrick is obviously swift, instinctual, subversive, a canny survivor—the Scottish equivalent, perhaps, of Robert Lowell's skunk or (more obviously) Ted Hughes's "Thought-Fox."[19] And W. N. Herbert in his essay "Morgan's Words" provides the following interesting gloss:

> The whittrick is, of course, the symbol of Morgan's interface, that point between languages at which new possibilities emerge. . . . [I]t might be suggested that the whittrick speaks in a language formed when standard English collides with spoken Scots. This third language appears to be what interested Morgan about concrete poetry. . . . (in ibid., 72)[20]

However one reads the metaphor of the whittrick, it certainly seems to correspond with something untamed in the Scottish poet's text, an ephemeral countercultural spirit that refuses to be trapped in the standard code of the dominant discourse of English.

It would be possible to argue at this point (without getting too caricatural) that Morgan evolves a kind of "Tweed English" equivalent of the "Green English" Loreto Todd talks about in Ireland. Undoubtedly the openness of his mind (and text) produces a multi-literary language far more various than the English English from which it diverges. The adoption of a particular Scottish regional patois is relatively uncommon in Morgan's work, though it's *one* of the tactics he uses at times: as he tells us in his essay "Glasgow Speech in Recent Scottish Literature," he "began using Glasgow speech in a few poems like 'Glasgow Green' and 'Good Friday,'" [1968] later "extending this through a range of different Glasgow voices in 'Stobhill' (1971)" (in *Crossing the Border*, 324).

When we turn to the poetry of Tom Leonard, though, we're struck by the full force of this accent in poem after poem, animated by a kind of hostile wit, both aggressive and subversive. In his essay on Glasgow speech, Morgan indicates how marginalized it has been up to this point, even (amazingly) in Scotland:

> In the fifty-page introduction to the first volume of *The Scottish National Dictionary*, virtually nothing is said about the language of Glasgow. . . . [T]he speech of this large conurbation containing half the

population of the country is dismissed in one sentence: "Owing to the influx of Irish and foreign immigrants in the industrial area near Glasgow the dialect has become hopelessly corrupt." (in ibid., 312)

A few lines later in the essay, Morgan brings this opinion more up to date by quoting J. Derrick McClure's comment of 1974 on "the impoverished and bastardised Scots spoken in present-day Glasgow."

However, such comments only add fire to Leonard's determination to articulate the "bastardized" diction, to enact the living speech of the milieu which has been so summarily and vindictively dismissed: clearly he would agree with Morgan's opinion that "to sweep speech under the carpet [as *The Scottish National Dictionary* and McClure try to do here] is to academize, and indeed tarmacadamize, systems of stasis and control that are perpetually in need of re-examination" (ibid., 328). Leonard responds precisely to this need, and subjects the governing linguistic control systems to savage scrutiny and review. To this end, as Morgan notes of Leonard's *Intimate Voices: Selected Work 1965–1983* (1984), "He uses English, or Glaswegian, or sound-poetry, as the need changes, but his book is a book of voices, and the city comes alive through what his characters say" (in *Crossing the Border*, 285): further, these voices express "Leonard's underlying and reiterated theme of the relations between language and power" (286).

And that relationship is a close one; and the villain in the piece— predictably enough—is the standard code imposed from the south. In his essay "On Reclaiming the Local" (in *Reports from the Present: Selected Works 1982–95* [1995]), Leonard talks about the Establishment's attempt "to create a bogus unified 'personality,'" a false consensus or illusion of uniformity by which dissent can be dismissed and *normalized*. He identifies a number of linguistic arenas in which this chicane operates, primarily mediated through the education system which continues to enforce "the dominant literary tradition" and "prescriptive grammar" (36).

In "Literature, Dialogue, Democracy," he amplifies this latter comment rather sourly (but legitimately) by pointing out that inequalities in the perception of the "status of diction has been one peculiarly British way of sorting people into a hierarchy of worth" (in ibid., 58). And in the same essay he underlines the dark political motives operating historically in the domain of education at large. He argues that the original creation of literature as a syllabus subject in practice turned it into an élite field operating *against* the principles of universal free education. What was enshrined in Literature with a capital "L" were the "rights and values of monarch and aristocracy"—values enforced in Scotland, though not of course in America, to which a number of fugitive Scots withdrew (Leonard singling out Tom Paine and Alexander Wilson, "the Paisley poet").

Scotland's loss was America's gain, as Paine and Wilson went to help formulate the New World Democracy of which Walt Whitman was to be such a strong enthusiast, while Britain continued to languish in the darkness of class privilege. Leonard, though, incorporates into his argument at this point an awareness that not all was ideal even in America since—in an uncomfortable paradox—the land of the free continued for a long time to tolerate slavery. He makes use of this datum to emphasize a link "between those nineteenth-century American—and Caribbean and African—slaves, and the British urban proletariat." As far as he's concerned, these radically disadvantaged groups on either side of the Atlantic are all victims of the same economic and industrial processes of capitalist manufacture, sharing a "historic link [that] survives in the language of the groups, and in the Literature of the children and grandchildren of those slaves and proletariat writing today" (55).

So the slaves of empire in the Caribbean and the (virtual) slaves of empire in or from Scotland share a common language of deprivilege—which accounts at least partly for Robert Crawford's poem entitled "The Gaelic Caribbean," dedicated to Fred D'Aguiar (the Anglo-Guyanese editor of the "Black British Poetry" section of *The New British Poetry*). At the beginning Crawford waits in a "silence" occasioned by the fact that the various refugees/immigrants have had their "tongues" torn out. Then, as the poem develops, he has a vision of "Guyanese Gaels" beginning to "Unslave themselves" in the historical process (in Crawford et al., *Contraflow*, 20).

The highly mixed referents here, as well as suggesting complex racial intermingling, and linguistic hybridity, metaphorically affirm an identity of suffering and colonization so that (symbolically, at least) Gaelic virtually becomes a part of the Creole continuum. In fact, as the editors of *The New Poetry* point out, there's a *real* "Scottish influence on Caribbean language and writing," and Edward Kamau Brathwaite has explicitly recognized the "Scots linguistic component in Creole" (Hulse, Kennedy, and Morley, 18). So the islands off the north and west coasts of Scotland are much closer to those of the West Indian archipelago than geography might suggest.

From the Glasgow perspective on all this, Albion is clearly the per-
fidious element in the pattern; and America (in spite of having slaves
—always a problem for the casual reader of the *Declaration of Independence*) is the potential redeemer. In an interview with Ken Cock-
burn, Leonard informs us that his choice of the title *Intimate Voices*
for the first selection of his work is an act of rebellious Anglophobia,
stressing that the book's voices ("plural") have "nothing to do with
the supposedly objective Public Voice nonsense" purveyed in English
poetry (in Crawford et al., eds., *Talking Verse*, 112). Instead, Leonard
has turned to "Cummings and Williams and various Americans"
(ibid.).

The most significant of these Americans seems to be William Carlos Williams, celebrated in Leonard's article in *Poetry Information* entitled "The Locust Tree in Flower, and why it had Difficulty Flowering
in Britain" (reprinted in *Intimate Voices*). Leonard begins with the
positive assertion, "What I like about Williams is his voice"; and then
proceeds immediately to the negative side of the ledger, to criticize
British notions of voice in the sterile or deflowered world of class
privilege. He notes that there are "basically two ways of speaking in
Britain" (95)—with a Received Pronunciation [RP] accent which lets
the listener/reader know that one is a product of the private (fee-
paying) school system; or *without*. And if the speaker is unlucky
enough to be in the "without" (or "have-not") category, the voice
available—as we discover in part 1 of Leonard's poem sequence "Unrelated Incidents"—will only be able to articulate "thi lang- / wij a thi
/ guhtr," a proletarian and deprivileged speech mode so different
from the "Inglish" of the affluent and well-educated (in *Intimate
Voices*, 86).

Williams, however, being American and therefore not involved in
the class system implicit (or, virtually, explicit) in RP, doesn't have to
buy into the standard code and all that goes with it. As Leonard puts
it rhetorically: "Why then should an American follow grammatical
rules of prose or poetry which in effect simulated a voice he not only
didn't have, but didn't want?" (96). There seems to be no reasonable
answer to this—either for Williams or anyone else for that matter.
Consequently, just as Williams explores a different way of saying in
his poem "This is Just to Say," so too may (for instance) *Leonard*, following the American lead—which is exactly what he does in the
poem "Jist ti Let Yi No (from the American of Carlos Williams)" (in
*Intimate Voices*, 37). In this poem Williams's American accent is re-

placed by a Glaswegian one; and the plums Williams purloins from the icebox become—in the hard-drinking Scottish culture—the bottles ("speshlz") stacked in the "frij" ready for a booze-up.[21]

Models are available for resistance to English English, then, not only in American but in Scottish literature too—as Leonard goes on to tell us. The examples he gives are Ian Hamilton Finlay as practitioner of Concrete Poetry (which plays with a "heightened awareness of syntax"); Hugh MacDiarmid for consistently crossing the "boundaries" appropriate to conventional lexis in poetry; and Edwin Morgan (ibid., 97). The problem is that the standard code remains formidably fixed in place linguistically, culturally, politically, and in terms of the accepted literary canon. Leonard notes that the central authorities in English poetry and criticism virtually speak "with one voice"—and that voice doesn't come from Paterson, N.J., or Glasgow.

Nevertheless, counter-examples offer themselves if the will is strong enough. Leonard concludes his article by drawing attention to the efforts made particularly by American poets throughout the twentieth century to undermine the status quo and facilitate the emergence of "new—and multiple—voices" in poetry in English (99). And as a parting shot he brings the article back full circle to Williams's poem "The Locust Tree in Flower" by quoting it complete as an act of defiance in the face of an English that is the reason "why it had Difficulty Flowering in Britain."[22]

So how can new flowers be persuaded to flourish in the hostile soil of English English? The nonstandard voice (in this case Scottish or, more specifically, Glaswegian) needs to be encouraged, certainly: but dangers lurk in the process. In "The Voyeur" (*Intimate Voices*, 23), for instance, Leonard dramatizes the danger of trivialization of the local accent. He does this by belittling (literally, since his target is the word "wee" [small]) overuse of Scottish verbal mannerisms. Repeated obsessively fourteen times in a poem of less than a hundred words, "wee" becomes something of a linguistic joke, producing (to adapt one of his own metaphors) a kind of kitsch of the larynx. And the joke's a dangerous one, considering that it identifies the vocabulary of Scotland with small size (insignificance?)—a theme we explored earlier with reference to Sylvia Plath's work.

But, Leonard persists (tongue firmly in cheek), having your own word like that "makes you proud." Or not. The poet isn't looking for a kind of language equivalent of the tartan shortbread tin, what he describes in another poem as the "Paroakial" approach (in ibid., 40).

Such preciousness merely does the work of the powers that be, by ghettoizing the local and relegating it to the margins where it can be ignored. Yet the Scottish voice *mustn't* allow itself to be ignored, because the issues are real and serious. In an article in *Scottish International* entitled "The Proof of the Mince Pie" (in *Intimate Voices*, 65), Leonard takes up—as a way of orienting his attack on the Establishment—an Eng. Lit. question on a university exam paper which, following the conventional form of these things, instructs the hapless student to "Discuss. . . ." Leonard's comment is that discussion may take place, "but not in a Glasgow accent," certainly not if the student is intending to graduate into well-paid employment. He proceeds to lambast the academic world by claiming that the university system enshrines "the notion that culture is synonymous with property"; that ugly political ideas of privilege underlie canonical thinking; and that the implication of all this is that non-RP users may safely be relegated to "the language of the gutter" —or, if you prefer, "thi lang- / wij a thi / guhtr" (86).

In part 3 of a poem I mentioned a couple of pages ago, "Unrelated Incidents," Leonard takes as his target another Establishment organization—the BBC. Predictably his remarks focus on (received) pronunciation, and he points out how a "BBC accent" is automatically privileged as a truth-telling mechanism—the corollary implication being that (say) a Glaswegian accent is automatically considered a vehicle for lying. So if (by some extraordinary surrealist quirk of circumstances) that monument to the Bureaucracy's public information-passing, "The Six O'Clock News," were to be broadcast in Glaswegian "yi / widny thingk / it wuz troo" (88). Interestingly, and carrying on the parallels Leonard (and Crawford, and others) have drawn between Scottish regional culture and the Caribbean, the Westindian-British poet David Dabydeen makes a very similar point. In the poem "Two Cultures" in *Slave Song* (1984), Dabydeen returns to Guyana from England, bringing with him (so the locals affirm) a significant accent—"Like BBC!" or "Like white maan" (42). What's particularly interesting here is the author's note on these comments: he explains that it's become a Guyanese custom (for those people who actually own radios) to listen to the BBC World Service broadcasts, an act almost of homage to "the superiority of the White Man in matters of seriousness and truth" (71).

Leonard's decision in nearly identical cultural circumstances is clear: he chooses emphatically *not* to talk "like BBC" since the truth he's seeking is other than that purveyed by the official voice of the Establishment. The record needs to be set straight in some other way. Maybe the inhabitants of Glasgow are "Ghostie Men" (the title of one of his best-known poem sequences, in *Intimate Voices*, 103 ff.)—but if so they need to be resurrected linguistically, a task he sets about accomplishing here with great energy.

As a Scot who's suffered the colonizing impact of the dominant (phallogocentric) discourse, Leonard can complain that he's been treated "izza wummin" (that is in this case, presumably, "fucked") by the authorities, represented in the poem by

> thaht basturd therr
> niz imperialist cock
>
> (106)

As a spectator of the historical atrocities visited on his people, he can retell in his own "lang- / wij" the old nursery-rhyme dishonesties[23]—in this case concerning a Scottish Humpty Dumpty who gets "trampld" by all the king's horses and all the king's men, rather than being safely put back together again (107). What happens here, effectively, is that the official BBC version of events (which would presumably report lawful police containment of a violent demonstrator —that is, Mr. Dumpty), instead of being "thi / trooth" becomes a pack of lies, and Leonard's "guhtr" version becomes the truth. So it's clear that the State "take" on affairs may be seriously misleading, and the reportage seriously biassed—the example Leonard takes from actuality (as opposed to children's rhyme) being "ulstir fur fucks sake" (111). And his conclusion, while admitting (as everyone tells him) that his "language is disgraceful" is that

> all livin language is sacred
> fuck thi lohta thim
>
> (120)

Leonard's defiance here is exemplary, as he refuses to fade away like a ghostie man or lie down and take the linguistic (and political) mistreatment meted out by the metropolitan center south of his border. Though his language is by some standards "disgraceful," it's only so by being heavily laced with swearing; whereas the language of the dominant discourse is "disgraceful" in a more profound way, because of the ruthless privileges and abuses it conceals. Perhaps not quite as wide-ranging as Morgan's Scottish English, Leonard's is certainly concentrated and focused on the key issues, offering (compelling?) a close scrutiny of the language and culture inherited from the south. Undoubtedly, in the texts themselves, his Glaswegian dramatizes a dynamic and feisty alternative to the standard code.

If the voice generated seems somewhat rough and barbaric by the genteel standards of metropolitan English, then so be it. Being a "barbarian," in fact, becomes a key issue, particularly when we turn to Douglas Dunn's collection entitled *Barbarians* (1979). At the beginning of our study we encountered Walt Whitman's "barbaric yawp," which set the ball rolling and has been duplicated in several Anglophone cultures since then. Earlier in this chapter we saw how Irish culture may be pushed "beyond the pale" into barbarism—a circumstance noted, incidentally, by Seamus Deane in his pamphlet *Civilians and Barbarians* where he argues, so Robert Crawford tells us, that "English norms of culture and civility had meant that differing Irish phenomena were defined as barbaric," creating the "idea of a barbarian un-English identity" (*Devolving English Literature* [1992], 286). Exactly the same strategy is visible in Scotland: John Nichols's *A Sketch of the Early History of Scottish Poetry* (1871) insists, so Crawford again tells us, that "'The words used in good English composition must be classic English words. Every violation of this rule is a **Barbarism**.'" He goes on to list "'The use of provincial or slang words or expressions' as one of 'the most frequent sources of Barbarism.'" (*The Scottish Invention of English Literature*, 230). Evidently the "pale" is being redrawn somewhat along the line(s) of Hadrian's Wall, if a little farther north! Whatever the demarcations, though, the term "barbarian" is already well-used by the time it comes down to Dunn.[24] A note on the rear cover of his book takes us back to Classical Greece for the original derivation and meaning of the term, which for the Greeks was "someone who did not speak their language." We're told that in the poems Dunn is to engage the term in the modern Scottish context of "nationality and imperialism."

Clearly, as the etymology emphasizes, we're in Leonard territory again here, where cultural and political assumptions are made on the basis of language and accent. As Crawford says, the book's title "announces a commitment to people and voices excluded from the dominant culture, particularly those whose speech is in some way non-standard or 'barbarous.'" (*Devolving English Literature*, 280). Like Leonard, then, Dunn inevitably sides with the "barbarians," turning the term from an insult into a compliment: in an interview in *Verse*, conducted by Crawford (who else?) he says "I am a barbarian," and goes on to define barbarians positively as "people who contest the Establishment and the degeneration of the State."[25]

*Barbarians* itself, as David Kinloch tells us, "takes both its epigraphs from the work of the French novelist and essayist Paul Nizan, while the opening poem, "The Come-on" is prefaced by a line from Albert Camus" (in Crawford and Kinloch, *Reading Douglas Dunn*, 157). This is an interesting tactic not only because it emphasizes the fact that Dunn by his own admission is "a Francophile" (Haffenden, *Viewpoints*, 30), thus to some degree sidestepping the authority of English in the Anglo/Scottish collision, but also because it helps to distance him somewhat from that eminently xenophobic and particularly Francophobic character who had been his boss at the University of Hull's library, Philip Larkin (about whom more presently).

"The Come-on" (Dunn, *Barbarians*, 13–14) begins on a highly negative note as the poet complains that he's been forced to witness a cultural violation—"the soul of . . . [his] people / Fingered by the callous"—*fingered* presumably meaning here not just "handled," but perhaps "given the fingers," or even marked out for extinction. Smaller callousnesses grate too, as the protagonist finds himself in enemy territory surrounded by the "Black traffic of Oxbridge" that purveys its "culture of connivance," exercising an " 'authority' " (in quotation marks) that "rules us." Among this power élite are the snobs who laugh at the lifestyle of the underprivileged, and the people who "mock at your accent." The lower class and the non-RP speakers are kept in their place by this mockery—and their place is, of course, beyond the pale, unless a rare exception is made and they're allowed through the sidedoor of the Establishment (or even of the literary canon). If the tradesman's entrance to the tradition is opened, then subversion may be possible; and the poet has a cunning plan which involves turning the oppressors' weapons back on them:

> We will beat them with decorum, with manners,
>     As sly as language is.

This may not be as direct and dynamic as Leonard's plan ("fuck thi lohta thim"), but could nevertheless be effective enough. Commentators tend to see Dunn's meticulous technical control in the light of the above tactic: that is, Kinloch reports, " 'The Come-on' is written in meter because, as Dunn has said, 'the style of the book hopes to portray a gesture of affront [returning the "finger"?] to readers who might be expected to approve of a metrical way of writing, while finding the meaning of *Barbarians* disagreeable'" (in Crawford and Kinloch, *Reading Douglas Dunn*, 158).

In the next poem, though, the subterfuge falters as the disguise slips. In "In the Grounds" (*Barbarians*, 15–16) we're once more (as in "The Come-on") on the edge of territory where we don't belong, but this time we're not invited in. Glyn Maxwell says of Dunn in the poem, "Now he is not the Decent; he is a Barbarian. Like Derek Walcott, like Tony Harrison, he is well aware of what he looks like among the Legislators, the white southern anglos of then and now" (in Crawford and Kinloch, *Reading Douglas Dunn*, 61). And what he looks like is not a pretty sight: rather, he cultivates the image of "barbarians, whose chins / Drool with ale-stinking hair." It's as if Dunn is playing with a common mis-etymology of "barbarian" here, that of the word being related to the Latin "barba" or "beard," so that being barbarian was to be bearded (unkempt)—in contrast to the Roman fashion of being well-clipped (or as Dunn himself puts it in the next poem, "Rome, . . . / The home of shave and soap and manicure" ([ibid., 17]). Irrespective of coiffure, though (and one wonders what the Rastafarians would make of this derivation of "barbarian"), on this occasion the "Barbarians" are not welcome in the "garden," sly as their language may be. Somehow in these texts the (well-groomed) owners nearly always seem to be English, and the interlopers come from the other side of the pale/border.

Which brings us back to (also well-groomed) Philip Larkin, who was in charge of the Brynmor Jones Library at which Dunn was appointed (lowly) assistant in 1969. I don't wish to imply for a second that Larkin abused his power in these circumstances—and in fact Dunn never suggests any such thing, being generally very generous in his remarks on Larkin's influence. And yet the situation is an interesting one, both in its practical ramifications and in its symbolism. On his side, Dunn understandably felt (as he put it in the *Viewpoints* interview) "pissed off by being referred to as Hull's 'other poet'" (14)—particularly as he considered that "That gentlemanly verse, towards which poets like Philip Larkin and Kingsley Amis have tended, is highly regrettable" (34). As well, he was frustrated at the way Larkin ran the library schedules, and the implications this had on his own budding writing career: Jane Stabler in *Reading Douglas Dunn* says, "Larkin's attitude to the working hours of his staff was inflexible, and he proved obstructive when Dunn requested time off to give

poetry readings. Larkin had little patience for much of the new poetry that was being published, and he disapproved of the idea of informal contact with an audience" (9). Symbolically, Dunn's situation
might be read in a poem written during his time in Hull, "A Dream
of Judgement" in his first collection, *Terry Street* (1969) to which
Larkin had significant input. Ostensibly, the text deals with the relationship between (the English) Dr. Samuel Johnson and (the Scottish) James Boswell. As one might expect, a certain hierarchy pertains, in which Johnson sits imperiously (imperially?) saying "No"
while Boswell, the "small Scotsman" is busy "Licking" the great dic-
tionary-maker's "boots." But is the poem *really* about two eighteenth-
century literary figures, or is it about Larkin and Dunn?

Robert Crawford doesn't think that Larkin, specifically, enters the
frame here, seeing the poem as dramatizing more generally "the apparently unshakeable dominance of metropolitan Englishness" (*Devolving English Literature*, 280). My own feeling, though, is that while
Crawford's general reading is entirely valid, surely the poem *is* about
Larkin; or at least, surely Larkin here (re)plays the historical role of
Johnson just as Dunn (re)plays that of Boswell? The Johnson/Larkin
identity is strengthened by the reference to "saying No"—a mannerism of negativity for which Larkin and the Movement were notorious: and this suggestion is supported still further by Dunn himself
saying in *Under the Influence: Douglas Dunn on Philip Larkin* (1987), "In
the literary world Larkin had the reputation of being difficult, saying
'No' . . ." (11)—surely a significant echo of "A Dream of Judgement"?

Whether or not it's Larkin who is the gatekeeper of the tradesman's entrance to the pale, though (and the cover photograph of
*Under the Influence* might be read as further evidence here),[26] Scotland seems obliged throughout history to bow to the dictates of England. This is obviously not a state of affairs Dunn condones, but one
that he feels obliged to face up to—if only because his accent (not to
mention his beard) marks him off as "barbarian." Whether by a
Leonard-like aggression or a Dunn-ish subtlety, English needs to be
broken, but remains a redoubtable opponent. Nevertheless, a
younger generation of Scottish poets—outstanding among whom is
Robert Crawford—is prepared to take it on, nothing daunted, on a
number of fronts.

Crawford's name has already occurred several times in my text,
engaging in matters Scottish as interviewer, editor, critic, and poet

(not to mention lecturer)—all endeavors bent on moving Scotland from the periphery of the cultural map to the center, and renegotiating/re-writing the hierarchical structure conventionally existent between English and Scottish literature. As much is evident from the titles of at least two of his volumes of critical comment—*Devolving English Literature* (1992) and *The Scottish Invention of English Literature* (1998). In the former he argues that Scotland has produced "heteroglot and multicultural kinds of writing which form not a peripheral exception to but a model for international writing in the English-speaking world." Using Bakhtin's model of heteroglossia as paradigm, he continues: "if discourse is always a blend of discourses (scientific, demotic, jargons, dialect)—then like Caribbean or Australian writing, Scottish writing, in which this blending is frequently explicit, becomes typical rather than eccentric" (in *Identifying Poets: Self and Territory in Twentieth-Century Poetry* [1993], 6–7). Crawford goes on to underline his claim that "Such Scots is a form of 'dialogized heteroglossia,'" and moreover that "it affects not only Scottish but English identity, in much the same way as does the superbly impure language of James Joyce" (7). Once more we're faced with a counterstatement to the Davie assertion of (the possibility of) purity of diction in English verse. Crawford, though, chooses to challenge not the Englishman's formulation of the notion, but (as it happens) a Scot's—Edwin Muir: he argues that Muir's desire for "a 'homogeneous language'" is misconceived since it's predicated on

> ideas of monoculturalism and linguistic purity which seem unhelpful and even offensive to many people today. Was the language of Shakespeare or Joyce pure and homogeneous? . . . We know that impurity of language matters as much as purity; because in impurity lies richness, imagination, and the seeds of new growth. Homogeneity—who needs it? (ibid., 162)

One answer to that rhetorical question might be, Davie (in the 1950s, at least), Larkin and The Movement. After all, a notion of homogeneity facilitates centrist consolidation and its corollary—the marginalization or sending into exile of the "other," banishing it beyond the pale where barbarism lives. It's not for nothing that chapter 6 of *Devolving English Literature* is entitled "Barbarians": Crawford, along with Whitman and Heaney and Deane and Leonard and Dunn, is having *his* say on the issue of cultural demarcations and on which side of the line it's more healthy to be located.[27]

Crawford, that is, is in the process not only of *Devolving English Literature* but also of redrawing the cultural map—much as does his fellow-poet W. N. Herbert in the poem "Mappamundi." Herbert constructs an atlas where Ireland gets "shuftit tae London," where Seamus Heaney takes up residence (or court), and where the only other bits permitted to survive are "Oaxfurd an Hull" (in Hulse, Kennedy, and Morley, *The New Poetry*, 291). England has obviously lost its empire and lost its grip, while Heaney takes over the center and Scotland perhaps waits in the wings to be written (large). In an interview with Richard Price, Herbert offers the following opinion about Scottish poetry: "I think that we're closer to a modern line than a lot of other nations, particularly England who've thrown that away quite deliberately. . . . Surrealism, the metaphysicals—it's what Dr. Johnson didn't like so it's alright by me!" (in Crawford, et al., *Talking Verse*, 96). It seems that Boswell's fortunes may be on the upturn after all, even in the citadels of the Legislators.[28] Herbert's and Crawford's Scottish project(s) in fact gained momentum while they were in the most unlikely of places, that heartland of dictionaries and orthodoxy, the University of Oxford. While there as postgraduate students they even got themselves published in an anthology which, as Richard Price tells us, was "entitled with typical humor, *Password: SCOP*" (in Crawford, et al., *Contraflow*, vi).

Whether or not Oxford was the appropriate venue for the "scop's / twang" (or in this case, perhaps that should be "scop's / tweed"), the location certainly caused some (Scottish) amusement. W. N. Herbert, for instance, spent some time working out (successful) strategies for getting into the conservative *Oxford Poetry* against the (cultural and class) odds—a story he tells with some relish in the Price interview in *Talking Verse* (Crawford, et al., 93). At the same time, there was a serious edge to the literary sport: Robert Crawford, while enjoying the fun of it all, notes of the magazine *Verse*, which he then edited, that it was important for the resident Scottish writers to beware "being confined by an Oxonian image." To avoid this fate he promoted an "internationalism" which was a way of "outflanking . . . Anglocentrism, not to mention Oxocentrism." And, he emphasizes, the people published in the magazine were usually "'alternative' figures" (in ibid., 8).

In addition, of course, Crawford had further "alternative" designs, as part of the maneuvering against Anglo- and Oxo-centrism, for the appropriation of Eng. Lit. itself—as his later title *The Scottish Inven-*

*tion of English Literature* does more than hint. On the first page of his introduction to that book he states his unequivocal case: "English Literature as a university subject is a Scottish invention" (1).[29] Curiously enough, though, this circumstance (which he documents copiously as well in *Devolving English Literature*—a volume dedicated, incidentally, "To Scotland") didn't automatically result in a raising of the profile of *Scottish* language and literature. In fact, as Crawford says, "the university study of English literary texts" that was invented by the Scots caused "an anxious emphasis on *Anglocentric* propriety in literary standards" (*The Scottish Invention*, 225, my emphasis); and— whether for economic, political, or cultural reasons—"the subject became a site of complex negotiations, and not infrequently conflicts between native and Anglocentric pressures" (ibid., 17)—in Scotland as elsewhere.

One of the ways of avoiding such pressures, or at least of getting a wider perspective on them, is to move from nationalism to internationalism—something that Crawford signals in his comments on the magazine *Verse*. This tactic might be seen as particularly suitable in any case for the Scottish, given their wide dispersal throughout the world partly as a result of what used to be the British Empire.[30] Certainly it's evident in Crawford's collection of poems entitled *A Scottish Assembly* (1990) which, among other things, celebrates instances of the Scottish diaspora—in Canada (and the United States), India, the West Indies, Australia, New Zealand, and so on. In the poem "Honeymoon" (16), Crawford even associates the most intimate moments of his private life with the global dispersal of his race:

> Let's be like Allan Murchie of Dunfermline
> Transported to Australia for wanting a Scottish republic. . . .

Here the anecdote (one of many Scottish tales in the book) tells of survival, resilience, persistence, independence—admirable qualities (not always associated with honeymoons) to complement the central datum of the poet's love. In fact, the whole volume is a kind of consciousness-raising exercise for Scotland (and for Crawford and his wife as part of that consciousness) in the international arena. In the poems "The Dalswinton Enlightenment" (21), and "Henry Bell Introduces Europe's First Commercial Steamship" (21) Crawford pays tribute to Scotland's pioneer inventors, and to the technology and heavy industry (especially maritime and railway construction) that it fostered.

This heritage represents a Scottish ideal that goes beyond the merely mechanical, creating what Douglas Dunn in his *Viewpoints* interview described as "that Clydeside mythology." Dunn tells us that this mythology "means a lot to me in terms of my imagination and I associate it with my own notional craftsmanship—'Clyde-built.'" (Haffenden, 25) As well as creating a tangible machine as end product, this ethos constructs in effect a linguistic mechanism, a Scottish "voice," that is "articulated" (like the "churning paddles" of Patrick Miller's newly invented steamship on the loch in Crawford's poem) "In triumphant meter." Moreover, this voice articulates both a literary vocabulary, and a technical one of "rivet" and axis and other engineering terms—just as Walt Whitman had predicted it would in emergent new-world America.

Perhaps not surprisingly, a *political* element is evident here too: so Henry Bell's "dream" of a steamship becomes not just realized in fact, but "Democratised by Watt's technology." That is, the miracle is available to everybody, not just to a privileged élite; and it *is* a kind of miracle—harnessing natural elemental forces (fire, air, water) transformed into a new magical power. Interestingly, for the boyhood Crawford (on the evidence of the poems in *A Scottish Assembly* an enthusiast of both model and full-scale railways), the combination of artistic magic and technological expertise was learned literally at his mother's feet, as we discover in the opening poem, "Opera" (9). The boy sits on the floor while she makes his new clothes on the "SINGER" sewing machine that—Crawford says—was her typewriter, just as the garments were "her songs." Looking through the eye [I] of the machine's "needle," the poet sees *himself* stitched into these songs, made part of a Scottish oral folk tradition—not traditionally popular in canonical English circles, perhaps, but nevertheless a doughty tool. So the modern "SINGER" brand name becomes related to the linguistic power of the ancient singer or bard or "SCOP."

The combination of down-to-earth pragmatism and something magical here (like language itself?) is a theme Crawford returns to regularly in the volume. One particularly suitable Scottish hero in this regard is the inventor of TV, celebrated in the poem "John Logie Baird" (23) and in "Man of Vision" (24). In the latter, based on a painting of Baird by Stephen Conroy, tele*vision* becomes a different vision at the end—mythic, magic, visionary, almost god-like (in spite of being anchored down to brute reality by "basic integers"). This seems to me to be (again) metaphoric of the poet's relationship to language.

The concentration on language that we saw in Leonard's poetry and polemic may not be quite as overtly evident in Crawford's work, perhaps—and yet it's fundamental just the same. Richard Price has noted that Informationist writing (with which Crawford has been associated, along with W. N. Herbert and David Kinloch) uses "linguistic scrutiny as a means of making poetry" (in Crawford, et al., *Contraflow*, x). This relates the Informationists to the American L=A=N=G=U=A=G=E poets, though—Herbert suggests (as quoted in *The New Poetry*, 20)—the label "S=C=O=T=S" might be more appropriate here given the nationalistically independent nature of the undertaking.

The traditional technologies and language to which Crawford pays homage in *A Scottish Assembly* get updated and combined with the information technologies that are now becoming such key elements in all our lives. One is perhaps reminded here of the technical (and technological) variousness of the work of Crawford's immediate forebear, Edwin Morgan. Crawford himself speaks of Morgan's sequences "Interferences" and "Unfinished Poems" where "language crashes like a computer, veers off-course into the alien, or suddenly dies into silence" (in Crawford and Whyte, *About Edwin Morgan*, 21). Certainly Morgan was one of the first "writers" (in Scotland or anywhere else) to see and exploit the phenomenon of the language-machine/word processor—a combination of American- and Japanese-generated technology that to some degree perhaps transcends the hegemony of English.

From a younger-generation perspective, Crawford offers us (in *A Scottish Assembly*, 42), an Informationist view of how Scotland fits into this picture. In a manner of which Walt Whitman would again have approved, he presents us with a new ("unpoetic") vocabulary for a new situation. Scotland becomes "Semiconductor country," its conurbations "superlattices, heterojunctive." The landscape is still recognizably Scottish (even down to the inevitable "tweed"), but worn now with a difference, made strange by an *other* language (of information technology).

And there's a new advantage in the changed dispensation. Conventionally, since size is power, Scotland has been the small and poor neighbor in the "United" Kingdom; but the microchip revolution has transformed the conventions, so that something small can be very powerful. If Scotland remains a "micro-nation," then all well and good, since that doesn't imply that it's weak or "small-minded." In fact, in a way somewhat reminiscent of Dr. Who's phone booth, what appears small may turn out on entry to be enormous (both physically and symbolically)—"boundless," as Crawford puts it, in spite of appearing only a "chip" of a country.

The attempt to use new technologies (of a much lighter kind than the traditional Clydeside ones) to liberate the poet and create a new language constitutes an interesting experiment. It's true that in *A Scottish Assembly* it plays against a more traditional backdrop, against the odds of a Scotland plundered and bereft. And yet in spite of the fact that an artist can be "Denounced from the pulpit" for playing Gaelic songs (34); in spite of the local language in "the Museum of Ethnology" (39) being "odd, undeciphered, quite alone"; in spite of Scotland being symbolically "in hock," with everything in "Edinburgh" (44) having a "pawnticket" attached to it in the fond hope of future "redemption"; in spite of being commoditized and consumed by the postcolonial tourist industry (in "The Land o' Cakes," 61)—still, there's some hope of "redemption" (in a nonpawnbroker-sense).

The hope lies, as we've seen in other contexts throughout this study, in *re*-viewing and *re*-writing, remaining (like "Allan Murchie of Dunfermline") focused but flexible. The re-writing of Scotland is released at least to some extent from the historical bind of the relationship with the tyrant (and tyrannical language) south of the border—not only by a new technology and vocabulary, but also by political maneuvering as the possibility of devolution and an actual Scottish National Assembly becomes more real. In *his* (culturo-political) version of *A Scottish Assembly* Crawford's voice joins the wide-ranging assembly of selected literary Scottish elders—(for instance) Sir James Frazer, R. L. Stevenson, James Murray (of *OED* fame) and J. M. Barrie (all appearing in a single poem, "Scotland in the 1890s" [22]). As well, the assembly he calls up in the volume includes—as we've seen—technological pioneers of Scotland's past, and looks forward to the new technologies available to the artist in the future. His own language is not just that of the poet's "meter," but as well the voice of the steamships and railways, the pragmatic nuts and bolts of an earlier Scottish heritage leading into the vision of Scotland taking its place in the new (internationalist) dispensation as the "chip" of a "micro-nation."

Ever an enthusiast of the notion of dialogism, Crawford in the epigraph to his collection *Talkies* (1992) quotes Bakhtin's dictum, "one's own language is never a single language" (9)—an idea that certainly applies to Crawford himself, and to Scotland more generally. The fact that in *A Scottish Assembly* he chooses to "assemble" two language-machines[31] entitled "Scotland" (one [on 41] a conventional lyric of "Intimate grasses [that] blur with August rain"; the other [on 42] an exposition of "Semiconductor country," explored above) is symptomatic of his heteroglossic approach to the reality he dramatizes in his texts. It's symptomatic too, as he points out in *Devolving English Literature,* of "the growth of L=A=N=G=U=A=G=E writing," which exhibits "an eclecticism of registers and textures that constantly draws attention to the materiality of language" (271).

꩜     ꩜     ꩜     ꩜     ꩜

As we've seen in this chapter, in the case of both Irish and Scottish "Englishes," a variety of "registers and textures" is formulated to deny the orthodoxies of the standard code—to break English, if you will. This effort may put the non-English writer beyond the pale, but that location can be interrogated and perhaps turned to good account. Robert Crawford, for instance, argues that (in spite of "the continuing strength of London metropolitan publishing houses and journals" and of the continued promotion of "Anglocentric literary history") "it is surely true that, for most creative users of the English language today, one of the fundamental questions is how to inhabit that language without sacrificing one's own, distinctive, 'barbarian' identity" (*Devolving English Literature,* 300).

Sean O'Brien echoes Crawford's notion of devolution in the title of his collection of essays, *The Deregulated Muse* (1998). Obviously both devolution and deregulation constitute attacks on the metropolitan or standard code from what's conventionally regarded as the periphery (whether that be the Caribbean, Ireland, Scotland, or anywhere else). In an essay subtitled "*Scotland! Scotland! Actual/Virtual,*" O'Brien notes (by quoting Herbert) that "Scots is a language capable of doing more than English, capable of doing something different from English that criticizes and, ultimately, extends English" (268). Precisely what this "more" and "different" entails (as we've seen in this chapter) is a subject of some debate, the more militant writers (such as Leonard) mounting full-frontal attacks, while the more accommodating (such as Heaney or Morgan) are prepared to be subtler. O'Brien, writing of the various possibilities in current Scottish poetry, particularly as regards the debate on whether or not it's desirable and necessary to invent and write a kind of "Scots," says (with a tinge of Anglocentric envy): "Out of and alongside such arguments, which are those of democrats rather than reactionary nationalists of the English sort, a multi-vocal nation makes a memorable contemporary poetry. England could do with such clarifying problems" (269). In our final chapter we may see some such "clarification" in the English camp. Before that, though, I want to turn to the example of Australia, as representative of literary "breakings" of English in a former British colony; so perhaps it's appropriate to close here with reference to an eminent literary *Australian*'s ideas on "English" (albeit mediated through the words of Robert Crawford)—Les Murray. In an interview with Crawford, Murray complained that the whole label of "English Literature" is unacceptably ambiguous, saying that "'English' ought to mean either exclusively *English,* or else work from the *whole* English-speaking world" (in *Devolving English Literature,* 302). Crawford's own comments on this stance, as a marginalized-culture fellow-traveller, are as follows: "Murray's unhappiness with the word 'English' here is the unhappiness of the non-English writer too easily kidnapped by the world of the metropolitan centres through the use of a term which may mean simply anglophone or anglographic, but which may also slip into an imperial Anglocentricity." Obviously, in postimperial Australia (not to mention postimperial Scotland), such a situation is unacceptable and needs to be changed.

# 6

## Colony/Dominion: Writing Back

Up to this point, our discussion—while ranging quite widely through the domain of poetries in English—has centered mainly on England. This is perhaps not surprising, since the fundamental cultural assumptions which we've been scrutinizing tend to originate from there: in a sense, England is seen and (like it or not) certainly sees itself, as the center—and nowhere has this been more evident traditionally than in the various colonies that formed the British Commonwealth. Before concluding this survey, therefore, it seems to me appropriate to engage with the contemporary poetry in English originating from at least one such "colony." My choice here is Australia, though my remarks would apply equally to several parts of the once British Empire: all are involved in the ongoing process of "breaking English," of literary and linguistic counterattack, as is suggested by the title of one of the seminal theoretical volumes in the area, *The Empire Writes Back*.[1]

The book's authors use as their starting point the historical phenomenon of British imperialism, which (they argue) is responsible for disseminating the English language geographically around the world—a dissemination assisted toward the end of the nineteenth century not only (as we've already seen) by the normative authority of the *Oxford English Dictionary*, but as well by trends in the British education system that was being imported into colonial countries as part of the colonizing dominant discourse. One negative aspect of this situation, as Ashcroft *et al* tell us, was that "A 'privileging norm'" was established whereby "the 'peripheral', the 'marginal', the 'uncanonized'" (3) were totally deprivileged—a template that was to prove remarkably durable, lasting at least until the Movement era of purity of diction in the 1950s and 1960s. Gauri Viswanathan (writing

196

about the situation in the Indian subcontinent) argues that Eng. Lit. actually became an overt political tool in the colonizing enterprise, being used as a way of "maintaining control of the natives under the guise of a liberal education" (quoted in *The Empire Writes Back*, 3).

However, as history tells us with monotonous regularity, nothing (including oppression) lasts quite forever; and even as the Movement literary imperium was marshaling its forces in one direction in the sphere of English poetry, elsewhere in another direction altogether other kinds of forces were causing a final disruption to Empire—Kenyatta's Mau Mau in Kenya; Grivas's EOKA in Cyprus; and perhaps most striking of all, Nasser's national movement in Egypt. And where Larkin and Amis may have tried to ignore the direction of the tide, desperately crying "stet" from Mr. Bleaney's high window, the (then) young Peter Reading, in his poem sequence "Stet" could see that something was up, even if not sure exactly what:

> I read the headlines **Suez** and **Crisis Point**—
>> crikey! I thought, there must be something
>> terribly wrong with the nation's toilets;
>
> soon if the Government didn't act there'd be all kinds of nasties
>> gushing up out of the drains, Britain would be [is] engulfed.
>>>                              (*Stet* [1986], n. p.)

In spite of the awful (but significant) pun here, the main problem for the conservative forces in Britain wishing for things to stay the same ("stet"), wasn't really the *plumbing*—though that might be a suitably messy metaphor for the increasingly leaky empire as colonies grew towards independence. The problem was adjustment to the dismantling of the English hegemony in what the editors of Bloodaxe's *The New Poetry* tag as "post-imperial Britain," involving the "hard, slow dying" of "the old British superiority complex" (Hulse, Kennedy, and Morley, 16). Such an adjustment needed to be made not only in the arena of global politics, with the admission that Britannia may no longer rule the waves (particularly as those became the *air*waves of rapid mass communication); but as well culturally and linguistically, with the admission that English may no longer mean a single indivisible thing, purified by the dictionary and sanctified by the University of Oxford.

So it will be necessary, as Ashcroft, Griffiths, and Tiffin suggest, to make a distinction between the one-time imperial standard code of

English (with a capital "E") and "the linguistic code, english [with a lower-case 'e'], which has been transformed and subverted into several distinctive varieties throughout the world" (8). My own feeling is that one might go *further* than this, totally refusing the implicit hierarchical superiority of *E*nglish by denying it a capital (Capital/ metropolitan) letter altogether and simply making it one of a series of possible englishes, all equally lowercase with noncapital letters, thus effectively dismantling any notion of hierarchy in favor of a postmodern multiplicity.[2]

The two-fold mechanism by which this dismantling, or decolonization, may take place is outlined in *The Empire Writes Back* (38 ff): it consists of what are known as *abrogation* and *appropriation*. The first stage, abrogation, is "a refusal of the categories of the imperial culture, its aesthetic, its illusory standard of normative or 'correct' usage, and its assumption of a traditional and fixed meaning 'inscribed' in the words" (41). This amounts, then, to a denial of the possibility of purity in English—a denial that needn't be seen in a particularly negative light, however, since it may result in what C. D. Narasimhaiah describes as "a fascinating combination of tongues" (quoted in *The Empire Writes Back*, 40).

The second phase in the process, appropriation, involves adapting the colonizing discourse so that it may be "utilized in various ways to express widely differing cultural experiences" (ibid., 38–39). Hopefully, what will thus be produced is "a world language called english [which] is a continuum of 'intersections' in which the speaking habits in various communities have intervened to reconstruct the language" (39–40).

Rejection of imperial notions of an exclusive and monocultural dominant discourse, by cutting English free from its colonizing history, then, is to be followed by an act of reclaiming the language for use in the postcolonial multicultural context. The monoglossic is transformed into the diglossic or even polyglossic, with an emphasis on the *crosscultural* character of the linguistic medium, and on the dynamics of language *change* (as opposed to imprisonment in origins, dictionary definitions, and derivations). In order to achieve this "Re-placing" of English, a number of tactics is available, ranging from the use of special rhythms considered to embody or evoke a particular culture (as we saw earlier, in the work of the Dub poets); the glossing of certain words to emphasize the process of language variation and construction in the text (as we saw in Heaney's poetry);

the transcription of local dialect forms and vernacular (in both monoglossic and polyglossic texts); the use of untranslated words to convey a sense of cultural distinctiveness; the use of code-switching, interlanguages, and syntactic fusion; and the creation of neologisms.[3]

Many of these strategies apply more obviously to the work of indigenous peoples who have historically been the overt victims of colonization and have had their own native language(s) threatened by the imposition of Received Standard English, either through total suppression or by progressive assimilation of their cultural and linguistic otherness. But, as we saw much earlier with the case of nineteenth-century America, even writers whose main (or only) language is English may be subject to (and even subjects of) the dominant metropolitan discourse: as Walt Whitman realized, a cultural declaration of independence was required in addition to a political one. Exactly the same was true of settler writers in Australia (and elsewhere); and in fact Whitman himself was to provide the role model for a key literary figure in Australia around the time of *its* first political assertion of independence or separateness (the act of Federation in 1901), Bernard O'Dowd. O'Dowd, following Whitman's strong advocacy of a democratic model far more egalitarian than the English-style class-based system, saw in the New World of America—which had already asserted its right not to be an inferior adjunct of the Old World—a suitable paradigm for emergent Australia. Here was the possibility of breaking with "the categories of the imperial culture" as required by the process of abrogation (Ashcroft, Griffiths, and Tiffin, *The Empire Writes Back*, 38). Perhaps the "barbaric yawp" would work "down under" as well as across the Atlantic, particularly since the linguistic vehicle—"English"—was shared by America and (settler) Australia, offering the possibility of a joint subversion of that other language "sharer," the metropolitan center, England. The situation seems to be that suggested by Ashcroft, Griffiths, and Tiffin, when they speak about a writing which "abrogates the privileged centrality of 'English' by using language to signify difference while employing a sameness which allows it to be understood" (51). Certainly, O'Dowd's suggested adoption of an American-style democracy as political paradigm, and of Whitman as culture hero, represented a significant shift in allegiance for Australia, which, at least throughout the first two-thirds of the nineteenth century, had (inevitably) sought its role models from the colonial center, England.

Up to this point, in terms of poetry, a slavish imitation of English late-Romantic nature poetry was fairly much the norm in Australia, even though such a tactic was apt to cause something of an embarrassment to local writers as they struggled to make the inherited northern hemisphere template fit the southern hemisphere experience. Most obvious (and awkward) was the "reversal" of the natural seasons, with summer when winter "should be," and vice versa. As well, there was the strange collection of antipodean flora and fauna to be dealt with (Henry Kendall at one stage actually rhyming "Australian" with "alien" as an indicator of cultural discomfort). One method employed to defuse the alienness of the environment was to "tame" it by using English terms such as "wold" and "brook" to label it poetically; or—failing that—humor might be used to alleviate the threat of an all too apparent otherness by mocking it.[4] But O'Dowd wished to have nothing to do with any of this. He wasn't content to copy the English, and in fact wanted to write a different kind of world—one not only new, but *Whitmanesque.* In a series of lecture notes, the manuscript of which is held in the State Library of Victoria in O'Dowd's home town of Melbourne, he asserts parallels between the American and Australian situation(s)—including their relative "newness," political constitution, ancestry, environment, and so on. So, for budding Australian poets, rather than following "the guidebooks of Europe or Asia" for clues on how they should conduct themselves, instead they should seek guidance from "the author of *Leaves of Grass.*" In particular O'Dowd suggests two of Whitman's poems— the "Song of the Answerer," and "By Blue Ontario's Shore"—the second of which he describes as "a veritable Declaration of Literary Independence." And if Australia needs to indulge in translation to bolster its culture (as it has done to this point in time), rather than targeting the European classics, it would be better to "set to work to translate these two poems into Australian."[5]

This seemingly unusual notion of translating from English into English, of course, has meaning as soon as the term "English" is dismantled as a standardized category and transformed into a multiplicity of englishes. For O'Dowd and his compatriates the process will involve the necessity to "absorb his country as affectionately and as thoroughly as Walt absorbed America; he must look at it through Australian eyes, and not through feudal . . . eyes, and he must write its national spirit into being" (in McLeod, *Whitman in Australia,* 141).

The "feudal" reference here is one of O'Dowd's favorites in his lectures, and almost certainly comes (again) from Whitman. In a lecture given in Melbourne in early 1899, and entitled "Walt Whitman: his Meaning to Victorians—Democracy v. Feudalism," O'Dowd promotes "Whitman's spirit" as an inspiration for future Australians, particularly in the face of an inherited (colonial) Old World dispensation and its attendant dangers:

> The institutions of England, the literature of England, the laws of England, the customs of England, are . . . so steep[ed] in feudalism, so founded on feudalism, so diverted from their true natures and purposes by feudalism, that they are dangerous for a Democratic, that is, anti-feudal people like the Australians to adopt in wholesale fashion.[6]

Much of the politico-cultural material in O'Dowd's lectures and notes comes from Whitman's various prose works (which we examined briefly in the introductory chapter), and particularly the preface to *Leaves of Grass*, which he valued very highly. On 16 September 1896, he delivered a lecture on it to the Australian Church Literary Society in Melbourne, describing it as "a land-mark in literature," seen by some as "the greatest preface ever written." He argues that "This great 'Preface,' voicing the demand of modern Democracy for an adequate means of expression, . . . says plainly that the old forms of poetry, good as they may have been in their day . . . are utterly incapable, on account of their limitations and shoddy ideas, of holding the hot pregeny of Democracy" (McLeod, *Whitman in Australia*, 96).

O'Dowd describes Whitman as a kind of New World culture hero—a literary Kepler or Kant, and even as a poetic precursor of Darwin's *Origin of Species* and of "the theory of evolution itself" (in McLeod, *Whitman in Australia*, 139, 137). At one point he goes as far as to call him (more poetically) "a Columbus of new continents of the soul" (ibid., 142). By raising Whitman's profile in Australia in such comments, O'Dowd was essentially establishing a platform for a different "English" from that imitated and imported from the metropolitan center, a newer, more democratic discourse as a vehicle to affirm growing independence from the colonial origin. As A. L. McLeod tells us, as part of this project, by 1890 O'Dowd had become "the mainstay of The Australeum, a small organization—. . . established after the pattern of the American chautauquas and lyceums so popular at the time—which brought together a group of people interested in social, literary, political, and economic affairs" (ibid., 11). In addition, O'Dowd belonged to the "Australian Natives Association," an organization dedicated to dismantling the nation's colonial character and achieving independence. He lectured regularly to this body, almost always on the subject of Walt Whitman. O'-Dowd's authority for these addresses came—as well as from a great familiarity with the original texts—to some degree from the correspondence he shared with Whitman during the last few years of the "Good Gray Poet"'s life. This correspondence has been enshrined in the periodical *Overland* of Autumn 1962 (8–18), and subsequently in A. L. McLeod's *Walt Whitman in Australia and New Zealand* (18–39). Unfortunately, Whitman's end of the dialogue seems to consist mainly of reciting his dinner menues, and of anxious inquiries about photographs of himself entrusted to the tender mercies of the international mail system; while O'Dowd replies with a rhetoric of effusiveness excessive even by his own standards ("Dear Walt, my beloved master, my friend, my bard my prophet and apostle . . . ").[7] Even so, there can be no doubt that the living legend of literary Democracy, albeit in serious physical decline by this time, was a genuine role model and inspiration for writers of similar philosophical and political persuasion in Australia. An indication of O'Dowd's commitment to the cause is his pledge to Whitman that "we will fight tooth & nail for you as long as we live" (though in quite which battle isn't entirely clear).[8] In token of this allegiance, O'Dowd is reputed to have taken "to wearing a piece of grass in his buttonhole as a symbol of loyalty to the *Leaves of Grass*";[9] and in an even more symbolic gesture, he decided to name his firstborn son Eric Whitman O'Dowd in honor of the American poet.[10]

All in all, the correspondence between the two poets (at least the remnant that has so far emerged) is rather disappointing. But when one turns to O'Dowd's own ventures into Whitmanesque prose, the power of the influence of the American is evident; and O'Dowd's pamphlet, *Poetry Militant* certainly shows him as one of Whitman's "soldiers," totally involved in fighting the good (verbal) fight for Democracy. *Poetry Militant: an Australian Plea for the Poetry of Purpose* was published in Melbourne by T. C. Lothian in 1909, almost twenty years after Whitman's death—but the spirit obviously lived on. Striking rhetorical poses remarkably reminiscent of his American mentor, O'Dowd writes, "It is Poetry Militant I preach" (12), and the mode is indeed preacherly or sermonic. Central to the "lesson" is the scrutiny of an undeclared but ongoing war—not exactly between evil and good, but (something similar) between the old order and the new. O'Dowd's initial diagnosis is scarcely optimistic: he sees the poet struggling in "a community hypnotised by commercialism" and seduced by "the guiding motif of . . . 'Pleasure for Pleasure's sake'" (8). In such an environment, tainted by European Aestheticism, lacking originality or a significant sense of specific place, "We chop the logs of yesteryear into regulation ballade lengths, and pile them before the throne of the Prince of Nowhere-in-Particular" (14)—a "throne," of course, reminding us of the hierarchical monarchies of the old world that are anathema to the democratic inclinations of the new. Here, and throughout *Poetry Militant* (as throughout much of Whitman's prose polemics), politics and literature become inextricably intertwined in a far-from-Aestheticist manner. Going onto the attack, O'Dowd asserts that, rather than look back to "yesteryear" the poet must be willing "to dare to express a new thought, or frame a new form," refusing to allow "the infant Past to govern the growth of the adolescent Present and the adult Future" (11).

The past, in a reversal of the usual paradigm, may be "infant," but it still has great power. Speaking of what he labels "the classical," O'Dowd warns us that "The evil of the classical consists in this, that in some hands it is an attempt to put twentieth century wine into first century bottles" (19); and he goes on to say that "the trend of the classical is towards rigidity, the beaten track" (20), leading us ineluctably into "the truculent, narcotizing and despotic past" (27). For the old world (including England) this may be acceptable; but Australia must march to a different imperative—towards the "adult Future," a future seemingly guaranteed by the (relatively) new rhetoric of scientific discourse. Like Whitman, O'Dowd is fond of incorporating new technical terms into his "English," speaking of the poet (in eminently anti-Aesthetic style) as "the projector of cell-forming ideals into the protoplasmic future"; and as "a living catalyst in the intellectual laboratory" at a time when our world view is being transformed by the light "of Evolution theories" (15–16).

This mention of evolution underlines the fact that the essence of O'Dowd's argument here (again like Whitman's, as we saw in the first chapter) is *cultural Darwinism*—the evolutionary process of natural selection applied to whole cultures, and the survival of the fittest (the new worlds of America and Australia) as the old world (principally, in these cases, England) slides down the entropic spiral. Using a favorite metaphor (which had helped to provide him with the title of his first book of poems, *Dawnward?*), O'Dowd sees local poets bathed in the light of a new day; he exclaims:

> The fact of evolution and the fact of Australia make Australian poets, if they will, essentially poets of the dawn—poets whose function is to chart the day and make it habitable—marching poets, working poets, poets for use, poets militant. . . . [T]his is the dawn of a new world—a newer, stranger, vista widens before us, since Darwin's great message reached us. . . . (17)

Standing in the way of the business of "chart[ing] the day" (a literary and cultural process somewhat akin to the physical pioneering work of geographical exploration and the mapping of the continent), are language-users squandering their breath (and textual space) in mere outmoded imitation and decoration: O'Dowd tells us with regret of "The misdirected energies of too many modern versewriters . . . being wasted in making crazy quilts out of pretty words" (15). Under these circumstances, the "Poet Militant" must act as a kind of detective agency for language crimes, a "Scotland Yard" whose duty is "the detection and unveiling of frauds that conceal . . . [the poet] from himself" (37).

Vigilance is necessary not only because "Such frauds are so subtle that we sometimes build codes of morality upon them, and buttress thrones, laws and religions by means of them" but because the problem is rife, "our language [being] . . . so infected with the glamour-producing vocabularies of the frauds" (37). As part of this process, even the great canonical writers may need to be rejected, though that might seem like "blasphemy, immorality" (38): one remembers that O'Dowd's model, Whitman (in the essay-review entitled "An English and an American Poet"), had harsh words to say about the highest god of all in the pantheon, Shakespeare.[11]

On the other side of the ledger (or parade ground) we have the roll call of the *non*-fraudulent (new, democratic, forward-looking) vocabulary users—O'Dowd himself (by implication at least); then "Walt Whitman, Henrik Ibsen, and . . . John Davidson" (41); and, later, "the two greatest poets of this age of the Evolution Dawn" (in spite of the fact that one isn't literally a poet) "Walt Whitman and Frederick Nietzsche" (49). Not only does Whitman get *two* honorable mentions in the ranks of the culture heroes; it is with *his* words that O'Dowd chooses to end his treatise, with the following homage:

I cannot better conclude this plea for the formative poet, and for poetry militant, than by quoting a passage, which, but for my own deficiencies, would summarise my case, from Walt Whitman's "The Answerer"—

The words of the true poems give you more than poems,
They give you to form for yourself poems, religions, politics, war, peace. . . .
                                                                        (54–55)[12]

Given O'Dowd's strong advocacy of an evolutionary cultural attitude, and his admiration (and importation) of that great poetic pioneer of free verse, Walt Whitman, one might reasonably expect his "true poems" to be radically experimental and varied in form; but this is not ostensibly the case at all. True, he adopted (and adapted) his own version of a form unconventional (unfashionable, and certainly unpopular) at the time—the Anglo-Saxon "fourteener"—but his dogged persistence with it rapidly achieved a degree of rigidity and uniformity which made the "fraudulent" imitations of his contemporaries seem downright sprightly and energetic by comparison. So, when he writes rhetorically at the conclusion of *Poetry Militant* of his "own deficiencies" in poetry, we should take him with deadly seriousness. It's not my purpose here, though, to demolish him aesthetically: this has anyway already been done with sharp efficiency by Judith Wright in her *Preoccupations in Australian Poetry*.[13] Rather, I wish to attempt a reading of a couple of O'Dowd's key poetic texts in the light of the lectures and essays we've already reviewed above, in an effort to show that, external appearances to the contrary, he *did* attempt a new "English" in Australia to break the old "English" imitated and established by the Australian poetic "language frauds" of his day.

The initial exhibit, almost inevitably, is the celebrated sonnet "Australia," which was the opening poem of O'Dowd's first collection, *Dawnward?* (a volume dedicated "To Young Democracy");[14] and was of significant historical note in being winner of *The Bulletin*'s prize for a poem commemorating Federation. Hugh Anderson in his book *The Poet Militant: Bernard O'Dowd* says of the volume as a whole that it "brought bright new words and fresh imagery to the timid conservatism of Australian poetry," yet as well clung onto an "old-fashioned . . . rhetorical tone and [the use] of outmoded 'poetic' words" (84). Something of this ambiguity, or what I'd prefer to call "doubleness," is certainly noticeable in the poem "Australia." It follows the traditional (English) sonnet form of octet and sestet, rhyming abba, abba, cde, cde, and (in keeping with the question mark in the title of the volume as a whole) it formally ponders the future fate of Australia—bright new world or merely old world repeated; guiding light of a new civilization or merely deceptive hallucination; millennial Eden or earthly hell? This may all be highly significant; but what I personally find particularly interesting in the current context is the way that the octet and sestet subdivide the poetic material into two different referential systems (or discourses). That is, the first eight lines are loaded with old world allusions—to biblical phenomena such as Eden and characters such as Mammon; to Greek Classical referents such as Delos and Apollo (the "Sun-God"), and Greek words such as "halcyon"; to Latin vocabulary such as "millennial" and "demesne" (via Old French). By contrast, the last six lines of "Australia" refer to the distinctive fauna (and flora) of the Great Southern Land, to lyrebirds, and to the Southern Cross, that marker of Australasian identity on the flags and consciousnesses of Australia and New Zealand.

What I'm suggesting here is that the poem functions as a site of hybridity, at a junction between the old world and the new. It would no doubt be overstating the case to describe it as diglossic; but it certainly articulates the cultural moment when one system of authenticity comes into contact with what the authors of *The Empire Writes Back* describe as an "alternative authenticity." If O'Dowd's notion of denying the language frauds corresponds to the first step in the process of "writing back"—that of "abrogation"—then "Australia" represents the very start (historically and otherwise) of the second step, that of appropriation. The same might be said, too, of the other O'Dowdian poetic text I wish to engage, his "The Bush" of 1912.[15]

"The Bush," as well as being much longer than "Australia" (over twenty pages as opposed to a single one), is more complex in its strategy of appropriation. Like "Australia," it retains the hybridity of reference to the local (and democratic) collocated with reference to the classical (and feudal); but it goes further. That is, as well as restating or re-enacting the relationship between colonial and national authenticities, the poem seeks to assimilate and transform an established and independent local genre (echoed in the poem's title) that had grown up in the years preceding Federation—the bush ballad. The phenomenon of the bush ballad in Australia is interesting because, although clearly part of the Anglo-Celtic settler culture (particularly the "Celtic" component therein), it was related neither to the canonically respectable area of traditional Eng. Lit., nor to the popular inherited late-Victorian "Art for Art's Sake" Aesthetic movement about which O'Dowd was so disparaging. In a sense, then, bush ballads are part of what would be perceived by the metropolitan center in a colonial era as a marginal culture, and might themselves be considered as an early Australian manifestation of the desire to "break English" with their colloquial diction, their use of local slangs and Aboriginal words, and their frequent mockery of traditional English values and mannerisms.[16] O'Dowd's treatment of the "bush"—that archetypal Australian setting—seeks to accommodate the work of his local literary forebears (several of whom are specifically named in "The Bush"), and to extend it in significance.

This extension involves the realm of the mythical, even epic. In most treatments in Australian ballads and tales, the bush features primarily as a landscape and a backdrop, providing literal local color for a simple narrative action. It occasionally serves a metaphorical or allegorical function, but only in the most basic and limited way. In keeping with the generally unpretentious air of the genre, the scale is most often kept small, and the referents simple, even humble, recording and (modestly) celebrating the everyday in an almost documentary manner—albeit with an inordinately large number of dogs and horses! But O'Dowd's approach is different: as Walter Murdoch says in the introduction to *The Poems of Bernard O'Dowd*, his treatment "struck a note not heard before in the Australian chorus," avoiding "action" and "the race-course," and aspiring to higher significance. Like the settler bush balladeers, he was "weary . . . of the second-hand poetic ornaments of England" (vi), but at the same time didn't wish to limit himself to the locale of the billabong.

Instead he saw the bush (as he suggested in the opening stanza of the poem itself) as a mystico-spiritual "matrix" on which the new Australia might be inscribed, a "mystery" in which "Tangible Presences of Deathless Things" may suddenly appear (187). Scarcely a wombat breaks the horizon of his landscape; and instead of clearly drawn local scenery, vividly seen and realized, we're presented with the bush as cultural potential, as text waiting to be written—silent and void yet somehow pregnant with spiritual possibility, at this stage of the project a statement waiting to be stated. The text O'Dowd has actually written here is articulated in a high rhetoric appropriate to an epic purpose, and very different from the driving down-to-earth diction of the bush ballads—a rhetoric, one might add, that made him the butt of many a critical jibe.[17] At times, admittedly, the high-falutin tone, and the cultural collocations he attempts, become risible—as when (in a famous example) he writes of "Homers . . . waiting in the gum trees now" (199); but if the results are sometimes absurd, the undertaking itself isn't necessarily so.

Taking on the role of bush raconteur, but raising it to a new dimension—the realm of "Deathless Things"—O'Dowd sets out to retell the story of (settler) Australia, rewriting it in an epic context. He *re-places* it with reference to traditional heroic stories (such as the "Troy tales" in the *Iliad*) so that it becomes not a marginal late addition to the master narratives of the past, but an equal partner, since "Australia is the whole world's legatee" (204). Consequently the cultural strictures put in place by the powers of the old world cease to pertain, as O'Dowd suggests with his rhetorical questions, "Who fenced the nymphs in European vales? / Or Pan tabooed from all but Oxford dreams?" (205). Henceforth, the "drover's tale of love" (and there are several available in the archive of nineteenth-century Australian bush stories) may stand beside that of "Isolde . . . [and] Tristram" or that of "Launcelot . . . [and] golden Guinevere" (188).

Finding the dictions currently available to him inadequate to tell this story, O'Dowd attempts to put together a suitable language that will simultanously reflect the historical and global ("Ilium," the "Minoan," the "Sumerian," "Chaldea," the "Viking," the "Hindoo," "Druids") and the immediately local ("Alcheringa," "she-oak," "bunyip," "squatter," "the Never Never"). The center of the textual time and place, though, to which all is drawn, and which is named and repeated throughout, is *Australia* ("Austral," "Australia," or "Australian" recurring ten times in the text). However, the act of re-placing the continent can cause disorientation as well as reorientation, so that the poet has to ask, "Where is Australia, singer, do you know?" (208). The somewhat unexpected answer (which we've actually been given a few pages earlier) is that Australia is "not yet" (197). As O'Dowd goes on to explain, the country (unlike, for instance, England) is not yet written:

> She is the scroll on which we are to write
> Mythologies our own and epics new. . . .
>
> (208)

The "infant Past," Australia's inheritance from the old world—over-written and over-determined—is to be transformed into a palimpsest for new inscription as the "adult Future" starts to happen. Once the "new" "mythologies" are written, then the culture will extricate itself from that uncomfortable old rhyme (used by Henry Kendall in his poem "Charles Harpur") of "Australian" and "alien."[18] O'Dowd, redeeming the rhyme by rewriting it in "The Bush," looks forward to a time when "we become ourselves distinct, Australian / . . . Stripped to the soul of borrowed garments, alien" (196). That is, Australia will no longer be alien to itself because Australians will "become *ourselves*" (my italics), no longer "frauds," no longer imitations of someone (and somewhere) else in "borrowed garments."

This line of argument is extended into the specifically literary sphere with the reiteration later in the poem (in the final stanza, in fact) of the metaphor of textuality (of the "scroll [roll, role?]" still to be written). The poet asserts that "What word *we* write shall she, the script, declare" (my italics): here, Australians take responsibility (and claim the textual space) for writing *themselves*, rather than being written by the (hitherto) dominant discourse. As a result, local writers will transcend the colonized space prescribed for them; and the concluding line of the poem prophesies that Australia's "silence [shall] flower in song" (209).

So O'Dowd ultimately imagines Australian culture transcending its "script[ed]" role and finding its true voice. His own part in this process is a key one, as advocate if not notably as practising poet. I don't wish to overstate the case, or overpromote his work, since in the end I tend to agree with Judith Wright that his poetry is eminently unrewarding to read (indeed often almost unreadable). Nevertheless, the historical position his writing occupies is a strategically significant one. As we've seen, just as Whitman had set about "breaking English" in the American continent in the mid-1850s, so O'Dowd, following closely in the master's footsteps half a century later (and borrowing extensively from him), set about the same task on the Australian continent. In so doing, he helped to establish a pattern for twentieth-century poetry in Australia that was to be followed (as we shall see later in the chapter) by poets as unlike O'-Dowd as (say) Michael Dransfield—a turning away from English cultural models towards American ones.

သြ    သြ    သြ    သြ    သြ

Before we get to that phase of the argument, though, I'd like to look at the work of another writer whose voice has significantly contributed to the contemporary development of Australian English in poetry, and whose somewhat tart critical remarks on Bernard O'Dowd I've already mentioned above, Judith Wright. As well as commenting on other writers occurring earlier in the development of the literary culture in Australia, Wright has had her own poetic things to say about some of the territory traversed by (among others) O'Dowd, particularly as regards the bush and the bush ballad. In the first part of her *Preoccupations in Australian Poetry* (1965), she acknowledges a "Double Aspect" (xi) to the settler literary consciousness, writing, "We are, and have always been, two people in one—a race of Europeans exiled from our own mainstream of development, yet carrying on that stream within ourselves, and a race different in themselves because their environment and their influences are different" (1). This doubleness that Wright perceives might be made to coincide with the two stages of decolonization suggested in *The Empire Writes Back*—*abrogation* and *appropriation* (the first suggesting the reaction of the exiled consciousness; the second, the positive articulation of difference). In her comments on that early pioneering Australian poet, Charles Harpur, she quotes a passage from his journals that (echoing Whitman's sentiments in "An English and an American Poet," and perhaps even borrowing Whitman's posture) centers the tactic of abrogation on the great Laureate of the Victorian dominant literary discourse, Alfred Lord Tennyson, of whom Harpur writes:

> My dislike . . . is founded not so much on special grounds of judgment, as on general dissimilarities of mental habit. He is an old-world "towney"—a dresser of parterres, and a peeper into parks. I am a man of the woods and mountains—a wielder of the axe, and mainly conversant with aboriginal nature; a man made stern and self-reliant. . . .
> (in *Preoccupations in Australian Poetry*, 8)

Wright, while admiring Harpur's achievements, doesn't see him going much beyond this stage, arguing that even in some of his "most ambitious poems" such as "The Creek of the Four Graves" his efforts—while spectacularly free of the Tennysonian drawing-room (or polite gardening) aesthetic—are "descriptive and narrative only" (15). My own feeling is that Harpur goes much further than this in his literary pioneering, and that by naming the hitherto nameless creek and telling the story of early settler history that furnishes the name, he is in fact making a significant linguistic mark on the landscape previously perceived as empty, void. Similarly, when the settlers in the poem start telling tales round the camp-fire, their conversations echoing from the nearby (silent) trees give a new voice to the land, to what Harpur calls "aboriginal nature." These strike me as more than merely aesthetic gestures, in fact as significant details that are part of an impulse to establish a new "English" in Australia, going beyond the purely descriptive or narrative, however dependent on these latter the poem may be.[19]

What mainly interests me here in the present context, though, is the somewhat self-conscious macho attitude purveyed in this literature—the way Bush Man writes himself as "wielder of the axe, . . . stern and self-reliant." Wright doesn't particularly criticize Harpur's work in this regard, but is much harsher on that aspect of the writing of Adam Lindsay Gordon.[20] Certainly the latter's poetry—and in fact the bush ballad and tale more generally—is notorious (in spite of excellent examples of bush literature penned by women writers)[21] for its male orientation. And this of course poses a problem for Wright since, as an Australian, she is naturally interested in the efforts made by local writers to assert independence from the metropolitan discourse; but as a woman she may feel excluded from the new discourse being evolved. That is, just as nineteenth-century Australian writers felt colonized by the impositions of English poetry, so now Wright (and other women writers) may feel themselves colonized by the impositions of a local literary culture that finds no place for women. As she herself puts it: "[As a woman writing in Australia] You had two problems to contend with always: (a) your whole surroundings, your whole background, was quite different from the stuff you were given to read; and (b) in any case, it was masculine" (quoted in *Poetry and Gender,* [ed. David Brooks and Brenda Walker, 1989], 146). In a way, then, Australian women may feel subject to a *double* colonization (a phrase, incidentally, taken as the title of an interesting collection of essays on colonial and post-colonial women's writing published in Sydney in 1986)[22]—firstly geographically by virtue of inhabiting a once-colonized territory; and secondly in terms of gender by virtue of inhabiting their own bodies (which occupy a marginalized position in the world of sexual politics). Something similar has been noticed by Maggie Humm in her book, *Border Traffic,* in which she argues: "An insistent theme in colonial writing is its tendency to abstract relationships as mappable geographic space. The map is the colonial signifier of a dominated race, its economy, and topography. It is also a trope for that other colonial geography—the body of woman" (74). In terms of generating a viable literary diction this means (as the editors of *A Double Colonization* point out) an initial recognition that "language itself has been colonized by male experience," followed by the effort "to find a language which can describe female experience adequately" (Petersen and Rutherford, 10). So, as Bronwen Levy puts it in her essay, "Women Experiment Down Under: Reading the Difference," "the values of masculine language and meaning" need to be "challenged at the level of words, grammatical constructions and literary form"—a challenge that "leads to a politics not just about words but of words: language itself becomes a major site of contest, of revolutionary struggle" (in Petersen and Rutherford, *A Double Colonization*, 170). This revolution will of necessity involve an *opening* and a *breaking* of masculinised "English": hence the title, for instance, of the Canadian feminist, Betsy Warland's book, *open is broken*. Warland, in her essay "untying the tongue" in *A Double Colonization*, writes, "what prompted me to write *open is broken* was the realization that the English language tongue-ties me." This results in a "restricted mobility" for the female writer (140), a problem exacerbated by the fact that "it is our native tongue, the only language we have." Warland's solution is, curiously enough, to embrace our old friend the dictionary—not as a normative regulator of the dominant discourse (of course), but as provider of original roots and derivations: she argues that "etymology nearly always remembers the feminine sensibility of our inner landscapes" (141). The tactic of tracing etymologies, of resurrecting "abandoned words" and meanings—she goes on—generates a salutary "reconstructive power" in English; and she concludes by citing Daphne Marlatt's notion in "musing with mothertongue" of a new relationship between women and the (hitherto) dominant discourse: "inhabitant of language, not master, not mistress, this new woman writer . . . in having is had, is held by it. . . . Inside language she leaps for joy, shoving out the walls of taboo and propriety, kicking syntax, discovering life in old roots" (quoted in Petersen and Rutherford, *A Double Colonization*, 143).[23]

While the above statement could have been custom-designed to perturb the Movement, it might at this point just be worth mentioning that (predictably enough) not all literary excursions into the dictionary down under have quite such happy outcomes, such success as subversions. Louise Katherine Wakeling, for instance, in her wryly witty poem on lesbanism, "The small personal voice" (in *small rebellions* [1984], 23–24), sees etymology as *bolstering* prejudice rather than undermining it. The poet reminds us that "The Oxford Dictionary" is an instrument of linguistic death, providing only "word-sepulchres . . . silent as all tombs" that "never give anything away" (thus being either ungenerous, or part of a secret code that refuses to yield clues, or both). Nevertheless, its authority remains potent, and as a result of its definitions we learn not only the classical "root" of the word, but the fact that lesbianism (from the Establishment's "normalizing" point of view, at any rate) is indeed "rooted" (that is, in Australian slang, "exhausted," "fucked").

The dictionary entry quoted in Wakeling's text is more than simple *de*scription, and amounts to *pre*scription (or, effectively, *pro*scription): overt objective definition slides into implicit masculist disapproval. Moreover, the word's position in the alphabetical list is strategically interesting (damning), coming between "leprous" and "lèse majesté." So the regulating and hierarchizing (alphabetizing) impulse of the phallogocentric discourse "places" (not only literally, of course) lesbianism between a highly contagious disease and a term meaning "high treason."

As if that weren't bad enough, toward the end of the poem the protagonist has to face another manifestation of patriarchal authority in the shape of that eminently canon-forming literary-critical figure F. R. Leavis (author of, for instance, *The Great Tradition, Towards Standards of Criticism,* and *Revaluation: Tradition and Development in English Poetry*). In the circumstances, the poet can only counsel herself not to give way under the pressure, not to show a weakness that will be construed (by Leavis and many others) as "female." Wakeling's literary excursion into dictionary-world, then, while subversive in its satirical tone, is far less satisfactory than that of Warland, who will have nothing to do with the negative vibes generated by the texts of the dominant discourse, and concludes *her* essay on a high note of elation, liberation, even triumph: "the language—my language—broke open. my tongue freed. to mark exceedingly" (143).

Judith Wright's orientation is clearly somewhat different from Wakeling's; and she may not seem quite as flamboyant as Betsy Warland, or such an iconoclastic figure. Yet she too, in her own way, seeks to engage with the language of the male canon, to open up (or appropriate) the masculinized literary structure (in her case, the bush ballad inherited from the period of Australian Federation), and to go back to linguistic origins—though (as we'll see in a moment) she chooses to go back much further than Warland or Marlatt.

As regards engagement with Australian literary history, one of Wright's most interesting tactics is evident in her justly famous early poem "South of My Days."[24] Formally divided into five stanzas, the work divides informally into three parts, the middle one of which is a brilliantly-written pastiche of bush balladry. This central section (stanzas three and four) is framed by the beginning and end that Wright marks as her own with the formula "South of my days' circle," the reiteration at the end indeed bringing the poem itself round full circle. At the outset Wright asserts her ownership of the language and the material articulated in it when she affirms that the (cultural) landscape about to be presented is "part of my blood's country"— the blood (apart from being an obviously female sign of the kind, for instance, Sylvia Plath favored) suggesting a visceral connection quite unlike anything to be found in male bush writing (which, surprisingly, turns out to be somewhat bloodless on close inspection).

Having firmly established her own identity in the text, Wright goes on to introduce the male lead, "old Dan," who here functions in a secondary and subordinate role (reversing the hierarchy one *might* have expected according to the conventions of this genre). Dan, the bush raconteur, though a storehouse of seventy-years'-worth of pioneering stories, appears rather fragile, even pathetic as he spins his "yarn[s]" into a "blanket" that he "clutches round his bones," clinging onto the past, and trying to wrap himself up against the onset of (inevitable) winter cold.

But when he starts to tell the tale, the language comes alive— though the words, of course, are put in his mouth by Wright herself (again, an inversion of what one might normally expect). The language is vivid, energetic, flexible, colloquial, even slangy, full of local color. Then the female poet's voice breaks in again, reasserting authority and undercutting the headlong flight of the narrative with the cold observation that nobody's listening anymore. Dan has lost his audience, and is reminded of his place—huddled by the fireside, but also huddled in the past: his time for speaking is over, and others have taken his position. What he remembers is not wholly discarded, but is transformed in an act of appropriation as the (new, female) poet introjects Dan's material and it becomes part of *her* dream:

> South of my days' circle
> I know it dark against the stars, the high lean country
> full of old stories that still go walking in my sleep.

So a dominantly male discourse is taken over and renewed: without wishing to labour the pun too much, it is Wright who writes, asserting her right to be heard, claiming her rightful place from which to speak, decolonizing herself and her "blood's country." Thus, in a sense, she's exploring new territory here—as she puts it in "Unknown Water" (a poem reminiscent of "South of My Days" in taking over an old man's tales), "helping to clear a track to unknown water" (110)—breaking new ground, however old historically the land itself may be.

And in fact that land is very old indeed, geological time (and the time scale of ancient flora and fauna) dwarfing the human (as, for instance, in another well-known Wright poem, "The Cycads" [39–40]). Wright actually takes advantage of this datum to place phallogocentrism in a significant perspective: that is, she draws attention to its ephemeral and impermanent nature,[25] undermining the primacy of the male voice in Australian English poetry by harking back to a universal pre-speech condition in which male and female are *equally* wordless: a kind of *subversion* by *reversion*. In section 5 of the poem "Habitat," for instance, she speaks of "Dumb/ sounds before words" (303).

On reflection, perhaps this state shouldn't be called a "pre-speech" condition as much as a pre-*human*-speech one, since nature itself retains an elemental voice (which we might have been able to apprehend once, and which may still be vestigially present in our dreaming consciousness, but which we've basically now evolved beyond). So in "Letter to a Friend," 4 (57) the "river voices," the writing of a "bending branch," and the message scrawled on the sky by a "flying bird" may come to us in "the less-than-childish language" of our sleep.

Nature can still provide us with texts in its own language, then, but translating them can be problematic: so in the poem "Scribbly-Gum" (131), the poet peels back the tree's bark in search of some textual truth, but is unable to "read" the "life" revealed thereby. Wright may not be able to access the information here, but elsewhere the implication seems to be that women have more chance of sharing this natural language (perhaps through the link between land and blood articulated in "South of My Days") than do men. Man (in the person of Adam), as we discover in "Eve to her Daughters" (232–34) has become "mechanical-minded" and even "turned himself into God, who is faultless, and doesn't exist." Thus the patriarchy turns away from a possible dialogue with reality, with (Mother) nature. Further (as Sylvia Plath asserts in "Daddy" with its references to "Luftwaffe" and "Panzer-man" [*Collected Poems*, 222–24]), men may even become a powerfully destructive mechanical force—a prognosis made by Wright in "The Two Fires" (119–20) in which the potentially fruitful "seed" of the atom is perverted "by the climate of man's hate" into nuclear holocaust.

Women, on the other hand, are linked by the cycle of blood into natural creativity, a theme Wright takes up on a number of occasions. In "Woman to Man" (27), for example, she speaks of the "selfless, shapeless seed I hold"—a phenomenon clearly antithetical to the egotistical and prideful male self(ishness) epitomized by Adam in "Eve to her Daughters," and to the destructive atomic seed of "the man-created fire" in "The Two Fires." Where these latter tend inevitably towards annihilation, her "seed" by contrast becomes the "blood's wild tree" and the "intricate and folded rose." And in the poem "Woman to Child" (28–29), which also carries on her insistent reference to both "seed" and "blood," Wright states categorically "I am the earth, I am the root."

The contrast between male and female imperatives is elaborated in a later poem centering on a specimen of flora perhaps not exclusively but certainly distinctively Australian—the eucalyptus tree (in "The Eucalypt and the National Character," 362). Wright once more persists with her vocabulary of symbols taken from local nature, establishing (among other things in the poem) a contrast between eucalypt (indigenous, naturally occurring, informal, noncommercial), and pine plantations (non-native, deliberately planted, carefully pruned to shape, part of a flourishing antipodean commerce and industry). The eucalypt (always referred to in the poem as "She") possesses a "graceful asymmetry," and is "flexible, spare," adaptable, fertile—able to flower herself, and also to nurture fecundity in others, accommodating both "seed and egg." The pine, on the other hand, standing (selfishly) alone in regulated military ranks, plays the male role to the eucalypt's female one: its name, of course (as well as its shape) is rather a giveaway—particularly in its Latin form of "*pinus*" (a near-homophone of penis). That focus of phallogocentrism, "stiff / symmetrical," here performs not an inseminating but a symbolically sterilizing function (in contrast to the eucalypt's fecundity), since the light can't penetrate the closely-packed ranks of trees, and the trees themselves have no flower. Instead, the pines are depicted as aggressive, greedy, colonizing: "green regiments that gobble our noble hills."[26]

But in the end it's the eucalypt, the female principle, that triumphs, "surround[ing]" the pines and becoming "all light" and love. If we need to speak in terms of hierarchies, then it's evident here that female takes precedence over male, growing round the phallic principle in an embrace that may be floral, sexual, or culturally appropriating. In the (textual) place Wright generates in the poem, it's the woman who is "at home." This goes back, again, to the notion of the "blood's country," and underlines the fact that, at least as Wright sees it, women seem to have access to a referential system, or natural language that men don't (or, rather, can't) speak. Such a language may involve an "English" superficially indistinguishable from that enshrined in traditional Australian (male) literature, but its roots go much deeper—deeper by far than even, for instance, Betsy Warland suggests in her exploitation of dictionary derivations and verbal provenance.

ॐ  ॐ  ॐ  ॐ  ॐ

Judith Wright, then, in her own version of "breaking English" appropriates a conventionally Australian male literary genre (the bush ballad) and the conventionally male discourse of "English." In the process she takes responsibility for (re)writing herself, and other women, often using the generic term "Woman" (or some close equivalent such as "Eve") in her poem titles—"Woman to Man," "Woman's Song," "Woman to Child." We saw earlier that Bernard O'Dowd had tried a similar act of rewriting (though of course from a different gender base), especially in his long poem "The Bush," during which he sought to re-place Australian culture relative to the epic and mythic referential systems of the old world ("Homers . . . in the gum trees"!). The next poet I want to consider, Diane Fahey, continues the trend, giving it her own particular spin, notably in her collection of 1988, *Metamorphoses*. In this book, Fahey sets about rewriting from a female perspective some of the Greek myths which had been so popular (and not only with O'Dowd) during the period of Australia's cultural domination by a European past. The effect, as we shall see, is a double *de*-colonization, radically changing the inflec-

tion of the original colonizing master texts, and at the same time redeeming Woman from her traditional role as culture victim—transformations that indeed deserve the title *Metamorphoses*.

In her essay, "Greek Mythology in Modern Australian Poetry" in
*Southerly* (1993), Fahey points to the high level of literary-cultural
traffic between Australia and Classical antiquity, not only during the
foundational period in the nineteenth century, but as well throughout the modern period. She begins by tracing in passing a pattern of
male readings of myth through the work of Norman Lindsay and the
"Vision" group, to Hugh McCrae and the young Kenneth Slessor in
the 1920s; then on to Hope and McAuley in the 1940s and 1950s.
What she notices here (and elsewhere) is the way "the Greek mythological inheritance is in various ways imprinted" with data of contemporary relevance, "the way these poems engage with issues of
power and powerlessness within men and women, and in relationships between them" (19). Included in the discussion is the work of
various contemporary women writers in Australia, who are aware
that the legacy from ancient Greece is "to some extent constructed
by patriarchal consciousness." As a result: "A feminist questioning of
the androcentric nature of many myths has informed poems on
Greek myth by a number of women poets including Dorothy Hewett,
Fay Zwicky, Jennifer Strauss, and Kate Llewellyn" (6). One name she
leaves out of the list of writers here is her own, though it seems to me
that in many ways some of Fahey's work provides the most compelling example of all. Taking her cue from the first century Ovidian
text (itself a construction of much earlier material), which was to be
such a seminal influence on Renaissance literature, Fahey updates
the tradition of mythic (literary/cultural) transformation one more
time. This culminates what amounts to a series of *language* metamorphoses—from the original Greek source of the myths; through
the Latin mediation of Ovid's poetry; on to Elizabethan early-modern English, and finally to the contemporary period in Australia.

Her approach stresses the fact that, for her at least, delving into
these ancient myths is not an escape into a safely-dessicated past, but
part of an on-going process of negotiation. In her *Southerly* article
Fahey writes:

> In the face of still prevalent nineteenth-century attitudes to Greek
> mythology which saw it as exhausted stock, to be appropriated or triv-
> ialized at will, I find myself pondering another image: that of the

seeds found in Egyptian tombs, preserved intact for millennia, which have proved still capable of germination. I sense something of the possibility of recovering and tapping into ancient images. . . . [M]yth too is protean, shape-changing. The strongest myths, continuing to evolve as human consciousness evolves, invite radically new interpretations, ask to be wrestled with. (19)

Myth, then, as Fahey describes it, is itself a metamorphic (protean) phenomenon; so that a collection of myths about metamorphosis should be *doubly* effective in enacting transformations. She goes on to speak of myth "as a tool of insight in critiquing and reshaping received cultural images of feminine and masculine experience" (19). This statement underlines the fact that, in her version, what's significant is not (of course) the literal change in shape of the *dramatis personae* themselves, who (following the original myths) shift from animate to inanimate or vice versa and encompass a veritable menagerie of fauna or a botanical gardenful of flora. Rather, it's the change in shape of what one might call the *moral* that compels our attention.

So, faced with a European tradition in which, for instance, Europa is made to seem quite fond of the bull, and very grateful, Fahey emphasizes that women who figure in myths of rape should *not* be "turned into the blessed recipients of ecstasy": on the contrary, it's necessary to see rape "clearly for what it is, and what it is not" ("Icons," in *Metamorphoses*, 73). The fundamental obscenity involved in the act of rape may be compounded culturally by the way in which it's read or viewed: in her notes to the poem "Icons" (101–2), Fahey uses another icon—*The Shorter Oxford English Dictionary*—to show with distaste how the notion of rape coinciding with (female) ecstasy seems "embedded" in etymological origins, the words "rape" and "rapture" sharing "the same Latin root." She proceeds to illustrate that it is not only artists but subsequent art-historians who allow themselves to be seduced by this idea, quoting Hugh Honour and John Fleming (from the Macmillan *A World History of Art* [1982]) as saying of Titian's painting of the "Rape of Europa" that the victim's "abandoned attitude" dramatizes simultaneously "resistance" and "surrender," both "terror" and "rapture." The notion is clinched, apparently, by the ambiguous swirl of Europa's red scarf!

Fahey's gloss on this gloss is: "Clearly, this is a Europa who could keep a whole zoo happy irrespective of whatever divine pedigree its

members might lay claim to." She goes on, this time targeting Tintoretto's "Leda with the Swan," to say that the famous painting "shows
a Leda who, in contemporary terms, has recently been in touch with
the Dial-A-Swan service (an unlisted number)." The facetiousness of
the tone here shouldn't deflect readers from the high seriousness of
the undertaking, which is essentially to assert that if the patriarchy
(whether it consist of gods or mere male critics) is responsible for
writing the female, inevitably that writing will be wronging: as long as
the female is identified with passivity and silence, anything may be
read into or inscribed onto her, however inappropriate. In the cultural metamorphoses which form the (female) "Icons" of Fahey's
text, by contrast, the female is shown (as a note on the back cover tells
us) moving on from patriarchy towards the reclamation of "her own
space and authenticity." We're warned that this places the reader "at
the centre of a battlefield"—not only literally (since much of the material comes from tales of the Trojan War) but figuratively, since what
is dramatized is in effect a battle between ways of seeing and saying—
the traditional (patriarchal) against the rewritten (feminist).

The point at which Fahey joins the battle is an historically interesting one, as she tells us in her "Notes" (87 ff.). The mythologies she
uses originate from classical Greece, from a literature developed by a
patriarchal dispensation that had imposed itself "on earlier matrifocal culture." Consequently "an all-powerful male god" (responsible,
it might be added, for a large number of the rapes recounted in the
book) replaced "a Goddess incarnating the creative principle as
Source and Giver of All."[27] The female power of the latter became
diffused through a number of lesser figures who were subordinated
to patriarchal principles, and became defined specifically in terms of
their roles relative to men: "Hera *is* wife, Athene *is* father's daughter,
Aphrodite *is* the responsive beloved. . . ."[28] The way Fahey tells this
history admits patriarchal primacy, but—coming from a context informed by the "matrifocal"—doesn't see it as inevitable and eternal
(since it was preceded by its *other*). Moreover, a significant amount of
the material in her book centers on incidents from the war in Troy, a
conflict of more than casual historical importance since (she tells us
in her note to "Helen" [99]) it "pitted patriarchal Greeks against matriarchal Trojans." We know the outcome of that war, which is one of
the data that can't readily be transformed or rewritten in the book:
but at least, I'd suggest, we enter history at a place where the patriarchy is distinctly challengeable.

And this, of course, is precisely the challenge which Fahey takes up in *Metamorphoses*. She pits her skills as a writer against the patriarchal weight of the past, rewriting one of the cornerstone texts of Western culture (and even appropriating its title). And if that culture has traditionally rendered woman silent (a notion metaphorically enacted in the cutting out of Philomela's tongue [14], and in Echo's plight at only being able to repeat in fragments what's said to her [24]), then perhaps one of her tasks is to confront that silence and—paradoxically—re-articulate it.

This will not involve succumbing to the passive silence of the victimized—though, as Fahey admits in her contribution to the "Statements" section of *Poetry and Gender* (33–36), she has experienced that too. Rather, it will accomplish the redemption of that negative "silence of engulfment," and a redemption of the silencing occasioned by patriarchal oppression. That is, women may achieve a kind of metamorphosis, and become subject to (not object of) a different sort of silence, a silence transformed, *not* arising out of exclusion from the dominant discourse. As Fahey puts it:

> When an eloquence is attained through which the real self can speak, there is a new kind of silence—one of resonance, able to render the relationship of self to self, to others, self to nature. . . . Poetry is nourished by silence: by the silence before creation, in which possibilities press into being; by the silence of empowered selfhood which enables the poet to fire and unify a poem; by the silence around the completed poem which has attained its own shape. (34)

Her inspiration for this comes not only from ancient Greece (Sappho being the obvious instance for feminist writers in Australia, as elsewhere), but also from "New World" writers closer to the present—Emily Dickinson being a choice almost as inevitable as Sappho in this regard. Fahey emphasizes that Dickinson provides a perfect role model of "the ability to transform disempowerment into empowerment through silence and poetry," going on to speak of Dickinson's poetry as offering instances of "the transformations by which one gains new freedoms" (34, 35).

One such transformation in Fahey's own work occurs in the poem "Philomela" (*Metamorphoses*, 14), which is based on the legend of Tereus and Procne (as well as the eponymous Philomela herself). Fahey's choice of this legend is an interesting one, at least partly because it had caught the attention of two of the father-gods of that eminently patriarchal poetry movement, Modernism—Ezra Pound and T. S. Eliot. Pound used the story as part of his intertextual *mélange* in "Canto IV"; while for Eliot it provided significant background detail to section 2 of *The Waste Land*.[29] But Fahey's usage is subversive of the male discourse, concentrating exclusively on the main (female) character: and the moral (predictably) is a feminist-oriented one, focusing on the pun/metamorphosis of the word "flight." At the start of the poem, Philomela is still in human form, and "in flight" (that is, running away) from Tereus, who wishes to rape her, and succeeds in so doing. To prevent her from telling anybody, Tereus cuts out her tongue (as many a male literary editor has no doubt done symbolically to any number of aspiring Philomels since) and disappears from the text. Then a process of "healing magic" begins, "bringing transformation / to the defeated one" who (changed into a nightingale [or swallow, depending on which version one reads]) really is able to fly away from the patriarch(y).

So horror can turn into peace, song, freedom, and reconciliation. A metamorphosis takes place whereby the act of having to run away from the abuse of hierarchical power (Tereus) is transformed into the ability to fly—an act of liberation identified by Hélène Cixous as being typical of the *female*: she writes, "Flying is woman's gesture—flying in language and making it fly" (quoted in Brooks and Walker, *Poetry and Gender*, 111). Thus "flight," through the language of the poem (moving from beginning to end), becomes "flight," transcending the strictures of the male discourse.[30]

Another transformation, whereby entrapment turns into freedom, occurs in "Weaver" (11), in which the woman Arachne, representing the distaff side of creativity, is turned into a spider locked in her web. Rather than being diminished by the metamorphosis, though, Arachne becomes a whole world, a "ringed planet, nucleus / of atom," spinning a web composed of the earth's primal elements. Although apparently "trapped" by the circumstances, like the earth itself (and a compulsive weaver, not to mention a spider) she "spins and spins and spins": and what she spins is highly significant, because it comes from "her self [which] is inexhaustible." This is particularly important to Fahey's telling, because in the course of the poem Arachne has become a symbol of the female creative artist. And, in spite of the malign intervention of the gods, she's able to claim her own self, her own story, and weave it endlessly, transforming a humble domestic skill into a world-spanning art (though whether or not a pun on that other communications web [www] is intended, is a matter of sheer speculation).

Elsewhere, Fahey's textual tactics offer any number of incidental felicitous anachronisms, and not-so-incidental feminist triumphs. In the former category we get "Andromeda" (23) as "pin-up" (literally, since she's stapled to a rock), a pastiche of the modern commoditization (and brutalization) of the image of woman. Then there's "Galatea" (25) as woman objectified and constructed by the male (in this case literally, by Pygmalion), later becoming a "famed hostess" and "a pillar of society" (again—presumably—literally, since she's made out of marble!). Or there's "Ariadne" (28–29), on the psychiatrist's couch, working her way (mentally) through the ins and outs of the Minotaur's maze.

More seriously, we have the triumphs in adversity of a number of heroines (as well as the ones mentioned earlier). "Polyxena" (50), for instance achieves "an adamantine possession of self" and finds the courage "to defy her own powerlessness." And in the significantly-titled "Phoenix-Woman" (59–60), Hades (in this text the honorary symbol of the patriarchy) realizes that he "cannot / possess" Persephone, who in the end will emerge "shining, to melt / [his] ... kingdom." Then there's Europa, the hapless maiden visited by the Zeus-bull in "That Other Shore" (70) who, after the rape, turns out not to be so hapless after all, and "will command the images that hold / her truth" and will "speak and shape them" in the face of (male) artistic renditions of her plight down through history. Europa here obviously acts on the advice given to another of Fahey's heroines, "Semele" (80–81) to "Be born from yourself" (and not from an image written or painted by some other).

An indication of this assertion of individual identity in the face of a civilization that assigns stereotypical roles and cultural spaces to the female is the way Fahey entitles her poems, in the vast majority of cases using the name of the female protagonist involved. The act of titular naming focuses readerly attention on the key dramatis personae (women), and shows that the author has appropriated the textual space, making it available for the female voice. Exactly the same argument might be made, of course, on the larger scale, as regards Fahey's titling of the volume as a whole: that is, by duplicating Ovid's own title of *Metamorphoses*, she asserts dominion over the cultural property involved. If I may make a passing comparison here, another book in English entitled *Metamorphoses*, and published in the mod-

ern period, came from the pen of that bastion of the British establishment, C. H. Sisson (1968). The difference between Sisson's and
Fahey's endeavors is that the former's engagement with the original
text results in a title-sequence that is not much more than a series of
tepid translations, merely reiterative; whereas Fahey's volume
amounts to an inventively daring and wide-ranging appropriation.
Her text is certainly *not* a translation—except, that is, in the broadest
sense of "carrying across" (and carrying away) the material from its
enshrinement as a key datum in the canonical literature of Western
patriarchy to an-other place where it can speak on behalf of the traditionally silenced and marginalized.

Clearly Ovid's original, changed in shape, offers plentiful possibilities for Fahey's sexual/textual politics, as the many instances above
attest. Before we leave the book, though, one further element needs
discussion—namely, the framing devices used for the text by the author, and their significance. The volume is introduced by a proem
entitled "But First . . ." (8), which immediately sets the direction of
our exploration by pointing attention to the male gaze traditionally
blamed for the cultural construction of the female in our civilization:
the first words are "Narcissus gazes," and this is followed immediately
by a reference to Argus with "his hundred eyes." Admittedly Narcissus is staring at a construction (reflection) of *himself*, but as I read
this detail here it simply indicates the way the male world is totally
self-absorbed in its fetishizing, addicted to its own gazing (much as
Pygmalion is, later in the book, with Galatea). After the obligatory
reference to metamorphosis (Argus being transformed into a pea-
cock, this time the change being instigated by a Godd*ess*, Hera) the
introductory poem turns into a formal invocation to the Muse of
epic poetry: "In short, Calliope, let it happen." This reminds us that,
while most editors and publishers down through the ages have been
male, the Muses responsible for the origination of texts, for inspiration and creativity, are that other gender.

When the book *has* happened, Calliope gives way at the end of the
volume to a segment entitled "Notes and Illustrations" (85 ff.), and
to a bibliography (115 ff.)—unusual details in a book of poems. The
term "Illustrations" is an interesting one, inasmuch as it sets up a hierarchy in which the written material takes priority over the visual
(something that could have been avoided by simply not using the
word, and substituting, say, "art works"). By implying that the works
reproduced in this section are merely illustrative of her own text,

Fahey is appropriating and recontextualizing a tradition of male art, (re)constructing its images for her own purposes in much the same way that Titian and Tintoretto and Rubens and Tiepolo had constructed images of the female. Fahey also introduces a degree of subversive humor at times, in her comments on these master art works, by deflating the macho element in the various abductions depicted. She implies, for instance, that Boreas (the personification of the North Wind) looks a bit puffed in his attempts to carry off the ample Oreithyia in Rubens's painting (reproduced on 111): her authorial gloss on this is the wry comment that the trip back to Thrace must have seemed "very long" for both parties concerned (102).

The notes and bibliography sections serve the immediately practical purpose, of course, of providing background information for the mythic characters portrayed and transformed in the main text. But it seems to me that they serve an additional, more significant structural purpose: that is, by offering fairly comprehensive explications and directing our attention to ancillary sources they seem to provide a *system* that somehow supports and validates the poems themselves. What I'm saying here, essentially, is that Fahey is generating a pseudo-academic environment and systematic approach which one might more readily identify (to lapse uncomfortably into binarism again for a moment) with male notions of knowledge rather than female ways of knowing. Her motive in this, I suspect, is an *ironizing* one, aimed at destabilizing the authority of the patriarchy and of establishmentarian tertiary approaches (of the kind in which I'm currently engaging!) to cultural texts. Inappropriate framing devices, as we'll see with some Aboriginal work presently, can severely compromise the integrity or authenticity of the original. Fahey, for her own purposes, has of course already significantly tampered with the "integrity" of her source narratives by ransacking them (like Cixous's *voleur*)[31] for stealable or satirizable content. By evolving a seemingly respectable academic frame for this action, she compounds the attack by undermining the apparent authority of such frames and pointing out their essential hypocrisy. Further, she satirizes a cultural environment in which an insistent phallocentric focus is made epic and heroic (generating the sort of text Cixous rather facetiously described as a "*Penisneid*" ["Laugh of the Medusa," 890]), and in which what amounts to an extensive catalog of rapes can be condoned and made intellectually respectable or at least acceptable by the mere addition of a handful of footnotes. So in a sense what she's doing here is using the paraphernalia of "Eng. Lit." *against* itself, and thus questioning its right to mediate her script.

Fahey's series of *Metamorphoses*, then, in radically reinterpreting and re-inflecting the original texts, opening them up for fresh use, act not merely as revisions but, borrowing a term from Adrienne Rich, as *re*-visions: in "When We Dead Awaken: Writing as Re-Vision" Rich (we may recall) asserted that "Re-vision—the act of looking back, a seeing with fresh eyes, of entering an old text from a new critical direction—is for women more than a chapter in cultural history: it is an act of survival" (in *Adrienne Rich's Poetry and Prose*, 167). In reviewing the myths from a feminist perspective, Fahey generates a new context in which the female characters (almost always victims; almost always virtually passive; almost always silent) are metamorphosed into something different: by retelling classical rapes from the perspective of the person raped, a new notion of female identity emerges, often unexpectedly triumphant. Fahey, in challenging the right of the classical gods to rape, is effectively challenging the dominant patriarchal discourse, and seeking to break an "English" that threatens to write her over the margin into silence.

ॐ॒ ॐ॒ ॐ॒ ॐ॒ ॐ॒

Re-viewing as survival, combating the coercion toward silence, and resisting the imposition of inappropriate framing devices (literary and cultural) are all features that characterise not only Fahey's work (and that of many other women writers around the world), but as well that of various Aboriginal writers in Australia. They too have been struggling to break into (or should that be *out of?*) English, challenging the dominant discourse imposed at first colonizing contact and consistently reaffirmed since then. They too feel the need to rewrite themselves in the face of inaccurate images of identity constructed by a hostile *other*.

At the beginning of this chapter I used the term "colonization" at least partly in a metaphorical sense to describe the relationship between settler and metropolitan cultures; and I used it similarly above to indicate the relationship between female writer and patriarchy; but when it comes to the fate of the indigenous peoples, the term of course becomes absolutely literal. And in Australia, as in many other places, the historical and geographical act of colonization has had disastrous consequences for the Aboriginal inhabitants. Earlier I mentioned the two "A's" used in the process of "writing back" against

the Empire—*abrogation* and *appropriation*; but to these it's now necessary to add a third and rather different term, anterior and more in-
sidious, and negative in its operation—that of *assimilation*. As many
commentators tell us, assimilation (rather than its evil twin, *annihilation*, which was also adopted unofficially by some settlers) was the solution favored from early on in Australian colonial history for
dealing with the Aboriginal "problem." J. J. Healy, for instance, in *Literature and the Aborigine in Australia: 1770–1975* (1978), cites Edward
Curr's report to the Victorian Royal Commission of 1877 defending
this policy in spite of setbacks and generally slow progress. Having
courteously likened the indigenous peoples to "a mob of wild cattle"
needing to be tamed and to "children and lunatics who cannot take
care of themselves" and who may therefore need to be "coerced,"
Curr goes on:

> Then we must remember that the views and habits of mind of the
> blacks are unlike ours, and cannot entirely assimilate to ours for
> generations. This will easily be allowed when we remember that nei-
> ther Irishmen, the Scot, nor the Welshman has as yet developed in-
> to an Englishman, though they have gradually adopted our langu-
> age. (17)

If Royal Commissions couldn't always transform the indigenes, in
spite of the gift of English, then literature might be able to lend a
hand, writing Aboriginal characters in an acceptably docile form.
The critic Colin Roderick suggests, for example, that the Aboriginal
sections of James Tucker's novel *Ralph Rashleigh* are "on the whole,
imaginary concoctions" (in Healy, *Literature and the Aborigine*, 37). So
the indigenous peoples became fictional constructions within fictional constructions, written by somebody *other*, and thus effectively
transformed into a literary manifestation of political policy as colonization and subsequent assimilation became a textual phenomenon. Healy points out that "Throughout nineteenth-century Australian considerations of the Aborigine, the names of Defoe and
James Fenimore Cooper recur" (47 n. 36): so the fictional models
imposed on Aboriginality were (inevitably) foreign, stressing the no-
bility (*and* tractability—*and* presumably ultimately therefore assimil-
ability) of the savage. As Mudrooroo Narogin points out in *Writing
from the Fringe: a Study of Modern Aboriginal Literature* (1990), this was
to cause problems for the reading public in the late-twentieth century when militant Aboriginal writers seemed to be offending the

*decora* thus established, reneging on their roles as Men Friday, and disconcerting the middle class "gentleman and gentlewoman" whose "special area" literature had traditionally been (166).

An alternative to writing Aboriginality in a way which wouldn't *"épater le bourgeois"* was to go one step further than assimilation and write it out completely from the text. W. E. H. Stanner in a series of radio lectures for the Australian Broadcasting Commission (subsequently published as *After the Dreaming: Black and White Australians— an Anthropologist's View* [1969]) spoke of the local habit of "forgetting" and "disremembering." In the lecture/chapter significantly entitled "The Great Australian Silence" he noted: "What may well have begun as a simple forgetting of other possible views turned under habit and over time into something like a cult of forgetfulness practised on a national scale. We have been able for so long to disremember the aborigines that we are now hard put to keep them in mind" (25). This mannerism of not perceiving (or ignoring) the Aboriginal peoples is, of course, a reiteration or extension into the present of that original failure to perceive that permitted the declaration of the continent as *terra nullius* and therefore ripe plunder for the Empire. Stanner points out that, in the modern period, "All land in Australia is held in consequence of an assumption so large, grand and remote from actuality that it had best be called royal, which is exactly what it was. The continent at occupation was held to be disposable because it was assumed to be 'waste and desert'" (26). The convenient capacity to ignore, willfully not to see the indigenous peoples, is highly developed, then—to such an extent in fact that, as Adam Shoemaker tells us in *Black Words, White Page: Aboriginal Literature 1929–1988* (1989), "it took almost two hundred years for the British settlers of Australia to grant full citizenship rights to Aborigines and to recognize them officially for census purposes [which happened as a result of a referendum in 1967]" (6). The legislation, of course, in itself by no means results in an end to the "forgetfulness." Stanner in *After the Dreaming* in 1969 was still looking forward to a time when the disremembered would be remembered, which would necessitate bringing to light "the other side of the story over which the great Australian silence reigns" (25). In fact, at least to some extent, this has now taken place, with the publication of (for instance) Henry Reynolds's *The Other Side of the Frontier: Aboriginal Resistance to the European Invasion of Australia* (1988).

In the end, though, the most effective response to literary assimilation is (as Fahey had obviously concluded at the time that she undertook her *Metamorphoses*) to write *oneself*, to take away from the
colonizing culture the right to generate images pertaining to the hitherto marginalized or silenced individual(s). A superficial yet significant indication of this determination among Aboriginal writers is the
fact that key figures have assumed ancestral tribal names in place of
their Anglo-Christian ones (Kath Walker renaming herself Oodgeroo
Noonuccal; and Colin Johnson rewriting himself as Mudrooroo Narogin). The process of self-writing, then, has certainly begun to happen
in Aboriginal literature in English—albeit late in the day, and although the process is beset by special problems. Kevin Gilbert indicates as much in his introduction to the volume *Inside Black Australia:
an Anthology of Aboriginal Poetry* (1988): "There are a number of difficulties in perception and analysis, the most difficult of these is to attempt rationalization of hundreds of thousands of years of oral
tradition against the last twenty years of limited access to white education and education in the alien English tongue" (xv).[32] Perhaps what's
most significant here is not the huge antiquity of the oral, but the relative rapidity with which the colonizing written language undermined
it, raping the local culture with all the virulence of one of Fahey's
Greek gods, and radically demoralizing the victims into a passive helplessness. Errol West's poem "Sitting, wondering . . ." in the anthology
(173–74) articulates precisely this sense of "hopelessness," which "another promise" and a "band-aid gimmick" won't help to dispel. The
reality is:

> it's
> getting late, red tape, budgets, strategies,
> Rape![33]

> (173)

So the bureaucracy and politicians may proceed in their accustomed (ineffectual) ways, but the brute fact of "rape" remains. What
West describes as the "backwater of despair" needs to be transformed, and the "rape" to be negated; but (as West again says, in the
poem "There is no one . . .") the damage may be irreversible, the
breach in the continuity of the culture impossible to bridge, since

> There is no one to teach me the songs that bring the Moon
>    Bird, the fish or any other thing that makes me what
>    I am.

> (166)

The indigenous "I am" needs to confront the daunting prospect of self-reconstruction from what amounts to an *absence*, then, of somehow *de*-assimilating the colonized culture, breaking English open to rearticulate the Aboriginal. Colin Johnson notes something of the sort in his essay "Guerilla Poetry: Lionel Fogarty's Response to Language Genocide" when he describes Fogarty as "a poet guerilla using the language of the invader in an effort to smash open its shell and spill it open for poetic expression" (74). This represents a transformation of the passive role into an attack mode, as we'll see presently.

Somewhat lower-key, though still effective, is Oodgeroo's approach in her justly-famous (if ambiguously-titled) poem "We Are Going."[34] Like some of Errol West's work, it presents a lament for a world seemingly in the process of obliteration, its sacred sites turned into rubbish dumps, its totems in the natural world banished or extinct, its "old ways / Gone now and scattered." The people have become estranged from their environment, and are denoted by the third-person pronoun "they" rather than the first-person "we": they appear as "strangers" in their own land, in spite of the fact that it's "the white tribe [who] are the strangers." The poem concludes with the grim and uncompromising statement:

> "The bora ring is gone.
> The corroboree is gone.
> And we are going."

However, desperate as the subject-matter may be, the very fact of the *telling* is highly significant, since it gives the indigenous a voice in the settler language arena, suggesting not a going away as much as a coming back. Oodgeroo herself pointed this out in an interview with Gerry Turcotte two days after—and in the context of—the Australian Bicentennial Celebrations (which saw the largest ever civil rights protest march in the country, thus providing another arena for the assertion of Aboriginality). She said of her book *We Are Going* (the first printing of which apparently sold out in three days, to be re-issued seven times in the next seven months): "its success was inevitable, I think, not because I'm a good writer, but because for the first time the Aboriginals had a voice, a written voice. I'm the highest selling poet in Australia" (Rutherford, ed., *Aboriginal Culture Today*, 19).[35] Furthermore, Oodgeroo notes that her greatest success occurs when she goes "Back to my culture," when she's "in my own culture."

She's much less comfortable when "dealing with a rotten language that's supposed to be a *pure* language . . . it's been pinched from the French, the Germans and everyone. It's a bastardized language the English language and it's a terrible language to work with. Terrible!" (ibid., 23). Of course, since English is the dominant discourse, however terrible it may be, it must be negotiated (with): Oodgeroo acknowledges this, admitting that it's necessary to use English "in order to be published" in Australia. In any case, as it happens, she can't speak her native Noonuccal because it was "flogged out" of her at school. She says: "It was forbidden, it was classed as a pagan language. You get rid of that pagan language and you learn the King's English. Which is a *Christian* language. In the name of Christianity! look at what they did to us" (ibid., 23). However, if the Noonuccal language has been beaten out of her, she still remembers the tribe's mythologies, and contrives ingeniously to write herself (albeit in English) into them—as we see in her story, "Paperbark-Tree," which appears adjacent to the interview in *Aboriginal Culture Today* (31–32). The paperbark is particularly significant to her because her chosen name of "Oodgeroo" is actually the Noonuccal word for the paperbark tree, which becomes her totem. In the story, the protagonist has lost her tribe, and is told by the good spirit Biami to go to the dead campfire of the tribe, and collect all the charred sticks there, and to repeat this action every time she comes across another dead fire, putting the sticks into her bag. Then she is to go to the paperbark trees who will give her their bark. Armed with the charcoal and "paper," she must write down the lost stories of the tribe; and thus will "Oodgeroo" find her way back "into the old Dreamtime" (32).

So the writer who was once Kath Walker manages to reestablish contact with her Aboriginality through a name and a story that amounts to a symbolic telling of the need to transfer an oral culture into a print culture to preserve the record. Interestingly, too, she passes the idea on to another important figure in the writing of Aboriginality, the one-time Colin Johnson, who renamed himself Mudrooroo, also after the paperbark tree. He says: "I spoke to Oodgeroo, and she explained to me that . . . as creative writers our totem, or dreaming should be the Paperbark tree. This seemed logical as the paperbark tree, or whitefella name *maleleuca*, or my country name, Mudrooroo, has always had an important place in Aboriginal life" (Rutherford, *Aboriginal Culture Today*, 36). As well as taking his cue from Oodgeroo, Johnson points to more aggressive attitudes to the language situation, particularly in his remarks on the militant Lionel Fogarty in the essay "Guerilla Poetry" published in the periodical *Aspect*. Using an uncompromising and reiterative rhetoric to resist the disremembering and the great Australian silence, he demands:

> What happened to the Aboriginal languages of Australia? The English invader sought to destroy them utterly. The native was to be forced into the state of English civilization, and this meant, as a corollary, the death and destruction of Aboriginal language and culture. In the settled areas there was imposed a deliberate policy of language genocide. . . . (Johnson, 72)

Fogarty, Mudrooroo argues, resists the contemporary consequences of this state of affairs, writing defiantly in the style of "an Aboriginal songman" in the face of this "genocide" and the "tyranny" of the colonizing culture. Mudrooroo, borrowing a term from sociolinguist M. A. K. Halliday, goes so far as to claim that Fogarty (in such poems as "White Tendency") is turning "the language of the invader" into "an anti-language" (75),[36] and even generating "an anti-poetry, a turning away of all that the critics hold dear, and in which the rhythms are flattened out, sometimes changed abruptly, often discarded" (79).

Certainly Fogarty's poetry is (often literally) a challenge; and it tends to resist interpretation by being sometimes asyntactic, slang, and generally *other*. It provides an energetic textual confrontation with standard English—a confrontation begun, according to Kevin Gilbert's introductory note to Fogarty's contribution to *Inside Black Australia*, in early childhood. Learning the rudiments of written English at primary school on the Cherbourg reserve (in southeast Queensland), Fogarty came to use this language "like a dervish wields a club." (156)

And in spite of what Gilbert sees as a conspiracy to silence the Aboriginal voice (or, in this case, writing), Fogarty's first book of poems, *Kargun*, was published in 1980 when the poet was only twenty-two, to be followed rapidly by *Yoogum Yoogum* in 1982. The latter was produced hurriedly by Penguin Books so that it could be launched at the Commonwealth Writers' Conference, held so as to coincide with the Commonwealth Games in Brisbane. In fact, recent Aboriginal works (and protests) have often been timed to occur simultaneously with events that draw worldwide attention to Australia, so as to achieve maximum exposure through the international media, and perhaps undermine the nation's self-image as friendly and sunny and easygoing. They thus constitute continuing efforts at breaking what W. E. H. Stanner described as the "Great Australian Silence." After *Yoogum Yoogum*, both Kevin Gilbert's *Inside Black Australia*, and the substantial *Aboriginal Culture Today* (a special issue of the magazine *Kunapipi*) appeared in 1988, the year of the Australian Bicentennial; and as I put my notes together in Sydney early in 2000, no doubt plans are underway for something to coincide with the holding of the Olympic Games here, and subsequently the Centennial of Federation in 2001.

History may accidentally provide the occasional forum for the breaking of English, then; but—Fogarty suspects—nothing really changes: he complains, in the poem "Will We See 1990: Land or T.V.," that in spite of mathematics suggesting otherwise, "2001 still adds up to 1988" (*Yoogum Yoogum*, 82). And, on the specifically literary-cultural level, the poet remains dispossessed, lamenting the fact that in order to compete in the arena of written texts he must use

> a medium
> that is not mine.
> ("Tired of Writing," *Yoogum Yoogum*, 1)

However, that doesn't stop the Aboriginal "I am" from surviving—affirming its indigenous identity and continuity with the local—in spite of an alien medium, and in spite of the poisons and residues of the colonizing régime. So, in the poem "Ecology" (*Inside Black Australia*, 164), while modern industrial (and cultural?) "pollution" may threaten the delicate balance of an Aboriginal relationship with the land and nature, the poet can still identify himself as traditional "digging sticks," as winnowed seeds, "bandicoot," "flying fox," and so on: *not* isolated and alone (as Errol West felt), but part of an indigenous community.

In fact, given the nature of Aboriginality, my labeling it "I am" is somewhat misleading, since high emphasis is placed on this *communal* identity (that is, "We are" rather than "I am"). Fogarty in the poem "In Transformation" affirms this when, speaking to future generations of his people he says, "I am all you as you are me"—a close-knit group "centered" in a joint destiny (in *Yoogum Yoogum*, 23). And the people, however dispossessed they may be materially, remain part of a *music* denied to the whitefella, whether it be instrumental ("flutes performing") or vocal:

> Again we half air chanted, enchanted by gripped still
>     extravaganza . . . .
>                    ("To Yubba Joey Geia," *Yoogum Yoogum*, 89–90)

The collocation of "chanted" and "enchanted" here underlines the magic quality of Aboriginal music (and words), a celebratory extravagance—not to mention a radically altered syntax—in marked contrast to the "barren" songs of the "white man."

In the poem "Have" (93–95), Fogarty again employs an energetic, urgent syntax, inciting his people to

> get surviving
> not reserved suicidal
> own your own borrowed indigenous depth. . . .

In a series of verbal plays typical of his poetry, the author insists that what has been merely borrowed (or lent) must be claimed, owned as one's own. To fail to do this is to be trapped (ghettoized) on Aboriginal reserves (such as the one in which Fogarty was reared at Cherbourg). To remain quiet and reserved (as an English fella traditionally might) is, for an Aboriginal writer, silently to assent to entrapment and therefore to cultural (as well as sometimes literal) suicide. Instead, the indigenous peoples must tap into their ancient origins, to find a voice (like an Aboriginal-style "barbaric yawp," perhaps) which will articulate a powerful affirmation of freed identity, assertive and (if necessary) aggressive and pointed:

> Renovate needles in teethed
> special howling dingoes, nostrils wide open. . . .
>
>                                                  (94)

The inspiration for this freeing gesture, as far as Aboriginal writers are concerned, may indeed come from the land of the barbaric yawp—not from Walt Whitman, of course, but perhaps from the tradition of rebellion he helped to originate, now transformed in the modern period by militant African-American writers. That is, the struggle against American racism provides a cultural model for a similar struggle in Australia. As Adam Shoemaker asserts in *Black Words, White Page:*

There is little doubt that the "Black Power" and "Black is Beautiful"
movements in the United States have had at least some effect upon
the format and the language of Black Australian political protests.
Similarly, the Black American vocabulary has also influenced the writings of some Aboriginal poets, such as Gerry Bostock, Lionel Fogarty,
and Aileen Corpus. (215)

So Fogarty may be forced into "a medium/ that is not [his]," but
at least he can adapt it by using appropriate models not wholly dependent on standard literary English or its canon. Like some Westindian-British poets, as we saw earlier, he decides to utilize the rhythms
and rhyme of popular music, and in particular reggae and *rap*. In the
first poem in his collection *Yoogum Yoogum*, for instance, he agglom-
erates a series of short lines with exaggerated singsong rhymes—
"wrote," "remote," "note," "Space," "pace," "race," "ace" (1)—in the
style of a pop rapster. This draws attention away from the traditional
high culture, denying its purity and subverting its primacy.

Colin Johnson remarks of this aspect of Fogarty's "Guerilla Poetry," "We know that English poetics touched him less than Afro-
American songs" (in "Guerilla Poetry," 75). More generally (and
with his new name of Mudrooroo) he said in *Writing from the Fringe:
a Study of Modern Aboriginal Literature* (1990): "a rhythm akin to Jamaican reggae is employed by some bands [in Australia] such as
Coloured Stone and Modern Tribe. This type of rhythm appears to
fit Aboriginal English speech patterns" (27). Later in the piece
(63–64), Mudrooroo notes that "One of the most successful and
popular Aboriginal Bands, No Fixed Address, saw themselves essentially as a reggae band, and could declare at one time that reggae was
Aboriginal music." This is presumably not just a matter of rhythm,
but of political orientation, since reggae animates "an identification
with oppressed people" far different from "European cultural influences."

The Aboriginal reggae connection shouldn't be *over*stated, however, since—for instance—the Rastafarian religious background of
Caribbean reggae (as Mudrooroo points out) isn't entirely appropriate to Aboriginality, except on the significant general level of raising
black pride in the face of a common colonizing discourse (a motive
that also may lie behind the publication of an article on the Rastafarians in the Aboriginal periodical, *Identity*).[37] As well, other forms of
music—notably country and western, and rock 'n roll—have proved

popular with Aboriginal listeners and performers. Nevertheless, the interest in reggae shown by writers such as Fogarty is certainly indicative of the desire to break away from the impositions of standard English into a discourse of subversion more politically appropriate to the colonized situation of Aboriginality. Mudrooroo argues that "the place for this development is among people least affected by assimilation," and he goes on to call for "a new Aboriginal literature away from the Metropolitan tradition." (30)

Reggae isn't the only route for Fogarty to follow in his subversion, though. In a poem "To Brother Gary Foley" (*Yoogum Yoogum*, 121), for instance, he uses a tactic that Sylvia Plath had found serviceable against the patriarchy—the adaptation of traditional (English) nursery rhyme to offer a message radically different from the original. So in *Yoogum Yoogum*, "Little Miss Muffet," "Bah Bah Blacksheep" and "Jack and Jill" put on an Aboriginal air, as a result of which there's *no* curds and whey, *no* wool, and in the end *no* "freedom."

Then, elsewhere (as in "Pastime Trip" [96], for instance), Fogarty moves beyond inherited nursery rhyme to combine a number of methods to transform the surface of his own poetic "English." Neologism and diglossia are used to emphasize the crosscultural innovative energies at play in the text, which becomes a complex mélange of standard code, Aboriginality, rhyme, pun, and slang—hard to decode without local glossing, but certainly a challenge to notions of purity and monoculturalism.

The surface of Fogarty's poetry compels an adjustment to conventional methods of reading, then—an adjustment that is perhaps symptomatic of a larger need, when dealing with Aboriginal texts, to re-view the whole business of reading and textuality, particularly since there's no Aboriginal written language in the sense that such things exist in Western cultures. Instead, Aboriginal texts have traditionally consisted of body painting, cicatrice patterns, dances, and the like: so an "English" "reader" is obliged to extend conventional notions of the category "text." An interesting experiment in this area was conducted by Krim Benterrak, Stephen Muecke, and Paddy Roe in their collaborative volume, *Reading the Country: Introduction to Nomadology* (1984), in which the land itself becomes the key text to be read—and a somewhat controversial one at that, given the contemporary cultural and political context of clashing notions of land rights and ownership (though these don't appear overtly in the foreground in this specific instance).

Stephen Muecke, who is responsible for theorizing the project, and for the written parts of the text, notes the "foreign" quality of the undertaking for someone who isn't indigenous when he says that "the ways in which many Australian Aboriginal people speak are free of the categories which articulate Western philosophies." Furthermore, in a traditionally collaborative medium, the governing notion of an author is transformed, so that "the imagination of the writer . . . eschews authority" (217). The foreignness of the undertaking is not confined to the European collaborators, though, since all members of the team are in one way or another on new ground: Muecke explains,

> We are all "foreigners." Krim and I are foreigners to the Plains [ie. Roebuck Plains, the country that becomes the central text], Paddy is foreign to the book as a European artifact, Paddy and I are foreign to painting, Krim and Paddy are foreign to the sort of writing and philosophy I have adopted to construct a unity or general direction for the book. (15)

The idea of foreignness is admitted, then, as part of the project, even welcomed as a challenge (in contrast to Movement-style xenophobia). Also embraced is the concept of nomadology: thus the sort of fixity we saw with the Movement's clinging to the last days of empire is inappropriate here. On the level of the language in *Reading the Country,* this is reflected in a turning away from normative notions of purity or monoglossia, and an acceptance instead of the text as a series of cultural and linguistic intersections. Muecke, following Lévi-Strauss and Derrida, applies to the narrative style of the book the term "bricolage" (which he defines as "the activity of roaming around in the ruins of a culture, picking up useful bits and pieces to keep things going or even make them function better" [148]). He argues that "Paddy Roe's storytelling, as it has been written down here, stands as a *bricolage* of standard English and Aboriginal languages" (150). Under the circumstances, our readerly response needs to be scrupulous, avoiding a significant "error" to which Muecke alerts us: this is

> the familiar mistake of seeing Aboriginal English as a "bastard" version of standard English; language fallen from grace. Such an attitude is supported by a traditional purist condemnation of any powerless varieties of English like the migrant Englishes or youth sub-cultures. These varieties lack the support of institutions like the ABC, dictionaries and grammars. (151)

Another "error" about which he cautions us (and himself) in handling this language is the urge "to over-correct it in writing it down," to normalize or standardize it. This would be a grave mistake since it would effectively "banish the Aboriginality from the text."

This is an important proviso because essentially it warns us against (re)colonizing the text/land through the writerly and editorial processes, thus resilencing the indigenous—something of which, for instance, the Jindyworobak movement of the 1930s might be accused, however unintentional their cultural colonization may have been.[38] Maneuvering in this area is particularly fraught with difficulties in view of various politicocultural implications, notably (as Mudrooroo points out from his position of *Writing from the Fringe*) an opposition between "the 'broken English' of the various Kriols which have developed and Standard English" (111–12).

Muecke's problem in *Reading the Country* becomes that of defusing this oppositional stance, or of dismantling the implicit hierarchy. He attempts this by evolving a special variant of the written language, which he explains in a section of *Reading the Country* entitled "Aboriginal English" (241–43). He uses the designation to cover a range of phenomena from "a mild accent to a full blown creole language" (Paddy Roe's speech being "somewhere between these two extremes"). Special features that Muecke discusses include "the lack of fricatives in Aboriginal languages"; the use of "[e]xtended vowels"; the dropping of the 'h' sound of English [which] is not used in Aboriginal languages generally"; and the use, in transcribing Roe's Nyigina language, of "a three vowel system (i, a, u)" rather than the European five vowel one. In addition, there are special pronounal uses in Aboriginal English (as—we remember—there are, too, in the Jamaican Creole of the Rastafarians);[39] and semantic variations, such as the "spacialization" of time, so that people may be described as "coming behind," rather than "afterwards" or "later."

Perhaps the most significant part of Muecke's exercise, though, is discussed in his subsection entitled "Establishing the Texts" (242–43), where he deals specifically with the problem of transferring the oral to the written in a way that will take account of pause, rhythm, and the relationship between speech and silence. As well, it will be necessary somehow to incorporate

> Gestures and other activities going on during the story . . . [which must be] included as part of the context. . . . Similarly, the role of the listener is important. The texts are essentially dialogues, even if Paddy

Roe is the main speaker. His narrative style solicits audience response, and this is supported by the tendency in his culture to *collectively* produce texts.

Muecke is thus transforming the conventions of "English" narrative to make it a suitable vehicle for a culture whose notion of language is "*dialogical*" and of text "polyphonic (an amalgam of different voices)." Coupled with Krim Benterrak's paintings and maps, which help to link the parts of the narrative to specific parts of the country being read, this amounts to a collaborative rewriting of the category "text" as it's normally understood in English.

Ingenious as *Reading the Country* may be, however, problems remain, as Mudrooroo asserts in *Writing from the Fringe*. While he applauds Muecke's method of transcription up to a point, he feels that Roe's discourse is still compromised and turned into "an interesting artefact which may be measured and deciphered using the methods of European criticism." Worse than that, though, "slabs of Standard English" in the book act as barricades inhibiting the (collaborative) commerce between speaker and listener, and in the end Roe's discourse "becomes imprisoned between slabs of academic prose resembling nothing more than the walls of a prison" (151).

For Mudrooroo, then, Muecke's interventions are too heavy-handed and—irrespective of intention—politically incorrect.[40] The metaphors of imprisonment used here have a particularly strong resonance and are particularly damning in the Aboriginal context, since—apart altogether from the common experience of being herded into reserves, Aboriginals make up an inordinately large proportion of the prison population, mistreatment and death in jail seemingly being a part of their ongoing legacy in twenty-first century Australia. Mudrooroo obviously doesn't see Muecke as culpable on quite this scale, but the metaphor nevertheless remains uncomfortably evocative; and he continues to be bothered by the (white) editorial function. Of prefaces and introductions to Aboriginal works in general he says:

I see them as not only introducing the writer to the reading public, but also inviting the reader to accept Aboriginal literary productions in certain ways. In effect, they are signals which often apologise for the Aboriginality of the texts which sets them apart from the grand tradition of European literature. . . . [They imply] that Aboriginal people . . . are fringe dwellers on the outskirts of the Metropolitan literary tradition of Europe. (20)

In fact, Mudrooroo argues, it's not only Europeans who intervene in this way: even Aboriginal editors can be similarly at fault. The case he cites is that of Jack Davis during the latter's period as editor of the Aboriginal periodical *Identity*, whom he quotes as saying: "anything that came to me that was not written clear enough for an English speaking audience, I had to use my skills to make the stuff readable, buyable . . ." (in Mudrooroo, *Writing from the Fringe*, 91).[41] The way Mudrooroo interprets this circumstance is that "in effect [it] meant that Aborigines accepted Standard English as the dominant discourse," thus fostering rather than combating "an assimilationist policy" (92).

Inappropriate editorial stances and inappropriate framing devices, then, can do significant politicocultural harm. Mudrooroo himself has explored framing tactics not only in his theoretical pronouncements (principally in *Writing from the Fringe*), but as well in his own creative writing, notably in the text *Doin Wildcat*, a kind of sequel to his groundbreaking novel *Wildcat Falling*. In the latter, the (fictional) narrator wrote his novel as a rehabilitation exercise while in jail. Now, out of jail, he's been commissioned to write the screenplay, and *Doin Wildcat* is—on the narrative level, at least—an account of this process and of the making of the film.

The project (*Doin Wildcat: a Novel Koori Script as Constructed by Mudrooroo Narogin*, 1988) appeared in the Bicentennial year and (like several other texts coinciding with that notable occasion) took the opportunity of raising some key Aboriginal issues. One of these, inevitably, is the jail motif, which continues to be metaphorically as well as literally potent, evoking not only actual incarceration but also the continued historical imprisonment of Aboriginality in a foreign culture and discourse. In *Doin Wildcat*, the way out of such entrapment and into a new freedom appears to lie in rewriting or retelling, moving diglossically from one language to another, flexibly from one genre (or medium) to another: one might say, carrying on the filmic reference in the text, from one frame to another.

This might seem straightforward enough; but the fundamental situation is problematized in a number of ways, reflecting the complexity of issues surrounding the textual expression of Aboriginality. The book acts as a study (one might apply Muecke's term bricolage) of multiple framing devices, ficitonalizations, story tellings, improvisations. The original storyteller (invented by Mudrooroo, of course) is actually present in the new fiction (of filmmaking), but not in control, since his literary-cultural property (his story) has been appropriated by the American movie director who is in a position to finance the whole arrangement. Wildcat's only possible response initially is one of frustration and rejection: "Well, fuck em, let em do what they want to do. Tired of the whole fuckin story anyway. What with the writes and the rewrites" (12). It seems in this passage that the "owner" has been bullied out of his rights (writes); but if one takes the argument a step further, the fact that Wildcat is now *telling the story* of the making of the film indicates that he's actually *reclaiming* it—or perhaps that, through him, Mudrooroo is reasserting his author-ity over the text. After all, the subtitle of the book reminds us that we're handling an artefact *"Constructed by Mudrooroo Narogin."* Moreover, it's a *"Novel Koori Script"* that we're dealing with here, bringing a significant play of double-meaning into the project. The "novel script" in question may be simply the screenplay adaptation of the prose narrative—which would indicate assimilation into the literary conventions of "English," an acceptance of the categories of the dominant discourse, and a buying into (or selling out to) Western commercialism and consumerism. On the other hand, though, "novel script" may indicate a whole new way of writing—an innovation or subversion that achieves a different creative language of the self. The fact that Mudrooroo labels it *"Koori"* (after his Aboriginal people and language) tends to prioritize this latter reading, claiming the text culturally; but it doesn't entirely suppress the former reading.

The double-meaning in the subtitle is carried over, interestingly, into the American director/producer of the film (again, both these terms being ambiguous given that the "real" director and producer of the text is Wildcat or—behind him—Mudrooroo). At face value, Al Wrothberg represents Western colonization, the force of cultural appropriation, the power of money; but as well as this he's Jewish, which (Wildcat/Mudrooroo emphasizes) makes him part of a victim culture, thus sympathizing with and in some sense even sharing Aboriginal experience: "those uniformed bastards standin over yuh with sticks an guns, an clubs an words. Yeah, em Jews ave known it too, so we decided that . . . [Wrothberg's] not just another Gubba, a Watjela wantin to rip us off, but a Jew, an that means sufferin an dispersal an all that" (4). The fact that "words" are part of the apparatus of oppression listed here is significant. On one level, of course, they're simply insults and obscenities, verbal violences to accompany physical ones; but as well they're the literal and metaphorical weapons of the dominant discourse, a key detail given that Mudrooroo's battlefield, the site where his drama is played out, is the arena of *language*. In this context, Wildcat/Mudrooroo draws further collateral support from a *Jewish* example. When Wildcat is talking to Renee, the actress playing his ("real life") beatnik girlfriend, he starts to quote the words of the archetypal "beat," Allen Ginsberg: "Ow's this for a beatnik poem: 'I saw the best minds of my generation destroyed by madness, starving hysterical naked, dragging themselves through the negro streets at dawn looking for an angry fix'" (73). This quotation is, as we already know, the opening of Ginsberg's great protest poem, "Howl"—a protest, a breaking of English, a "barbaric yawp" of wrath (echoing the first syllable of Al *Wroth*berg's name), which Mudrooroo here enlists in support of the Aboriginal cause.[42]

Ginsberg's voice, while one of the most sympathetic, isn't by any means the only verbal guest appearance in this text. As Wildcat discovers, following any number of postcolonial and feminist literary theorists, in order to survive in a world dominated by a colonizing discourse, "Yuh know, yuh ave to be like a chameleon in yer speech. Mimic their style of talkin" (79).[43] One such "style of talkin," of course, more of an intruder than a guest, is the *English*—symbolized in Mudrooroo's text by the imported education system represented in the *university*. Wildcat complains that the university has "all the fakeness of istory seekin to perpetuate itself," enshrined "in acclimatized mid-twenties British empire architecture." For him, the clinching datum is "[the campus] clock tower reflectin itself in a murky pool flaccid with carp. It too looks like a movie set" (61). In this view, the empire clings on, its monuments (the clock tower that might be telling it that its time is over) lost in a narcissistic insularity (the murky pool), glittering yet effete (the carp in the flaccid water). Above all, its most distinctive quality in the contemporary world is its "fakeness." As Mudrooroo writes it here, the dominant discourse becomes a construction (as he indicates in the book's subtitle) of a construction (the empire) of a construction (the "fake" university) of a construction (the "movie set"). At this point, a reader may begin to wonder who's writing whom, and to what end? Or, one might ask— as do Bob Hodge and Vijay Mishra in their comments on the *Oxford History of Australian Literature* in *Dark Side of the Dream: Australian Literature and the Postcolonial Mind* (1991), "What is literature? What is Australianness? What is history? And finally, where does Oxford fit in?" (2). All of these questions need to be consistently re-asked at every point.

As *Doin Wildcat* unfolds, we quickly become aware of the author's tactics to alter the surface of the language used—the changed spelling and rhythm from standard English, the incorporation of Koori words, slang, the variety of voices and narrative styles, code-switching, and so on. These are part of the wider project of breaking out from the dominant discourse into an authentic and self-sustaining Aboriginality, a genuine writing of self in which the ultimate author-ity lies with the Aboriginal culture, unmediated by the outdated (but tenacious) colonizing structures: as Wildcat/Mudrooroo puts it, "Yer stop pretendin an be yer natural self when yuh want out" (79).

This is clearly more easily said than done, since working out what "yer natural self" might be under the circumstances, and then finding an appropriate literary vehicle for it, leads us into a highly vexed area of somewhat contesting opinions. Obviously some rethinking (and rewriting) of current circumstances is required, in the process of which it appears necessary to negotiate a changed relationship between standard and kriol languages. Though Mudrooroo might not agree, it seems to me that both *Reading the Country* and *Doin Wildcat* set up interesting tactics that might be employed. Both conceive language (unlike Donald Davie and the original dictionary writers) as *un*fixed (Muecke would presumably say "nomadic").

Both evolve systems which (like the theorists of the "Creole continuum") undermine "static models of language formation" and overturn "'concentric' notions of language which regard 'Standard' English as a 'core.'" (Ashcroft, Griffiths, and Tiffin, *The Empire Writes Back*, 47). It seems, after all, that the university's phallic clock tower may not be the center of the universe any more, and the fat carp may be wallowing in vain! So the breaking of English can go on, in the outback as elsewhere.

ॐ  ॐ  ॐ  ॐ  ॐ

Mudrooroo's images of "acclimatized mid-twenties British empire architecture," and of the university's "c[l]ock tower" offer all manner of appealing areas to examine in the context of colonizing discourses operating against Aboriginality; but rather than laboring *that* point any further I'd like to turn instead to another consideration, already hinted at in passing in my mention of the character Al Wrothberg, the Jewish film director in *Doin Wildcat*. Wrothberg's (like Ginsberg's) is an interesting case, which reminds us that not all representatives of victim cultures in contemporary Australian literature are Aboriginal. To conclude this survey of ways of "breaking English" in a former colony, therefore, it might be appropriate to mention an instance in which the marginalized protagonist was both white and male—that of Michael Dransfield.

Dransfield's poetry comes principally from what one might call the American side of English, his affinities (particularly later in his short career) being with the protest/confessionalist line of which Lowell, Ginsberg, and Plath have been my main examples in this present study. Like these writers, Dransfield found himself operating on the peripheries of his culture, even over the edge into a counterculture. Like Ginsberg he experienced life on the streets, drug addiction, and periodic incarceration in institutions of one sort or another. Like Plath, he frequently portrayed himself as the victim of his sensibilities, his art, and of the hypocritical ostensibly paternalistic society that surrounded him.

The reactivation of the influence of America in Australian literature (an influence that I earlier traced from Whitman through O'-Dowd, though I'm not of course suggesting that Dransfield's work is anything like that of the latter), and the consequent rejection of English models—yet another break with the erstwhile empire—is very much a phenomenon of the 1960s. Key elements here are the availability in Australia of two anthologies of contemporary American poetry (which I argued in Chapter 2 were also highly significant in the Americanization of the literary counterculture in England);[44] and, in a nonliterary dimension, Australian involvement supporting the Americans in the Vietnam conflict. Dransfield, as well as being a strong advocate of Donald M. Allen's *The New American Poetry*, was a strong opponent of the war, protest against which was often identified with what was sometimes called "the Dransfield generation."[45] Certainly Vietnam reminded Australians that events in Southeast Asia and on the Pacific rim were (symbolically as well as geographically) closer to home than any older allegiances with Britain (whose interest in Vietnam was of course nowhere near as rigorously pursued as was the American interest in that country and in likely adjacent friendly bases for R&R).

Dransfield's own contact with American culture (as well as via the Allen anthology) came primarily through two literary events held in Australia—the May 1968 Armidale Writers' Retreat, and the Ade-

laide Festival Writers' Week in March 1972. The former was important because it put him in contact not only with Rodney Hall, who
was to become his editor after Dransfield's death in 1973, but as well
with Alfred Alvarez, that English Plath-advocate who wished to direct
contemporary English poetry beyond the gentility principle and in
the direction already taken by some American writers. Both Hall and
Alvarez were tutors at Armidale and, as Patricia Dobrez says in her
*Michael Dransfield's Lives: a Sixties Biography* (1999), they "provided
Dransfield with a bridge to his own generation, by helping him to
face the pain within and to make of it not escapist but confronta-
tionalist poetry" (227). Robert Lowell, described by Alvarez as "a
courageous man determined to 'walk naked' without evading the
profound disturbances of his life" (in Dobrez, 229–30), was a key figure in this regard; but even more significant was the Plath connection. Dobrez explains that at the time of contact with Dransfield,
Alvarez was working on *The Savage God: a Study of Suicide*, which initially focuses on Plath; and he'd recently revised *The New Poetry* to include a selection of her work. As a result, "Dransfield went out of his
way to find copies of [Plath's] *The Colossus* and *Ariel*, which he had
not owned previously—a fact which witnesses to the effect Alvarez
had on him in Armidale" (233). In March 1972, Dransfield came
into contact with another writer in English eminently prepared to
trespass across the boundaries of gentility—Allen Ginsberg. The
Beats had been offering a radical alternative to the English literary
status quo since the mid-1950s, not only in America, but (subsequently) in England and Australia (as elsewhere). Dransfield would
have been familiar with their work through the Allen anthology, but
by being present at the Adelaide Festival he actually had the opportunity to market himself alongside them as a younger generation antipodean manifestation of the originals. Ginsberg and Ferlinghetti
attended the Festival, Ginsberg at the "Town Hall Happening" playing his harmonium, singing Blake, and (as Dobrez tells us) involving
"a group of Aboriginal dancers and song-men in his performance"—
a phenomenon that was "a cultural revolution for South Australia" at
that time (339). Dransfield for various reasons wasn't there on that
particular occasion, but his volume of *Drug Poems* was published simultaneously by Geoffrey Dutton's Sun Books with Ginsberg's *Open
Head* and Ferlinghetti's *Open Eye*—a unique publicity opportunity of
which Dransfield took advantage, getting himself photographed
alongside the visiting American greats.

This was distinguished company indeed—but the problem is that the poetic impulse with which Dransfield is here aligned (and allied) may not be a very comfortable fit. What I want to argue at this point is that while he's clearly attracted by a countercultural urge (both as regards his writing and his lifestyle), at the same time he feels a strong pull towards a more traditional brand of literary culture, and ultimately falls through the gap between the two. On the one hand is allegiance to a radicalizing, iconoclastic impulse which, however, causes him discomfort by being deracinated (nomadic?). On the other hand is allegiance to an inherited "English" discourse of Romantic aestheticism, stable yet—for want of a better phrase—old fashioned (out of touch, no longer viable?). These two disparate options, neither entirely satisfactory, create a dilemma of *choice* (had he been a Movement poet, of course, there would have been no dilemma because there would have been no choice). To put it slightly differently, I'd suggest that when we read Dransfield's poetry we see that he's being written by conflicting discourses—a circumstance that conspires, in the end, to silence him. The poet, in simultaneously embracing and rejecting the inheritance of a traditional culture, creates a situation in which his poetry enacts the effective breaking (down) of English. This seems to me to be the essential message (if it's possible to talk of such a thing) of Dransfield's complicated and fascinating fiction of Courland Penders.

Patricia Dobrez analyzes this fiction with great ingenuity, suggesting that "Courland Penders was not merely the family estate he invented as part of his personal history, it was the symbol of his cultural inheritance as an Australian." This inheritance, like so much in his life and work, is profoundly ambiguous, since the name Courland Penders includes "the words 'our land' and 'end'" (426). It functions, then, as a multi-layered system of signs, both positive (belonging to "our land") and negative (reaching the "end" of the line) —what Rodney Hall in his introduction to the *Collected Poems* speaks of as a "complex . . . icon" (xix).[46] When Hall asked Dransfield about the property, apparently "He said this was his 'heartland' and left it at that. Such syllable-twisting from *cour* to *coeur* was very much to his taste" (*CP*, xix). Irrespective of fictional inventions, though, at the level of the text, Courland Penders acts as the "ancestral" stately home that the poet invents as an enabling or empowering device in his work. Coupled with a fictionalized coat-of-arms and lineal descent from European dukedoms, it has some connection—as Livio

Dobrez points out in *Parnassus Mad Ward: Michael Dransfield and the New Australian Poetry* (372)—with Rainer Maria Rilke's protagonist in *The Notebooks of Malte Laurids Brigge,* who fantasises about living in a closed-up country house and writing poems among "my old things, the family portraits, the books. . . ."

However, as well as enabling the writing process, Courland Penders acts ultimately (and simultaneously) as a cul-de-sac into which the poet writes or traps himself. Livio Dobrez describes the place as the site of an "endgame," in fact "The Aesthete's endgame" (376): he argues that

> It is, in short, aesthetic art we are talking about. . . . Courland Penders itself, part homestead, part chateau or schloss, meeting ground for Europe and Australia, is the House of Art, that is, of Aestheticism. . . . More precisely, it is a *museum* of a world that has decayed. Its end is the end of a whole way of seeing. . . . (375–76)

I agree with this assertion, though I'd be inclined to take it somewhat further: that is, in my reading of Dransfield's text at least, Courland Penders represents not only "the end of a whole way of seeing" but as well of a whole way of *saying.* Thus it functions as an allegory of *the dominant discourse* at large, privileged and historically sanctified (in Davie's terminology, "pure," perhaps), yet superannuated and inhibiting in a contemporary decentered world of multiple voices and cultures. So, in "Portrait of the artist as an old man" (*CP,* 17–18), the house may look "as though it grew out of the ground," having a permanence and solidity, a rightness and a rootedness that provides a foundational site of writing. And yet the cultural inheritance in "my father's house" is not—as the Bible would have us think—many mansions, but instead "many cobwebs," suggesting dereliction, absence of (human) life.

The cobwebby quality appears again in one of the most powerful country house poems, "Courland Penders: going home" (*CP,* 39–40), in which "All the corners have spiders," the furniture is shrouded in dust covers, and the key to the main door is "rusty from disuse." The house has become a derelict culture-museum with its "portraits" and "anthems," everything seen in a constricting perspective down the narrowing driveway. The dwelling/poem/frame contains only "a dead family" with no offspring, so that fertility and continuity are negated: if it isn't already, soon the ancestral home (which becomes increasingly like the House of Usher the more we explore it) will be-

come a "mortuary." As regards a viable literary discourse, this is disastrous because "poems are stillborn, / anachronists, insubstantial,"
and the situation's evidently terminal: we really do seem to be "At the
end of the road."

In another poem, "Tapestry at Courland Penders" (*CP*, 40–41),
things at first appear more hopeful. We seem at one point to have a
delicate and evocative echo of W. B. Yeats (also providing an intertextual context for the fascination with stately homes, one of Yeats's
preoccupations as well as Dransfield's) when a woman is described as
moving over the lawn the way "a gazelle" moves.[47] Unfortunately, this
echo, this hint of a continuing life in the long line of Romanticism,
dissipates; the colors fade; and an unfashionable art form turns into
mere illusion: "the dream a tapestry the tapestry a dream." Dransfield's poetic language here (repeating Yeats's) becomes a reflexive
structure, turning round on itself like a trap, or canceling and negating itself by mere repetition, meaningless reiteration. By the end of
the poem, as the winter night closes in we're stranded in an "old /
metaphor" (at the end of the road again), with a dead art-work, a
"Still Life With Roses."

Previously, the Romantic roses were still alive for Dransfield, the
lushness of his early writing at times affording an extraordinary contrast with the skeletal last works (of which more presently). Rodney
Hall notes how "Flouting the conventions of good taste by his love of
excessive images and archaic vocabulary, he openly claimed a place
for himself in a bardic tradition avoided by his peers" (*CP*, xviii). So
Dransfield sometimes allows himself the self-indulgent flourish of a
seductive mellifluousness (as, for instance, in "Abydos" [*CP*, 9–10]
with its evocation of "the crystal / octagony" of a wineglass in which
"Leander drowns, drowns"). Or, on occasions he lets himself be carried away by his own raptures—as with his description of the hair of
a young woman on a bicycle in "River road, forenoon, autumn, a cul-
de-lampe" (*CP*, 14) as "windspun miraculous lightcaught."

Such textual gestures are, on one level, quite beautiful—but hard
to justify as anything but escapist in a contemporary society racked
with violence and ugliness. Sooner or later (and in Dransfield's case,
regrettably, it's sooner), the young woman will cycle round the corner where the poet can't follow her with his male gaze, and tired old
Leander will have to be plugged back into his Greek mythic past.
Dransfield in fact satirically explores the latter case in "Colonial
poet" (*CP*, 101), where at the start we meet the protagonist playing

with the spectrum of aesthetic subjects at his disposal: perhaps he'll choose to write about his "travels," or "roses," or some "mythological topic." But essentially it doesn't make much difference, because whichever topic he selects and exploits (or colonizes, since he *is* after all, a "Colonial poet") *really* what he's writing is *himself:* as he gazes lovingly into the "still pool of his verse" he sees only "a clear reflection of himself as god."

The artistic process here achieves only a narcissism in which the colonizing cultural patriarch merely recreates his own image—enshrined as icon and divinized. What makes the situation particularly complicated (and interesting) is the double-edged nature of the poem: that is, by not specifying the exact identity of the "Colonial poet," Dransfield may be satirizing someone established and conservative, such as A. D. Hope (one of his favorite targets); or he may be satirizing *himself,* his own commitment to the colonizing discourse. Clearly he disapproves of the colonial poet's literary conduct; but at the same time he's ineluctably implicated in it, upholding what may be a redundant, and undesirable, yet *unavoidable* cultural and political heritage.

The situation is exacerbated by the parlous condition of modern Australia that (as Bernard O'Dowd had indicated much earlier in the century, with his call for the Poet Militant) may require more than an old-fashioned and self-regarding aestheticism. This condition is examined in Dransfield's apocalyptic "Endsight" (*CP*, 79), a protest poem about the pollution caused by multinational companies that seem to have colonized the whole earth sometime in the near sci-fi future. As a species, no longer enlightened, we've become engulfed in a darkness not only physical but metaphorical, as the "consciousness" is assailed by encroaching gloom. In a surrealist nightmare-scape, blinded owls fly into buildings and the cadavers of horses putrefy in the streets.

This is a world in the malign grip of giant industrial conglomerates; but—surprisingly—Dransfield seems to reserve his strongest spite not for these, but for the mediators of the dominant literary discourse who've somehow shirked their responsibility by omitting to protest the situation very aggressively. So, as the world rots, the target to which we're directed is the writing of the "Official Poets" playing with their "genteel / iambics." Presumably (given the poet's association with Alfred Alvarez) the use of the word "genteel" is significant here, since (like Alvarez in England) Dransfield is accusing

his literary peers (or elders) of not reaching *beyond* the gentility principle. In any event, the discourse of which Dransfield feels himself
part has obviously failed to make itself heard effectively, and we end
(again) with the grim vocabulary of sterility, emptiness, and death, as
"life [is made] extinct."

The direction here is clear: it's downward (and emphatically not
*Dawnward*), into what Dransfield describes elsewhere as the "ill
depths" of our culture (*CP*, 347), where "displaced Romantics" languish (*CP*, 305). Under the circumstances, the key question seems to
be, "Which text can the superannuated Romantic poet occupy?,"
and the answer is, "None." The discourse represented (as I've argued above) by Courland Penders seems doomed to deteriorate. So,
in "Birthday ballad, Courland Penders" (*CP*, 51–53), in spite of the
promise of fantastic escape offered by Coleridge's "XANADU" written (ominously) "in pinprick visions down your arm," we're sen-
tenced instead to wander through sterile and sepulchral "corridors
of dusty marble." Similarly, in "Only the sun was gone" (*CP*, 59–62),
the house is no more than "an enchanted prison" in which "The
dead become white/ fragments—disfigured." Not only are these
white fragments the skeletons of the dead—as well, they're blank
pages from which the writing has disappeared—literally dis-figured
(in a pun somewhat reminiscent of one we encountered earlier,
when Sylvia Plath spoke of the urge to "efface" herself in "Tulips").[48]

The inevitable *terminus ad quem* of all this is *silence*, a state we can
see foretold in some of Dransfield's best-known poems, and enacted
in his last ones—a Plath-like phenomenon with none of the redemptive possibilities Diane Fahey can see. Nowhere is the urge to disfig-
ure and (self) efface, to disappear into the silence of the literally
deconstructed text, more powerfully expressed than in "Bum's rush"
(*CP*, 30–31). We begin with reference to the literary discourse from
which Dransfield is being given (or gives himself) the "bum's rush"
(ejection)—the lyric aesthetic tradition as evoked in the poem's epigraph from Swinburne about the seductive power of the god of poetry, Apollo. A fix of "beautiful" lyric gives the poet a drug-user's
"rush," but is unavoidably followed by the "bitter" process of addiction, of coming down, of withdrawal. Courland Penders, as we saw,
could turn into a prison or trap, but in "Bum's rush," the phenomenon is even more severe, enacted by the arctic reference of
igloos and eskimos and (most significantly for the addict) "snow." We
end up in an imagined "devils island," a penal colony reference fa-

miliar throughout the (white) history of Australia, but here symbolic of an updated solitary confinement within one's own consciousness, from which there is only a single escape.

As Livio Dobrez perceives, Dransfield with his seductive dreams and fictions of privilege now turns into "a *crystal duke* in an igloo ('Blue all year like a duke's veins'), following a long-standing aesthetic obsession with the fantasy of Courland, now transformed into a drug image" (412). The power of this "image" is undeniable: in a landscape of ice and snow the poet falls into a "morphine blue" crack, and begins to freeze to death. Apollo (the sun god's) potency turns into a "midnight sun" in which the poet's identity starts to erode as he becomes "the last of . . . [the] species"—a sort of negative statement of cultural Darwinism in which the least fit must perish. In a truly chilling, if memorable, final image in the poem, the protagonist advises us to turn into "human lemming[s]," finding a spot where "the ice is thinnest" and letting ourselves "vanish." The ice sheet from which human identity disappears (effaces itself) threatens to turn into an empty page, a silence negating the voice of the literary discourse to which Dransfield has subscribed (or to which he's addicted).

In the process towards silence in Dransfield's last poems, the text becomes an articulation of fragments, the fragmentation itself being a form of confession and protest. Hodge and Mishra say of the work of writers such as Dransfield that "the disordered syntax and fractured forms that were the signature of this writing expressed a sense of alienation and pointlessness" (154).[49] Dorothy Hewett in her article "The Voyage out from Xanadu" takes the argument a step further when she writes that

> Dransfield's later voice is like a ransom paid in the kingdom of the silent. His defenses have broken down, he is the romantic without a country, so that the effect is like reading the private diary of a poet who has lost his outer skin. The diary is coming to us in broken phrases, sometimes almost monosyllables. . . . Apart from the power of this . . . language there is immense value in it because Dransfield is reporting back from the boundaries of human alienation. . . . (quoted in Patricia Dobrez, *Dransfield's Lives*, 17–18)

Certainly the end of "Bum's rush" represents one such "boundary" from which Dransfield is "reporting back." The same might be said, a little later, of his "M Ward" poems, during the period of his treatment for withdrawal symptoms,[50] and even of his frightening last poems. Of the latter, "A waste of time / A time of waste" (*CP*, 346) reports (or enacts) a savage dismantling of the Romantico-aesthetic English literary convention, a demolition that is, in view of Dransfield's split allegiances to the discourse in question, almost sado-masochistic in intensity. The poem is reduced to a mere skeleton, language stripped to the bone. The dominantly monosyllabic words printed in long columns, of course, on one level represent the "tracks" of Dransfield's mainlining habit; but as well they indicate his addiction to a literary form that he here takes apart before our eyes. The cult of aesthetic beauty is undermined, deprived of all sense of rhythm or "music" (*melopoeia*), all sense of verbal interplay or complexity (*logopoeia*), all imagery and symbolism (*phanopoeia*). The three ingredients Ezra Pound (borrowing from the Greeks) asserted as being essential to poetry-making are all deliberately absented here.[182] If, as the poem's title tells us (and as was suggested too in the polluted landscape of "Endsight"), we live in a time of waste, then everything becomes *abject*: even art is simply a waste of time and should be thrown away. It's as if we're being invited into an absence, or an English broken to such a degree that its energies spill away into the spaces between the words. This writing back to the silence may be an ironic mimicry of the silence imposed on its margin-dwellers by conventional society; but ultimately it remains a silence nevertheless.

ॐ  ॐ  ॐ  ॐ  ॐ

Dransfield's case is undoubtedly an extreme one, though it clearly has affinities with others in this chapter—the feminist, for instance, and the Aboriginal. Breaking English in what I'd ideally prefer *not* to call postcolonial Australia takes many forms, as we've seen. The endeavor has been going on a long time, certainly for at least the whole of the twentieth century; and the points of attack have been various and multiple. Bernard O'Dowd, inspired by the politics of democracy and the prior example of New World cultural rebellion in the form of Walt Whitman, sought at Federation in 1901 to break the stranglehold of the dominant colonizing discourse by writing (however unsuccessfully) an independent Australian self. Almost fifty years later Judith Wright joined in, rescrutinizing the gendered nature of this self—a project to which many other notable women poets were subsequently to lend their energies, re-viewing the English available to feminist writers in Australia at that time. In the late-

1980s, Diane Fahey undertook the task of rewriting and transforming the phallogocentric discourse she found at the foundation of Australian culture (and inherited from a European tradition mediated through English). The cultural metamorphosis she achieved is somewhat similar to that necessitated by the plight of some indigenous poets, seeking to articulate their Aboriginality in a kind of English which would allow them to write themselves, without overly compromising with the (racist) colonizing discourse inherited from a xenophobic imperium. And finally we saw Michael Dransfield caught between discourses and ending up with an English not broken by the struggle against sexism or racism, but by the urgent necessity to voice what would be conventionally perceived as a marginal or peripheral way of living (and dying), generating virtually an anti-language which is almost no language at all.

In the final chapter I wish to turn back again to England—fifty years further on historically than when we first visited it in the preliminary chapter—to look at some recent developments there in the ongoing project of breaking English.

# 7

## Conclusion:
## The "matter of England/
## ... the matter with England"?

The British Isles had not been invaded since that famous day in 1066; so an incident occurring in the late-1980s came as something of a surprise to many. Jane M. Jacobs reports the unlikely event in her fascinating study, *Edge of Empire: Postcolonialism and the City* (1996). She writes:

> In 1988, the year in which Australia "celebrated" the bicentenary of its founding as a settler colony, an Aboriginal activist visited Britain. On a windy day on Brighton beach, surrounded by invited journalists, Burnam Burnam raised the Aboriginal flag and declared the British Isles to be Aboriginal territory. This colonial return mimicked Governor Phillip's hoisting of the Union Jack at Sydney Cove on the east coast of Australia 200 years before. (157)

This action didn't (of course) right—or even rewrite—colonial history, whatever that may be. It certainly didn't provide Burnam Burnam with the chance to declare Britain *terra nullius* (though such a declaration would have been about as honest as the original one); but it nevertheless indicated a change of direction in cultural traffic that had been going on for many years. As Bill Ashcroft, Gareth Griffiths, and Helen Tiffin put it, *The Empire Writes Back*—not just from Australia, but from many countries who have taken their lead from the rebellion (linguistic and otherwise) of that original New World nation, America. And as well, as we've seen, "writing back" may be from a site not just geographical, but also—frequently—*gender*-based.

254

This cultural phenomenon has dramatized, in various ways, profound dissatisfaction with the status quo, even on the part of such relatively moderate writers as Seamus Heaney. Heaney in his essay "Englands of the Mind," for instance, indicates that not all of these "Englands" (or all of these "Mind[s]," for that matter) are particularly healthy ones: so he can note that

> English poets are being forced to explore not just the matter of England, but what is the matter with England. I have simply presumed to share in that exploration through the medium which English has, for better or worse, impressed upon us all, the English language itself. (in *Preoccupations*, 169)

The language may be "impressed upon" a number of writers (and nations), but not all are equally impressed *by* it: that is, certainly not all share the presumptions underlying that language, as we've seen throughout. Several authors, in fact, far from silently assenting to the (cultural) imperialism embedded in what was once the dominant colonial discourse, have undertaken the project labeled by Chris Tiffin and Alan Lawson as "De-Scribing Empire," in which (as Jo-Ann Wallace puts it) it may be necessary to engage in "the writing, unwriting, and re-writing of imperialist texts."[1] Tiffin and Lawson actually begin their study by "unwriting" a notable act of flag-raising—not that of Burnam Burnam, but of another "antipodean," Edmund (later Sir Edmund) Hillary. The venue is not Brighton beach but the (even windier) summit of Chomolungma, or Mount Everest as it was (and still is) better known in Coronation-Day Britain. The editors unwrite this imperial text by restoring the mountain's local and traditional name (as opposed to its imposed British colonial one); by emphasizing that Hillary is a New Zealander (not an Englishman); and by elevating to prominence the name of the Himalayan sherpa, Tensing Norgay (whom Hillary himself has always fully acknowledged, but who was given a remarkably low profile by the British press of the day). Tiffin and Lawson note the complexity with which the event has been "incorporated into imperial discourse":

> Both the start and end of the [newspaper report] . . . assert a frame of the coronation. The successful ascent is a "conquest" of a foreign and "unknown" geographical space. . . . The conqueror is of British (in the Greater Britain sense) birth and breeding. The nineteenth-cen-

tury figure of the Empire as crown (with India as its principal jewel) is redeployed as a new crown constituted by the courageous deeds of the sons and daughters of Empire. (2)

While a certain amount of jingoism might be understandable on Coronation Day itself in 1953, almost fifty years on this "England of the Mind" is clearly out-of-date, however appealing to British conservatism. Tom Paulin in his article "Into the Heart of Englishness" (in *The Times Literary Supplement* of 20 July 1990), writing about Philip Larkin's vision of the mother country at the time of the Queen's Silver Jubilee, notes that "Because things rich and splendid are now at an end, life on the island is unheroic, routine, toadlike" (779). The conclusion of Paulin's open heart examination is that there may in fact no longer *be* a heart at all, that as a result of our surgery we will witness only "the maybe missing centre" of "Englishness" (ibid.).

Paulin's remarks are directed primarily at the deployment of these notions in *textual* space; but the debate about an essential lack revealed here, and about the whole status of "English"(ness) is echoed throughout the fabric of the culture, even in physical *urban* space, as Jane M. Jacobs recounts in the first part of her study *Edge of Empire*, providing interesting parallels with the literary and linguistic case that is our main concern in the present volume. Jacobs talks about the construction in the metropolis of a new "ethnoscape" in which "ambivalent new communities are thrust together with anxiously nostalgic old ones." At this point, and subsequently, she might be talking (as of course she *is*, in part) about *linguistic* communities, in which "Xenophobic fears and gentler fantasies of a surer past of imperial might manifest as a politics of racism, domination and displacement which is enacted, not on distant shores, but within the very borders of the nation-home" (24)—the empire "writing back" with a vengeance! As Jacobs emphasizes, this is a significant change of venue, since "During the height of nineteenth-century imperialism Britain's colonized Other resided a safe distance from the imperial heartland" so that "Geography was set in favor of preserving neat imperial divides between Self and Other" (70–71)—the size of the globe furnishing a kind of super-*Pale*, as it were.

Chapter 3 of Jacobs's book (38–69) is entitled "Negotiating the Heart: Place and Identity in the Postimperial City," and it deals with the notorious Bank Junction redevelopment project in the very center of the city of London. Here the questions of England's (and English's) colonial and postcolonial identities come into sharp focus literally at the heart of affairs. The commercial block involved was a monument to high Victorian Empire affluence, situated in the primary business and banking district, flanked by the Mansion House, the Midland Bank, the Bank of England, and the Royal Exchange— a territory to which one might well apply Fred D'Aguiar's term, "capitally British" (in Allnutt et al., *The New British Poetry*, 3).

The fundamental topic to be addressed was whether or not this "sacred" symbolic area should be redeveloped at all, or whether at least the external fabric of the imperium should be preserved. The debate was given extra piquancy by manifestations of *post-Victorian* xenophobia in view of the development group's and architects' nationalities. That is, opponents of the modernization scheme pointed out the irony of the fact that this area had survived the German Blitz, but was now to be demolished by a partly-German consortium whose reconstruction plans involved an (if not absolutely alien, then definitely Scottish) architect whose best-known building is the Neue Staatsgalerie in Stuttgart, and whose design for the Bank Junction block has been likened to a German control tower on wartime Alderney.[2] All of this reflects, as Jacobs puts it, the desire to promote "a domesticated memory of empire constructed in opposition to a demonized European other" (49).

World War II and the subsequent European Community aside, we can see in this debate many of the characteristics surrounding our own exploration of "broken English" and "breaking English" in the contemporary period. On the one hand is the Movement-style desire to maintain the status quo at all costs, to promote an ongoing (if absurdly outdated) notion of superior—and "pure"—Englishness, predicated on a (once enormously significant) imperial power, and bolstered by xenophobic exclusivity. On the other hand, in the face of these lingering imperial wish fulfilments, is the desire to update, to reflect changed "ethnoscapes," to *accommodate* difference (quite literally in one case Jacobs raises—the development plans for Spitalfields in east London with its high Bengali population),[3] and to achieve a social fabric flexible in word and brick. Whichever "side" one chooses, Englishness has clearly become a contested category in many manifestations of the culture—as indeed David Gervais suggests in the title of his study *Literary Englands: Visions of "Englishness" in Modern Writing* (1993).

At the end of chapter 5 we briefly saw the eminent Australian poet Les Murray's own particular vision of the matter, and his suspicions about the heart of Englishness—not that it may not exist any longer (as Tom Paulin suspects) but that it continues to lure writers unwittingly into "an imperial Anglocentricity."[4] Whether the heart is absent or continuing as an unseen malign influence, though, the obvious tactic for non-*writers* of English is *centrifugal*—as Robert Crawford suggests in his study *Devolving English Literature*. Commenting on Murray's reservations about the inclusiveness of the label "English," Crawford advocates:

> a constant awareness of the need for *devolutionary* readings—readings which are alert to all the nuances of the "provincial," "barbarian," and "colonial," to the subtle accents and strategies of the marginalized who have all too often been smoothly absorbed or repressed by being designated "English Literature." (302, my italics)

As anyone who has met Murray will attest, smoothly absorbing or repressing him is scarcely a viable strategy; and indeed in the interview with Crawford Murray emphasizes the active *difference* of Australian English, saying that "I think the real identity of Australia which potentially and even actually exists is creole." He adds that "when you look at it closely there are hundreds and hundreds of *words* that are different, and differently used"; and he even goes as far as to assert that "every word in the English language has a different meaning in Australia" (in Crawford et al., *Talking Verse*, 165). When asked if "as a poet" he has a particular "mission," his reply is " . . . only to decentralize the English language. Which is happening" (in ibid., 172).

Where Murray chooses the term "decentralize," Tiffin and Lawson offer the notion of "De-Scribing"; Alan Robinson prefers tracing "*Instabilities* in Contemporary British Poetry"; Robert Crawford insists on "Devolving"; and Janet Batsleer et al. go for the more basic "*Rewriting* English"[5]—all occupied in similar if not identical projects, all (as it were) clearing the ground around Bank Junction. Batsleer et al. might be commenting on the scenario sketched by Tiffin and Lawson of the scaling of Mount Everest on Coronation Day when they write, "we are living out the dotage of an imperial culture, and . . . our dreams are peopled by ghosts" (10). And their suggested remedy would, one imagines, appeal to (say) Murray and Crawford: they argue, intriguingly, that "the rewriting of English" will require "its formal *dis*organization as a school and university subject" (my italics), involving the development of "connection[s] that cut across and challenge the authority of [existent] . . . boundaries" (175).

This subversive act of deconstruction—aimed at the pedagogical process—seeks to undermine, too, other "ghosts" of the "imperial culture" such as the much-abused *Oxford English Dictionary*, that logical extension of Dr. Johnson's original normative linguistic endeavor. Roy Harris reports a part of this history in his study *The Language Machine*, telling us that

> In 1862 one appeal for volunteer helpers in the national dictionary project refers explicitly to "the race of English words which is to form the dominant speech of the world." The connexion between the myth of standard English and Victorian imperialism could scarcely be plainer. (117–18)

One might think that *Victorian* imperialism shouldn't concern us in the present study, and shouldn't matter too much to writers in English in the last part of the twentieth century—but in fact in some circles the Victorian seems to *hang over* for a very long time, as one of the "ghosts" in dire need of exorcism. The same might be said of the OUP's grip on the canon, a phenomenon gaining significant authority through the literary examples cited as correct usage in the *OED*, and proliferated through the number of influential anthologies and histories published under the Oxford imprint. Adrian Mitchell comments on this colonization of Eng. Lit. in his poem, "The Oxford Hysteria of English Poetry."[6] Out-canoning the canon, he charts the English poetic spirit from "the caveman days" at "Wookey Hole" right through to the contemporary period of tertiary institution patronage. In the latter, a literary-academic Establishment is generated—the narrator himself winning "the Chair of Comparative Ambiguity/ At Armpit University, Java"—and at the end of the day "It seemed like poetry had been safely tucked up for the night."

Safe packaging does wonders for the domestication of poets through the ages, then. But not everyone can fit into the pack, apparently: a notorious instance is Eric Mottram in his untamed struggles with the Arts Council of Great Britain. Mottram was editor of the "British Poetry Revival" section of the Paladin anthology *The New British Poetry* (1988), which he entitled "A Treacherous Assault on British Poetry" to commemorate his (earlier) dealings with the literary Establishment. He asserts that in the late 1970s the British Arts Council was responsible for dissolving the editorial board of *Poetry Review* (of which he was a member) because of the board's "inclusion of 'foreign poets,' particularly Americans" in its publication: this inclusion was the "treacherous assault" in question (Allnutt et al., *The New British Poetry*, 133). For those interested, Mottram goes into more detail when he deals with the situation again in his chapter ("The British Poetry Revival, 1960–75") in Peter Barry and Robert Hampson's compilation, *New British Poetries: the Scope of the Possible* (1993, 15–43). He even appends to his essay a report issued by the "Poets Conference, 11 December 1978" entitled "Poets and the Arts Council of Great Britain" (45–50), so that we can see just *how* contested some of the categories really have been over the last part of the twentieth century.

The report voices a number of grievances, many of them centering around funding. It complains that the allocation of grants has been governed by a "narrow and personally-biassed" approach; and that there has been discrimination against publications and events that didn't "'adhere to existing standards'" (46). Particularly mentioned in the report as going financially (and presumably morally) unsupported are the "flourishing group of concrete and sound poets whose work is consistently recognized abroad"—but not in England, evidently. In a prime example, an application for funds to mount the Eleventh International Sound-Poetry Festival (in London) was turned down by the Arts Council on the grounds that it fell "'outside the field of literature which [should be] . . . recommend[ed] for support'" (48).

The Mottram affair is a reminder, in case one was needed, that a poet doesn't necessarily have to be Antipodean, Gaelic, colored, or female to incur displeasure and activate prejudice in the literary arena. Nevertheless, as we've seen, old-fashioned authoritative assertions or prescriptions of what "English" should mean, and what a "poem" should embrace have failed to stop a proliferation of Englishes and poems emphatically *not* in the Movement mold. That mold, whether the Arts Council concurs or not, seems to be "broken" as the "Empire" (literal and figurative) not only "Writes Back" but *fights* back too.[7] The result, in spite of a strong conservative desire for orthodoxy, is a *hetero*doxy voiced by and serving a number of cultural communities, effectively devolving authority from the metropolitan Establishment. Even in the world of publishing, as Robert Crawford tells us, devolution is a reality; and "the power of the English cultural centre is under increasing challenge"—not only from American takeovers of traditional British houses ("Chatto, Cape, the Bodley Head, and Hutchinson"), but "from the 'provinces' and barbarian regions, home of such innovative houses as Bloodaxe Books" (*Devolving English Literature*, 301).

ॐ    ॐ    ॐ    ॐ    ॐ

The "pagan" north of England, then, is to play its part in what Edwin Morgan called the "de-Londonization" of English (*Crossing the Border*, 21); and the Viking marauder Eric Bloodaxe, his weapon advanced to the attack in the publisher's logo, is to have his "barbarian" say. Perhaps the most prominent writer to emerge under this aegis is Tony Harrison, in his own words not just "barbarian" but "Rhubarbarian"; not just "scop" but bard—in fact, "Permanently Bard."[8] The pun here underlines the outsider or deprivileged status he enjoyed from boyhood days at school (though in fact it might be more accurate to say "*lack of* status" that he certainly *didn't* "enjoy"). As one of "The Rhubarbarians" (*PB*, 63), Harrison knows that he's basically been cast in a nonspeaking role in the play that is English culture, marginalized (upstaged?), and relegated to a crowd scene where his only contribution can be to mumble "rhubarb rhubarb" in the background without even the release of a "barbaric yawp" from time to time.

This is, of course, also the well-known scenario of "Them & [uz]" (*PB*, 33–34). In the poem, Harrison recounts how an early contact in the classroom with the English literary canon is also an early contact with class prejudice and arrogance; and (budding poet though he may be) his voice is from the outset ridiculed and marginalized. Because of his northern accent, he's labeled by his English teacher as "barbarian," unfit to utter Keats's immortal (canonical) "Ode to a Nightingale." Though Keats himself didn't speak RP, his work has been appropriated by those who do, and "normalized" accordingly, a process that suppresses accent variations (both Keatsian and Harrisonian). So the (upper class) voice of the teacher in the poem warns Harrison that "your speech is in the hands of the Receivers"— that is, in the eyes (and ears) of the literary and academic Establishment, bankrupted and confiscated. As a result, in his formative years the scholarship boy Harrison is reduced to "prose," having to read the part of the drunken porter in *Macbeth*, and denied the glories of Shakespeare's blank verse and tragic heroes. According to at least one commentator, his subsequent poetry-writing career has been "an act of slow revenge upon that original English teacher."[9] Whether or not this is true, certainly a great deal of his art (and probably his heart) has been involved in dramatizing the conflict between "Them & [uz]." That is, battle lines are drawn between those who "own" standard RP English (who are, of course, "nicely spoken") and whose hegemony needs to be broken; and those who *don't*, who own nothing (whose affairs, linguistic and otherwise, are always on the edge, waiting to be sequestered by the "Receivers"). These latter (as we learn in part 2 of "Them & [uz]") must become iconoclasts prepared to "occupy / your lousy leasehold Poetry" (become language squatters in the domain of the privileged) in order to gain a voice and make themselves heard.

Otherwise, unless "[uz]" are prepared to fight back (linguistically at least), the message is clear: once a victim, always a victim—not only in the classroom but as well in the ironically-titled "National Trust" (*PB*, 62). As we discover, to "trust" the power-élite in this "nation" is not merely to have one's heritage (including the entrenched class system) preserved by an Establishmentarian institution, but to be forced down a hole until we go insane! The poem recounts the tale of a convict lowered by the gentry (for a bet) into a deep pit so as to gauge its depth—an exercise that, it seems, drove the hapless victim mad and unable to speak. Harrison suggests a similar tactic be employed for a National Trust site in Cornwall, except that the individual despatched down the mineshaft should be a scholar rather than a jail-bird. The moral he adduces from all this is in the form of a Cornish proverb, which he translates as "the tongueless man gets his land took." One might add that the man's language is "took" as well; and Carol Rutter in a note to the poem points out that the chasms featured here are "like the black holes of history into which the dumb disappear" (in *PB*, 145).

As Terry Eagleton says of Harrison, "No English poet has shown more finely how the sign is a terrain of struggle where opposing accents intersect, how in a class-divided society language is cultural warfare and every nuance a political valuation" (in Astley, *Tony Harrison*, 349). I suggested a few moments ago (taking my cue from the title of Harrison's well-known poem) that the "warfare" is between "them & [uz]"; but it seems to me that that's not exactly right. Rather, the conflict's between [ʌs] and [uz], between differently-accented constructions of how we see and claim ourselves ("us")—a phenomenon we saw earlier in the apparently very different environment of Rastafarian language with its "I-n-I."[10] So, in Harrison's account, the privileged will use the power-language of RP, describing themselves as "[ʌs]"; while the nonprivileged who talk with a "foreign," nonstandard accent (almost—if one can speak of such a thing—a kriol from Leeds), pronounce themselves as "[uz]" or some alternative variant. Whatever we call ourselves, though—at least the way Harrison tells it in part II of "Them & [uz]," "[uz]" must triumph in the end: our own "name" and "voice" will occupy the textual territory, as a result of which it'll be "RIP" for "RP" (*PB*, 34).

An interesting and perhaps unexpected ally of this intransigent assertion of northern dialect is another "foreigner"—David Dabydeen who, like Harrison, prides himself (as we've already seen) "On Not Being Milton."[11] Dabydeen, we remember, draws analogies between his own Guyanese creole and the "lawlessness of the primarily oral form" of northern dialect Middle English (in *Sir Gawain and the Green Knight*), as if the latter were yet another linguistic element in the Caribbean continuum of languages (in "On Not Being Milton," 4). That is, a parallel evidently exists between the Guyanese creole's relationship to standard English, and that of the Gawain-poet (who is Harrison's northern cultural ancestor) to Chaucerian metropolitan English. Dabydeen elaborates the analogy, as Rick Rylance notes in yet another work entitled "On Not Being Milton,"[12] as follows:

> The language problem [experienced by many black writers in Anglophone areas] is symptomatic of the wider political and cultural situation in a way which is true for users of variant forms within "English" [and England] also. Thus Anglophone Caribbean writers are creating a "nation language" which uses English elements but draws on a wider repertory of popular forms . . . to express a Caribbean identity distinct from that offered by the English education system. (in Astley, *Tony Harrison*, 125)

The kinship between writers (such as Dabydeen, and Brathwaite) "working in the Caribbean" and writers (such as Harrison) working "outside the mainstream in England itself" is underlined by rebellion against the canonized high rhetoric of perhaps the greatest English epic writer, John Milton. As Rylance continues,

> Dabydeen contrasts Milton's language with Caribbean creole. "Milton's ornate, highly-structured, Latinate expressions . . . are still the exemplars of English civilization against which the barbaric utterances of black people are judged," he argues. Creole, on the other hand, expresses black experience authentically without the imperialist distortions of "standard English." It is energetic, lyrically and sexu-

ally lively and draws vitally on ordinary speech. Interestingly, Dabydeen makes an analogy between the black experience of language and "the ancient divide between north and south in Britain." (in Astley, *Tony Harrison,* 125)[13]

So perhaps it's *not* so surprising after all to find, for instance, that Dabydeen's *Coolie Odyssey* (1988), a book celebrating a particular West Indian occasion—the one hundred and fiftieth anniversary of an Indian presence in the Caribbean—should begin with reference to the "North" of both Heaney and Harrison:

> Now that peasantry is in vogue,
> Poetry bubbles from peat bogs,
> People strain for the old folk's fatal gobs
> Coughed up in grates North or North East
> 'Tween bouts o' livin dialect. . . .[14]

What's happening here, as we've seen so often in the course of this study, is a forging of new alliances against a common "enemy" (the standard code) that effectively remakes the postcolonial cultural world of English. As Benita Parry puts it in her essay on Dabydeen's poetry entitled "Between Creole and Cambridge English," this project "estranges customary English usage" and "redraws the map of territory charted by a European cartography."[15]

Douglas Dunn, that expert on *Barbarians,* is prepared to redraw the linguistic map further, or at least in a slightly different way, when he argues in the essay, "Formal Strategies in Tony Harrison's Poetry" that the "linguistic dominion" contested by writers like himself (or for that matter Dabydeen) may also be an object of combat for native English writers such as Harrison. He comments that, as poets from Ireland, Scotland, and Wales know only too well, "the phrase 'the English Language' tends to promote a British 'national unity' that has never existed." Such nonexistent unity may be challenged by, for instance, using Gaelic; but it can also be contested "through the astute use of English itself." And this is where, Dunn believes, Harrison comes in: in the face of an "English" literary institution that requires respect, even "love," Harrison would retort, "Go to blazes" (in Astley, *Tony Harrison,* 129).

The point is well made, though one suspects that Dunn's gentility in the exclamation "Go to blazes" is probably misplaced, and Harrison himself would have preferred (and used) something more astringent that might have come from Tom Leonard's mouth—

Leonard and Harrison having a great deal in common in their approaches to literary (and "bad") language. Harrison would certainly
concur with Leonard's bitter observation in the essay "Literature, Dialogue, Democracy" that "Inequality of status of diction has been
one peculiarly British way of sorting people into a hierarchy of
worth" (in *Reports from the Present*, 58).

One thing the two writers clearly have in common is the link expressed here—and made on all relevant occasions—between language (and accent), class, and politics. Ken Worpole in his essay
"Scholarship Boy: the Poetry of Tony Harrison" writes that the class
conflicts that bedeviled Harrison's grammar school days revolved
most obviously around "spoken language," working-class pupils
being judged by the standards of RP "('form of speech used by the
majority of cultured people,' *Concise Oxford Dictionary*) . . . and found
badly wanting" (in Astley, *Tony Harrison*, 65). Subsequent to his scholarship days Harrison has stated a preference (on the strength of his
experience at school) for "language that communicates directly and
immediately" without any mediation by Established authorities: he
opts for the notion of "men speaking to men" rather than men working via "Oxford's anointed" (in ibid., 9).

This would perhaps account for his "Not Being Milton," and not
wishing to be! Again one perhaps thinks of Tom Leonard's embracing of "thi lang- / wij a thi / guhtr" rather than subscribing to the
"'Received Pronunciation' of . . . Oxford," that tertiary institution
(which, Leonard asserts, like the whole university system) "is a reifi-
cation of the notion that culture is synonymous with property."[16] In
all of this, the educative process of the Establishment seems bent on
the status quo, canceling out any accidental benefits (such as Harrison's grammar school scholarship) that it temporarily grants. Douglas Dunn, speaking of Harrison's sequence of poems entitled *v.* in
his brief article "Abrasive Encounters," sees the poem sequence as
confronting the plight of all the people striving to make themselves
heard in a system that "disinherits as many of those as its democracy
manages to educate" (in Astley, *Tony Harrison*, 347).

At this point, the dictionary surprisingly crops up again—but this
time not as a tool of the enemy. That is, rather than being a normative device of the Establishment and RP, it becomes a means of self-
education (when the system itself fails) and of self-improvement.
The volume *v.* (1985, n. p.) takes as its epigraph a quotation from
that northern folk-hero (to some) the leader of the National Union

of Mineworkers, Arthur Scargill, who apparently said in the *Sunday Times* of 10 January 1982: "*My father still reads the dictionary every day. He says your life depends on your power to master words.*" Certainly here, as the linguist John Honey has been aware, *Language Is Power*—a proposition taken up also in Harrison's poem "Wordlists" (*PB*, 38–39) which deals with the power immanent in the dictionary. The epigraph on this occasion, similar to that of *v.*, albeit from a somewhat different source, gives us the dying words—or word—of Joseph Wright: the word in question is, of course, "*Dictionary.*" Carol Rutter in her notes to the poem tells us that Wright, who was a northerner and in his youth worked in a woolen mill, eventually "became professor of comparative philology at Oxford and the editor of the *Dialect Dictionary*" (in *PB*, 128–29). As a member of the working class, the example of Wright inspires Harrison, because the power to which Wright's education gave him access has also been made available to Harrison. If, as Arthur Scargill's father asserted, the power to master words is indispensable, then—as Harrison himself says in "Wordlists"—the dictionary can become "A bible paper bomb"—and even the "OED" may be pressed into service in the good fight to gain "other tongues."[17]

Not all Oxford dons need to be mugged, then! In fact it's typical of Harrison's approach that he's prepared to use whatever instruments are at his disposal (from Leeds Grammar School onwards) to articulate his position more forcefully. This is one of the reasons he almost always uses traditional poetic forms for his work—not (of course) as a slavish kowtowing to the conventions of the Established canon (after all, he doesn't want to be Milton); but to test out several ways of saying, in order to determine what still works and what's broken. In an interview with Michael Alexander, speaking of the formal traditions he airs in his poetry, Harrison says his tactic is "to subject them to a sort of maximum strain as . . . for example in *v*, where I take a very classical form but inhabit it with the most profane language," thus applying to it "all the stresses and strains of modern existence, modern thought, modern attitudes" (in Crawford et al., *Talking Verse*, 85).

A few pages later, he makes reference to a very different phenomenon surviving into the modern period and also subject to all sorts of stresses and strains—Hadrian's Wall! Harrison notes that he lives "near the Roman wall" (which, as well as being another inherited formal structure is, of course, on one level just another version of the Pale, designed to exclude the barbarian). However, he doesn't see this as altogether a negative site: if the wall represents "a past imperialism," nevertheless it may be turned to present constructive effect (if only relatively modestly) by being "requarried into the limekiln or made into pig-troughs or barns." He goes on, "I am interested in the way things are recycled," and he mentions not only "material things," but "spiritual things" too (in ibid., 90): and surely one might add here "language" as well.

Clearly Harrison would be on the side of the developers of Bank Junction (not to mention Stephen Muecke's bricolage)! The old order may still be of some use, then; or it may need to be replaced or recycled (re-viewed and re-written): either way, nostalgia and a desperate clinging to the past for past's sake is not a viable alternative. His literary-linguistic tactics, though, require a careful balancing act: Terry Eagleton notes that Harrison's particular skill is in "just subduing colloquial raw materials to some semblance of iambic order without civilizing them out of sight" (in Astley, *Tony Harrison*, 349)—a conjuring trick managed not without controversy at times (as notoriously with the 1987 televized adaptation of *v.*), but with vigor and in a wide range of writing.

Of late, Harrison has concentrated more and more on translation, a writerly act whose "politics," as Joe Kelleher suggests, "straddles issues of cultural conformity and cultural resistance," staging "a series of political negotiations" in addition to the obvious one of "'crossing linguistic barriers'" (*Tony Harrison* [1996], 22). Even early on, Harrison was interested in experimenting with such challenges, and Sandie Byrne in her compilation *Tony Harrison: Loiner* (1997) tells us that while at Ahmadu Bello University in Nigeria he collaborated in a production of Aristophanes' *Lysistrata* that "used Standard and Pidgin English to re-create the linguistic and social division between Attic and Doric Greek" (5–6). This gives us an indication of the resources—and resourcefulness—at the poet's disposal, the way he can create a variety of "Englishes" appropriate to each textual occasion, without being hamstrung by notions of purity or decorum, or for that matter by a single homogeneous view of Englishness that must be defended at all costs.

Tony Harrison is just one of a number of poets to have emerged from the north of England in the de-Londonization of British poetry in the second half of the twentieth century. Undoubtedly the very best known of these has been Ted Hughes—but when he became

Poet Laureate (and probably well before that date), he ceased to be an inspiration for the younger generation of poets, even from his native north. In fact he became, in some quarters, an object of embarrassment, even ridicule. This phase of his career, when—as Official State Poet—he morally (if not literally) *re*-Londonized himself, has been wickedly, and very astutely, satirized by Ian McMillan in his poem "Ted Hughes is Elvis Presley" in *Dad, the Donkey's on Fire* (1994, 19–21).

The incommensurate hugeness of Ted ("'He was too, too big,' I said"), his celebrity and macho Elvis-the-Pelvis-like gyrations, all feed into a text where the line between pop stardom and Laureateship becomes blurred and eventually obliterated. At the beginning of the poem, the Elvis voice has cheated death and moves to England where, somewhat after the fashion of the Momo-Lumb in Hughes's *Gaudete*,[18] it takes over Hughes and becomes a grotesque combination figure:

> I am Elvis Presley.
> I am Ted Hughes.

This composite "stride[s] the moors / in a white satin jump suit" and then, gathering the appropriate Hughesian creatures around him/them/it—foxes, jaguars, pigs, crows—buckles down to the task of being Poet Laureate and writing a Royal memorial. Regrettably, it doesn't quite work, because bits of Presley's favorite hits—"Wooden Heart," "Blue Hawaii"—keep intruding. The tragic fate of this pop idol/ famous poet who throws such "a huge shadow on the wall" and was at the outset substituted by "a barrage balloon" is that he somehow gets punctured (deflated) and begins to shrivel away until the "Elvis, Ted" is only "three inches long." It would be unworthy, I think, of the great man's memory, to speculate on just how far this is really a fiction; but certainly one message is clear: Hughes, who was the significant voice of the north as far back as the 1950s, is certainly *not* that voice in McMillan's opinion now. In fact the two presumably don't "speak the same language" at all, in spite of the circumstance of sharing English as a mother-tongue.

In any event, in the four or so decades that separate them, the two poets' norths are quite different places. Hughes's is (or was) a bracing Yorkshire of near-caricatural, invigorating wildness and dark natural mystery (later reduplicated regularly, and finally tamed for Laureateship duties); while McMillan's is a semiderelict, semiurban

Thatcherite world of unemployment and hopelessness. Not surprisingly, then, the younger poet won't countenance the high culture English into which Hughes bought; and he deliberately plays down any loftiness that might attach to his own calling: so a note on the rear cover of McMillan's *Selected Poems* (1987) can describe him as "A tennis ball packer who turned professional poet. . . ." This is in keeping—with all due respect to tennis ball packers—with his projection of himself as a sort of combination standup comedian (something which Harrison flirted with too)[19] and northern Surrealist. As advocate and writer, he presides over an accelerating textual slippage which is the verbal equivalent of a mined-out industrial terrain—what the anonymous "blurb"-writer of the *Selected Poems* calls "an odd perspective," from "an unusual corner" of the language.

McMillan's work is as arresting as the television series *Boys from the Black Stuff* and, the surface humor aside, ultimately about as funny in its implications (which is *not at all*). The poetry is played out against what sometimes appears to be a casual or incidental backdrop of industrial dereliction, seemingly indicated in passing, but which in the end accumulates to overwhelm the foreground ("On the Closure of Cadeby Colliery"; "Pit Closure as Art"; "The er Barnsley Seascapes"; "The Grimness" [*Dad, the Donkey's on Fire*, 73; 12–13; 82–86; 89–92]). So, even in what might have been the idyllic setting of "Postmodernist Summer Nights in the Dearne Valley" we're faced with an extraordinarily unsettling elegy in which the language the poet must use collapses inwards

> on itself. A dead fish falling
> in the bath. . . .
>
> (ibid., 129)

The surrealist catachresis here turns McMillan's favored comedic patter into something more obviously dark. It destabilizes our readerly response to the local landscape and language in a world where reason, stable order, and rationality may not pertain any longer. As he suggests in the poem "Responses to Industrialization" (*Selected Poems*, 26–27), "Purity of diction is one thing," but we live in a different world, a "now" which just may not register in terms of such "purity."

৵    ৵    ৵    ৵    ৵

In the work of McMillan and Harrison we see the language of English poetry marshaled to reflect and articulate new (though not necessarily desirable) "Englands of the Mind," whether they be what David Gervais describes in *Literary Englands* as "post-English" or not.[20] Outside England, as we've seen in the course of this present study, the category "English" has been similarly contested, and effectively dismantled as a single entity. As early as 1948, William Carlos Williams in his essay "The Poem as a Field of Action" (in *Selected Essays* ) had suggested that while "To the English, English is England" (291), the New World perspective on the matter might be rather different. Looking back a further century to the example of Walt Whitman, Williams saw that Americans, "yawping speakers of a new language" were in a "privileged" position from which they might "sense and . . . seek to discover . . . unknown elements [that] would disturb" the received wisdom and the status quo (286).

Demographically, of course, the situation of English has changed markedly in the period about which Williams was commenting. As Sidney Greenbaum says in his essay "Whose English?":

> it is difficult to justify England's distinctive claim to English: there are four times as many speakers of English in the United States as in the whole of the United Kingdom, and there are probably more English speakers in second-language countries than there are in mother-tongue countries. (in Ricks and Michaels, eds., *The State of the Language*, 23)

The endpapers of the volume from which Greenbaum's essay comes are of interest in this regard because one of the editors, Christopher Ricks, uses them to take the opportunity to deconstruct the *OED* definition of "ENGLISH." He interrogates (for instance) the *Dictionary*'s citing of the phrase **"the King's, the Queen's English"** by demanding (among other things) whose property this really is, assuming that for the sake of argument such a thing even exists at all.

And yet perhaps one shouldn't be *too* tough on the *OED*. E. S. C. Weiner, one of the coeditors of the *Dictionary* and previously a worker on the *OED Supplement*, writes in *The State of the Language* that the vocabulary of "English" has become "federated rather than centralized." He adds that every English-speaker is "to some extent 'multilingual' within English" (501).

While Tom Leonard and Tony Harrison might doubt the absolute veracity of such liberal democratic linguistic sentiments, certainly this statement represents a significant step forward in *OED* editorial enlightenment. The acceptance of variations here is reflected in the more directly literary world by the contents of the 1998 anthology *The Penguin Book of Poetry from Britain and Northern Ireland since 1945*, which—in addition to the usual and expected—has embraced someone who came from the United States (Sylvia Plath) and someone who went there (Thom Gunn); includes poems in Welsh as well as Scottish and Irish Gaelic; and even finds a few pages for concrete poetry of mild (Edwin Morgan) to moderate (Ian Hamilton Finlay) concreteness—not to mention marginal drawings by Stevie Smith. All in all, this constitutes a various and pleasurably stimulating experience for the reader. One element, however, that the publication *can't* accommodate, purely on practical grounds, is that of *performance* poetry, though here too there have been significant developments, as we've seen. Sean O'Brien in his "Afterword: *In Search of an Audience*" in *The Deregulated Muse* contrasts the earlier experience of poetry readings—"held in university lecture theatres, where the somnambulent addressed the catatonic in a religiose torment devised in the interests of 'culture'"—with more recent "theatrical and celebratory" events put on by "performance poets such as John Agard, Grace Nichols, Linton Kwesi Johnson, Jackie Kay and Benjamin Zephaniah" (272). Obviously, things are re-energizing all over!

Throughout this present study we've seen various Englishes generated in a wide variety of cultural circumstances to challenge the hegemony of "English"—from Whitman's "barbaric yawp" to Ginsberg's "Howl"; from Rich's "dream of a common language" to Heaney's "green English"; from Johnson's "dub" to Fahey's *Metamorphoses*. All are liberations from a centrist ideal of a "pure" English diction; all subvert and undermine the positing of a single (dominant, colonizing) English. As we see in the most recent Penguin anthology (*PBPBI*), that old notion appears to have been broken, so that new Englishes are constantly breaking out of the silence. Perhaps it would be appropriate, therefore, to conclude with the profound words of one of the younger generation writers to have broken through in the closing decade of the century—Robert Crawford—who, in his volume *Identifying Poets: Self and Territory in Twentieth-Century Poetry* (162) writes: "Homogeneity—who needs it?"

# Notes

## 1. Introductory Discussion

1. London: Chatto and Windus, 1952. The volume was reissued several years later with a new postscript (London: Routledge and Kegan Paul, 1967). For chronology's sake, I shall restrict my quotations and comments to the earlier edition, which preceded the Movement anthology, *New Lines* (1956).

2. Perhaps the first academic to make use of this double meaning of "Broken" was Colin MacCabe, in an introductory article entitled "Broken English" to a special issue of *Critical Quarterly* 28, nos. 1–2 (Spring, Summer 1986): 3–14. Therein MacCabe talks about, on the one hand, the academic discipline of English "hopelessly broken in its attempt to assure a uniform language or literature"; and, on the other, "the enormous varieties of cultural forms in English" liberated by such a breakage (14).

In passing, one might note a somewhat similar usage, not in the purely academic world this time, but in the realm of popular culture: the English singer Marianne Faithfull titled her LP of 1979 *Broken English* (Island Records Ltd., L-38772).

3. In a public lecture given at the University of Canterbury (New Zealand) on 1 November 1999, Dr. John Simpson, Chief Editor of the *OED*, made the important point that he saw the publication's contemporary function as *descriptive*, not *prescriptive*. However, with the best will in the world, given the *OED*'s (and for that matter the OUP's) historical status, irrespective of editorial intention in this particular case, the descriptive tends to assume the status of the prescriptive in view of the *Dictionary*'s widely conceded authority, now and earlier. The book may find it hard to live down its history—a history shrewdly charted by John Willinsky, who writes:

> The dictionary contributed to Rule Britannia by equipping the conquering language with a coherent history that ran back through the nation's best writers. . . .
> It was not long before an educational version of this virtuous literary heritage was used to arm the "colonial spiritual policemen." . . . The *OED* was but one of many vehicles that formalized aspects of English culture in preparation for advancing the Anglicizing mission. . . . As it turned out, the actual [original] editing of the *OED* spanned the last great gasp of British imperialism. (202)

4. This passage is the beginning of the final section (section 52) of Whitman's "Song of Myself" (*Walt Whitman: Complete Poetry and Collected Prose* [New York: Viking Press, 1982], 87). Unless otherwise stated, all future references to Whitman's work will be from this text.

5. This text (along with the other anonymous review mentioned here) is conveniently available in the Penguin Critical Anthology, *Walt Whitman*, edited by Francis Murphy (Harmondsworth: Penguin Books, 1969), 37–42. Subsequent reference to this volume will be to "Murphy."

6. Whitman's talk of the "free play of the muscle" here is symptomatic of the sheer physicality of his reference frequently. It was to influence the subsequent "Objectivist" writers (such as, notably, William Carlos Williams), who set great store by the world of material objects immediately around them as a primary reference system. Whitman seems to have gone further in this regard, equating bodily (sexual) health and vigor with cultural and spiritual health. In "Walt Whitman and his Poems" he goes on to claim of the great American poet (that is, himself): "The body, he teaches, is beautiful. Sex also is beautiful." (Murphy, 33). One need hardly point out how much such a statement was at odds with Victorian England's public reticence about such matters.

7. "MAKE IT NEW" is actually Ezra Pound's famous formulation, and became a catchphrase for early modernism. Though used in a number of places, it is most conveniently to be found in "Canto LIII" (*The Cantos of Ezra Pound* [London: Faber and Faber, 1975], 265).

8. "Slang in America" appeared as an article in the magazine *North American Review*, November 1855. It appears in the Viking *Collected Poetry and Collected Prose* which is my primary source for quotations from Whitman. "An American Primer" was a series of notes for a lecture never delivered, but probably dating from 1855 to 1860, and eventually published in 1904. My source for the quotations from this document is Murphy, 64–79.

9. Unless otherwise indicated, all quotations from Williams's work are taken from *The William Carlos Williams Reader*, edited by M. L. Rosenthal (New York: New Directions, 1966). This quotation, from the section of *In the American Grain* entitled "The Fountain of Eternal Youth," appears on 330.

10. This and the following passage I quote are part-paraphrased and part-quoted in James Scully's interesting anthology, *Modern Poets on Modern Poetry* (London: Fontana, 1966), 69.

11. Like its American cousin, Objectivism, Imagism (as the name implies) focussed the energy of the poem on the image, cutting out extraneous narrative and elaboration. Pound prescribed the following:

1. Direct treatment of the "thing" whether subjective or objective.
2. To use absolutely no word that does not contribute to the presentation.
3. As regarding rhythm: to compose in the sequence of the musical phrase, not in sequence of a metronome.

("A Retrospect," in *Literary Essays of Ezra Pound*
[London: Faber and Faber, 1954], 3)

Seen in the context of popular late-Victorian long narrative poems, Imagism and Objectivism become antidotes to that nineteenth-century fashion, seeking to review and reposition poetry in the modern cultural matrix.

## 2. GENTILITY AND ITS ALTERNATIVES

1. See, for instance, *The Course of English Surrealist Poetry since the 1930s* (New York: Edwin Mellen Press, 1989), chapter 12; or "Ted Hughes: Surrealist?" *Dada/Surrealism*, 8 (1978), 134–45.

2. The sanest and most comprehensive study of the "Movement" is undoubtedly Blake Morrison's *The Movement: English Poetry and Fiction of the 1950s* (Oxford: Oxford University Press, 1980). Perhaps the most solid commentary on Larkin is Terry Whalen's *Philip Larkin and English Poetry* (London: Macmillan, 1986); or, to be really appalled, read Andrew Motion's *Philip Larkin: a Writer's Life* (London: Faber and Faber, 1993). My own remarks on Larkin occur in chapter 3 of my book, *A Study of Cultural Centres and Margins in British Poetry since 1950: Poets and Publishers* (New York: Edwin Mellen Press, 1995).

3. In *The Poet in the Imaginary Museum: Essays of Two Decades* (Manchester: Carcanet Press, 1977), 48. This interesting collection of essays charts Davie's own gradual move away from notions of purity and gentility, though that move lies beyond the scope of the present book. For Davie's later opinions on some of the issues raised here, see his *Under Briggflatts: a History of Poetry in Great Britain 1960–1988* (Manchester: Carcanet Press, 1989). My own remarks on his change of direction may be found in *A Study of Cultural Centres and Margins*, particularly 152–53 and 159–60.

4. See above, 13 ff.

5. As an alumnus of that rival institution, the University of Cambridge, perhaps I should be more careful to hide my glee at this point. Or perhaps I should at least divert attention from it by directing readers, for further comment on the subject of the University origins of various twentieth-century poetry groups, to Donald Davie's article, "The Varsity Match" in *Poetry Nation*, no. 2 (1974), 72–80. Therein Davie notes that, unlike the Boat Race and other sporting engagements between Oxford and Cambridge over the last half-century, which have come out relatively even, in the literary stakes one side is unrivaled: he says, "each new generation of English poets . . . was formed or fomented or dreamed up by lively undergraduates at Oxford, who subsequently carried the group-image to London and from there imposed it on the public consciousness" (73). He also points out that "because the [literary] positions that matter [in London] are so few, it is entirely feasible for a group to secure one or two sub-editorial chairs and a few reviewing 'spots,' so as to impose their shared proclivities and opinions as the reigning orthodoxy for a decade" (74)—which is clearly what Larkin and his peers did (and more): Davie quotes Ian Hamilton as saying of the "Movement" initiative, "'it was a take-over bid and it brilliantly succeeded'" (77). As a result of all this, Davie concludes, "We really are a small nation, aren't we?" (80).

6. Alvarez's remark about the "gentlemanly ideal" here arises in the context of a far-from-gentlemanly "debate" that was currently going on in that rival institution, Cambridge University, centring on the redoubtable personage of F. R. Leavis. At this time it was possible to see eminent members of the English faculty at Cambridge storming in and/or out of lecture- and common-rooms with monotonous regularity, in a manner very "public" and far from "mild."

7. As John Willinsky tells us (3), the dictionary-making urge at the Clarendon Press was, in fact, triggered during the days of late-Victorian empire, in January 1884, with the serial publication of a seven thousand word word-list.

8. My initial information here comes from John Honey's significantly-titled volume, *Language Is Power: the Story of Standard English and its Enemies* (London: Faber and Faber, 1997), 62. Honey summarizes Harris's argument, which concludes that "before the publication of the famous multi-volume *Oxford English Dictionary* . . . hardly anyone had heard of standard English at all. . . ." This conclusion is one with which Honey entirely disagrees, countering it with the assertion that the concept had actually existed for centuries, even if the specific term hadn't. For Harris's "take" on the matter, unmediated by Honey's criticism, see *The Language Machine* (London: Duckworth, 1987), 115–23, and particularly 117–18, where he writes: "In 1862 one appeal for volunteer helpers in the national dictionary project refers explicitly to "the race of English words which is to form the dominant speech of the world." The connexion between the myth of standard English and Victorian imperialism could scarcely be plainer."

9. To say that John Honey "disagrees violently" with this argument is perhaps to *under*state the case! With typical combativeness he describes Crowley's book as "a disreputable work and, what is more serious, a dangerously mischievous one" (117). A few pages before this outburst, he countered Crowley's assertions by pointing out that something that might be called a canon had existed since the sixteenth century in samples of Eng. Lit. to be found in school textbooks; and that from about 1700, anthologies for school use began to appear (see *Language Is Power*, 95).

10. For a different perspective on the OUP, and an extended account of the heroic struggles of Oxford lexicographers to bully the vast undertaking of the *OED* into shape, see Peter Sutcliffe's *The Oxford University Press: an Informal History* (Oxford: Oxford University Press, 1978).

11. For a more detailed list of Larkin's contacts, honors, and positions of responsibility, see my book, *A Study of Cultural Centres and Margins*, 144 ff.

12. See above, 35.

13. As I've already suggested earlier, I can do no better than commend to the reader Blake Morrison's study of *The Movement* (1980), and Terry Whalen's *Philip Larkin and English Poetry* (1986). Or, for discussions more consonant with the present argument, consult my *A Study of Cultural Centres and Margins* (1995), chapters 2 and 3. The case of Larkin is, as most commentators concede, far more complicated than that of the Movement; but limitations of space and a different objective in this current study prevent me from going into these complexities (though I do so in *A Study*).

14. Unless otherwise indicated, all quotations from Larkin's poetry come from the 1990 revised paperback edition of *Collected Poems* (London: Marvell Press and Faber and Faber, originally 1988).

15. Coventry was one of the first major English cities to suffer the blitz. For a more overt handling of this theme by Larkin, see his novel, *Jill* (London: Faber and Faber, 1975 [originally published by the Fortune Press in 1946]), 211 ff.

16. *The Less Deceived* is the title of Larkin's volume of poems (Hessle: The Marvell Press, 1955) which came out the year before *New Lines*. The phrase became a sort of slogan or rallying point for Movement writers, indicating their refusal to

get carried away and make fools of themselves (as the "Deceived" poets of the New Apocalypse movement had done a decade earlier).

17. Unless otherwise indicated, my references to Thomas's poetry all come from the *Collected Poems 1934–1953* (ed. Walford Davies, London: J. M. Dent, 1988).

18. Elsewhere, both Blake Morrison and I have done extended analyses of these comparisons. See Morrison, *The Movement*, 150–54; and Jackaman, *A Study of Cultural Centres and Margins*, 73–82.

19. Amis's poem entitled "Against Romanticism" appeared in *New Lines* in 1956 and—in the same year—in his first full-length book of poems entitled (with remarkable lack of Romantic idealism or sense of divine inspiration) *A Case of Samples*. In the poem, in spite of being tempted by "gods," a "unicorn," and "frantic suns," the protagonist opts for "a path" that leads to "a temperate zone" and a "decent surface" with "roads that please the foot" (see *Collected Poems 1944–1979* [London: Hutchinson, 1979], 35–36).

20. See above, 45.

21. In "Gerontion" the people say "Signs are taken for wonders. We would see a sign!" (*Collected Poems 1909–1962* [London: Faber and Faber, 1963], 39)—but of course in the Movement poem there are no "wonders," and the signs have no mystical significance!

22. References to Lowell's poems will, where appropriate, be cited from *The New Poetry*; but since not all the quotations I use come from poems that appeared in that anthology, I shall also cite them from Robert Lowell, *Robert Lowell's Poems: a Selection,* edited by Jonathan Raban (London: Faber and Faber, 1974). "The Quaker Graveyard" appears (in rewritten form) in Lowell, *Selection,* 38–41.

23. The Lowell family had arrived a few years later (1639), but still early enough to be part of the New England Establishment. Randall Jarrell claims that "Of New England Mr. Lowell has the ambivalent knowledge one has of one's damned kin" (in Thomas Parkinson [ed.], *Robert Lowell: a Collection of Critical Essays* [Englewood Cliffs, N.J.: Prentice-Hall, 1968], 44); and he goes on to catalog some of the things against which Lowell rebelled: "the Old Law, imperialism, militarism, Calvinism, Authority, the father, the 'proper Bostonians'. . . . " (59) Hugh Staples, also in Parkinson, argues that "For Lowell, the Quakers symbolised inhuman cruelty—which has for its cause spiritual alienation and for its motive economic greed" (66): one can see the continuity with *In the American Grain* here.

24. As Marjorie G. Perloff points out in *The Poetic Art of Robert Lowell* (Ithaca: Cornell University Press, 1973), there are close formal similarities between the two poems (particularly when Lowell's poem was in its original version—which it isn't in Alvarez's anthology). She writes, "Even the verse form of 'The Quaker Graveyard' resembles that of 'Lycidas': its 194 lines . . . are divided like the 193 lines of 'Lycidas' into a loose structure of pentameter lines, varied by an occasional trimeter. . . ." (141).

25. See, for instance, *New Lines—II*, xv, where Conquest enlists the somewhat unlikely support of A. E. Housman to voice his distaste for the complexity and obscurity of the Metaphysicals. Lowell's allegiance to the English Metaphysical poets is perhaps best articulated in his brilliant "Waking Early Sunday Morning" (Lowell, *Selection,* 101–4), generally agreed as being based on Andrew Marvell's

"The Garden," though ending not with "delicious Solitude" but with a "Bible chopped and crucified," "the blind/swipe of the pruner" (a transparent reference to Marvell's "Mower" poems), and "our children" falling "in small war on the heels of small/war."

26. Ginsberg's poem (to which we shall return presently) begins famously, "I saw the best minds of my generation destroyed by madness, starving hysterical naked,/dragging themselves through the negro streets at dawn looking for an angry fix" (*Collected Poems 1947–1980* [New York: Harper and Row, 1984], 126). Henceforth, unless otherwise indicated, all my quotations of Ginsberg's poetry will be from this edition.

27. The main writers among the "Beats" or "Beatniks" are probably Ginsberg himself, Lawrence Ferlinghetti (founder of City Lights Books), and Jack Kerouac (author of the famous Beat novel, *On the Road*). The group got its name not (as one might expect) from an enthusiasm for music, particularly jazz, but because it tended to identify with the dead-beat, down and out members of the community, living on the edge of established society. Thomas Merrill offers a slightly different explanation when he writes that "the Beatnik feels that the demands of society are . . . pointless and without purpose. . . . Society represents an authority from without; the Beatnik seeks an authority from deep within. . . . As a result, from the social point of view he is beat, tired, 'fed up' " (in *Allen Ginsberg* [New York: Twayne, 1969], 17).

28. The reader may recall that I quoted parts of this passage in my own comments on Williams in chapter 1 (see above, 27).

29. In *On the Poetry of Allen Ginsberg*, ed. Lewis Hyde (Ann Arbor: University of Michigan Press, 1984), 26. Further quotations from this volume will be indicated in the main text as "Hyde, *Poetry of Ginsberg*."

30. See above, 55.

31. This is one of the Beats' "in" locations. In New York's East Village, it was to be the setting for Jack Kerouac's *The Subterraneans* of 1958.

32. In this section of the text Ginsberg actually talks about the urge "to recreate the syntax and measure of poor human prose." What I take him to mean by this rather ambiguous statement is that he wishes to communicate without any fake "poeticism," without the enriched vocabulary of the apocalyptic writer (which he certainly uses elsewhere). His emphasis on prose here is in line with a similar emphasis to be found in the theoretical pronouncements of Pound and William Carlos Williams, who considered the discipline of prose writing as essential also to the poet. The "poor human" voice in "Howl" is the voice of the outsider to Moloch's kingdom, the dispossessed and therefore (from Ginsberg's perspective) uncorrupted.

## 3. GENDERED SPACES AND THE NEW POETRY

1. See, for instance, Amis's interview with John McDermott in 1975, as reported in McDermott's *Kingsley Amis: an English Moralist* (London: Macmillan, 1989), 29; and extracts from Philip Larkin's letters as published in Andrew Motion's *Philip Larkin: a Writer's Life*, passim (and particularly 61, 62, 119, 143). Al-

ternatively, I provide a résumé of this material in my book, *A Study of Cultural Centres and Margins*, 104–6 (Amis), and 119–22 (Larkin).

2. This statement is reported in Alfred Alvarez's essay, "Sylvia Plath" (originally written as a memorial broadcast for the BBC Third Programme following Plath's suicide in 1963). The essay is reprinted in his *Beyond All This Fiddle: Essays 1955–1967*, 45–58. Plath's comment on Lowell occurs on p. 50.

3. For the Plath poems I deal with here I shall offer, where possible, a double reference system—to Alvarez's *The New Poetry*, and (for convenience's sake) to Plath's *Collected Poems* (henceforth *CP*) edited by Ted Hughes (London: Faber and Faber, 1981).

4. The exception, predictably enough, I suppose, is pornography-fan Kingsley Amis. His poem "Fair Shares for All" (*Collected Poems*, 51)—as well as undermining notions of egalitarianism and democracy by smutty innuendo in the title itself—revolves around the prurient metaphor of "nude steak posing behind gauze" in the butcher's shop as analogous to the commodity purveyed in "girly" magazines and striptease joints. One should perhaps add at this point that historically Amis's poem was written well before the "beefcake" shows of male strippers, so that the gender of the commodity here is unambiguous!

5. Without wishing at this point to resort to chauvinist clichés such as hair being a woman's crowning glory, it might not be irrelevant to mention the care that Plath herself is reported to have taken with her coiffure. In Ted Hughes's much-overrated *Birthday Letters* (London: Faber and Faber, 1998), for instance, in the poem "The Shot" he talks about her propensity for changing her hairstyle frequently and suddenly, including finding ways of obscuring the scar on her cheek that was a result of her earlier suicide attempt. Irrespective of what Hughes says, though, my suggestion here is that "hair" was indeed something to which Plath herself gave significance, both inside and outside her poem "Lady Lazarus."

6. In *Dad, the Donkey's on Fire* (Manchester: Carcanet Press, 1994), 19–21. We shall have recourse to this wickedly amusing (and deflating) text on a number of occasions: see, for instance, above, 268.

7. For a much more detailed discussion of the metaphor of red blood and white sheets in the context of women's writing, see Susan Gubar's interesting essay, "'The Blank Page' and the Issues of Female Creativity" in *Writing and Sexual Difference*, ed. Elizabeth Abel (Brighton: The Harvester Press, 1982), 73 ff. Gubar deals specifically with Plath in an efficient if highly compressed passage on pp. 86–88.

8. This is one of the categories supplied by Jeni Couzyn in her introduction to *The Bloodaxe Book of Contemporary Women Poets* (Newcastle upon Tyne: Bloodaxe Books, 1985). She speaks of "three basic stereotypes" by which women poets can be contained and subsequently discredited and dismissed by the literary patriarchy: *Mrs. Dedication* (such as Elizabeth Barrett Browning, talented but subordinated to a superior husband); *Miss Eccentric Spinster* (such as Emily Dickinson, talented but out of touch); and *Mad Girl* (such as Sylvia Plath, talented but insane) (15).

9. Quoted in Alfred Alvarez's *Beyond All This Fiddle*, 52; and also quoted by Alvarez in the appendix to Edward Lucie-Smith's anthology *British Poetry since 1945* (Harmondsworth: Penguin Books, 1970), 391.

10. See *A Study of Cultural Centres and Margins in British Poetry since 1950*, 311–13.

11. See above, note 8.

12. See, for instance, the *Journals*, 212, where Plath looks forward to Rich being "eclipsed" by the poems on which she herself was currently working; or 219, where she complained about not being "recognized" in spite of writing poems "richer than any [of] Adrienne Cecile Rich." The rivalry Plath expresses here undoubtedly went back to W. H. Auden's having chosen Rich's *A Change of World* for the prestigious Yale Younger Poets Award in 1951.

13. Claire Keyes in *The Aesthetics of Power: the Poetry of Adrienne Rich* (Athens: University of Georgia Press, 1986) traces many of the parallels and similarities between individual poems of Plath and Rich, seeing in Rich's work "a distillation of the general tone of many of Plath's poems" (85).

14. In Barbara Charlesworth Gelpi and Albert Gelpi, eds., *Adrienne Rich's Poetry and Prose* (New York: Norton and Co, 1993), 177. Unless otherwise stated, all subsequent quotations from Rich's work will be from this collection, indicated as *P and P*.

15. Mimicry is in fact a tactic that two of Rich's culture heroines used regularly—though rather in the sense of assuming a "little girl" diction than of satirically imitating the male voice itself. Sylvia Plath, as we've already seen, does this in some of her best-known poems; but so too does Emily Dickinson, as Rich notes when speaking of "Dickinson's 'little-girl' strategy" as a masking device for concealing the poet's subversive power (*P and P*, 187).

16. In *P and P*, 176–77; also in *On Lies, Secrets, and Silence*, 49.

17. See *P and P*, 12 n. 9.

18. In fact a preoccupation with her origins, particularly the Jewish part of her genealogy, has been a significant element in Rich's work. In "Sources" at one point she describes herself as "*split at the root* white-skinned social christian/ *neither gentile nor Jew*" (*P and P*, 103). The place in her *corpus* where she explores this most fully (other, of course, than "Sources" [*P and P*, 101–14]) is in, "Split at the Root: an Essay on Jewish Identity" (*P and P*, 224–39). Evidently she felt the need to confront this material in order to emerge (as she does at the end of "Sources") "powerful; womanly." (*P and P*, 114).

19. See "The Knight" (*P and P*, 8). At the beginning of the poem the knight rides in shining in the sun (son) in all the "gaiety of his mail" (male); but by the end, the macho figure has been deflated—if anyone in armor can be said to deflate—and reduced to a victim trapped in "walls of iron, the emblems/ crushing his chest with their weight."

20. Adrian Oktenberg in his essay "'Disloyal to Civilization': The *Twenty-One Love Poems* of Adrienne Rich" (in *P and P*, 329 ff.) argues ingeniously that the male perspective is not so much irrelevant as held in a kind of dialectical structure, as thesis to the female perspective's antithesis. Thus (to borrow Rich's metaphor) every "peak" may be read antithetically as a "crater": Oktenberg claims that Rich "is concerned with not one but two civilizations; the constant play of her mind is between (and beyond) them" (*P and P*, 330).

21. For more precise details of the quite striking parallels, see Humm's *Border Traffic*, 175–80. Or, in the context of what Humm describes as "the issue of Lowell's misogyny among that of other twentieth century men of letters faced with

the feminisation of American culture" (179), see Sandra Gilbert and Susan Gubar, *No Man's Land: the Place of the Woman Writer in the Twentieth Century, Volume 1* (New Haven: Yale University Press, 1988), 153–60.

22. For Duffy's poems, I shall where possible offer a double reference system for the works cited—to the anthology from which the poem comes, and also for convenience's sake to her *Selected Poems* (Harmondsworth: Penguin Books, 1994). "Foreign," for instance, may be found in Allnutt et al., *The New British Poetry: 1968–88*, 92; and in *Selected Poems* [henceforth *SP*], 54.

For a rather different view of Duffy's work, including some of the poems I deal with here (notably "The Dolphins" and "Psychopath"), see Ian Gregson's chapter "Carol Ann Duffy: Monologue as Dialogue" in his *Contemporary Poetry and Postmodernism: Dialogue and Estrangement* (Basingstoke: Macmillan, 1996), 97–107.

23. See above, 98.

24. The formulation comes from the title of a poem by Tony Harrison, and will be discussed further in chapter 7, below.

25. For those interested, I cover the topic of women's publishing houses in England in much more detail on 235 ff. of *A Study of Cultural Centres and Margins in British Poetry since 1950*. Chapter 5 of that book (213–50) offers a different perspective on, and selection of, women poets in English from that of the present chapter.

## 4. Ethnic Spaces in the Empire of Words

1. While there are a number of small variations in current use of the term "Westindian-British," I persist with this label on the authority of James Berry, editor of the anthology of Westindian-British poetry entitled *News for Babylon* (London: Chatto and Windus, 1984), who used the term as the title of his essay in *Poetry Review* (vol. 73, no. 2 [June 1983], 5–8). In specifically selecting Westindian-British poetry as the center of my exploration here, I'm aware—along with Fred D'Aguiar—of the reductivist dangers of generalization: as he cautions us in his editorial statement about "Black British poetry" in Allnutt et al., *The New British Poetry*, "a variety of discourses and ideologies" (4) are involved in such umbrella categories. In spite of this, it seems to me that meaningful broad statements can still be made, given that the various individual authors—and in fact the various ethnic minorities in England—are working against identical (literary) prejudices and often using similar tactics in seeking to combat them.

2. See above, 94–95. What's perhaps lacking in Marson's work that Rich perceives in Walcott's is "an integrative kind of anger" (*Adrienne Rich's Poetry and Prose*, 271) to weld the various components together at a high temperature—an anger of the kind that we'll see amply demonstrated in the work of Linton Kwesi Johnson presently.

3. See Bill Ashcroft, Gareth Griffiths, and Helen Tiffin, *The Empire Writes Back: Theory and Practice in Post-Colonial Literatures* (London: Routledge, 1989). This collaborative volume is a significant guide-book to the map of postmodernism, and features prominently in chapter 6, above, passim.

4. Dabydeen's term is borrowed from a poem by Jimi Rand entitled "Nigger Talk," which Dabydeen quotes on p. 10 of his essay (and which is also available in James Berry's *News for Babylon*, 112–14). Rand writes:

> Dis na white talk;
> Na white talk dis.
> It is coon, nignog samba wog talk.

5. The term "nation language" is Brathwaite's invention to describe what (roughly) corresponds to the linguists' notion of the "Creole continuum." Labels and descriptions in this area are tricky to establish since it's necessary to avoid the implications of (for instance) hierarchical ranking, and precedence. Paula Burnett applauds Brathwaite's term since it avoids any suggestion that Westindian-English is merely a "dialect" of the standard code, a lower subsidiary of "a 'high culture' norm" (*The Penguin Book of Caribbean Verse in English*, xxv). The same problem arises, of course, with the commonly-used term "postcolonial" itself, which arguably implies in a politically incorrect way that post-coloniality is in some sense contingent on and indebted to (in more than purely historical terms) a prior colonization.

6. In spite of Donald Davie's insistence on "purity of diction" as a governing linguistic criterion, a number of other commentators see hybridity (which Davie would presumably have considered *im*pure) as a key *virtue*. Burnett obviously fits into this category—and so too does C. D. Narasimhaiah, who (working in the context of the Indian subcontinent) sees the benefits to his own "composite culture" of an English which is a hybrid of "Celtic," "Scottish," "Saxon," "Welsh," and even "American" (see Ashcroft, Griffiths, and Tiffin, *The Empire Writes Back*, 40; and above, 198).

7. As regards the study of "Accent," Honey notes with interest that "all three of the 'representatives' of the immigrant community who were invited on to a BBC *Panorama* television programme in 1981 to discuss the Brixton riots" exhibited RP accents—as did three of the four "black MPs elected in 1987" (162). Quite what one makes of this data is another issue, of course—except perhaps to acknowledge that "Accent" does indeed seem to "Matter," or at least gets noticed.

8. For an extended discussion of the religion of Rastafarianism, see Joseph Owens's study, *Dread: the Rastafarians of Jamaica* (London: Heinemann, 1979). "Jah" [possibly derived from "Jehovah"] means "God"; "Ras" is an honorific meaning "Head" or "Prince"; and "Tafari" was Selassie's proper name, meaning "self" in Amharic. Further, "Rastafari" means "Head Creator"; and "Haile Selassie" means "Power of the Trinity." Embedded in these titles and names are a series of complex puns (such as, for instance, "fari" in "Rastafari" as "Far Eye" [vision] and "For I" [belonging to the elect]).

9. See above, 229, 235–36. As regards the tactics of naming in Rastafarianism, Joseph Owens emphasizes that "Names have a special importance and significance for the Rastafarians; a name or a title is not an arbitrary sound, but rather conveys in some way the reality of the person or the thing signified. Every name, indeed every word, is pregnant with significance for the Rastafarians, and they delight in scrutinizing every syllable for possible meaning" [see, for instance, footnote 8, immediately above] (*Dread*, 119).

10. For a list of the commonest examples, see Owens, *Dread*, 66–67; and for his further remarks on Dread Talk, see the whole section of *Dread* from 64–68.

11. The notion of Caribbean immigration to England as an act of colonizing in reverse has an obvious appeal for many Westindian-British writers, as does the cultural merging of the British Isles into the West Indian island chain. E. A. Markham, for instance, writes that West Indian poetry is mainly generated from a series of offshore islands—Jamaica, Trinidad, Britain (prefatory quotation to *Hinterland*, n.p.); and David Dabydeen can claim that England, with a current West-Indian population of over half a million, has become the largest West-Indian island except for Jamaica and Trinidad ("On Not Being Milton," 12).

12. Petersen and Rutherford, eds., (Sydney: Dangaroo Press, 1986). This collection, as we'll see, traces parallels between the situations of women writers in a number of anglophone cultures, and is of particular significance to our argument later in discussing the phenomenon of "double colonization" in contemporary *Australian* women's writing (see above, 211 ff.).

13. Apart from being one of her most popular performance pieces, "Riddym Ravings" has been widely published. It appeared as the title poem in Breeze's collection, *Riddym Ravings and Other Poems* from Race Today Publications in 1988; and was reprinted in her collection, *Spring Cleaning*, from Virago Press in 1992 (19–22). As well, it has been anthologized in *The New British Poetry* and in *Voiceprint*, edited by Stewart Brown, Mervyn Morris, and Gordon Rohlehr (Harlow: Longman, 1989). There are small variations of spelling and lineation in these various printings: my source for quotations in this chapter will be the Virago Press version.

14. The incidental detail of the poem admittedly offers a Jamaican setting; but it seems to me that the "foreignness" of the situation of the "Mad Woman" applies equally to the plight of immigrants in that other "Kingsto[w]n"—London. This reading is consonant, too, with the mobility across boundaries and borders of many West Indian (British) writers in the last part of the twentieth century.

15. See above, 56–57.

16. Anyone who, like me, was brought up in the early 1960s in the East of England could attest to the undermining of state-controlled musical tastes and standards of conduct (hitherto mediated by the stuffy old BBC) by Radio Caroline and other "pirate" radio stations moored in the North Sea just outside the territorial limit—dramatic days indeed!

17. This is according to J. Edward Chamberlin in his study, *Come Back to Me My Language: Poetry and the West Indies* (Toronto: McClelland and Stewart, 1993), 145.

18. This section of Kay's poem is conveniently available in Hulse, Kennedy, and Morley, *The New Poetry*, 297–300. The sequence as a whole forms a fascinating dramatic interaction of female voices that resist the categories of the masculist dominant discourse.

19. It also appears in *The Penguin Book of Poetry from Britain and Ireland since 1945* [*PBPBI*], 318–19.

20. I realize that in my reading here I'm making the (racist) assumption that the "Don" in question *is* white; but it seems to me that the satirical direction of Agard's poem makes such an assumption symbolically inevitable—just as Plath's

(and Breeze's) doctors *must* be male in their texts (though in everyday life there are of course many female doctors, not to mention dons). In fact, forcing the racist (or sexist) assumption onto the reader may itself be part of the satirical or subversive tactics of the writers in question.

21. See *Mangoes and Bullets: Selected and New Poems 1972–1984* (London: Pluto Press, 1985).

22. Derek Walcott, *Midsummer* (New York: Farrar, Straus, Giroux, 1984), n.p. The poem also appears in Walcott's *Collected Poems: 1948–1984* (New York: Farrar, Straus and Giroux, 1986), 483. For Rich's comments, see her interview of 1991 with David Montenegro (in *Adrienne Rich's Poetry and Prose*), 270–71. See also above, 94–95; 113; and 281 n. 2.

23. J. M. W.Turner's paintings seem to figure extensively as a symbol of (cultural) colonization in the late-twentieth-century Caribbean literary consciousness. His "Slave Ship" (more properly, and more shockingly, titled "Slavers Throwing Overboard the Dead and Dying, Typhoon Coming On" [1840]) is the inspiration for the long title-poem in David Dabydeen's *Turner: New and Selected Poems* (London: Jonathan Cape, 1994), 1–40. An anonymous blurb writer says (on the inside of the book's front cover) that "Dabydeen has written a dynamic, redemptive riposte to the picture, and to imperial legacies in general." Dabydeen himself is clearly aware of the enormity of his undertaking. He notes of the drowning African in the foreground of Turner's painting that "Although the sea has transformed him . . . he still recognises himself as 'nigger.' The desire for transfiguration or newness or creative amnesia is frustrated. [He wishes to describe himself] anew but . . . [is] indelibly stained by Turner's language and imagery" (ix–x). In the face of this situation, this construction imposed by another culture, Dabydeen obviously decides to take responsibility in his own text for reconstructing, rewriting what has been essentially misrepresented in the painting. A somewhat similar circumstance pertains—we shall discover—in Australian poet Diane Fahey's collection *Metamorphoses*, in which she sets about re-viewing the rape victims "celebrated" in male Renaissance painting.

24. The concept is, of course, more complicated than that; but, put at its simplest and most basic, as Breiner describes it, "The Negritude movement" proffers "the argument that blacks [are] . . . not marginal, but centrally human (in contrast to the congenitally alienated whites)" (158).

25. These details, and further anecdotes, are available in Johnson's prefatory interview to his contribution to Markham, *Hinterland* (250–61).

26. See above, 48.

27. "Di Great Insohreckshan" (which was first published in *Dread Beat and Blood* [London: Bogle-L'Ouverture Publications, 1975], 55) appears in *Hinterland*, 271–72, and in *Tings an Times: Selected Poems* (Newcastle upon Tyne: Bloodaxe Books, 1991), 43–44.

28. In Rastafarian Dread Talk, "Babylon" ("babylan") represents the oppressive non-Rastafarian Western world in general. Sometimes the term is used more specifically to indicate, for instance, the British Empire, or the police force.

29. Printed in Hulse, Kennedy, and Morley, *The New Poetry*, 183–84; or see *Tings an Times*, 45–46.

30. This appropriation of a line from The Lord's Prayer reminds us that the Church is regarded—at least by Rastafarians—as part of the oppressive Estab-

lishment of Babylon, both in helping to perpetrate the horrors of the colonial period and in condoning the inequities faced by ethnic minorities in contemporary history.

31. See, particularly, my remarks on Diane Fahey's *Metamorphoses*, above, 217 ff.

32. These inclusions are never, of course, enough to satisfy the advocates of Caribbean verse. E. A. Markham, for instance, laments in *Hinterland* that "Caribbean heritage poets are still not accorded dual-citizenship when it comes to entry into prestige collections of British poetry" (39, n. 1). For a more extended discussion of Caribbean content in British anthologies, see my *A Study of Cultural Centres and Margins in British Poetry since 1950: Poets and Publishers*, 274 ff.

## 5. "English" across the Gaelic Frontiers

1. The essay appears under this title in the collection edited by Robert D. Hamner entitled *Critical Perspectives on Derek Walcott* (Washington D. C.: Three Continents Press, 1993), 304–9. Previously it was published under the title "The Murmur of Malvern" in Heaney's collection of essays entitled *The Government of the Tongue: the 1986 T. S. Eliot Memorial Lectures and Other Critical Writings* (London: Faber and Faber, 1988), 23–29. My own references will be taken, for convenience's sake, from the latter (indicated henceforth in the text as *Government*, xx).

2. In *Government*, 29. Walcott's brilliant original is conveniently available in *Collected Poems 1948–1984*, 345–61, this particular line occurring on 350.

3. In an interview with John Haffenden, published in his *Viewpoints: Poets in Conversation* (London: Faber and Faber, 1981), 64. By restricting myself to Heaney's work up to and including *North*, I'm aware that I'm skewing the overall record somewhat, and that—as Bernard O'Donoghue points out in his more extensive survey—the "Irish" experiments of Heaney's earlier work tend to be abandoned subsequently. This abandonment is signaled surprisingly strongly in an interview with Brian Donnelly for Danmarks Radio in 1977 when Heaney says: "I have played with notions of Irishness and so on, but that's almost literary convention now to talk about the loss of the Irish language—place names and so on. All that's true, and yet somehow it's all over, you know." (in Edward Broadbridge, ed., *Seamus Heaney* [Copenhagen: Skoleradioen, 1977], 61). For O'Donoghue's very clear statement of how he himself "places" Heaney culturally, see *Seamus Heaney and the Language of Poetry*, 153 ff.

4. For convenience's sake, where possible my references will be taken from Heaney's *New Selected Poems: 1966–1987* (London: Faber and Faber, 1990), henceforth *NSP*, xx. "Digging" is reprinted in *NSP*, 1–2.

5. See Frank Kinahan, "An Interview with Seamus Heaney," *Critical Inquiry* 8, no. 3 (Spring 1982): 412. The interview (405–14) was conducted on 8 March 1981 at the University of Chicago. Heaney spends some time praising the "music" of English poetry, and only feels compelled to launch an attack on the hapless iambic pentameter as a result of the guilty pleasure he got from composing the lyric "Glanmore Sonnets," 3. He justifies his reservations about the melodious English line in the face of *North*'s "tight line" (411) by saying that as

regards the "Glanmore Sonnet" in question, "its sweetness disabled it somehow" (412).

6. For Whitman, see above, 21 ff.; for Williams, see above, 26 ff.; for Pound's "MAKE IT NEW" see above, 274 n. 7; for Pound's "To break the pentameter" see Canto LXXXI (*Cantos*, 1975, 518); for Brathwaite, see above, 115–16, 134.

7. See *Preoccupations: Selected Prose 1968–1978* (London: Faber and Faber, 1980). The "essay" entitled "Belfast" is actually an agglomeration of three articles (from the *Honest Ulsterman* [1978]; the *Listener* [1971]; and the *Guardian* [1972]). The passage quoted here (from the *Guardian* of 25 May 1972) is also printed under another title (which Heaney used elsewhere for a different piece of work), "Mossbawn," in Edward Broadbridge, ed., *Seamus Heaney*. To avoid any confusion, I shall quote wherever possible from the Faber *Selected Prose* (henceforth *Preoccupations*, xx).

8. *High Windows* was the title of Larkin's collection of poems from the early 1970s (London: Faber and Faber, 1974)—virtually the same period as Heaney's *North*. Larkin for some years lived in a flat whose high windows allowed him to observe the people passing below him without having to be in any sort of actual contact with them. Windows (particularly train windows) are a common device in his work to provide framing structure and distance for the topics he chooses—a very different artistic milieu from that of Heaney with the sten gun poked into his eye!

9. Mahon's "spent / Cartridges" and "bombed bathroom" are to be found in "Poem Beginning with a Line by Cavafy," conveniently available in Ormsby's *Poets from the North of Ireland* (Belfast: Blackstaff Press, 1979), 163.

10. Paulin's "Settlers" is conveniently available in Blake Morrison and Andrew Motion's *The Penguin Book of Contemporary British Poetry* (Harmondsworth: Penguin Books, 1982), 116. The passage quoted here from Paulin's "Under the Eyes" may be found in *Poets from the North of Ireland*, 189. For my more extended remarks on the broader context of writing in late-twentieth-century Ireland, see *A Study of Cultural Centres and Margins*, 169 ff: my comments on the poems by Paulin and Mahon mentioned here are to be found on 177–78.

11. See above, 152.

12. To be fair, Heaney gives Larkin more due in the essay than I've suggested in my selection of quotations here. As well, he suggests that—just as there are a number of "Englands"—so too are there a number of Larkins. For a brilliantly discerning and far more positive view of Larkin, see Heaney's essay "The Main of Light" in *The Government of the Tongue*, 15–22.

13. For extended discussion of this form, see O'Donoghue, passim, and particularly chapter 1 ("English or Irish Lyric?" [1960s Heaney]), 25 ff.

14. See *A Study of Cultural Centres and Margins in British Poetry since 1950*, 199 ff.

15. The useful (if somewhat ponderous) term "reterritorialization" is borrowed by Lloyd from Gilles Deleuze and Félix Guattari's *Anti-Oedipus*, though Lloyd uses the term—as he admits—"in a more literal sense" than do its originators (38, n. 9).

As regards Lloyd's disparagement of Heaney's aesthetic cast of mind and desire for harmony ("synthesis," "resolution"), I agree with Peter McDonald when he says in *Mistaken Identities: Poetry and Northern Ireland* (Oxford: Oxford University Press, 1997) that "Lloyd, like other post-colonial theorists, is more concerned with what he calls 'The real basis of the present struggle in the economic and social conditions of a post-colonial state' than with the different 'here and now' of poems." McDonald goes on to say, somewhat tartly, "It is also important in such an argument that support for 'the present struggle' should legitimize the adverse criticism of a popular poet; the critique of identity-discourse offered by Lloyd and others must be at all costs (and at any cost) a radical one." (9). McDonald's own (less radical) remarks on identity-discourse in Northern Irish poetry at large are well worth reading.

At one point, McDonald cites a passage from the unfinished epilogue of W. R. Rodgers's *The Character of Ireland* that echoes Heaney's remarks on the Northern Irish "twang": speaking of "the 'sharp, expulsive, jerky' Ulster accent" McDonald quotes Rodgers as saying:

> I am Ulster, my people an abrupt people
> Who like the spiky consonants in speech. . . .
> (in McDonald, *Mistaken Identities*, 33)

16. *Contraflow on the Super Highway: Poems by Robert Crawford, W. N. Herbert, David Kinloch, Peter McCarey, Richard Price and Alan Riach* (henceforth indicated in the text as Crawford et al., *Contraflow*, xx) [London: Southfields Press and *Gairfish*, 1994].

17. For the most vivid recounting of this phenomenon see Pound's Canto I (*Cantos*, 3-5) a translation/reincarnation of the *nekuia* episode in the *Odyssey*, where the poet/hero (Odysseus-Pound) performs the act of ritual bloodletting to gain contact with Tiresias (universal wisdom).

18. Morgan's sentiments here echo, of course, the more famous case of Seamus Heaney, who objected to being labeled as a "British" poet in *The Penguin Book of Contemporary British Poetry* (Harmondsworth: Penguin Books, 1982). Heaney's response was the poem "An Open Letter" where he asserted that "be advised / My passport's green." The Heaney incident is covered in Ronald Tamplin's *Seamus Heaney* (Milton Keynes: Open University Press, 1989], 75; and in Bernard O'Donoghue's *Seamus Heaney and the Language of Poetry*, 26.

19. See Ted Hughes's "The Thought-Fox" in *The Hawk in the Rain* (London: Faber and Faber, 1957), 14. One might easily argue as well, I think, that Morgan's whittrick is close kin to Hughes's "Otter" (*Lupercal* [London: Faber and Faber, 1960], 46-47).

20. We remember that Morgan, in the *Akros* interview with Marshall Walker, speaks of searching for "some kind of common ground" between concrete poetry and conventional poetry, a "half-way house" between the two kinds of text (*Edwin Morgan: an Interview*, 3–4). Perhaps the language "interface" is one of the things that fascinates Morgan, following Walter Benjamin, about the act of *translation*: see Peter McCarey's essay, "Edwin Morgan the Translator" in Crawford and Whyte, *About Edwin Morgan*, 90–104, and particularly 97–99.

21. As the reader will no doubt recall, we came across W. C. Williams's poem in the opening chapter: see above, 27.

22. Leonard uses version 1 of the Williams poem (in *Intimate Voices*, 99). Both this and the second—slightly "filled-out"—version are conveniently available in *The Collected Earlier Poems of William Carlos Williams* (New York: New Directions, 1951), 93 and 94.

23. One is perhaps reminded here, in a not-totally-different situation, of Sylvia Plath's recycling of nursery rhymes.

24. The examples I've given here are only a selection, of course. Tony Crowley in his study *The Politics of Discourse* tells us that "in early-twentieth-century Britain" it was common for British society to be divided "in linguistic terms into the articulate and the barbarians"—the latter being "those stolid young [people] . . . who appear to have absolutely no interest in literary expression" (214): see particularly 214–22. Other specific cases that might be added to the list are the north of England writer Tony Harrison's "Rhubarbarians" (in *Permanently Bard: Selected Poetry* [Newcastle: Bloodaxe Books, 1995], 63) whom we'll meet in the final chapter; and Lilian Mohin's *Beautiful Barbarians: Lesbian Feminist Poetry* (London: Onlywomen Press, 1986).

25. See *Verse*, no. 4 (1985): 26–34. These parts of the interview are reported in Dave Smith's essay "Them and Uz: Douglas Dunn's Technique" in *Reading Douglas Dunn* , ed., Crawford and Kinloch (Edinburgh: Edinburgh University Press, 1992), 80–93.

26. In the photograph Larkin—clean-shaven and shiny, in dark suit and tie, complete with Remembrance Day poppy in buttonhole—sits higher than and slightly forward of Dunn (bearded, sports-jacketed and sweatered, un-poppied).

27. Crawford evolves a daring argument to trace a line of "barbarians" through twentieth-century English poetry, using the unlikely character of Philip Larkin as "One of the clearest bridges between the work of the Modernists and these barbarians" (*Devolving English Literature*, 271). The argument is ingenious, but—for me at least—ultimately not convincing. I question, for instance, the overall appropriateness of his labeling Modernism as provincial; and in the end I'd go along with the conventional wisdom and argue that Larkin (complicated though his case may be) remains an enemy of Modernism and retreats behind the centrist Movement pale, rendering all outside it as "barbarian." I don't really see Larkin on the same side as Leonard, or Dunn—or Crawford.

28. This is not to say that the younger generation of Scottish poets takes Dr. Johnson or the Establishment too lightly, or underestimates its power. Ian Duncan, in the essay "Adam Smith, Samuel Johnson and the Institutions of English" in Crawford's *The Scottish Invention of English Literature,* notes that Johnson in his various endeavors—the *Dictionary* (1755), the edition of Shakespeare's works (1765), and the *Lives of the Poets* (1781)—"definitively erects the institutional superstructure of 'English Literature,' a national vernacular language regulated by a native canon of classical authors" (39).

29. This is a theme Crawford takes up not only in this volume, but as well in his earlier one, *Devolving English Literature*. Basically he argues (as Ian Duncan puts it) that Adam Smith's *Lectures on Rhetoric and Belles Lettres*, given at the University of Glasgow between 1751 and 1763, "constitute the first significant university programme devoted to the analysis of English literary discourse." (*The Scottish Invention*, 37). The *exportability* of Scottish teaching expertise (which is mentioned in Crawford's poems as well as his prose) has done much to proliferate Scotland's influence in this regard, Andrew Hook discussing "Scottish Academia and the Invention of American Studies" (ibid., 164–79) and Chris Worth "Scotland and the Early Teaching of Literature in Australia and New Zealand" (ibid., 207–24).

30. In this regard, what might be considered as a joint responsibility for the evils of empire has caused feelings of guilt in some Scottish writers: W. N. Herbert, for instance, in his poem "Letterbomb" speaks of Scots blaming themselves for "complicity in colonialism" (in *Contraflow*, 46).

31. Inevitably one remembers here William Carlos Williams's famous "objectivist" slogan that a poem is "a machine made of words" (in the *Selected Essays of William Carlos Williams* [New York: Random House, 1954], 256; and also quoted by Randall Jarrell in the introduction to Williams's *Selected Poems* [New York: New Directions, 1968], xv). Objectivism in fact seems quite close kin to Informationism in some ways, and to L=A=N=G=U=A=G=E poetry more generally. Certainly Williams acts as a model (as we've seen throughout) for twentieth-century poetic avant-gardism in English—and in *Scotland*. Earlier we saw Tom Leonard's version of Williams's poem "This Is Just to Say" (see above, 180–81); and Crawford also echoes the same poem (combining it with the lyrics of a recent pop song) in "A Saying" (*A Scottish Assembly*, 29).

# 6. Colony/Dominion

1. See Ashcroft, Griffiths, and Tiffin, *The Empire Writes Back: Theory and Practice in Post-Colonial Literatures*, which remains essential reading for studies in this field. It takes its title (*Star Wars* movies aside) from Salman Rushdie's comment, quoted as epigraph to the volume, that "the Empire writes back to the Centre" (ix).

2. The authors of *The Empire Writes Back* in fact comment somewhat uncomfortably on their use of upper and lower case, applied to English/english: see 217.

3. For further discussion of these various tactics, including analysis of specific examples, see chapter 2 of *The Empire Writes Back*, "Re-Placing the Language: Textual Strategies in Post-Colonial Writing" (38–77).

4. As regards the awkwardness of antipodean seasonal cycles, it's still not uncommon to find Australasian Christmas cards laden with snow and robins in spite of the fact that it's too hot to snow in midsummer, and that the English robin doesn't exist in the southern hemisphere. It must be admitted, too, that "Here we go gathering nuts in *November*" doesn't quite have an authentic ring to it: or, as Henry Kendall put it with some awkwardness in his famous "Bell–Birds," "They sing in September their songs of the May-time" (in G. A. Wilkes, ed., *The Colonial Poets* [Sydney: Angus and Robertson, 1974], 102). Kendall's significant rhyming of "Australian" and "alien" occurs in his poem in memory of another "bush" writer, Charles Harpur:

> So we that know this singer dead,
>   Whose hands attuned the Harp Australian,
> May set the face and bow the head,
>   And mourn his fate and fortunes alien.
>
> (Wilkes, Colonial Poets, 87)

As regards the attempt to "normalize" the landscape by the use of English pastoral terms, again Kendall is perhaps the most obvious example, or perhaps one should say the gravest offender—though Charles Harpur and several others were guilty of the same mannerism regularly too. The use of humor to defuse the threat of Australian difference is most notable in such gems as Barron Field's "The Kangaroo," in which the poet rhymes "Australia" with "failure," satirically suggesting that the beast in the title is all that saves the continent from being a total write-off (see Wilkes, *Colonial Poets,* 7–8).

5. A great deal of O'Dowd's manuscript material, and his correspondence with Walt Whitman, is conveniently gathered in A. L. McLeod's *Walt Whitman in Australia and New Zealand: a Record of his Reception* (Sydney: Wentworth Press, 1964). This particular passage occurs on p. 141. Throughout, in my use of this volume I've retained (as McLeod does) the sometimes idiosyncratic punctuation and phrasing of the original.

6. In McLeod, *Whitman in Australia,* 109. The lecture text quoted here actually appears as an article in the Melbourne publication, The *Tocsin* of 13 April 1899, with the subtitle "Excerpts from a recent lecture by 'Gavah the Blacksmith' [a pseudonym of O'Dowd's]."

7. Letter to Whitman of 3 December 1890, in *Overland,* no. 23 (Autumn 1962): 9; also in McLeod, *Whitman in Australia,* 19.

8. Letter to Whitman of 6 September 1890, in *Overland,* no. 23 (Autumn 1962): 11; also in McLeod, *Whitman in Australia,* 23.

9. This observation is reported in Hugh Anderson's study, *The Poet Militant: Bernard O'Dowd* (Melbourne: Hill of Content, 1969), 35. In the course of the book, Anderson quotes extensively from O'Dowd's letters and lectures.

10. O'Dowd reported this to Whitman in a letter of 9 January 1890 (*Overland,* 12; McLeod, *Whitman in Australia,* 26). The circumstance may seem of slim literary relevance; and yet the naming of a son can have potent symbolic significance, since it indicates a continuity and a future growth (as opposed to a nostalgic return to past ancestry). The New Zealand critic, C. K. Stead, in an essay entitled "From Wystan to Carlos" has suggested that the naming of sons by New Zealand poets indicates a reorientation of literary interests—Allen Curnow naming his son after the (then) English poet Wystan Hugh Auden; while a poet of a later generation, Ian Wedde, chose to name his son Carlos after the American poet William Carlos Williams, thus emblematizing the shift from English role models to American ones in New Zealand poetry in the second half of the twentieth century (see Stead, *In the Glass Case: Essays on New Zealand Literature* [Auckland: Auckland University Press, 1981], 139–59, and particularly 154).

11. Whitman wrote that "In the verse of all those undoubtedly great writers, Shakespeare as much as the rest, there is the air which to America is the air of death"; and he goes on, "What play of Shakespeare, represented in America, is not an insult to America, to the marrow in its bones?" (in Francis Murphy, ed., *Walt Whitman,* 38; and see above, 19).

12. The quotation from Whitman (predictably enough) goes on much longer than I've thought fit to cite here. The passage O'Dowd uses is one of Whitman's famous catalog sequences, a device O'Dowd borrowed for his own poetry from the "Good Gray Poet" from time to time. The reader may perhaps remember that the "Song of the Answerer" was one of the texts O'Dowd felt should be "translated" into Australian for the benefit of "the great Australia of the future" (in McLeod, 141).

13. (Melbourne: Oxford University Press, 1965.) See particularly chapter 5, "The Reformist Poets" (68–79). As Wright puts it succinctly, in a comparison of Henry Lawson and Bernard O'Dowd, "Lawson at his worst can still move us, and O'Dowd at his best cannot convince us"; and, later on the same page, in another comparison, "O'Dowd in fact was not a poet; Whitman was" (73).

14. (Sydney: The Bulletin Co., 1903), 9. The theme of "Young Democracy" is taken up and pursued further in a poem of that title later in the collection (39–42).

15. My references to "The Bush" are taken from *The Poems of Bernard O'Dowd* (Melbourne: Lothian Publishing Co, 1941), 187–209.

16. Perhaps the most obvious example of the use of slangs and Aboriginal words in a bush ballad is "Banjo" Paterson's unofficial Australian national anthem, "Waltzing Matilda"—the existence of such an enthusiastically-received national song owing nothing to "God Save the Queen" or "Rule Britannia" being in itself an indication of the desire to break with England—(see *Songs of the Bush: A. B. "Banjo" Paterson, Complete Works 1885–1900* [ed. Rosemund Campbell and Philippa Harvie], Sydney: Lansdowne Press, 1983, 250). The satirical approach to (upper-class) English values and character is evident in a number of places— such as, for example, Paterson's "The Geebung Polo Club" (ibid., 206–8) or Henry Lawson's "Middleton's Rouseabout" (*Henry Lawson: Collected Verse, vol. 1, 1885–1900*, ed., Colin Roderick, [Sydney: Angus and Robertson, 1967], 62–63).

17. As usual, Judith Wright proffers trenchant opinions here. She finds O'Dowd, compared to Henry Lawson, "more rhetorical, . . . more programmatic" (*Preoccupations in Australian Poetry*, 71). She goes on to complain that "Abstractions like Democracy and High Ideals were the natural habitation of his mind" (71), the result being not sublimity, but "the confusion of his rhetoric and the pedagogy of his half-assimilated information" (73). On the level of poetic technique, she finds him equally deficient, voicing the opinion that "it is more than doubtful whether O'Dowd ever produced . . . anything that could be regarded as verbal music at all" (74). Moreover, as a writer he "begins at the level of abstraction, of the intellect" and "gives no hint of possessing a pair of eyes and the capacity to use them" (73).

18. See above, 200, and also n. 4, above.

19. See "The Creek of the Four Graves" (*The Poetical Works of Charles Harpur*, ed. Elizabeth Perkins [Sydney: Angus and Robertson, 1984], 161–72). The "echo" passage occurs on p. 163:

> The Echoes of the solitary place,
> Came as in sylvan wonder wide about
> To hear, and imitate tentatively,
> Strange voices moulding a strange speech. . . .

The act of naming (and thus asserting dominion over, as Adam did with the animals in Genesis), and of giving a voice to an "empty" land, of course, have unfortunate political connotations given the Crown Law's argument that Australia was *terra nullius* (land belonging to nobody), and therefore ripe to become British "property." In spite of the fact that, from a twenty-first century reading, Harpur in this poem is unconsciously (?) implicated in the enterprise of colonizing through language, for present purposes I prefer to see him as the earliest

Australian poet seeking to assert a local language variant/name/voice as an initial step in the process of appropriating the colonizing discourse and of decolonizing the culture.

20. Wright speaks of Gordon's "swaggering emptiness" (*Preoccupations in Australian Poetry*, 62), of "the fundamental hollowness of his outlook," and "his fake-masculine recklessness and flamboyance" (ibid., 63).

21. See, for instance, Barbara Baynton's famous *Bush Studies* (Sydney: Angus and Robertson, 1980).

22. See Kirsten Holst Petersen and Anna Rutherford, eds., *A Double Colonization: Colonial and Post-Colonial Women's Writing.* As we saw earlier, the phenomenon of "double colonization" affects not only Australian women but potentially *all* postcolonial female writers; and in some cases it may be exacerbated by racism and (in the case of Westindian-British female poets, for instance) immigrant status (see above, 122).

23. Here, and throughout in my brief quotations from Warland and Marlatt, I've retained what appears to be the somewhat idiosyncratic syntax of the original on the grounds that syntactic and punctuational variations are part of the language "revolution" that shouldn't be normalized or rewritten—particularly by a male academic.

24. Throughout, my references to Wright's poetry will be taken from *Judith Wright: Collected Poems 1942–1985* (Sydney: Angus and Robertson, 1994). "South of My Days" occurs on pp. 20–21.

25. In the sixth of "Seven Songs from a Journey," Wright uses one of the traditional metaphors for such impermanence: "No sign on the clean sand / will stay to remember you by" (*Collected Poems*, 138).

26. I'm aware that this is not the only possible interpretation of this particular text, and that my personal reading of the poem is not an entirely conventional one. Most previous readings identify (as Wright indeed invites us to do in the title) the "Eucalypt" with the Australian "National Character" ungendered: it seems to me, though, that the gendered nature of the writing and of the argument becomes more and more explicit as the poem develops, only being subordinated at the beginning and the very end.

27. Here Fahey is quoting Marija Gimbutas's *The Goddesses and Gods of Old Europe. 6500–3500 B.C. Myths and Cult Images* (London: Thames and Hudson, 1982).

28. Here Fahey is making use of the argument formulated by Christine Downing in *The Goddess: Mythological Images of the Feminine* (New York: Crossroad Publishing Co., 1981).

29. See Pound's *Cantos* (1975), 13–14; and Eliot's *Collected Poems* (1963), 66.

30. The somewhat truncated quote from Cixous is used in *Poetry and Gender* by Veronica Brady in her essay "Over the Frontier." Cixous herself uses the flying reference a number of times in her interesting essay, "The Laugh of the Medusa" (in *Signs: Journal of Women in Culture and Society* 1, no. 4 [Summer 1976]: 875–93). In addition to the reference to flying being woman's gesture (887), she notes that woman "doesn't 'speak,' . . . she flies" (881), and that "Women take after birds and robbers" ["voleurs"] (887). This latter instance uses a pun on flying (just as Fahey uses the "flight"/"flight" pun in "Philomela"—though of course Cixous's pun is quite different, being in another language): the French

verb "to fly" ("voler") also means "to steal." This is a happy circumstance for Cixous (though not a pure chance or accident, she maintains), who goes on to talk about women stealing the text from men (which is essentially what Fahey does, of course, with *Metamorphoses*), and untidily subverting the discourse much as one might ransack a room one has broken into.

31. See above, n. 30.

32. One might argue that contact with the alien English tongue has lasted *two hundred* rather than twenty years, although Aboriginal access to the education system certainly didn't seem to be uppermost in the minds of the early settlers. Gilbert probably bases his timeframe here on the actual history of Aboriginal publications (which he catalogs in his introduction): apart from David Unaipon's *Native Legends* of 1929, the first book of note on the list is Kath Walker's [Oodgeroo Noonuccal's] volume of poems *We Are Going* (1964); quickly followed by Colin Johnson's [Mudrooroo Narogin's] novel *Wild Cat Falling* (1965).

33. The horrors of this "Rape" are described in Gilbert's introduction to *Inside Black Australia*, xx–xxiii; in Henry Reynolds's *The Other Side of the Frontier*; and to a lesser degree in Robert Hughes's general picture of the convict era, *The Fatal Shore: a History of the Transportation of Convicts to Australia 1787–1868* (London: Pan Books, 1988).

34. See *My People: a Kath Walker Collection* (Milton, Qld.: The Jacaranda Press, 1970), 78.

35. "Recording the Cries of the People: an interview with Oodgeroo (Kath Walker)" in *Aboriginal Culture Today*, ed. Anna Rutherford (Sydney: Dangaroo Press, 1988), a special issue of the periodical *Kunapipi*, vol. X nos. 1 and 2, 1988.

36. See M. A. K. Halliday, *Language as Social Semiotic: the Social Interpretation of Language and Meaning* (London: Edward Arnold, 1978), 164 ff. Halliday tells us that an antilanguage "exists solely in the context of *re*socialization, and the reality it creates is inherently an alternative reality": thus it is "the language of an antisociety." He goes on (in a remark that might be applied, for instance, to Diane Fahey's work) to cite Harold Garfinkel's claim in 1967 that "the language . . . of femaleness was . . . an antilanguage, since it was required to construct . . . a counter-identity" (171). For a succinct yet somewhat extended discussion of Halliday's theory of antilanguages with specific reference to Australian literature (and particularly to Aboriginal literature), see Bob Hodge and Vijay Mishra, *Dark Side of the Dream: Australian Literature and the Postcolonial Mind* (North Sydney: Allen and Unwin, 1991), 205–11.

37. My information here comes from Mudrooroo's *Writing from the Fringe*, 64. The article on the Rastafarians is printed in *Identity*, vol. 5 (1982). Mudrooroo points out that culturally, as regards music to listen to, Aboriginals tend to be at the mercy of local radio stations, since the people generally can't afford discs or videos.

38. The Jindyworobaks were the first group of Australian poets to try to raise the profile of the Aboriginal peoples and culture. Led by Rex Ingamells, they produced a series of anthologies duing the 1930s and 1940s. The name "Jindyworobak" is an Aboriginal term which translates (roughly) as "to join together": it was used to signify both a joining of indigenous with nonindigenous peoples, and a joining of human with natural worlds. Admirable as these projects may have been in theory, in practice the literary results were disappointing, and

amounted to an (accidental) reappropriation of Aboriginal cultural property. For a more sympathetic view of the movement, and a selection of its best products, see Brian Elliott, ed., and intro., *The Jindyworobaks* (St. Lucia: University of Queensland Press, 1979).

39. See above, 120 ff. Muecke explains the Aboriginal usage as follows: "Different forms are used to codify whether or not the speaker includes himself or herself or the listener in the pronoun. For instance, *mintupella* excludes the listener while *yunmi* includes the listener" (241).

40. For a more positive and enthusiastic assessment of Muecke's methods see Bob Hodge and Vijay Mishra, *Dark Side of the Dream*, 83 ff. The whole section of the book entitled "The Politics of Mediation" (77–86) is of interest here.

41. As regards "buyability," Mudrooroo is aware of the complexity of the situation, and of the dilemma Jack Davis had as editor of a publication that was struggling to be financially viable. In *Writing from the Fringe*, he notes that the Aboriginal population is small and economically underprivileged, so it doesn't provide a realistic commercial market. Consequently any book with Aboriginal content, to be fiscally profitable, will have to be "written to conform to the dictates of the marketplace" (26). In fact, Aboriginals make up less than two percent of the total Australian population and—for some of the reasons already outlined—might be seen as the literary *other*, having little commercial effect on the dominant taste of the book-buying public.

42. For my earlier reference to the opening of "Howl" see above, 65. One might be excused for thinking that my assertion of a howl of *wrath* here is rather stretching too far the fact of the Jewish director's name; but Wildcat/Mudrooroo himself (themselves?) actually directs our attention to its translation on the very first page of the "Script," noting that Wrothberg says his name means "Anger of the Mountain" (3).

43. Obvious choices for commentators on mimicry are Jacques Lacan, and Homi BhaBha: see, for instance, BhaBha's "Of Mimicry and Man: The Ambivalence of Colonial Discourse," which he prefaces with a significant quotation from Lacan on the tactics of mimicry (in *Modern Literary Theory: a Reader*, ed., Philip Rice and Patricia Waugh, [London: Edward Arnold, 1992], 234–41). Or, to trace the theme (circuitously) in feminist literary theory, see Claire Keyes's discussion of Mary Jacobus's exploration (probably via Luce Irigaray) of mimicry in the poetry of Adrienne Rich (in Keyes's *The Aesthetics of Power: the Poetry of Adrienne Rich* [Athens: University of Georgia Press, 1986], 31 ff.). See also above, chapter 3, n. 15.

44. See above, 67.

45. Harry Heseltine in *The Penguin Book of Australian Verse* (Ringwood, Vic: Penguin Books Australia, 1981) speaks of a "Dransfield generation," adding that it was also known as the "generation of 68." (xxvi) The latter label seems to be from John Tranter, probably via Andrew Taylor and Tom Shapcott.

46. See *Michael Dransfield: Collected Poems*, ed. Rodney Hall (St. Lucia: University of Queensland Press, 1987), xvii–xxiii. All quotes in my text from Dransfield's poems are taken from this edition and will be indicated henceforth as (*CP*).

47. In "In Memory of Eva Gore-Booth and Con Markiewicz" (*The Collected Poems of W. B. Yeats* [London: Macmillan, 1950], 263) Yeats wrote of "Lissadell" where "Two girls in silk kimonos, both/ Beautiful, one a gazelle" walked in the

garden. This is by no means the only echo of Yeats to be found in Dransfield's poetry. Dransfield, for instance, favored the rose as an emblem, just as Yeats did (notably in his early volume entitled *The Rose* [1893], but passim). And one feels that Dransfield would have allied himself strongly with Yeats when the latter wrote "We were the last romantics" (from another country house poem by Yeats, "Coole Park and Ballylee 1931," [*Collected Poems*, 276]). As well, of course, both Dransfield and Yeats spent much time tracing semifictional genealogies linking themselves with an ancestral land-owning gentry.

48. See Plath, *Collected Poems*, 160–2; and above, 76 ff.

49. Hodge and Mishra's argument here (though not directly relevant to mine) is an interesting one, and their pivotal comparison somewhat surprising. They liken Dransfield's technique and vision to that of Henry Lawson (see *Dark Side of the Dream*, 153–55), asserting that the writing is "akin to Lawson's through similar syntactic forms"; and they go on to argue that "the central consciousness . . . constructed, the drug-addict as hero, was a direct successor of the alcoholic Lawson" (154).

50. "M Ward" in Canberra hospital was where Dransfield underwent treatment during September and October 1972. Livio Dobrez suggests that: "M Ward may be said to be the poetic destination of the Long Voyage. It corresponds to Courland Penders, Dransfield's other house. Where the first was the refuge of the terminal aesthete, this one is the refuge of the terminally religious" (421).

51. Pound wrote about these "three 'kinds of poetry'" in his essay "How to Read" (in *Literary Essays of Ezra Pound* [London: Faber and Faber, 1954], 25).

## 7. CONCLUSION

1. See Chris Tiffin and Alan Lawson, eds., *De-scribing Empire: Post-colonialism and Textuality* (London: Routledge, 1994). Jo-Ann Wallace's comment appears on 171.

2. This was actually the second version of the scheme proposed, in which James Stirling was the leading architect. The original proposal had involved the (even more "foreign") Mies van der Rohe. For a more detailed account of the fascinating machinations see Jacobs, chap.3, and particularly the section entitled "Continental Entanglements" (58–64).

3. See chap.4 of *Edge of Empire*, entitled "Eastern Trading: Diasporas, Dwelling and Place" (70–102), and particularly 80 ff. It should be pointed out here that the "accommodation" of the Bengali minority in the Spitalfields Market area was by no means all sweetness and light, and that many of the outcomes of the development reflected a racism more subtle than, but not entirely unrelated to, that of the National Front.

4. See above, 195. Murray's opinion, given in interview with Robert Crawford, is reported in Crawford's *Devolving English Literature*, and the actual phrase "imperial Anglocentricity" is Crawford's, to be found on 302.

5. See Alan Robinson, *Instabilities in Contemporary British Poetry* (Basingstoke: Macmillan, 1988); and Janet Batsleer, *Rewriting English: Cultural Politics of Gender and Class* (London: Methuen, 1985).

6. Conveniently available in George MacBeth's anthology *Poetry 1900–1975* (London: Longmans, 1979), 318–20.

7. I'm aware here that, in a sense, the Mottram affair is "ancient history," since it occurred in the late-1970s. However, the fact that Mottram was still dining out on it in the late-1980s (in *The New British Poetry*, published in 1988) is an indication that the attitudes enshrined therein persist—if not as strongly then at least to some degree—perhaps into the late-1990s. To set the record straight, it should perhaps be noted as well that the Arts Council funding of countercultural literary phenomena improved during this period—from zero to nothing much! Michael Horovitz, for instance, notes in *Grandchildren of Albion* in 1992 that "for the first time in its three decades, *New Departures* has received support from the Arts Council," albeit amounting to "only a small fraction" of likely publication costs (18).

8. See *Permanently Bard: Selected Poetry,* ed. Carol Rutter (Newcastle upon Tyne: Bloodaxe Books, 1995). Part 1 of the poem "The Rhubarbarians" is to be found on 63. Unless otherwise stated, my quotations from Harrison's work will be from this volume (henceforth *PB*, xx). My remarks, in this chapter, on Harrison's *corpus* are by no means meant to constitute a general survey, since a large number of commentators—most notably in Neil Astley's monumental *Tony Harrison: Bloodaxe Critical Anthologies: 1* (Newcastle upon Tyne: Bloodaxe Books, 1991)—have worked on him in recent years. Rather, I shall simply select aspects of Harrison's writing which are germane to my main argument.

9. Carol Rutter, the editor of *Permanently Bard*, makes this suggestion in her introduction (9–30), attributing the remark (possibly) to Harrison himself (17).

10. See chap. 4, above, 120 ff.

11. See chap. 4, above, 131. See also n. 12, below.

12. In Neil Astley, ed., *Tony Harrison: Bloodaxe Critical Anthologies: 1,* 114–28. Subsequent references to this volume will be indicated in the main text as (in Astley, *Tony Harrison*, xxx). Harrison's own poem "On Not Being Milton," the introductory work to the ongoing sequence "The School of Eloquence" is to be found in his *Selected Poems* (Harmondsworth: Penguin Books, 1984), 112.

13. Dabydeen's original, from which I quoted a number of times in chapter 4 above, is to be found in Ricks and Michaels, *The State of the Language*, 3–14.

14. The poem is conveniently reprinted in *The New British Poetry*, 27–31. This passage occurs on 27.

15. See Benita Parry, "Between Creole and Cambridge English: the Poetry of David Dabydeen" in *Kunapipi*, vol.10, no. 3 (1988): 1–14. The quotations I've used here occur on 13–14.

16. See Leonard's *Intimate Voices*, 86, 95, 65; and chap. 5, above, 182.

17. As many commentators have noted, the one tongue of which Harrison's education deprived him was "mi mam's" (*PB*, 39). The divisive nature of a privileged education forms a key component to the drama of his early work, though it stands somewhat outside my present argument.

18. See *Gaudete* (London: Faber and Faber, 1977). Hughes's sequence of poems and prose pieces tells of how the Reverend Nicholas Lumb, an Anglican clergyman from the north of England, is taken over by an itinerant demon and becomes a sort of surrealist "Momo" substitute, subverting his congregation, or at least the female constituents thereof, in an unambiguously nonspiritual man-

ner. I suggest elsewhere that essentially what Hughes is dramatizing here is the takeover of the superego by the undeniable dark forces of the id (for discussion of such a takeover see my article "Ted Hughes, Surrealist?" in *Dada/Surrealism*, no. 8 [1978]: 134–45). So Hughes and McMillan share not only northerness, but a surrealist bent as well—though that isn't enough, obviously, to persuade McMillan that in any meaningful way they share a voice or common purpose!

19. In Harrison's dedication to "Them and [uz]," for instance, the music-hall comic, "Professor" Leon Cortez, stands alongside Professor Richard Hoggart as dedicatee and inspiration (*PB*, 33). The choice of northern music-hall comedian as hero and role model is not so surprising when one considers that professional comedy was one of the (few) ways for northerners to extricate themselves from the unenviable choice of poverty or going down the pit.

20. Gervais uses this term with less-positive connotations than I'd be tempted to adduce. In his chapter on "Larkin, Betjeman and the aftermath of 'England'" (in *Literary Englands*, 185 ff.), he sees Betjeman's England as essentially "more real" than Larkin's (191). By comparison, he finds Larkin's England is fabricated out of "nostalgia . . . sustained by a relatively impoverished sense of history," and considers that "its drama is reduced to only pathos" (185). Consequently he proffers for it the label of ("merely") "post-English" (185).

# Bibliography

Abel, Elizabeth, ed. *Writing and Sexual Difference*. Brighton: The Harvester Press, 1982.

Agard, John. *Mangoes and Bullets: Selected and New Poems 1972–1984*. London: Pluto Press, 1985.

———. *Man to Pan: a Cycle of Poems to be Performed with Drums and Steelpans*. Havana: Ediciones Casa de las Américas, 1982.

Allen, Donald, ed. *The New American Poetry 1945–1960*. New York: Grove Press, 1960.

Allen, Donald, and Robert Creeley, eds. *The New Writing in the USA*. Harmondsworth: Penguin Books, 1967.

Allnutt, Gillian, Fred D'Aguiar, Ken Edwards and Eric Mottram, eds. *The New British Poetry: 1968–88*. London: Paladin, 1988.

Alvarez, Alfred. *Beyond All This Fiddle: Essays 1955–1967*. London: Allen Lane, 1968.

———. "The New Poetry or Beyond the Gentility Principle." See Alvarez, Alfred, ed. *The New Poetry*.

———. *The Savage God: a Study of Suicide*. London: Weidenfeld and Nicolson, 1971.

———. *The Shaping Spirit*. London: Chatto and Windus, 1958.

———. ed. *The New Poetry*. Harmondsworth: Penguin Books, 1962.

Amis, Kingsley. *Collected Poems 1944–1979*. London: Hutchinson, 1979.

Anderson, Hugh. *The Poet Militant: Bernard O'Dowd*. Melbourne: Hill of Content, 1969.

Armitage, Simon, and Robert Crawford, eds. *The Penguin Book of Poetry from Britain and Ireland since 1945*. Harmondsworth: Penguin Books, 1998.

Ashcroft, Bill, Gareth Griffiths, and Helen Tiffin. *The Empire Writes Back: Theory and Practice in Post-Colonial Literatures*. London: Routledge, 1989.

Astley, Neil, ed. *Tony Harrison: Bloodaxe Critical Anthologies: 1*. Newcastle upon Tyne: Bloodaxe Books, 1991.

Barry, Peter and Robert Hampson, eds. *New British Poetries: the Scope of the Possible*. Manchester: Manchester University Press, 1993.

Batsleer, Janet et al. *Rewriting English: Cultural Politics of Gender and Class.* London: Methuen, 1985.

Baynton, Barbara. *Bush Studies.* Sydney: Angus and Robertson, 1980.

Benterrak, Krim, Stephen Muecke, and Paddy Roe. *Reading the Country: Introduction to Nomadology.* Fremantle: Fremantle Arts Centre Press, 1984.

Berry James. "Westindian-British Poetry." *Poetry Review,* 73, no. 2 (June 1983): 5–8.

Berry, James, ed. *News for Babylon: the Chatto Book of Westindian-British Poetry.* London: Chatto and Windus, 1984.

BhaBha, Homi. "Of Mimicry and Man: the Ambivalence of Colonial Discourse" In *Modern Literary Theory: a Reader,* edited by Philip Rice and Patricia Waugh, 234–41. London: Edward Arnold, 1992.

Borroff, Marie, ed. *Wallace Stevens: a Collection of Critical Essays.* Englewood Cliffs, N.J.: Prentice-Hall, 1963.

Bradley, D. D. "Ted Hughes 1930–1998." *Pembroke College Cambridge Society Annual Gazette* 73 (September 1999). 22–30.

Brathwaite, Edward Kamau. *History of the Voice: the Development of Nation Language in Anglophone Caribbean Poetry.* London: New Beacon Books, 1984.

Breeze, Jean Binta. *Spring Cleaning.* London: Virago Press, 1992.

Breiner, Laurence A. *An Introduction to West Indian Poetry.* Cambridge: Cambridge University Press, 1998.

*British Poetry from the 1950s to the 1990s.* See Day, Gary and Brian Docherty, eds.

Broadbridge, Edward, ed. *Seamus Heaney.* Copenhagen: Skoleradioen, 1977.

Brooks, David, and Brenda Walker, eds. *Poetry and Gender: Statements and Essays in Australian Women's Poetry and Poetics.* St. Lucia: University of Queensland Press, 1989.

Brown, Stewart, Mervyn Morris, and Gordon Rohlehr, eds. *Voiceprint: an Anthology of Oral and Related Poetry from the Caribbean.* Harlow: Longman, 1989.

Brown, Stewart, and Ian McDonald, *The Heinemann Book of Caribbean Poetry.* Oxford: Heinemann, 1992.

Burnett, Paula, ed. *The Penguin Book of Caribbean Verse in English.* Harmondsworth: Penguin Books, 1986.

Byrne, Sandie. *Tony Harrison: Loiner.* Oxford: Oxford University Press, 1997.

Chamberlin, J. Edward. *Come Back to Me My Language: Poetry and the West Indies.* Toronto: McClelland and Stewart, 1993.

Cixous, Hélène. "The Laugh of the Medusa," *Signs: Journal of Women in Culture and Society,* no. 4 (Summer 1976): 875–93.

Cobham, Rhonda, and Merle Collins, eds. *Watchers and Seekers: Creative Writing by Black Women in Britain.* London: The Women's Press, 1987.

Conquest, Robert, ed. *New Lines: an Anthology.* London: Macmillan, 1956.

———. *New Lines—II: an Anthology.* London: Macmillan, 1963.

Couzyn, Jeni, ed. *The Bloodaxe Book of Contemporary Women Poets.* Newcastle upon Tyne: Bloodaxe Books, 1985.

Crawford, Robert. *Devolving English Literature*. Oxford: Oxford University Press, 1992.

———. *Identifying Poets: Self and Territory in Twentieth-Century Poetry*. Edinburgh: Edinburgh University Press, 1993.

———. *A Scottish Assembly* [Poems]. London: Chatto and Windus, 1990.

———. *Talkies* [Poems]. London: Chatto and Windus, 1992.

Crawford, Robert et al. *Contraflow on the Super Highway: Poems by Robert Crawford, W. N. Herbert, David Kinloch, Peter McCarey, Richard Price and Alan Riach*. London: Southfields Press and *Gairfish*, 1994.

Crawford, Robert, ed. *The Scottish Invention of English Literature*. Canbridge: Cambridge University Press, 1998.

Crawford, Robert, and David Kinloch, eds. *Reading Douglas Dunn*. Edinburgh: Edinburgh University Press, 1992.

Crawford, Robert, and Hamish Whyte, eds. *About Edwin Morgan*. Edinburgh: Edinburgh University Press, 1990.

Crawford, Robert et al. eds. *Talking Verse*. St. Andrews: *Verse*, 1995.

Crowley, Tony. *The Politics of Discourse: the Standard Language Question in British Cultural Debate*. Basingstoke: Macmillan, 1989.

Dabydeen, David. *Coolie Odyssey*. London: Hansib/ Dangaroo, 1988.

———. "On Not Being Milton: Nigger Talk in England Today." In *The State of the Language*, edited by Christopher Ricks and Leonard Michaels, 3–14. Berkeley: University of California Press, 1990.

———. *Slave Song*. Sydney: Dangaroo Press, 1984.

———. *Turner: New and Selected Poems*. London: Jonathan Cape, 1994.

Daly, Mary. *Beyond God the Father: Towards a Philosophy of Women's Liberation*. Boston: Beacon Press, 1973.

Davie, Donald. *Collected Poems 1950–1970*. London: Routledge and Kegan Paul, 1972.

———. *The Poet in the Imaginary Museum: Essays of Two Decades*. Manchester: Carcanet Press, 1977.

———. *Purity of Diction in English Verse*. London: Chatto and Windus, 1952.

———. *Under Briggflatts: a History of Poetry in Great Britain 1960–1988*. Manchester: Carcanet Press, 1989.

———. "The Varsity Match." *Poetry Nation*, no. 2 (1974): 72–80.

Day, Gary, and Brian Docherty, eds. *British Poetry from the 1950s to the 1990s*. Basingstoke: Macmillan, 1997.

Dobrez, Livio. *Parnassus Mad Ward: Michael Dransfield and the New Australian Poetry*. St. Lucia: University of Queensland Press, 1990.

Dobrez, Patricia. *Michael Dransfield's Lives: a Sixties Biography*. Carlton South: Melbourne University Pess, 1999.

Dransfield, Michael. *Michael Dransfield: Collected Poems*. Edited by Rodney Hall. St. Lucia: University of Queensland Press, 1987.

Duffy, Carol Ann. *Selected Poems*. Harmondsworth: Penguin Books, 1994.

Dunn, Douglas. *Barbarians* [Poems]. London: Faber and Faber, 1979.

———. *Terry Street.* London: Faber and Faber, 1969.

———. *Under the Influence: Douglas Dunn on Philip Larkin.* Edinburgh: Edinburgh University Library, 1987.

Eagleton, Terry. "New Word Train." In *Poetry Review*, 74, no. 2 (June 1984): 57–59.

Eliot, T. S. *Collected Poems 1909–1962.* London: Faber and Faber, 1963.

Elliott, Brian, ed. *The Jindyworobaks.* St. Lucia: University of Queensland Press, 1979.

Enright, D. J. *The Apothecary's Shop: Essays on Literature.* London: Secker and Warburg, 1957.

Fahey, Diane. "Greek Mythology in Modern Australian Poetry." *Southerly*, 53, no. 1 (March 1993): 5–20.

———. *Metamorphoses.* Sydney: Dangaroo Press, 1988.

———. "Statements," *Poetry and Gender*, Edited by David Brooks and Brenda Walker, 33–36. St. Lucia: University of Queensland Press, 1989.

Faithfull, Marianne et al. *Broken English.* London: Island Records (L-38772), 1979.

Fallon, Peter, and Derek Mahon, eds. *The Penguin Book of Contemporary Irish Poetry.* Harmondsworth: Penguin Books, 1990.

Fogarty, Lionel. *Yoogum Yoogum.* Ringwood, Vic.: Penguin Books, 1982.

Fraser, G. S., ed. *Poetry Now.* London: Faber and Faber 1956.

Gervais, David. *Literary Englands: Visions of "Englishness" in Modern Writing.* Cambridge: Cambridge University Press, 1993.

Gilbert, Kevin, ed. *Inside Black Australia: an Anthology of Aboriginal Poetry.* Ringwood, Vic.: Penguin Books, 1988.

Gilbert, Sandra, and Susan Gubar. *No Man's Land: the Place of the Woman Writer in the Twentieth Century. Volume 1: The War of the Words.* New Haven: Yale University Press, 1988.

Ginsberg, Allen. *Collected Poems 1947–1980.* New York: Harper and Row, 1984.

Gregson, Ian. *Contemporary Poetry and Postmodernism: Dialogue and Estrangement.* Basingstoke: Macmillan, 1996.

Haffenden, John. *Viewpoints: Poets in Conversation.* London: Faber and Faber, 1981.

Halliday, M. A. K. *Language as Social Semiotic: the Social Interpretation of Language and Meaning.* London: Edwin Arnold, 1978.

Hamilton, Ian. "A Mismatched Marriage." *Sunday Telegraph*, 25 January 1998, 7.

Hamner, Robert D., ed. *Critical Perspectives on Derek Walcott.* Washington D.C.: Three Continents Press, 1993.

Harpur, Charles. *The Poetical Works of Charles Harpur.* Edited by Elizabeth Perkins. Sydney: Angus and Robertson, 1984.

Harris, Roy. *The Language Machine.* London: Duckworth, 1987.

Harrison, Tony. *Permanently Bard: Selected Poetry.* Edited by Carol Rutter. Newcastle upon Tyne: Bloodaxe Books, 1995.

———. *Selected Poems.* Harmondsworth: Penguin Books, 1984.

———. *v..* Newcastle upon Tyne: Bloodaxe Books, 1985.

Healy, J. J. *Literature and the Aborigine in Australia: 1770–1975.* St. Lucia: University of Queensland Press, 1978.

Healy, Maura, ed. *Fire the Sun: an Anthology of Poems.* Harlow: Longman, 1989.

Heaney, Seamus. *Among School Children: a Lecture Delivered in the Memory of John Malone.* Belfast: John Malone Memorial Committee, 1983.

———. *Death of a Naturalist.* London: Faber and Faber, 1966.

———. *The Government of the Tongue: the 1986 T. S. Eliot Memorial Lectures and Other Critical Writings.* London: Faber and Faber, 1988.

———. *New Selected Poems: 1966–1987.* London: Faber and Faber, 1990.

———. *North.* London: Faber and Faber, 1975.

———. *Preoccupations: Selected Prose 1968–1978.* London: Faber and Faber, 1980.

———. *The Redress of Poetry: an Inaugural Lecture Delivered before the University of Oxford on 24 October 1989.* Oxford: Oxford University Press, 1990.

Heseltine, Harry, ed. *The Penguin Book of Modern Australian Verse.* Ringwood, Vic.: Penguin Books Australia, 1981.

Heymann, C. David. *American Aristocracy: the Lives of James Russell, Amy, and Robert Lowell.* New York: Dodd, Mead and Co., 1980.

Hodge, Bob, and Vijay Mishra. *Dark Side of the Dream: Australian Literature and the Postcolonial Mind.* North Sydney: Allen and Unwin, 1991.

Honey, John. *Does Accent Matter?: the Pygmalion Factor.* London: Faber and Faber, 1989.

———. *Language Is Power: the Story of Standard English and its Enemies.* London: Faber and Faber, 1997.

Horovitz, Michael, ed. *Children of Albion: Poetry of the "Underground" in Britain.* Harmondsworth: Penguin Books, 1969.

———. *Grandchildren of Albion: an Illustrated Anthology of* Voices and Visions of Younger Poets in Britain. Stroud: New Departures, 1992.

Hughes, Robert. *The Fatal Shore: a History of the Transportation of Convicts to Australia 1787–1868.* London: Pan Books, 1988.

Hughes, Ted. *Birthday Letters.* London: Faber and Faber, 1998.

———. *Gaudete.* London: Faber and Faber, 1977.

———. *The Hawk in the Rain.* London: Faber and Faber, 1957.

———. *Lupercal.* London: Faber and Faber, 1960.

Hulse, Michael, David Kennedy, and David Morley, eds. *The New Poetry.* Newcastle upon Tyne: Bloodaxe Books, 1993.

Humm, Maggie. *Border Traffic: Strategies of Contemporary Women Writers.* Manchester: Manchester University Press, 1991.

Hyde, Lewis, ed. *On the Poetry of Allen Ginsberg.* Ann Arbor: University of Michigan Press, 1984.

Jackaman, Rob. *The Course of English Surrealist Poetry since the 1930s.* New York: Edwin Mellen Press, 1989.

———. *A Study of Cultural Centres and Margins in British Poetry since 1950: Poets and Publishers*. New York: Edwin Mellen Press, 1995.

———. "Ted Hughes: Surrealist?" In *Dada/Surrealism*, 8 (1978): 134–45.

Jacobs, Jane M. *Edge of Empire: Postcolonialism and the City*. London: Routledge, 1996.

J. C. "NB." *Times Literary Supplement*, 23 January 1998, 16.

———. "NB." *Times Literary Supplement*, 6 February 1998, 16.

Johnson, Colin. [Mudrooroo Narogin]. "Guerilla Poetry: Lionel Fogarty's Response to Language Genocide," *Aspect*, no. 34 (August 1986): 72–81.

Johnson, Linton Kwesi. *Bass culture*. London: Island Records (ILPS 9605), 1980.

———. *Dread Beat and Blood*. London: Bogle-L'Ouverture, 1975.

———. *Dread beat an blood*. London: Virgin Records (FL 1017), 1978.

———. *Tings an Times: Selected Poems*. Newcastle upon Tyne: Bloodaxe Books, 1991.

Kay, Jackie. *The Adoption Papers*. Newcastle upon Tyne: Bloodaxe Books, 1991.

Kelleher, Joe. *Tony Harrison*. Plymouth: Northcote House Publishers, 1996.

Kendall, Tim. "The Salmon in October." *Times Literary Supplement*, 16 July 1999, 26.

Keyes, Claire. *The Aesthetics of Power: the Poetry of Adrienne Rich*. Athens: University of Georgia Press, 1986.

Kinahan, Frank. "An Interview with Seamus Heaney." In *Critical Inquiry* 8, no. 3 (Spring 1982): 405–14.

Kinsman, Judith, ed. *Six Women Poets*. Oxford: Oxford University Press, 1992.

Larkin, Philip. *Collected Poems*. London: Marvell Press and Faber and Faber, 1990.

———. "A great parade of single poems." Interview with Anthony Thwaite. *Listener*, 12 April 1973, 472–74.

———. *High Windows*. London: Faber and Faber, 1974.

———. *Jill*. London: Faber and Faber, 1975.

———. *The Less Deceived*. Hessle: Marvell Press, 1955.

———. *Required Writing*. London: Faber and Faber, 1983.

Larkin, Philip, ed. *The Oxford Book of Twentieth-Century English Verse*. Oxford: Oxford University Press, 1973.

Lawson, Henry. *Henry Lawson: Collected Verse, vol. 1, 1885–1900*. Edited by Colin Roderick. Sydney: Angus and Robertson, 1967.

Leonard, Tom. *Intimate Voices: Selected Work 1965–1983*. London: Vintage, 1984.

———. *Reports from the Present: Selected Works 1982–95*. London: Jonathan Cape, 1995.

Lloyd, David. *Anomalous States: Irish Writing and the Post-Colonial Moment*. Dublin: Lilliput Press, 1993.

Lowell, Robert. *Robert Lowell's Poems: a Selection*. Edited by Jonathan Raban. London: Faber and Faber, 1974.

Lucie-Smith, Edward, ed. *British Poetry since 1945*. Harmondsworth: Penguin Books, 1970.

MacBeth, George, ed. *Poetry 1900–1975*. London: Longmans, 1979.

MacCabe, Colin. "Broken English." *Critical Quarterly* 28, nos. 1–2 (Spring, Summer 1986): 3–14.

Markham, E. A., ed. *Hinterland: Caribbean Poetry from the West Indies and Britain*. Newcastle upon Tyne: Bloodaxe Books, 1989.

Marsh, Edward, ed. *Georgian Poetry*. London: The Poetry Bookshop, 1912.

McDermott, John. *Kingsley Amis: an English Moralist*. London: Macmillan, 1989.

McDonald, Peter. *Mistaken Identities: Poetry and Northern Ireland*. Oxford: Oxford University Press, 1997.

McGuinn, Nicholas. *Seamus Heaney: a Student's Guide to the Selected Poems 1965–1975*. Oxford: Arnold-Wheaton, 1986.

McLeod, A. L., ed. *Walt Whitman in Australia and New Zealand: a Record of his Reception*. Sydney: Wentworth Press, 1964.

McMillan, Ian. *Dad, the Donkey's on Fire*. Manchester: Carcanet Press, 1994.

———. *Selected Poems*. Manchester: Carcanet Press, 1987.

Merrill, Thomas, ed. *Allen Ginsberg*. New York: Twayne, 1969.

Mohin, Lilian, ed. *Beautiful Barbarians: Lesbian Feminist Poetry*. London: Onlywomen Press, 1986.

———. *One Foot on the Mountain: an Anthology of British Feminist Poetry 1969–1979*. London: Onlywomen Press, 1979.

Morgan, Edwin. *Collected Poems: 1949–1987*. Manchester: Carcanet Press, 1990.

———. *Crossing the Border: Essays on Scottish Literature*. Manchester: Carcanet Press, 1990.

Morrison, Blake. *The Movement: English Poetry and Fiction of the 1950s*. Oxford: Oxford University Press, 1980.

Morrison, Blake and Andrew Motion, eds. *The Penguin Book of Contemporary British Poetry*. Harmondsworth: Penguin Books, 1982.

Moss, Stephen. "Private Lines," *Guardian*, 20 January 1998.

Motion, Andrew. *Philip Larkin: a Writer's Life*. London: Faber and Faber, 1993.

Mudrooroo [Narogin]. *Doin Wildcat: a Novel Koori Script as Constructed by Mudrooroo Narogin*. Melbourne: Hyland House, 1988.

———. *Writing from the Fringe: a Study of Modern Aboriginal Literature*. Melbourne: Hyland House, 1990.

Mulford, Wendy. "Notes on Writing: a Marxist/Feminist Viewpoint." In *On Gender and Writing*, edited by Michelene Wandor, 31–41. London: Pandora Press, 1983.

Murphy, Francis, ed. *Walt Whitman*. Penguin Critical Anthology. Harmondsworth: Penguin Books, 1969.

O'Brien, Sean. *The Deregulated Muse*. Newcastle upon Tyne: Bloodaxe Books, 1998.

O'Donoghue, Bernard. *Seamus Heaney and the Language of Poetry*. Hemel Hempstead: Harvester Wheatsheaf, 1994.

O'Dowd, Bernard. *Dawnward?* Sydney: Bulletin Co. 1903.

———. "O'Dowd to Whitman/Whitman to O'Dowd." *Overland,* no. 23 (Autumn 1962): 8–18.

———. *The Poems of Bernard O'Dowd.* Melbourne: Lothian Publishing Co, 1941.

———. *Poetry Militant: an Australian Plea for the Poetry of Purpose.* Melbourne: T. C. Lothian, 1909.

Ormsby, Frank, ed. *Poets from the North of Ireland.* Belfast: Blackstaff Press, 1979.

Owens, Joseph. *Dread: the Rastafarians of Jamaica.* London: Heinemann, 1979.

Parkinson, Thomas, ed. *Robert Lowell: a Collection of Critical Essays.* Englewood Cliffs, N.J.: Prentice-Hall, 1968.

Parry, Benita. "Between Creole and Cambridge English: the Poetry of David Dabydeen." *Kunapipi,* vol.10, no. 3 (1988): 1–14.

Paskin, Sylvia, et al., eds. *Angels of Fire: an Anthology of Radical Poetry in the '80s.* London: Chatto and Windus, 1986.

Paterson, A. B. "Banjo." *Songs of the Bush: A. B. "Banjo" Paterson, Complete Works 1885–1900.* Edited by Rosemund Campbell and Philippa Harvie. Sydney: Lansdowne Press, 1983.

Paulin, Tom. "Into the Heart of Englishness." *Times Literary Supplement,* 20 July 1990, 779.

Perloff, Marjorie G. *The Poetic Art of Robert Lowell.* Ithaca: Cornell University Press, 1973.

Petersen, Kirsten Holst, and Anna Rutherford, eds. *A Double Colonization: Colonial and Post-Colonial Women's Writing.* Sydney: Dangaroo Press, 1986.

Plath, Sylvia. *Ariel.* London: Faber and Faber, 1965.

———. *Collected Poems.* Edited by Ted Hughes. London: Faber and Faber, 1981.

———. *The Colossus.* London: Heinemann, 1960.

———. *The Journals of Sylvia Plath.* Edited by Frances McCullough. New York: The Dial Press, 1982.

Pollard, Velma. "Dread Talk—the Speech of Rastafari in Modern Jamaican Poetry." In *From Commonwealth to Post-Colonial,* ed. Anna Rutherford, 215–26. Sydney: Dangaroo Press, 1992.

Pound, Ezra. *The Cantos of Ezra Pound.* London: Faber and Faber, 1975.

———. *Literary Essays of Ezra Pound.* London: Faber and Faber, 1954.

Reading, Peter. *Stet.* London: Secker and Warburg, 1986.

Reynolds, Henry. *The Other Side of the Frontier: Aboriginal Resistance to the European Invasion of Australia.* Ringwood, Vic.: Penguin Books, 1988.

Rich, Adrienne. *Adrienne Rich's Poetry and Prose.* Edited by Barbara Charlesworth Gelpi and Albert Gelpi. New York: Norton and Co, 1993.

———. *On Lies, Secrets, and Silence: Selected Prose 1966–78.* New York: Norton and Co. 1979.

Ricks, Christopher, and Leonard Michaels, eds. *The State of the Language.* Berkeley: University of California Press, 1990.

Robinson, Alan. *Instabilities in Contemporary British Poetry.* Basingstoke: Macmillan, 1988.

Rodrigues, Fay, et al., eds. *ARTRAGE: Inter-Cultural Arts Magazine*, no. 1 (November 1982).

Rosenthal, M. L., ed. *The William Carlos Williams Reader.* New York: New Directions, 1966.

Rutherford, Anna, ed. *Aboriginal Culture Today* [special issue of *Kunapipi*, 10, nos.1 and 2 (1988)]. Sydney: Dangaroo Press, 1988.

———. *From Commonwealth to Post-Colonial.* Sydney: Dangaroo Press, 1992.

Scully, James, ed. *Modern Poets on Modern Poetry.* London: Fontana, 1966.

Shoemaker, Adam. *Black Words, White Page: Aboriginal Literature 1929–1988.* St. Lucia: University of Queensland Press, 1989.

Sisson, C. H. *Metamorphoses.* London: Methuen, 1968.

Stanner, W. E. H. *After the Dreaming: Black and White Australians—an Anthropologist's View.* Sydney: A[ustralian] B[roadcasting] C[ommission], 1969.

Stead, C. K. *In the Glass Case: Essays on New Zealand Literature.* Auckland: Auckland University Press, 1981.

Sutcliffe, Peter. *The Oxford University Press: an Informal History.* Oxford: Oxford University Press, 1978.

Tamplin, Ronald. *Seamus Heaney.* Milton Keynes: Open University Press, 1989.

Thomas, Dylan. *Collected Poems 1934–1953.* Edited by Walford Davies. London: J. M. Dent, 1988.

Thurston, Scott, and Andrew Duncan, eds. *Angel Exhaust*, no. 9 (Summer 1993): *Tyranny and Mutation. New Radical Poets.*

Thwaite, Anthony. "Commentary: Ted Hughes Remembered." *Times Literary Supplement*, 13 November 1998, 16–17.

Thwaite, Anthony, ed. *Larkin at Sixty.* London: Faber and Faber, 1982.

Tiffin, Chris, and Alan Lawson, eds. *De-Scribing Empire: Post-colonialism and Textuality.* London: Routledge, 1994.

Todd, Loreto. *Green English: Ireland's Influence on the English Language.* Dublin: O'Brien Press, 1999.

Viner, Katherine. "The Blood of Poetry: on Plath as Feminist Heroine." *Guardian*, 20 January 1998, 2–3.

Wagner-Martin, Linda. *Sylvia Plath: a Biography.* London: Chatto and Windus, 1988.

Wain, John. *Essays on Literature and Ideas.* London: Macmillan, 1963.

Wakeling, Louise Katherine and Margaret Bradstock. *small rebellions.* Sydney: Wentworth Books, 1984.

Walcott, Derek. *Collected Poems 1948–1984.* New York: Farrar, Straus and Giroux, 1986.

———. *Midsummer.* New York: Farrar, Straus, Giroux, 1984.

Walker, Kath. *My People: a Kath Walker Collection.* Milton, Qld.: The Jacaranda Press, 1970.

Walker, Marshall. *Edwin Morgan: an Interview.* Preston: Akros Publications, 1977.

Wandor, Michelene, ed. *On Gender and Writing.* London: Pandora Press, 1983.

Warland, Betsy. "untying the tongue." In *A Double Colonization: Colonial and Post-Colonial Women's Writing,* edited by Kirsten Holst Petersen and Anna Rutherford, 140–43. Sydney: Dangaroo Press, 1968.

Whalen, Terry. *Philip Larkin and English Poetry.* London: Macmillan, 1986.

Whitman, Walt. *Walt Whitman: Complete Poetry and Collected Prose.* New York: Viking Press, 1982.

Wilkes, G. A., ed. *The Colonial Poets.* Sydney: Angus and Robertson, 1974.

Williams, William Carlos. *The Collected Earlier Poems.* New York: New Directions, 1951.

———. *Selected Essays.* New York: Random House, 1954.

———. *Selected Poems.* New York: New Directions, 1968.

———. *The William Carlos Williams Reader.* Edited by M. L. Rosenthal. New York: New Directions, 1966.

Willinsky, John. *Empire of Words: the Reign of the* OED. Princeton: Princeton University Press, 1994.

Wright, Judith. *Judith Wright: Collected Poems 1942–1985.* Sydney: Angus and Robertson, 1994.

———. *Preoccupations in Australian Poetry.* Melbourne: Oxford University Press, 1965.

Yeats, W. B. *The Collected Poems of W. B. Yeats.* London: Macmillan, 1950.

Yorke, Liz. *Adrienne Rich: Passion, Politics and the Body.* London: Sage Publications, 1997.

# Index

ML                    6/05